New Mexico Baseball

ALSO BY L. M. SUTTER

Ball, Bat and Bitumen: A History of Coatfield Baseball in the Appalachian South (McFarland, 2009)

New Mexico Baseball

Miners, Outlaws, Indians and Isotopes, 1880 to the Present

L. M. SUTTER

McFarland & Company, Inc., Publishers
Jefferson, North Carolina, and London

LIBRARY OF CONGRESS CATALOGUING-IN-PUBLICATION DATA

Sutter, L. M., 1959–
    New Mexico baseball : miners, outlaws, Indians and isotopes, 1880 to the present / L. M. Sutter.
        p.   cm.
    Includes bibliographical references and index.

    ISBN 978-0-7864-4122-8
    softcover : 50# alkaline paper ∞

    1. Baseball — New Mexico — History. 2. New Mexico — Social life and customs. I. Title.
GV863.N6S88   2010
796.35709789 — dc22   2010014906

British Library cataloguing data are available

©2010 L. M. Sutter. All rights reserved

No part of this book may be reproduced or transmitted in any form or by any means, electronic or mechanical, including photocopying or recording, or by any information storage and retrieval system, without permission in writing from the publisher.

On the cover: Albuquerque Indian School baseball team, 1911 (National Archives and Records Administration)

Manufactured in the United States of America

McFarland & Company, Inc., Publishers
  Box 611, Jefferson, North Carolina 28640
    www.mcfarlandpub.com

To the players and fans, past and present,
of this most splendid state.

Table of Contents

Preface and Acknowledgments   1

Introduction   5

   1. The Land of Enchantment   9
   2. Base Ballists in the Territory of New Mexico   24
   3. Picks, Shovels and Bats   52
   4. Doing Time: The Penitentiary Players   83
   5. A League, a Town, a Legend   96
   6. The Flying Kellys   116
   7. Soldiers, Cowboys and Baseball Players: African Americans in New Mexico   126
   8. The King (No Asterisk)   136
   9. The Connie Mack World Series   146
   10. The Rio Abajo   156
   11. Making the Ball Sing   174

Epilogue   217
Chapter Notes   221
Bibliography   231
Index   235

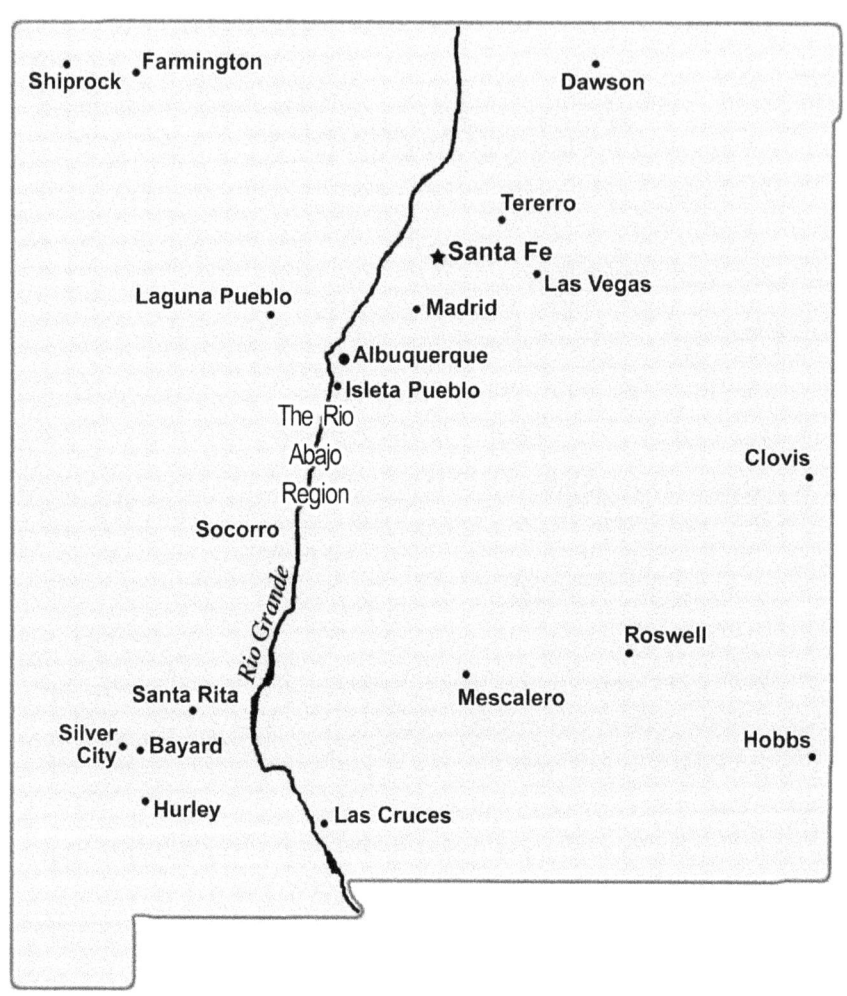

Map of New Mexico

Preface and Acknowledgments

Having lived in New Mexico for many years, I can say with conviction that there is no place in this country with a richer or more dramatic history, and the residents of the state are justly proud of it. Whether it be a tale of the Wild West or one concerning the Manhattan Project, New Mexicans, who are innately good storytellers, are happy to offer up their living breathing history to anyone smart enough to seek it out. A couple of years ago, having just spent a good deal of time studying baseball in the Appalachian coalfields, I began to wonder about the myriad mining camps of the West, particularly in New Mexico, and if they had played the game with the same fervor as the eastern teams. It didn't take long to find many a mining camp team, and their infinite variety of competitors. In fact, I found that the state enjoyed a thriving baseball culture that began when it was still a territory, its deserts and mountains a haven for some of America's most beloved criminals. Further digging yielded more surprises: from territorial days onward, the game crossed ethnic and cultural boundaries; it was played, and played hard, by every group that called New Mexico home.

What I find most compelling about baseball is that it is never played in a vacuum, always mirroring what is going on in the world around it. Every ball game takes place in a social or political or cultural milieu that affects it in some fashion. The New Mexico baseball stories, by necessity, have to be told against the backdrop of the state's many cultures—Native American, Hispano American, African American and Anglo American—and the way that they have intertwined to create a uniquely complex populace. While race sometimes affected play in the state, it was more often disregarded (sometimes to a revolutionary degree) and leagues—even individual teams—could be represented by multiple groups. Throughout the decades in which the face of the national pastime was unerringly waspish, the teams and leagues of New Mexico were often multi-colored, multi-cultural and even multi-lingual.

While the state's largest city of Albuquerque has a recent history in the high minors, the emphasis in this book is on the state's lower minor and semi-pro circuits, exceptional amateurs, and an outlaw league that featured some of Kenesaw Mountain Landis' most celebrated victims. These New Mexico teams featured a diversity of players ranging from soldiers and convicts to miners and women. The physical environment of the state makes it a long-ball heaven; the neighboring states and Mexico also enjoy high altitude and aridity, thus providing the same caliber competition. It would be an incomplete survey if it didn't touch on some of the impressive out-of-state teams that began making their way into New Mexico as early as the nineteenth century. The early fair tournaments in Albuquerque routinely attracted some of the best players from the Colorado teams of the Western League. The Copper League boasted not only New Mexican teams but also those from southern Arizona, Juarez, Mexico, and El Paso. Indeed, Texas was the most consistent provider of rivals beginning in the 1880s with El Paso and continuing the trend with strong teams, both black and white, from the High Plains.

Although the very first reports of baseball in New Mexico come from the 1860s, I have begun (following an overview of the state's history) by looking at the 1880s, when the game was a novelty to a smitten territorial population. The chapters then follow in loose chronological succession, from the early twentieth century to present day. The focus is less on a rigid timeline of players' careers, the beginning and end of teams or leagues, or the life span of an institution (such as the Farmington Connie Mack World Series) and more on what I deemed to be crucially important years for each. When a story seems to fall out of any predictable chronological succession (the story of the Laguna Pueblo mining teams, for example) it is because it needed, by virtue of the subject matter, to go in a very specific chapter.

The last two chapters stand outside any timeline because they cover not just one team or player or a moment in time, but the enduring affect of baseball in the lives of New Mexico's Native American and Hispano populations. These are histories in themselves, tales of the game in cultural settings that may be new to the reader. For these two peoples, it was a profoundly important part of their traditions, a multi-generational manifestation of community and continuity. Besides the simple joy it provided, for ethnic groups, who were intensely patriotic even while being marginalized by Anglo America, I believe there was a subtle symbolism involved in playing the American game as well as those who felt more entitled to it because of lighter skin and Eastern pedigrees. The final chapter, that on Native American baseball, is the longest simply because their history in the game is as neglected (besides the study of the immortal Native major leaguers) as it is unique. The earliest reference to baseball in New Mexico regards the Navajo people learning it in the 1860s as prisoners of the federal government. When the game was foisted upon them as students in the government boarding schools, they not only embraced it, but adored it. Today's annual Native American All-Star game, between young Pueblo and Navajo players, is both a celebration of the matchless quality of New Mexico baseball and a hopeful portent of more Native players at the professional levels in years to come.

There is very little written history of New Mexico baseball. Dr. Lynn Bevill has probably contributed the most with his work on the Copper League; for anyone with an interest in the White Sox scandal, his research merits deeper investigation. The West Texas–New Mexico League produced so many minor league stars and records that one can find a few scattered sources (not surprisingly in this era, there are quite a few on the remarkable Joe Bauman). It was not until the Albuquerque Dukes entered the Pacific Coast League in 1972 (the year in which Tommy Lasorda managed the club to the championship) that New Mexico baseball finally began to garner any consistent limelight outside its own borders. Thus, the bulk of actual research data in this book was drawn from local and regional newspapers prior to 1970 and, of course, interviews. On the other hand, if this meager introduction to the overall history of this state sparks the reader's interest, there are countless fine surveys to be found, along with many informative works that emphasize a single aspect of this riveting saga.

A suggestion before starting: whereas a separate section of notes can be irksome and sometimes rather disruptive to the "flow," I urge the reader to check the one included here. There were so many intriguing bits and pieces of history—some directly related to the baseball story being told, others less germane but nonetheless fascinating—that I was compelled to include them.

In acknowledgments, it is customary to say that a project could not have been completed without a particular person. But I can, with complete truthfulness, say this of photographer Belinda Winn. Her unobtrusive and gentle manner put every subject at ease, allowing her to capture what makes each face remarkable. The reader will enjoy her reproductions without any knowledge of the many hours she worked to restore their clarity and beauty. And she was a true companion of the road, content with the endless driving and sometimes dubious hotels, and she was not above leaping from a still-rolling car in pursuit of the perfect shot. Stephen Grillo was always there for technical support and no cartographer ever worked so carefully or so lovingly on his creation.

The debt I owe the many people who shared their memories with me is beyond reckoning. Not only did they patiently put up with frequent phone calls and endless questions but they also opened their homes and their communities to me. Some of them did me an additional service by leading me to others who had stories to tell. So many others went out of their way to help me with this project. Garet and Mardi von Netzer and Mike Haynes of the Panhandle Sports Hall of Fame in Amarillo, Texas, went far above and beyond in assistance. Nancy Brown-Martinez at the Center for Southwest Research at the University of New Mexico was endlessly patient and helpful, as was the entire staff of the Silver City Museum. Terry Humble of Bayard was more than generous with his own scholarship and Susan Holmes was not only extremely helpful in ongoing research assistance, but incredibly enthusiastic. Thanks go to Robert Turner of Hobbs, Tomas Jaehn of the Fray Angelico Chávez History Library in Santa Fe, Loni Manning and Debbie Doggett of the Farmington Museum, and Cathy Baca-Soto and Leonela "Leo" Murphy of the Owl Bar and Café in San Antonio, New Mexico.

Personal thanks go to Terry "Salty" Smith (despite his continuing misguided team loyalties), Alfred Stites, the rest of the Grillo clan, Mark Gardino, Tim Sampson, Cindy Sutter, Thomas Harding, David Sutter, Lottie Robinette, Eric Hicks and Debbie Abeita. Special thanks to Jimmy "Ace" Abeita who helped me through the process, not only with information, but with humor as well. In the long process, he became a dear friend. And to T who, once again, was the force behind it all.

Introduction

In 1880, the United States of America was a modern and well-ordered country. Having survived the crucible of civil war, it now enjoyed peace and stability which, in turn, fueled innovation. For the cities of the eastern United States, it was the Industrial Age and the working classes filled the factories, stoking the country's economic fires with their labor. Enjoying the benefits of that industry, a rising middle class began to tumble over the boundaries of those cities and into newly formed suburbs. For a fortunate few, it was the Gilded Age. The well-to-do lived in urban palaces in which maids removed the city dust with the recently invented carpet sweeper. Or perhaps the wealthy family chose to reside in one of New York City's luxurious apartment buildings, replete with elevators and located on a broad thoroughfare that defied the night with electric street lights.

Even the average citizen enjoyed a sense of privilege as he witnessed a boom in American population, industry and power. Every state from the Atlantic Ocean to the Mississippi River boasted several solid cities of brick and stone where streets were swept daily. Horse-drawn omnibuses and streetcars carried consumers to department stores where a growing variety of manufactured items was readily available. From general stores and markets, shoppers bought food (some of the first canned goods were made available that year) supplied by the patchwork of handsome farms that made up the rural areas. Wide rivers and their tributaries ensured healthy crops and verdant pastures for fat cows.

In the industrious Northeast of 1880, the descendants of patriots still basked in the glow of the recent centennial celebrations. In the South, Reconstruction having come to an official end, wounds were licked and cities rebuilt. In the Midwest, former settlements on important waterways had bloomed into substantial towns, their vigorous inhabitants grappling for their fair share of the ample American pie. From Boston to Houston, Minneapolis to Mobile, America celebrated its proud membership in the great club of democracy. Despite its comparative youth, the country in 1880 was an orderly place with timetables and city ordinances, bricked avenues and multi-storied buildings, municipal parks and opera houses that swelled its citizens with pride.

As the eastern half of the United States thrived on all the modern amenities and opportunities of post-bellum civilization, its population began to strain at the western borders like an adolescent in last year's clothes. Many a hopeful entrepreneur or impoverished family looked across the virtual boundary between East and West and saw opportunity in the unsettled frontier. However, what those who embarked on the grueling journey frequently found when they arrived in the foreign world now known as "the Old West" was a throwback to the feudal past. Ruled primarily by the strong and unscrupulous, the West was a place where violence won the day and the weak learned to keep their heads down, humbly pecking out a meager existence from the parched soil or a gold-flecked stream. It was a combustible mix of cultures, lawlessness, avarice, harsh climate and countless guns. Despite the scattered islands of statehood (California, Colorado and Texas), in 1880 the western half of the country was a vast expanse of untamed land, in many ways entirely disconnected from the America of the East. While the East contentedly preened its civilized feathers, the West was a roiling petrie dish of conflicting elements.

The territory of New Mexico was the epitome of the Wild West. From the arid Chihuahuan and Sonoran deserts of the south to the cool grandeur of the lower Rockies in the north, legendary characters of every breed rode the land, terrifying the gentler folk of the growing townships while titillating the tabloid readers of the East. By 1880, for instance, although most of New Mexico's other Native American tribes had been subdued, the United States government was facing the last armed resistance from Apaches in the southwestern part of the territory. To protect the burgeoning numbers of settlers and miners in the area, a series of forts had been established, many of their ruins still dotting the southern deserts. The most famous problem for the soldiers stationed in southwest New Mexico was the remaining Indian resistance fighter Geronimo, the wily captain of a group of Chiricahua Apaches. He led the soldiers of the United States cavalry on a very merry chase until his eventual surrender in 1886.

In late nineteenth-century New Mexico, miscreants vastly outnumbered lawmen, and justice was often administered outside the law — on a whim, with a noose. Some of those men, serving variously on one or both sides of the badge, still have the power to fascinate, and the year 1880 witnessed the antics of some of the biggest names. Crack shot and deft wit Doc Holliday came back to Las Vegas, New Mexico, in that year after an extended absence. He owned a saloon there but had abandoned it after running afoul of local law enforcement. Returning to attend to business matters, he killed a man, making it necessary to yet again abruptly depart town. He would cement his place in history a few months later at the infamous OK Corral in Tombstone, Arizona, with his friends the Earp brothers.

Undoubtedly, Doc Holliday would have often run into gunslinger-cum-lawman Bat Masterson around that time, as the latter was playing cards for a living in a circuit that included Tombstone (he left shortly before the famous shootout), Leadville, Colorado, and Trinidad, Colorado, which sits within a few miles of the shared border with New Mexico. Masterson would eventually serve as marshal of Trinidad before ending up in the East, as a writer for the sporting publication, the *New York Morning Telegraph*.

It was most likely in 1880 that at Fort Sumner, New Mexico, Henry McCarty, also known as William Bonney and, ultimately, as Billy the Kid, posed for his iconic only photograph. Slope-shouldered and leaning on his rifle, he seems both contemptuous and intrigued by the camera. It is also likely that it was near that time that he first met Pat Garrett, the man who would become his destiny.

Then there were the men who gained their reputations in more civilized fashion. In the few short years that The Kid wandered New Mexico, he was a thorn in the side of the territorial governor, Lew Wallace. A seasoned military man, Wallace had been appointed to put an end to the bloody Lincoln County Wars, in which Billy the Kid played an integral part. During the time that he was negotiating possible amnesties with many of the gunfighters involved in that conflict, including Billy, Governor Wallace was also busy penning the final chapters of a novel which would catapult him to fame. *Ben-Hur*, published in the fall of 1880, would become an immediate success and sell more copies than any American novel of the nineteenth century.

Certainly the territory of New Mexico had little in common with the states of the East. An early evening stroll through the capital city of Santa Fe, in the spring of 1880, would have proven that. The unpaved streets teemed with livestock, the incessant honking of dozens of burros combining with rooster crows in deafening chorus. The majority of buildings were made of adobe, the feminine curves of their rooflines glowing gold and rose in the setting sun. Within a stone's throw of the plaza, scattered small fields of beans and corn could be found between houses. Massive carved doors set into high adobe walls swung open to reveal lavish courtyard gardens. The rich incense of *piñon* smoke mingled in the air along with the whispers of evening prayers from the many *santuarios* in this heavily Catholic community. Flying in the very face of that godliness were the myriad saloons, brothels and gaming houses that kept the town's economy rolling.

But amidst the amorphous adobes and twisting alleys of what was lovingly called the Ancient City rose a few ambitious buildings of brick or stone, complete with Grecian pediments and mansard roofs, bespeaking the desire of some citizens to impose straighter lines and a more modern face on the town and hence the territory. To the north of the plaza stood the gray stone federal building, a monolithic reminder of the constant presence of Uncle Sam. To the east, a complex of ecclesiastical buildings bore witness to the European sensibilities—and authority—of the diocese's French archbishop. A recently erected sanatorium stood as a potent lure to eastern consumptives. Mercantiles, which up until two months earlier had received their inventory from wagons that had rumbled along the Santa Fe Trail, now boasted goods delivered in record time by the newly-arrived Atchison, Topeka and Santa Fe Railroad. Somewhere near the plaza, the rhythmic clack of the printing press signaled that the city boasted a newspaper, the lifeblood of any modern municipality.

The people that mingled in the dusty streets, speaking an eclectic mix of tongues, were a combination of Native Americans from a variety of tribes, descendents of the Spanish conquistadores and colonists who had arrived almost three centuries earlier, and Anglo Americans from the East. By the year 1880, New Mexico had been a United States territory for thirty-four years and those Anglos, more dismissive than intrigued by the territory's antiquity and its disparate cultures, wanted nothing less than complete Americanization. It became their *raison d'être* (and that of some well-to-do Hispanos) and they set to work in towns across the territory, building eastern-style communities. It was hoped that tidy, red brick towns would convince the rest of the United States that New Mexico was not only civilized but also one hundred percent American and absolutely worthy of statehood.

So on that evening, in the budding spring of 1880, several pillars of the Santa Fe community gathered at a popular local spot, the Parlor Restaurant. There, in the din of the crowded bar and the monte tables, in the fog of countless cigarros, these civic-minded citizens of the West huddled together in conversation. They had come to organize a great institution for their city, indeed an essential for any city in the United States. It was one that would lay to rest any assumption that a westerner was less a son of the Stars and Stripes than his eastern brethren. They had come to organize a venture that would prove that, amidst the territory's exoticness, the ubiquitous signs of its antiquity and the almost medieval barbarity with which outlaws controlled the wilds, there beat a thoroughly modern, thoroughly American heart.

They had come to organize the Santa Fe Base Ball Club.

1
The Land of Enchantment

Perhaps it is only the painter, able to wrest an infinite number of colors from just three primary ones, who can aptly describe the varied landscapes of New Mexico. The diversity of vistas is such that, traveling from one end of the state to the other, one might easily imagine oneself on different continents. From creosote and diamondback desert to an arctic-alpine environment which can support little more than the tundra-loving pika, the only climate that New Mexico cannot claim is tropical. But there is a common denominator that ties all these varying environments together: the brilliant light of a sun much closer to the soil of New Mexico than to land at sea level. With the rays burning intensely through the thin air, the result is an unmistakable luminescence that makes the strata of rock faces glow lemon and salmon and puce. It is fierce enough to throw the slightest geological scar — a hair's breadth of mineral matter — into dramatic relief.

New Mexico is rarely a place of subtle geology; instead, it is a pageant, showcasing the raw violence that has molded this planet. From the early Paleozoic onward, the geologic history of the area is a brutal and churning one of receding seas, earthquakes and volcanoes that sent multi-ton boulders hurtling hundreds of miles away. What the carnage left behind are the state's unmistakable landmarks. The lights of the growing city of Las Cruces twinkle beneath the canine-sharp Organ Mountains. The canyons of Bandelier National Monument are made of volcanic tuff so soft that early inhabitants easily carved dwellings from it using stone tools. Shiprock (Tsé Bit'a'í or "winged rock" to the Navajo) is a massive volcanic plume that rises in desolate beauty from the surrounding plain. Hidden beneath the Guadalupe Mountains of the southeast are Carlsbad Caverns, some of the largest in the world, and at nearby White Sands, evaporation of a late Paleozoic sea left massive deposits of gypsum so white as to almost reflect the cerulean skies above. And for the first-time visitor, emerging from a canyon in the Sangre de Cristo Mountains, the view of the Rio Grande Gorge snaking its way across the Taos Plateau easily elicits a gasp.

Eventually, into this high desert landscape came the first human inhabitants, hunter-gatherers who, ten thousand years ago, used primitive weapons very successfully on now extinct creatures like sloth and elephant. Millenia later, anthropologists tell us, the descendents of those hunter-gatherers learned

New Mexico stepped suddenly and inexorably from its Old West history into the atomic age with the development of the atomic bomb. A stage for ongoing research in space age warfare and defense is White Sands Missile Range, the largest military installation in the United States and home to Trinity Sites, where the atomic bomb was first tested (Belinda Winn).

to cultivate crops, like corn, beans and squash — the "three sisters" — that still comprise a substantial part of the New Mexican diet. Soon these early Americans began to build settlements close to their precious crops and not just flimsy, above-ground dwellings, but pit houses, ideally suited to protect them from the harsh local climate. But it was the pottery of these people, today referred to as the Mogollon, that makes them truly remarkable. Starting out simply, the work advanced in sophistication until, by the end of the first millennium, the potters of the Mimbres River Valley were creating a style that is now one of the most coveted in the world of collectors. Named by modern archaeologists for a mountain chain in southwest New Mexico (although the area they inhabited stretched from present day Chihuahua to Colorado and from New Mexico into Arizona), the Mogollon thrived in the area for almost fourteen hundred years. Around the thirteenth century, at approximately the same time that the their culture was peaking in the southwestern corner of New Mexico, another culture was rising to the north and the two undoubtedly influenced each other, especially in the realms of agriculture and art. This new culture was expanding across what is now called the Four Corners, and would leave its mark seared across the Southwest and into the consciousness of millions of curious and captivated people. They were called the Anasazi by the Navajo, which roughly translates into "the ancient enemies." To today's descendants of these people, that's a bit insulting, like the Capulets changing the Montagues' family name to the Bad People. A more accurate appellation is "Ancestral Puebloans" because the heirs to their genius are today's Pueblo peoples of New Mexico and Arizona. The Ancestral Puebloans would leave behind them dramatic evidence of a highly developed civilization, one that built elaborate cities of stone across the San Juan River basin, the most sophisticated of which are found at Chaco Canyon and Mesa Verde. Their art, whether in the form of exquisite pottery or haunting petroglyphs, is without equal. Scientists theorize that severe drought forced them to abandon their remarkable cities roughly seven hundred years ago, most of them migrating eastwards toward the life-giving Rio Grande River. Today, anthropologists say, their descendents live in nineteen Pueblo villages in New Mexico, from the northernmost, Taos, to Isleta which is south of Albuquerque, to Zuni in the western part of the state. The twentieth existing Pueblo, Hopi, is situated (some would say uncomfortably) in the midst of Arizona's sprawling Navajo reservation. Today many Puebloans accept the scientific explanation of their lands and ancestry, believing that the current Pueblos were settled when the Four Corners area was deserted after 1200 C.E. Others, following traditional beliefs, maintain that their ancestors occupied the sacred lands upon which they now live hundreds of years earlier than science allows.

New Mexico is also home to a large population of the Navajo, who are a branch of the Athapascan ethnic family, to which also belong the Apache, also native inhabitants of the state. Archaeologists suggest that the Athapascans are relative newcomers to the American Southwest, arriving after 1000 C.E. when the Ancestral Puebloans were well established in their exquisite cities (ironically, the name Navajo is also one that was foisted upon one group by another, this time by the Spaniards who took it from the Zuni. In their own language, the people that history calls the Navajo, are "Diné" or "the people" and their cherished land is "Dinetah"). Like some of the Ancestral Puebloans, the Diné initially settled along the San Juan River where they grew corn to supplement their diet of hunted and gathered food. As for their more nomadic cousins, the Apaches, three distinct groups of them claimed parts of what is now New Mexico—the Jicarilla, who now live along the border with Colorado, the Mescalero, found in the south-central part of the state, and the Chiricahua, whose lands once extended from southeastern New Mexico across the border into Arizona. Their tribal lands having been taken in years of warfare with the United States, today most of the Chiricahua live in Oklahoma (where their ancestors were held as prisoners of war) or on the Mescalero reservation.

The Native Americans of New Mexico share intersecting histories and the Pueblos share similar cultures. But every nation is unique unto itself, despite

Just north of the rich mining area around Silver City is the Gila Wilderness. Long before the Spanish and the Anglo Americans discovered the vast mineral wealth there, it was home to the ancient Mogollon people and the Chiricahua Apaches (Belinda Winn).

the tendency among invaders of every ilk to conveniently lump all the tribes into a generic category labeled "Indian." For instance, there are many different Native languages and although some are related, most are mutually unintelligible. The religious rituals among the Indians also vary enormously, and while those of the Pueblos may share similarities, one Pueblo's rites and rituals can differ dramatically from the next and neither will bear any resemblance at all to those of the Navajo and Apache. What all the nations share is the history of invasion and subjugation by outsiders, the Spanish and the Americans. Their continued existence is much more a testimony to their resolve as a people than to benevolence on the part of either of those foreign governments. Today, the reservations of New Mexico are sovereign nations, self-governing and industrious. For each tribe, the land remains the beating heart of their society.

Into this Native America of Pueblo, Apache and Navajo came the Spanish in the sixteenth century, on horses, an animal unknown to the New World. Up from the viceroyalty of New Spain, or Mexico, they sought treasure, primarily in the form of gold and other precious metals. It is said that the very first of the Spanish explorers, Fray Marcos de Niza, saw the multi-storied adobe structures of Zuni Pueblo, burnished to gold in the setting sun, and assumed that he had found the mythical Cíbola or Seven Cities of Gold. He hurried

1. The Land of Enchantment

back to Mexico City with his false impression and set the town abuzz. Soon conquistadores, soldiers and friars were headed north, only to find that the walls of the Pueblo weren't made of gold but of sun-baked mud. Gravely disappointed, the Spanish still saw promise in the arid landscape, believing that it might hold a wealth of riches underground. And, in addition to ore, there were thousands of Indian souls to be mined, a task the padres approached with vigor. The first Spanish capital of northern New Spain was founded in 1598 near Ohkay Owingeh Pueblo, north of present day Santa Fe, by Don Juan de Oñate, a man with a compulsion to map new territory and to leave graffiti.

> Oñate in his explorations also would reach into Kansas as well as south-westward to the Gulf of California at the mouth of the Colorado River; with the same curious motivation that drives tourists yet today, Oñate would pause at El Moro (Inscription) Rock to carve his name there and the message *'Paso por aqui'* ['I passed here'].[1]

Around 1609, Oñate's capitol having been deserted during one of his many expeditions, another capital of New Spain was founded in the bosom of the Sangre de Cristo, or "Blood of Christ," Mountains, the southernmost tip of the Rockies. Impressively christening it "La Villa Real de la Santa Fé de San Francisco de Asís" (the Royal City of the Holy Faith of Saint Francis of Assisi), the new Governor, Don Pedro de Peralta, set about building a seat of royal authority. His Palace of the Governors, which is the focal point of Santa Fe tourism, is the oldest public building in the United States still in use. Through the Palace, New Mexico was ruled by the viceroy in Mexico City who, in turn, was ruled by the king of Spain, himself often subject to the will of the Spanish Inquisition. (Few Americans realize that the Inquisition has a place in the history of their country, yet at one time a seat of that dark entity was located at Kewa Pueblo, twenty-five miles south of the capital city.)

To build an annex to the empire required lands, labor and wealth, all of which could only be supplied through the subjugation of the Pueblo Indians. The Spanish conquest of them is like that of any colonization effort the world wide; at its worst, it is an ugly story, filled with the blood of the native people. The foreigners' arrival was a violent one and the century that followed witnessed the formation of a chary relationship, in which laboring Indian regarded Spaniard with quiet distrust, while Spaniard considered the other his property, to be Christianized and controlled for his own best interests. Of the crimes committed against the Native peoples of New Mexico, it was those of the Catholic church that eventually tipped the scales, culminating in the Pueblo Revolt of 1680. The Pueblos were unhappy but could survive the hated systems of *encomienda*, by which they were required to pay tribute, and *repartimiento*, by which they were required to labor, all for the benefit of high-ranking Spaniards. Yes, they could bear those burdens. What they could not abide was the religious inflexibility of the Spanish friars who had outlawed their sacred practices and brutally punished less than complete adherence to Catholicism. In 1680, a series of well-coordinated attacks resulted in the deaths of several hundred Spaniards and the complete vanquishing of them from what is now New Mexico. For thirteen years the exiled Europeans awaited a chance to return to their settlements in northern New Spain. When they did, under the leadership of Don Diego de Vargas, it took more years of battles and bloodshed to secure the territory once again. But in the ensuing decades, attitudes of both Pueblo and Spaniard to one another became, if not friendly, at least more cooperative. The new government in Santa Fe was considerably more sympathetic to the needs of the Pueblos and the friars toned down the enthusiastic enforcement of religious doctrine. While still expected to be good Catholics, the Natives could quietly practice their own long-cherished beliefs. Although still not entirely trusting of one another, the mingling and marriage of Hispano and Pueblo grew more common, giving rise to the multilingual, multicultural society that makes the state so uniquely attractive to today's tourist.

The Mexican War of Independence in 1821 brought little substantial change to New Mexico. Just as when it was under the auspices of Spain, the capital at Santa Fe was too distant for its inhabitants to feel any real control by authorities in Mexico City. The most dramatic act of the new government, as far as New Mexicans were concerned, was to open the borders of the province to American traders, something the government of Spain had assiduously guarded against. The result was the Santa Fe Trail, which brought more into New Mexico than just better-made and more affordable goods. It opened the gates to Anglo American adventurers, mercantilists and fur trappers, who frequently found the environment of New Mexico enticing and lucrative enough to settle there.

But it was the Mexican-American War of 1846–48, ending with the Treaty of Guadalupe-Hidalgo, that brought the largest changes, and would make Native American and Hispano the first casualties of manifest destiny. Among other provisions of the treaty, Mexico ceded most of present-day New Mexico, portions of Colorado, Wyoming and Arizona, and all of what is now the states of Utah, Nevada and California. Leading the Army of the West into what would soon be named an official territory of the United States was General Stephen Watts Kearny. Kearny was genuinely sympathetic to the New Mexicans' natural suspicion of the Americans, and his "Kearny Code" attempted to institute just and equitable laws of governance. But he wasn't able to keep his soldiers' basic prejudices entirely subdued, nor force them or the new white settlers to a fair and broadminded perception of the New Mexicans. To the Anglo newcomer — soldier and layman alike — the Pueblo Indians, whose villages lay in such close proximity to the new territorial capital, didn't seem like the inheritors of a sophisticated civilization — they were simply a quaint bunch whose lands held interest. Much more dangerous, it was thought, were the Navajo and Apache, who seemed to the Americans like nothing more than

1. The Land of Enchantment

Near the Mexican border. Sitting in such close proximity to the United States, through the years Ciudad Juarez sent many a strong team across the border to play and actually belonged to American baseball leagues like the outlaw Copper League and the Arizona-Texas circuit (Belinda Winn).

wild animals. As for the local Hispanos, many of them descendents of the original conquistadores who lived on land granted to them by the King of Spain centuries earlier, their pedigrees didn't make a dent in the Anglo estimation of them. They were simply thought of as "Mexicans," natural relatives of that same Santa Ana who had spilled American blood at the Battle of the Alamo. Hurling himself into the contained and wary dance that Indian and Hispano had engaged in for three centuries, this new American partner would exercise little regard for the toes of the other two. His arrogance and presumption of privilege would insult and harm the Hispanos and Pueblos, and very nearly destroy the Navajo and Apache.

After his arrival in Santa Fe, General Kearny called for the construction of a fort just to the north of the plaza and in short order, forts were being built throughout the new territory, most, of necessity, located along rivers, like many of the Pueblo and Spanish villages before them. After the end of the Civil War, some of these forts housed troops of the Colored Infantry or Buffalo Soldiers. Indeed, the 125th Colored Infantry built the initial structures at Fort Bayard, in the southwest corner of the territory. That installation was the first line of defense against some of the most mythical of the Native American warriors, the Apaches Mangas Coloradas, Victorio and Geronimo.

Back in the eastern United States, the news of the annexation of New

Mexico met with real qualms on the part of certain factions. The main objection — and it had many vocal supporters— was to the adoption of so many brown-skinned people into the country (General William Tecumseh Sherman famously suggested that another war be started with Mexico to force it to take New Mexico back). But some trailblazers saw opportunity in this very old "new world" and immediately started packing their trunks for the journey west. "Then, besides the merchants and soldiers, there were the lawyers in frock coats and bat-wing collars. They descended in swarms, after the conquest, eager to their shoe-soles for political power and a slice of New Mexico's vast real estate, which presented the country's most visible form of wealth."[2]

When Anglo newcomers entered the new territory, they discovered a growing population of German Jews who had begun settling there as early as the 1840s and had established a vibrant merchant class.[3] With the arrival of Solomon Jacob Spiegelberg to Santa Fe, the first in a handful of dynamic Jewish dynasties formed in the urban centers; they would influence New Mexico culture and politics for decades. Indeed, the drawing rooms of prominent Jewish families were bastions of culture and polite society in places like Albuquerque, Las Vegas, Las Cruces and particularly Santa Fe, where the Catholic archbishop Jean Baptiste Lamy found fast friends in the Spiegelbergs, the Seligmans and the Staabs. And in one of the oddest tales to emerge from nineteenth-century New Mexico, a Prussian-born Jew was once elected governor of the Acoma Pueblo.

Meanwhile, as the native Indian, acclimated Spanish, and newly arrived Anglo populations of New Mexico found their bearings with each other, the borders of the territory were being hammered out by bureaucrats in Washington. The Compromise of 1850 made it an official territory, and a whopping big one it was, including at that time all of what is now Arizona and part of southern Colorado. Three years later, the Gadsden Purchase added a sizable chunk of land along the Mexican border, stretching from the fertile Mesilla Valley in southern New Mexico all the way to Yuma (Arizona) on the western edge of the territory. Ambitious men saw huge promise in the addition, particularly as part of a railroad route that would run from Texas to the Pacific Coast. And there were some men involved in the planning of the line who had ulterior motives. They would make the young territory an unwitting participant in the darkest hour in American history and add yet another government's flag to the list of those that have flown over the capital at Santa Fe.

In 1861, the New Mexico Territory seemed ripe for the picking to the Confederate States of America. First, it was a question of attitudes, and the Confederacy rightly assumed that the southern half of the territory would fall in lockstep with it philosophically. In addition, there was the mineral wealth of New Mexico and adjacent Colorado, not to mention the gold to be found in California, and the strategic importance of her ports. The Confederacy envi-

1. *The Land of Enchantment*   17

The landmark mountain, Cerro Pedernal, or "flint mountain," near Ghost Ranch. One of the most famous buttes of the American Southwest, it has been immortalized by countless artists and photographers, most notably the local legend Georgia O'Keeffe (Belinda Winn).

sioned the Old South stretching laterally to the Pacific.[4] In 1862, New Mexico was invaded by three regiments of Texas rowdies who headed up the Rio Grande and managed to win the Battle of Valverde, south of Socorro. But the further up the river the Confederates headed, the more cut off from supplies at their base in El Paso they were. When they pushed on to Albuquerque in hopes of an easy victory and provisions, they were met with their first taste of the actual northern New Mexican loyalties, which in fact lay solidly with the Union. Everything the Confederates needed to continue the fight had been removed or destroyed. Capturing a small post nearby, they exacted enough necessities to continue their quest for the capital, where, for a few bleak days, the "stars and bars" flew over the august Palace of the Governors. On March 26, 1862, en route to seize the arsenal at Fort Union, the Texans met the Colorado Volunteers in the Battle of Glorieta Pass, referred to as "the Gettysburg of the West." While day one saw no clear victor, the Confederates definitively won the second day's fighting. But stealthy maneuvering through the mountains led a contingent of Union loyalists to the poorly guarded Confederate supply train, which they obliterated in short order, leaving the Texans with nothing to fill their empty bellies but defeat.

With the end of the Civil War, many former soldiers (mostly Confederate), out of uniform and with no prospects in the smoldering cities of the South, made their way to the frontier. And they brought guns—lots and lots of them. In New Mexico these men found countless saloons, offering gaming tables, "soiled doves" and an endless flow of spirits. One of the most promising locales for a reprobate lifestyle was Las Vegas, New Mexico, roughly sixty-five miles east of the capital on the Santa Fe Trail. Today's Las Vegas has picture-perfect Old West charm with its vast number of buildings dating from that period. Its dramatic scenery, perfect nineteenth-century architecture and rich history (which includes Teddy Roosevelt and his Rough Riders) make it an essential stop on any tour of northern New Mexico. But in those days the town had a ruling population of thugs because of its proximity to Fort Union. "Many soldiers, upon being discharged or dismissed from the army, settled in the Las Vegas area, and when the tracks of the Santa Fe Railroad reached the town in the early 1870s, it brought in an even rougher element, along with the inevitable army of camp followers."[5] As these men plied their trades, upstanding local citizens attempted to lead normal lives in the increasingly amoral environment.

While the territorial and municipal governments attempted to quash the general lawlessness, and while those entities joined forces with the federal government to push the Indians toward complete containment, New Mexicans of Spanish descent were facing their own destruction at the hands of land-hungry ranchers and cattlemen. To these acquisitive Anglo newcomers, land grants that had been awarded centuries before by the monarch of an ancient country across the sea were of no consequence. A perfect example of this was the Las Vegas Grant, a valuable tract of 500,000 acres that had long been held intact, according to Hispano law and custom.

> Nevertheless, Anglos accustomed to taking what they wanted on the public domain moved in with their flocks and herds and either took what they wanted or bought land from the families that had no legal right to sell it. By enclosing the holdings, some of which encompassed as much as 10,000 acres, the new owners denied the Mexicans access to timber, water, grazing land that they had enjoyed for generations.[6]

In bids for greater power throughout the territory, the Anglos also fought each other. The famous Lincoln County War of the late 1870s was a result of wealthy cattlemen and a contingent of political-machine-backed thugs, slugging it out over land, riches and full authority in the eastern territory. Murder was rife, as were the predictable retaliatory strikes. The most famous combatant in that conflict was of course Billy the Kid.

All of these elements raised red flags for politicians in Washington who were wrangling with the issue of statehood for the territory, something widely sought by the more law-abiding citizens of New Mexico. But one obstacle in particular loomed in the path, at least in the eyes of the redoubtable eastern congressmen: the people. The people of New Mexico, in their opinion, were simply too dark-skinned, too foreign, and far too Catholic to allow the territory to be granted statehood, hence able to elect its own representatives. This eastern prejudice, plus a certain internecine bickering regarding statehood, meant that no concrete progress was made until 1911, when a constitutional convention was held in Santa Fe, resulting in New Mexico's admission as the nation's forty-seventh state on January 6, 1912.

With a pristine new mantle of statehood, New Mexico's politicians and civic leaders toyed with ideas to attract more inhabitants, business and industry. While they concocted their development schemes, a movement was already afoot that would succeed in turning the world's eyes to New Mexico but in a distinctly counter-cultural way. It had begun in 1898 when two young artists, Ernest Blumenschein and Bert Phillips, stumbled (as the result of a broken wagon wheel) upon the mountain village of Taos, about fifty miles from the Colorado border. For generations this lovely hamlet had been home to a strong Hispano community and for centuries before that, the Taos Pueblo Indians, who lived (and many still do) in two picture-perfect versions of the Pueblo "apartment building." Each is five stories high, and each was inhabited long before Christopher Columbus ever dreamt of seeking a new route to the Indies, and probably even before he was born. Blumenschein and Phillips were immediately smitten with Taos and settled there, Blumenschein even playing shortstop on the town baseball team.[7] And they put out a general call to American and European artists and writers to come see this Eden for themselves. Seventeen years later, the Taos Society of Artists was formed and the rest of the world came to be introduced to the stunning vistas of New Mexico and its handsome people through this assemblage of talent. Not only did they convey the state's natural beauty to the cognoscenti of the art world but also to the average American, in the form of advertisements for the Santa Fe Railroad.

Following on the heels of the Taoseño school came the artists of the capital city seventy miles to the south. Vibrant personalities, and frequently quite wildly behaved, they set about transforming Santa Fe into a seat of the avant garde. As the wave of their followers swelled, the interest in other types of New Mexican art did as well. Collectors the world over discovered the perfection of a Pueblo pot, the symmetric beauty of a Navajo rug, the profound sincerity of Spanish devotional art, not to mention Western art, with the cowboy's all–American saga told on canvas or bronze. For the train traveler, inexpensive rugs or pots could be purchased from Native American artisans at depots or Harvey Houses. For monied types, private studio tours could be arranged with bohemian artists on Canyon Road in Santa Fe. The artists of New Mexico helped give birth to, and still nourish, the tourism which supports the state today. Their uniquely personal urge to recreate what New Mexico reveals to them has been parlayed into a multi-million dollar industry.

It is safe to say that, even after achieving statehood, New Mexico stayed well below the radar of twentieth-century American consciousness. Not until after the end of World War II and tales began to emerge of the Manhattan Project, were many citizens of the United States fully aware of the state's exis-

A volcanic plume on the Navajo reservation near Shiprock. These dramatic geologic formations rise from the arid New Mexico landscape like ancient castles, providing rare shade for nearby residents (Belinda Winn).

tence. Even today, there is rampant confusion as to whether or not a passport is required to visit.[8] For many years it remained a closely held secret among the few who were born there, the few who relocated there and the few who visited occasionally. Only in the last twenty-five years has it become one of the world's hottest tourist destinations.

The visitor to New Mexico—whose official nickname is "the Land of Enchantment"—is quickly struck by the dichotomy of ancient and modern and by the casualness with which its residents cross from one realm to the other, every day. Many of the Pueblo people find their lands abutting the pollution and racket of the twenty-first century urban metropolis, yet still find renewal in their centuries-old traditions. To reach the tranquility of the deserted Ancestral Pueblo cliff dwellings at Bandelier, one must drive past the guarded fortress of Los Alamos National Laboratory, birthplace of the atomic bomb. And the San Ildefonso Puebloans, the living descendents of those vanished canyon inhabitants, live "in the shadow of Los Alamos, the mushrooming shadow of violent change in which all of us now must go on living."[9] Likewise, in the center of the state, the twenty-seven antennas of the Very Large Array burr and click as they scan the cosmos while, less than one hundred miles to the north, the inhabitants of Acoma Pueblo, this country's oldest continuously inhabited city, sit atop their spectacular mesa at night and also watch the night sky, but reverently and with silence. But their grandchildren are just as likely to be living in large cities, as students, professionals, or artists, with one foot fully in the twenty-first century and the other in their ancient past.

1. The Land of Enchantment

A family chapel in northern New Mexico. Catholicism is still a powerful force in New Mexico, and nowhere is that as evident as in rural areas where lovingly maintained private houses of worship can still be found (Belinda Winn).

For many an eastern tourist, weaned on tales of pilgrims and Jamestown, it can be a revelation to learn that their Anglo-Saxon ancestors were still under the large and oppressive thumb of Henry the Eighth when the Spanish first arrived in the American Southwest. The descendents of those early settlers revere their ancestry and nowhere is this more evident than in the churches that decorate the state. The Santuario de Chimayó is the site of a yearly Good Friday pilgrimage which attracts thousands of devout Catholics, most walking more than thirty miles to pray there. And even in hip and trendy Santa Fe, home to movie stars and billionaires, Hispana communicants of St. Francis Cathedral can be found in a small side chapel of "La Conquistadora," changing the robes of that oldest statue of the Virgin Mary in the country, with tenderness and real affection. An hour spent in one of these churches is a journey to another time and place, one rich in almost medieval pageantry and yet comfortingly simple at the same time. But as older Hispanics focus on the old Spanish inheritance, the younger Hispanos throughout the state, while respecting the antiquity of their families, celebrate a more contemporary culture. It is a dynamic movement most vividly illustrated in its visual and performing arts. This young blood also celebrates its connection with other children of Spain in the New World and proudly waves a New World Latino banner more often than that of Iberia. Soon, these modern Hispanos will be able to catch a flight at the Virgin Galactic Spaceport, which will be situated just off the Camino Real, the "royal road" that their ancestors established between Mexico City and Santa Fe nearly five centuries ago.

The resident Anglos are the beneficiaries of both of these cultures and have contributed their own spirit to the mix. They have historically been the independently minded — the trapper, the scout, the cowboy, the pioneer — unintimidated by the loneliness that was usually their lot on the frontier. For some, their ancestors made the grueling journey westward 150 years ago, carrying little but dreams of open spaces and big skies. Today, their spreads still line the highways, from the vast expanses of the big-time rancher to the third-generation plot with its humble house and ribby cows, gathered around the rare watering hole. Some early Anglos came as prospectors, independently chasing a mother lode of rare minerals, while others signed on with companies to dig out the treasure for them. Route 66 opened the state to the casual roadtripper, many returning to make their contribution to the youthful energy of cities like Albuquerque and Las Cruces. Always a destination for artists, another brand of bohemian began migrating into New Mexico in the 1960s, settling in communes and working small farms. One legacy left by the hippies of years past is environmental responsibility, as they were pioneers in organic farming, green architecture and clean energy. Later, other Anglo Americans were lured by the state's burgeoning high-tech culture and its relaxed lifestyle.

The Anglo urbanites and suburbanites work and struggle alongside their Native American and Hispano neighbors, as they balance mortgages, kids and diminishing 401ks. All three groups want fundamentally the same American dream but some feel that they have sacrificed far too much for the benefit of others, and memories are long. So there remains a degree of tension between these three groups that is obviously not mentioned in tourist brochures.

> Despite exaggerated and widely disseminated reports of threes cultures dwelling in harmony, New Mexico is a land of many conflicts. These include conflicts among cultural groups, conflicts over land use, conflicts over scarce water, conflicts between stability and change. These clashes stem from conflicting legal and religious traditions, conflicting views of the individual's place in society, and opposing values concerning civilization and progress.[10]

New Mexico, with its exotic history and climes, might seem an unlikely place for baseball to have taken root, especially so early and so profoundly. But the territory was engaged in earnest and widespread competition by at least the 1870s. As for the men who played there, they have been as varied as the state's disparate peoples and the games waged in circumstances as extreme as the landscape. There have been Spanish teams and African American teams, teams of Anglos and teams of Native Americans and, in a place that is credited with more than the usual amount of racial tolerance, many a mixture of all these groups. Cavalry teams played those of the infantry while both were guarding New Mexicans from the Apaches. Navajos still meet Pueblos in an annual all-star tilt at the home of the Albuquerque Isotopes, the Los Angeles Dodgers' affiliate. A few of the state's leagues have been havens for outlaw players. One league opened its arms to a team made up of men serving time for real crimes. Miners of lead have tangled with those who mined coal. There have been a number of low-level professional teams and leagues in New Mexico, with many a dispiriting tale of years of hard slog getting a man no closer to the Show. But then, some of the sport's biggest names—Hershiser, Valenzuela, Piazza—called the state home for a season, while whetting their talents to a keen edge on the Triple A club in Albuquerque.

The familiar curves of Santa Fe style. Starting in the early twentieth century, elements of ancient Pueblo and Spanish colonial architecture were combined to create Pueblo Revival, a style that would be unique to the City Different. This is part of the New Mexico Museum of Art, and was the first to be built in that landmark fashion (Belinda Winn).

In the history of baseball in New Mexico, there is one truth: it has never been easy. In a state where the lowest elevation is almost 3,000 feet above sea level and desiccating desert conditions prevail, keeping players on their feet and grass alive is a struggle. Southern New Mexico ball clubs have been sunburned playing in December and northern ones have had to postpone summer games because of a freak snowfall. Yet these conditions could also provide a distinct home field advantage. Many a local team could relax while visiting players lost consciousness from altitude sickness, stepped into prairie dog holes or attempted to field while dodging tumbleweeds. And the dry thin air that can make playing in New Mexico a torment has also rewarded players and fans with the delight of seeing what would be a double anywhere else turn into a towering Ruthian blast that sails through the turquoise skies, seemingly into the next county. With a built-in boon like that, New Mexico was tailor-made for baseball.

2

Base Ballists in the Territory of New Mexico

In September of 1882, the town of Albuquerque was atwitter about the upcoming fair or, as it was called, "The Great Exposition." Among the many catch phrases employed to advertise it was "Antiquity Resurrected and Young America Represented." A large ad in the *Albuquerque Journal* told of the numerous delightful "firsts" that would be available to what organizers predicted would be monster crowds. Included was an event that — decades later — would bring international recognition to the city ("For the first time in the Territory, for most of them, they will see a grand genuine gas balloon ascend to the clouds, freighted with humanity"). Also on display would be a group of people that was, at that time, considered one of the territory's oddities: "Many of them, for the first time, will witness the wonderful races, curious dances, and queer antics of the aborigines of New Mexico." In addition, the might and muscle of Uncle Sam would be showcased: "For the first time, the military of the Territory, including an Indian company, and the crack company of Arizona Territory, will come together and in friendly rivalry show us what they know about Upton's Army Tactics."[1] And one enticement that would have attracted much attention was this: "For the first time the several base ball clubs of the Territory will engage in a grand tournament in view of the visitors."[2]

By the time of that 1882 fair, baseball was all the rage in every corner of the territory. No one could ever say with certainty just when the game had arrived in New Mexico although it was played by the soldiers of at least one fort in the territory by the end of the Civil War. It might have been introduced shortly after the United States took possession of New Mexico, by the disciples of Alexander Joy Cartwright who, at the century's midpoint, made his way across the frontier toward California and its promise of riches. From the jumping off point at Independence, Missouri, Cartwright traveled the Santa Fe Trail until it reached the junction where it met the Oregon Trail, which he then followed to California. Since he was known to start a game whenever he could find eighteen willing men, perhaps Cartwright taught it to fellow travelers before they said goodbye at the divergence of the two famous routes.[3] At any rate, an early mention of the game was made in an 1873 newspaper from the mining boomtown of Silver City:

Mr. Kidder brought with him from Santa Fe the necessary collateral's [sic] for this bone breaking, joint dislocating sport, and on Thursday evening a goodly number of the boys were out practicing. Only one of these was laid out for the evening. Which argues well for the proficiency of all concerned."[4]

The tone of this snippet suggests that the sport was still a fairly novel way to pass a few hours in southwestern New Mexico. However, by 1884, the citizens of the territory were familiar enough with baseball that antipathy directed at umpires had become a natural state of affairs, as proven when a Las Cruces newspaper offered a cheeky take on a singularly unfortunate event. "A base ball umpire has been struck by lightning in Colorado. This is as it should be."[5]

Whenever the game took root, it bloomed in that period and place glamorized by television and movies as the Wild West. For the people who lived there, life was rugged and difficult. In 1878, for example, the general populace was thrilled that the kidney-pounding stagecoach journey from Santa Fe in the north of the territory to La Mesilla in the south, a distance of two hundred and eighty miles, had been reduced to a mere sixty hours, provided it was not held up by bandits.[6] A train ride from Las Vegas, New Mexico, to Trinidad, Colorado, one hundred and thirty miles away, took eleven hours and set the rider back $12.65.[7] Bath tubs were available in towns, but for the most part, only at public bath rooms, which were usually operated by the local barber. It was suggested by thinking people that bathing was a practice that should be engaged in sparingly and then only if "the doctor should not deem it inadvisable."[8]

But modern technology was beginning to make its way into the territory, particularly in the form of communications. A telephone was installed in Las Cruces in 1879 and the first call was placed between parties there and in nearby Mesilla, to the delight of all witnesses. "Singing, conversation, a jewsharp, a violin and bugle were distinctly heard three miles."[9] But even nineteenth-century technology wasn't immune to the brilliant Geronimo who, with his men in 1885, cut telegraph lines and, to delay their repair, spliced them back together with rawhide "...with such attention to detail that many hours were required to find it — hours during which hostiles got a long jump on pursuing soldiers."[10]

For recreation, one of the most popular pastimes was drinking. Alcohol was readily available at any mercantile and heavily advertised in the local papers as tidbits of actual news, such as the following description of a certain brand of spirits: "Their 'Stonewall' brand of whiskey is 'ne plus ultra.' It is warranted to make drunk come 'quiet as a nun' and leave you next morning 'fresh as a bridegroom.'"[11] The same journalistic attention was paid to local drinking establishments: "If you *will* drink, go where they set out liquor fit for the Gods. The Monarch Saloon is where they produce the article."[12] Of course, it took very little advertising or urging to get most men into saloons, and those of the larger towns had much to offer including women who "...in their fine frilly clothes, lent a touch of gentility to an otherwise drab and harsh existence — altogether a civilizing influence whether the males were aware of it or not."[13]

Unfortunately, along with liquor, the mercantiles also stocked plenty of guns and ammunition and the combination of firewater and firepower was a lethal one. In Las Vegas, where on December 18, 1878, there were thirty saloons[14] and one week later, thirty-six,[15] every news cycle brought accounts of more shootings. In a story to gladden the heart of any harried modern restaurant worker, one Las Vegas waiter grew irritated enough to shoot a complaining customer.[16] The towns of the territory were for the most part held captive by gunslingers. And law enforcement and the territorial judicial system were famously unable — or unwilling — to attempt serious reforms. "Little wonder New Mexico won the reputation as the worst-governed place in the United States, a reputation that continued far into the twentieth century."[17]

Gradually, however, the law-abiding citizens of the territory began to fight back against the unbridled violence. Fittingly, it was the people of Las Vegas — one of the most violent towns in the history of the United States — who, despairing of any real action on the part of law enforcement, united to face down the thugs themselves. In 1882, they swathed the town in the famous (threatening) invitation to a "Grand Neck-Tie Party," a poster now available at any dealer of Western collectibles. Eventually, men like Pat Garrett and Bat Masterson espied a brighter future on the legal side of the gun and donned the sheriff's silver star.

Towns that were situated in close proximity to raiding Native Americans often had the advantage of more lawfulness in their communities because of the nearby forts; the presence of soldiers could discourage even the most brazen of outlaws. And newspapers also helped tamp down bad behavior by naming and excoriating the perpetrators of violence. While doing their part to fight lawlessness, the papers also made a point of hailing the underpinnings of polite society that were beginning to appear, including literary, musical and debating societies and exclusive schools for young ladies and gentlemen.

The newspapers — along with many citizens in this frontier society — wishing to curb the baser instincts of its young men, saw great promise in baseball. As a sport whose appeal at that time lay largely in its promotion of "manliness over boyishness,"[18] it must have seemed tailor-made for the wilds of the West and the papers began full coverage of the burgeoning sport locally. It wasn't long before passionate town team loyalty arose, and each paper began firing salvos over the bow of other towns' teams — and their dailies.

Albuquerque was one of the first, most enthusiastic territorial towns to adopt baseball. Located in central New Mexico, on either side of the legendary Rio Grande River, the area was once home to the ancestors of the nearby Pueblo Indians. Eighteen families of Spanish settlers arrived in 1706, and the city was named in honor of Don Francisco Fernández de la Cueva, the Duke of Alburquerque (an additional "r" in the original spelling), a small town in western Spain. As a result of this notable namesake, the New Mexican Albu-

2. Base Ballists in the Territory of New Mexico

The Albuquerque Browns around 1890. The Duke City was one of the first New Mexican towns to enthusiastically embrace baseball. It proudly hosted the yearly tournament at the territorial fair (Image 000-119-0439.tif, ZIM CSWR Pict Colls PICT 000-119, Cobb Memorial Photography Collection, Center for Southwest Research, University Libraries, University of New Mexico).

querque is commonly referred to as the "Duke City." Originally a farming and sheep-herding community, with the arrival of the Atchison, Topeka and Santa Fe Railroad in 1880, the community boomed. Bypassing the established city plaza by two miles, the railroad automatically divided Albuquerque into Old Town, then a collection of weathered adobes and a few brick structures, and New Town, which at that time consisted of "a few tent saloons and dance halls."[19] Trains were not its only claim to transportation fame; in the twentieth century, Albuquerque earned distinction as an important stopping point on the original Route 66. Today, it is New Mexico's largest city, a vibrant mix of many cultures. Because it has developed a variety of business and industry, and a large population to support them, it is a bustling working town, hence a bit less twee than the capital city to the north.

One of the city's earliest forays into baseball can be traced back to 1882 when a Kentucky-born gentleman by the name of William T. McCreight organized Albuquerque's first real team.[20] McCreight, a printer-journalist who had allegedly played for the National League St. Louis Browns (1876–1877), loyally christened the new club for his major league experience. In 1882, when the *Albuquerque Daily Journal* announced the organization of the club, it was clear that the boys might not be well-practiced, but they would be grandly equipped:

> The baseball association met last night, the president in the chair and most of the members present. It was decided to have the secretary write some firm dealing in base ball outfits and inquire the prices of balls and bats, toe plates, masks, caps, gloves, etc. The name decided on was the Albuquerque Browns. Their practice day is Thursday.[21]

The Browns hosted home games at their diamond which was located inside the racetrack at the fairgrounds, or they ranged far and wide to compete, away games limited almost exclusively to towns on the railroad lines. While Santa Fe was a mere sixty miles away, other towns were much farther. San Marcial, today a ghost town, was over a hundred miles south of Albuquerque, just west of the infamous stretch of desert appropriately named Jornada del Muerto, or "Journey of the Dead Man" by the early Spaniards. Las Vegas, home of the Optics (named for the local newspaper), was just as far to the northeast. Years later, McCreight told a reporter that the team went as far south as El Paso and as far north as Raton. He added that, at those early games, "Damsels with bustles mingled with tinhorn gamblers who bet their last dimes on the Browns."[22]

Typically, the entire baseball team would turn out to meet a visiting nine at the railroad station and escort them to a local hotel, the first of many niceties that were part of the overall experience of nineteenth-century competition. Accompanying the team was usually an entourage of rooters, and nothing set off the local newspapers more feverishly than a poor showing by a visiting fan base. If no fans came along, the writers commiserated with the players to their faces and then promptly returned to their presses to produce scathing reports on towns that didn't support their teams. Santa Fe, long considered a place far too big for its proverbial britches by other territorial communities, always drew harsh criticism from other town dailies, and there was nothing better than quoting dispirited remarks from its players. An 1883 visit of a disgruntled Santa Fe team drew this report:

> They [the team] ceased their labors long enough to make a vigorous "kick" in the presence of a reporter and declare they were disheartened at the lack of interest the citizens of Santa Fe generally were taking in the match to be played at Albuquerque tomorrow. They drew a strong contrast between the two cities, and said that while Albuquerque people were pushing their club to the front and doing everything possible to bring about a successful game, and victory for them in the end, Santa Feans to the number of twenty ... had not even agreed to go with them for the purpose of witnessing the match.[23]

After a couple of seasons of play, the Browns began coming up against some talent that was no longer strictly amateur. In a match played with a team of workers from the Atlantic and Pacific Railroad, they found themselves up against a Mr. Rickard, referred to as a former member of the St. Louis Grand Avenue Club (making him a Brown Stocking between the years 1875 and

1880).²⁴ But the Albuquerque Browns were producing some big-league-bound players of their own. By early spring of 1884, four of their 1883 players had, according to the *Albuquerque Journal*, joined the newly-minted Union Association, an outlaw league that enticed players by functioning without the reserve clause. The most heralded of the foursome was a gentleman named Whitehead who had graduated to the St. Louis team, the pennant winners of that league's single year in existence. "Whitehead, the catcher of last season's Browns, is the daisy shortstop for the champion St. Louis Unions," crowed the *Journal* in June.²⁵ This daisy was undoubtedly Milton Whitehead, who helped steer the Maroons (the actual St. Louis team name) to a 94–14 record and then disappeared from the records of the major leagues. But of all the Browns to jump to the majors, the *Journal* was most delighted with a pitcher named Crawford who had once been employed by the paper as a pressman but was lured from Albuquerque by the St. Paul team with an eye-popping season salary of $1,500.²⁶

As the Browns honed their skills on the diamond, other teams were doing the same, the inevitable consequence being an informal league of towns, ranging from El Paso, Texas, across the border from Las Cruces, to Las Vegas. As the teams began to meet with greater consistency and develop fiercer rivalries, wholesale warfare erupted between the newspapers of the towns they represented. Up to that point, most of the lesser towns had traditionally lined up together — on most issues — against the capital city. Santa Fe, an established township since before the pilgrims put the first buckled shoe on Plymouth Rock, had developed a certain highhandedness in its dealings with its fellow territorial settlements (*Thirty-Four*, a Las Cruces newspaper, once suggested that "...the City of Holy Faith has a holy faith in being able to wind the twelve counties of New Mexico around her finger and imagines that she carries the suffrages of the whole Territory sewed up in a corner of her scapulary."²⁷) But no longer was it just Santa Fe singled out for ridicule — now it was a journalistic donnybrook, with every paper in every town seizing every opportunity to lambaste the next paper and team down the line. When a west Texas paper jumped the *Las Cruces Democrat* on a matter of scoring, the *Rio Grande Republican* came to its sister paper's defense with a sniff: "The writer of the above [from the *El Paso Times*] should learn how to score before criticizing a scorer. He evidently is ignorant of the art, and so we shall try to explain those 'remarkable facts' in order to enlighten him."²⁸ In 1884, the *Albuquerque Journal* took umbrage at what the *Socorro Chieftain* had to say about a match that the Browns had lost to the Red Stockings of that city: "It must be remembered that our club went down there with a crippled nine, and, although in such a fix, outplayed, outbatted and outfielded their opponents...."²⁹ When a rematch was proposed, the threat was hardly veiled: "If the Reds are possessed of grit, they will put up or cease their blowing."³⁰ Derision of an opponent's town and its community endeavors was common, aptly illustrated by the *New Mexican*'s take on Albuquerque's 1887 territorial fair. "The base ballists and about 150

The Albuquerque Browns in 1894. Standing at left is William McCreight, the father of Albuquerque baseball. He named the team after the St. Louis Browns for which he was said to have played (Image 000-742-0212.tif, ZIM CSWR Pict Colls PICT 000-742, William A. Keleher Collection, Center for Southwest Research, University Libraries, University of New Mexico).

of their friends got home from Albuquerque today, and all declare that, outside of this contest yesterday, there was little or nothing at the fairgrounds to excite the slightest interest."[31] And in an instance of a winning team's paper defending the losing team against its own press, the *New Mexican* chastised the *El Paso Times* for suggesting that its own players had lost a game because they had taken liberal advantage of all the saloons of New Mexico's capital city.

> In attempting to account for the defeat of its home team the El Paso Republican does its club gross injustice when it hints that while in Santa Fe they drank and caroused and hence were not in physical condition. At such a groundless charge the team and its friends are justly indignant and well they may be.... They are gentlemen and deserve every consideration and support at the hands of their home people.[32]

And every newspaper, the *Rio Grande Republican* of Las Cruces included, delighted in mocking the skills of another team. "The Santa Fe base ball club knocked the Albuquerque Brown's [sic] out Sunday last 13 to 1. Oh, why don't they come to our city and play a good club?"[33]

2. Base Ballists in the Territory of New Mexico

A motley crew of Phats, date unknown. Not surprisingly, William McCreight is standing in the center (Image 000-742-0209.tif, ZIM CSWR Pict Colls Pict 000-742, William A. Keleher Collection, Center for Southwest Research, University Libraries, University of New Mexico).

When the *Republican* boastfully suggested that its town team could offer real competition to the Browns, it wasn't mere braggadocio. Las Cruces consistently fielded good teams in the last twenty years of the nineteenth century. Located in the fertile Mesilla Valley of Doña Ana County, the city is wedged into what was at that time a geopolitically volatile corner bordering Texas (at El Paso) and Mexico (at Juarez). When the Treaty of Guadalupe-Hidalgo ended the Mexican-American War in 1848, a flood of Anglo settlers poured in over the small Hispano settlement. Each American pioneer was anxious to snag himself a plot of the rich, undeeded soil. Soon a settlement sprung up at the base of the jagged Organ Mountains and would be called Las Cruces— "the crosses." With the arrival of the railroad in 1881 and the establishment of a college in 1890 that would later become New Mexico State University, the sky was the limit for this farming and ranching community. But it is doubtful that the community would have prospered so without the soldiers at Fort Seldon, who not only helped protect the Mesilla Valley but were also instrumental in making baseball the favorite form of recreation.

In the 1880s, Fort Seldon was just one of several military installations in the territory, put there to protect American holdings from Native Americans and any lingering insurgents from the old Mexican government. Baseball was a common pastime for soldiers who had finished their drills and desert excursions and, when they were able, they engaged the town teams. In the north of the territory, Fort Union played the Las Vegas Optics and Fort Marcy the Santa Feans; in the south, Fort Bayard played the mining teams from Silver City. Fort Seldon was no different. Built in 1865 to safeguard Mesilla Valley settlers from raiding Apaches and outlaws, it was named for Colonel Henry Raymond

Seldon who had been a hero for the Union during the Confederate invasion of 1862. In 1883, a colorful news item, mixing weather and sports, ran in the local paper showing that, while the soldiers worked diligently in the service of their country, they also knew how to have a good time.

> Another rain has visited us with the usual results; making holes for the water to come in, and for the tarantulas to go out, and dampening everything but the spirits of the soldiers. In a base-ball match played today, between picked nines from the companies here, Co. B, 13th Infantry and Troop B, 4th Cavalry, some very fine work was shown.[34]

As it was July, in an area where the average temperature for that month easily approaches 100 degrees, that game — between the Blue Jays and the Rising Suns of Fort Seldon — lasted only three innings before it was called on account of temperature.

By 1885, the township of Las Cruces had its own team and correspondence was published in the *Rio Grande Republican* between a Mr. Fitzgerald, secretary of the fort club, the "MacArthurs," named for the commanding officer, and Mr. Williams, of the town team. In it, the two men attempted to schedule a game for the Fourth of July, and in the politest, most gentlemanly terms possible. As it was going to be a holiday and everyone was feeling very celebratory, the teams agreed on a doubleheader. As for the first game: "The Williams club did some good playing, gave their opponents a white-wash and the game stood at its ending 16 to 11. The stakes were two kegs of beer." There is no record of when the winning nine enjoyed their beer but they did go on to take the second game as well, "in a manner which won the admiration of even their opponents."[35] The winners were gracious in victory; in the same edition, the newspaper praised the behavior of the MacArthurs at the game, saying, "The soldier boys, who played base-ball last Sunday, were a nice lot of gentlemen, who conducted themselves in an orderly manner while in the city. Such soldiers are a credit to the army."[36] (It is highly likely that, when the day of competition arrived, in the stands was the five-year-old future general and Medal of Honor recipient Douglas MacArthur, whose father Arthur was the fort's commanding officer.)

The next month, the final game in a series saw the Las Cruces team (now called the "Montezumas") wing their way to a 3–1 victory over the soldiers. The military boys, who had graciously supplied tents for the spectators — who included women — "conducted themselves well, proved game as fighting cocks to the last, and took their defeat with good grace." A literal play-by-play account ended with a series of "Diamond Dots," revealing more about the actual timbre of the match and the times than the game itself. "And the good looking ladies were there in force." "We sigh for more worlds to conquer. Set 'em up in the other alley." "Morrison is a regular old bushel basket on the catch, and throws a rifle shot." "Base hits were numerous, and every one of them knocked the neck off a bottle of beer. Shoot me again brother, right in the neck."[37]

As the *Republican* frequently noted, a loyal segment of the Las Cruces fan base was women and they were well taken care of at local matches, with tents and special seating provided for them. As baseball historian Warren Goldstein has pointed out, the presence of the "fair sex" at baseball games meant that players on the field were held to strictest behavioral account. Misbehavior sullied not only each man personally but the sport at large.[38] But good behavior at a ball game was probably also an attempt by the town to introduce chivalry as a habit, the surest way to stamp out the barbarous reputation of West.

The MacArthurs of Fort Seldon wasn't the only team to compete against the Las Cruces town boys. The Montezumas were making a name for themselves by taking on teams throughout the region. And the more they played, the more exuberant the reporting on their exploits and on the game in general. A fierce competitor, frequently played, was the "saucy" team of miners from nearby Organ, who in turn considered the Las Cruces boys "a lot of dudes."[39] After one disastrous tangle with the Organians, in which the Las Cruces team lost 41–12, the *Rio Grande Republican* put the best face possible on the situation with a few colorful descriptions. "Henry Buchoz and Johnnie Rouiller are daisy batters.— Welch makes things quite lively.— As a catcher Melvin surprised the boys.— Rynerson is the dandy muff."[40] And the paper never failed praise the distaff side of the town's population for its unyielding support of the boys, as in this report of a game played in December 1884 (the median January temperature in Las Cruces is a balmy 58.1 degrees). "The ladies of Las Cruces, many of whom were on the grounds, clapped their fair hands whenever a brilliant play was made and laughed when some unfortunate fellow went to grass."[41] A Fourth of July game against Organ, during which the temperature hit 108 degrees, was celebrated in this bit of poetry:

> Our left fielder is sick; our catcher is lame;
> Our shortstop is playing a very poor game;
> Two pitchers are used up, the other is wild;
> The basemen can't play when the weather ain't mild;
> The man in the right field is suffering from chills;
> The 'sub' has a queer complication of ills;
> Just what bothers our captain the doctor can't tell—
> But that is the reason they beat us like h—-!

Despite the heat, the game was well-attended by women, who "risking all the dangers of exposure to the fierce rays of old Sol, clapped their kid gloved hands in appreciation of the lively work on the diamond field." The Organ miners carried the day, 22–10, the Las Cruces team being gently chided by the press for bad throwing and obvious lack of practice. But all's well that ends well: "At the conclusion of the match, and during the evening, the two nines were engaged in a vigorous attack on the prize — a barrel of beer; and subsequently demolished a basket of champagne at Lapoint's saloon...."[42]

In 1885, after a year after the National League did away with the Cartwright underhand pitching rules, and a few months after the American Association concurred, the *Rio Grand Republican* published an indignant denunciation of the new style that showed that is was not only local matches that drew attention but national ones as well.

> The base ball clubs of this country are making a mistake by their adherence to the present pitching rate. Since the practice of throwing was adopted the game has lost its chief interest, for batting is wellnigh out of the question. If the aim is to secure a method of delivery which will render it impossible for the striker to hit a ball, and occasionally kill one, an ordinary fieldpiece might be put in the pitcher's hand for the purpose of discharging the ball according to the rules of warfare.... A game won on passed balls, wild pitches or called balls is a poor game and that is what most of the leagues are now.[43]

It appears that, as far as the Las Cruces press was concerned, the game simply was not what it used to be, both nationally and locally. Like an old man remembering his first love, one writer for the *Republican* took an occasion to wax elegiac on the virtues of an earlier, purer game — town ball — which had employed "none of the foppishness of polished bats and comic opera costumes" of baseball.

> Young Americans will please to understand, then, that there was a pastime, played with a bat like a paddle, in which the striker ran around four bases while the outside tried to fire the ball between him and the base he was running towards; thus one could be "crossed out," or, what was better, he might be struck with the ball while running if the thrower was a good marksman, and the harder he was hit the more funny.

He went on to mourn the loss of a game so sensible that it needed no umpire, all questions settled by brawling. "There used to be an almost superstitious reverence for the result of the ordeal by combat, which always proved that 'cheatin'' never thrives."[44] One assumes that the writer rolled his eyes when, at the National League meeting that year in Chicago, the sissies decreed that all home plates should now be made of rubber instead of stone.[45]

It wasn't just the local press that seemed to lose steam for baseball. For whatever reason, Las Cruces' community interest in the gentlemanly game was not what it had been; in 1886, a team wasn't organized until late July.[46] One of the last lengthy articles devoted to the Las Cruces team concerned a game played against El Paso, a town to which the geographical focus of the game was shifting — the nearby Texas town would burst forth as a major player when the new century dawned. The reporter wrote, "All the Las Cruces boys lack to make them quite proficient ball players is more training in the way of coaching and base running. Their fielding was fair but they seem to lack the confidence that is characteristic in good ball players."[47]

One reason for the loss of interest may have been the closing of Fort Seldon in 1890, thus the end of one of the area's few truly competitive teams. Local baseball coverage continued to decline. It was mostly limited to sandlot Sunday afternoon nines like the Fats and the Leans, married men and bachelors and those teams comprising boys. By 1892, the situation had reached its lowest point when, in July, a line ran simply stating, "There is talk of organizing a base ball club in Las Cruces."[48] Occasional stories from the larger world of the game were still published. An 1891 story on the Omaha team of the Western Association merited a full column, including portraits of the players (which appeared next to the latest account of the fiendish Whitechapel murderer, dubbed the "ripper"[49]).

By 1900, it seemed that baseball had come under the exclusive domain of the College of Agriculture and Mechanic Arts. In one edition, while the newspaper devoted most of a page to a recent visit by Sheriff Pat Garrett, it did find the ink to mention that the college had just enrolled "a crack base ball player from Santa Fe,"[50] and later that month, reported on a game between college teams with the unlikely — and questionable — names of the Prettyboys and the Windpounders.[51] But the most compelling baseball news around that time, and that which garnered the most attention, dealt with the formation of two girls' teams at the school.

> The fair damsels of this institution, by organizing two baseball clubs, have once more shown to the good people that they are not going to let the boys stand alone to claim athletic honors. Many of the ruder boys appear greatly amused at the queer capers of these, the beauties of our college, but we wish to add that many of them are sufficiently acquainted with the game, so that with little practice they will be able to put to shame a few of the would be ball players. The dormitory lassies were the instigators.[52]

It seems as though women, who for years had loyally attend all the matches in Las Cruces, had peeled off their kid gloves and taken to the field for the honor of the grand old game.

* * *

New Mexico's first territorial fair was held in Albuquerque in 1881. The livestock display consisted of a bull and two cows. Two or three small adobes housed a meager agricultural exhibit (which was actually dinner for said livestock), a mechanical exhibit of a few pumps and a "hall" for fine arts. This hall was packed to its *vigas* (or rafters) with crafts created by the ladies of the town. The night before the fair was to open, a rare desert downpour began and lasted for days, the rainwater reconstituting adobe walls into mud. The deluge, which at first just delayed the event, eventually caused it to be cancelled altogether.[53]

Twenty-two years later, however, the organizers of the territorial fair of 1903 predicted the kind of glorious weather only to be found in New Mexico in October. Autumn in the Southwest may lack the bright and blazing palette of the wet and fertile East, but is no less magical in its subtlety. The fall flora is mostly silvers and golds, any additional colors would be overkill, almost too much for the eye to bear. The purple mountains are streaked with the brilliance of aspens and ravens circle idly against the boundless skies of an even deeper blue than usual; crisp mornings give way to warm afternoons.

These were exactly the conditions for which the fair organizers prayed. Every aspect of the event must go off without a hitch — New Mexico's very future as a state might depend upon it, for the most prominent invited guest was none other than William Randolph Hearst, congressman from New York, who was making a tour of the western territories. Accompanying him would be a huge group of luminaries and their wives from the eastern world of politics and high society. It is not surprising that the *Albuquerque Journal* was leading the charge to impress the visitors, considering that a permanent part of its editorial banner read, "New Mexico of right ought to be a free and independent state of the Union of the United States of America, and its people demand admission at the hands of the Fifty-eighth Congress." But it wasn't just Albuquerque that was poised to make deep obeisance to Hearst — Santa Fe and Las Vegas also prepared to greet him with all the pomp they could muster. After all, the scuttlebutt suggested that he was the probable Democratic Party nominee for the presidency in 1904. His was deemed the voice that could convince the rest of the country that the territory deserved statehood. Because of this, Albuquerque pulled out all the stops in its welcome of the distinguished entourage and one of those stops was a group of people that New Mexico higher-ups now considered a natural resource.

By 1903, any issue of Native Americans in the territory had been tidily dealt with. The people of the Pueblos quietly went about their business as they had done for most of the time that Europeans had been in the Southwest. The Apache and Navajo were attempting to rebuild their devastated populations. With the Native Americans no longer seen as a threat, Anglo New Mexicans had begun to envision their worth — particularly the Pueblos — as a tourist draw. One man, a Londoner by birth, certainly understood the drawing power of the Old West and its original inhabitants. Fred Harvey started building his line of restaurants and hotels strategically situated on the railroad lines. In New Mexico, he would incorporate the romance of Native America into his Fred Harvey Indian Detours, in which eager tourists were taken by faux-cowboy guides on perfectly choreographed (and comfortable) tours of the existing Pueblos and the ruined cities of the Ancestral Pueblos. And at any given Harvey House, an easterner could find local Indians selling their arts and crafts. At the time of the 1903 Territorial Fair, Albuquerque was beginning to understand just how lucrative an attraction some of the native citizens could be. Thus, part of the escort that met the Hearst party at the train was a "band of Navajos ... decked in blankets and feathers and mounted on their ponies" who would escort the contingent to the fairgrounds where it could witness "a realistic war dance" and then be spirited off to a ball. The next day, the visitors would see foot and mounted races by the Indians and, after that, more Indians would be trotted out for yet another dance.[54] White visitors always seemed to enjoy this type of fare because, as one writer put it, "There is always

2. Base Ballists in the Territory of New Mexico

a fearful pleasure about that creepy feeling that meanders up and down the backbone when the painted savages unite in that blood curdling wailing moan and whoop which is the invariable accompaniment of their dances and these performances are very fascinating."[55] After enjoying the "fearful pleasure" of many Indian dances, and the more staid delights of the banquet and following ball, Hearst and his nabobs then attended an event that was of infinitely more importance to the average New Mexican fairgoer — the opening of the baseball tournament.

The tournament that year was to be a three-way tangle among teams from the host city of Albuquerque, Santa Fe and El Paso. Each team was to rely primarily on homegrown talent although they were allowed three professionals to pad their rosters. The Santa Fe club had managed to secure a pitcher by the name of Lempke from the Denver team of the Western League, and another by the name of "Kid" Nichols, as well as a catcher named Baerwald, also from the Colorado capital. (This was Rudy Baerwald who played outfield for a brief while with the New York Highlanders in 1907. After that, he played for the mining town of Hurley, New Mexico, in the old Copper League.[56]) El Paso was coming with their two pros, pitcher Adams and catcher Markley, the latter deemed something of "a wonder" behind the slab.[57] Albuquerque had reached a bit higher and snagged pitchers Oscar Jones and Henry Schmidt of that year's Brooklyn Superbas on their way to winter vacation in California. The *Albuquerque Journal* gleefully described the ringers as "considered the fastest of the new men in the business."[58] But the real star came to the fair in an umpire's uniform: Captain Adrian C. "Cap" Anson, former Chicago White Stocking player and manager, bowler, vaudevillian and vociferous racist. While he was not met at the station by the large numbers that met Hearst, he was honored by an informal reception.

> Almost every man in the club at the time, and there were a number, knew him by sight and a few of them knew him personally so that he did not come among strangers. Indeed it is doubtful if there is a city or town in all the United States where this veteran favorite of the diamond would not find one of a dozen friends and admirers.[59]

Indeed, Anson would not have been a stranger to New Mexico given his close association with Albert Goodwill Spalding. In the early 1890s, Spalding and Andrew Graham, also from Chicago, had invested in a small resort built around a hot springs near Silver City, in the southwest corner of the territory. Long a proponent of the benefits of geothermal waters (the Chicago White Stockings properties included land in Hot Springs, Arkansas), Spalding had ambitions to expand the resort into a massive hotel. The locals of Silver City and nearby Deming were elated by the plans for the $100,000 hotel and, for a while, it looked as if the railroad line would have to be shifted to better accommodate the expected hordes.[60] Spalding was also involved in a corporation called the Rio Mimbres Irrigation Company which eventually sold off much of its real estate in seventy-acre parcels. "Settlers are already locating around the new town of Spalding and at the present rate within a very few weeks all the land which the company will place under irrigation this year will be sold."[61] (One wonders how many people in Luna County understand the name origin of tiny unincorporated Spalding, located off U.S. 180.) Albert Spalding remained a frequent visitor to New Mexico for a number of years. As late as 1913, he talked of building a baseball training college south of Silver City, name-dropping the talented coaching and playing prospects he was lining up. "For instance ... I believe that at the present time I can get Anson of Chicago as one of the trainers for my camp," he told the *Silver City Enterprise*.[62] Eventually, however, his interest shifted away from the area and westward to Point Loma in San Diego and the teachings of Madame Blavatsky.

Just as Spalding and Anson were familiar with the climes of southwestern New Mexico, so were the professional ballplayers known, according to year, as the White Stockings, the Colts or the Orphans, because of the loss of Anson. In 1899, Spalding brought the Orphans to spring training near Silver City, accompanied by a throng of reporters.[63] While there, they even played the local nine. (That Chicago roster included catchers Frank Chance and Tim Donahue, Jack Katoll on the mound, Bill Everitt, Gene De Montreville, Clark Griffith, and Harry Wolverton in the infield and Sam Mertes, Bill Lange and Nixey Callahan in the outfield.[64])

The fair opened on Monday, the twelfth of October, with games planned for every afternoon that week with the possibility of morning tilts as well. The Santa Fe manager, aptly named Billy Martin, "vouchsafed to enter a team that will not only win, but beat every team it crosses bats with, to a fare-you-well," and the capital city had come through with the funds necessary to bankroll their team's entry in the tournament.[65] El Paso was also optimistic about winning the purse, having just come off a victorious series over Fort Worth the week before.[66] And Albuquerque had the confidence that having two Superbas on the team could inspire.

The contests were heated ones and the fans showed their enthusiasm throughout. "They did some rooting from the bleachers that would have done justice to any league game,"[67] boasted one writer who went on to add, "They stood on their heads and turned handsprings and summersalts [sic] and in short simply went wild."[68] Midweek, the *Albuquerque Journal* saw fit to favorably editorialize on the enthusiasm shown — in hollering and attendance — at the tournament fair.[69]

After a week of play, by Saturday, the unexpected had occurred: each team had won two games. The managers and captains of the three teams huddled that afternoon, deciding to hold a series of games, the team with the most wins taking the fair purse and gate receipts as well. The teams were going into it for blood, the *Journal* dramatically announced in the issue going to press and fan excitement swelled, for the devotees of the game were always ready for more sport.[70] But somewhere between announcing the series and the promised spilling of blood — in fact within just a few hours of the managerial meeting — the arrangement took a different turn. The managers, in a private meeting, changed their minds and decided to forego the series (without informing the press) and divvy up the purse. Santa Fe went home. The managers of El Paso and Albuquerque decided, probably because they couldn't disappear so easily, to throw the fans a bone in the form of one final contest on Sunday. And that, between the two decidedly unenthusiastic teams, was one "superlatively awful" game.[71] Everyone was left to howl, and howl they did. Referring to the pitiful final tilt, Oscar Jones told the *Journal*:

> After they pulled me out of the sporty plan to play ball for it all I was not going to throw my arm out of business for a little bunch of gate receipts. I would have been willing to carry out the plan announced Saturday and play for the whole purse for the winning team and nothing to the other, but somebody got cold feet and then it was all off. We did not try to play baseball.[72]

The paper gave Santa Fe a pass because the team left without having disappointed the spectators with a sham game. But the other two teams felt true journalistic wrath. "It would have been much easier and more dignified to have called the game off yesterday than to have exchanged for coin of the realm so particularly punk an article of the national game."[73]

Cap Anson had left Albuquerque on Saturday night, full of praise for the fair association and its good work. Due to a few bad calls on his part during the games, he might have left Albuquerque with fewer friends than he had when he arrived.[74] Schmidt and Jones left Sunday evening, their destination the Pacific Coast, for a winter's rest before spring training and another season with Brooklyn.[75] William Randolph Hearst, after buying a "crack cow pony" named Frisky left with his trainload full of important people.[76]

New Mexico was proud of the success of the thirty-fifth territorial fair. The *Journal*, in a moment of self-satisfaction, wrote:

> It might be interesting to some of those easterners who talk about Darkest New Mexico to know that there were congregated in this city during the fair some scores or even hundreds of typical cowboys and that not a single one of them "shot up" the town during the whole week ... no one was even strung up to a telegraph pole or scalped or made to dance to the tune of a "forty-five."[77]

Upon returning to his world, William Randolph Hearst and his entourage praised the territory — the sights they had seen and the reception they had received there. With the benediction of that titan, New Mexico crossed her fingers and waited for statehood to magically be granted. She would have a long wait.

* * *

Setting the stage for the upcoming season, the *Albuquerque Journal* editorialized in 1911: "There is an inseparable connection in the minds of a large population of the citizens of this land between boosting and baseball, bleachers and business, prosperity and gate receipts. The amount of advertising given a city by a live baseball team is astonishing."[78]

An Albuquerque Indian School team from around 1900. The Indian boarding school system was considered the best way to assimilate Native Americans into white society and sports were deemed an essential tool in the process (Image 000-119-044I.tif, ZIM CSWR Pict Colls Pict 000-119, Cobb Memorial Photography Collection, Center for Southwest Research, University Libraries, University of New Mexico).

After several balmy days in late March, the first week of April 1911 (and the unofficial opening of baseball season) saw northern New Mexico cursed with violent weather. While snows delayed games that week at Santa Fe, players in the Duke City began one Sunday afternoon tilt in clement comfort, then found themselves racing for cover when a blinding sandstorm blew in, reducing visibility and temperature to distinctly uncomfortable levels. As one reporter, who anthropomorphized the tempest into "proud Boreas," put it, "Down the canyons west of the river it came, pushing loose sand before it in a cold, keen gale ... it struck the city of Albuquerque, strenuously enjoying her Sunday rest, with a vengeance, as if intending to make up for all the pleasant days of the spring."[79] This resident Shakespeare of the *Albuquerque Journal* was a sportswriter who anonymously covered local baseball that year with enormous relish, forever outdoing himself in the creation of crackling headlines and subheads and colorful accounts of the games. He was the nameless, faceless voice of a sport that kept the attention of the territory engaged.

He had a good deal to cover, for even with the official start of the season still a month away, most of New Mexico was headed for the local diamond and the teams ran the gamut. In Santa Fe, the Apprentices were employees of the Atchison, Topeka and Santa Fe Railroad.[80] In Las Vegas, the teenage Giants were born of the marriage of two former teams, the Sluggers and the Eat-em-alives. The Giants would routinely travel to Albuquerque that season to challenge the youngsters of the Happy-go-luckys, the Old Town Browns and the Swastikas.[81] Varsity teams from the University of New Mexico and Santa Fe's St. Michael's College went up against the players of Albuquerque's Menaul School, a boarding school for Spanish speaking boys, and the Albuquerque Indian School, as they raced to complete the abbreviated season before summer break.

In Raton, businessmen met in early spring to discuss forming a Southern Colorado/Northern New Mexico League, a proposition that was abandoned early on because, while most of the teams of the prospective circuit would be considered semipro, others were unabashedly professional. The coal camp of Dawson, New Mexico, for example, began their season with a completely salaried team, a rarity even in the annals of mining camp baseball. While it was a common occurrence for excellent pitchers and catchers to be brought in to the camps as ringers, the Dawson brass went a large step further, allotting the unheard of sum of $1,500 a month for a winning nine.[82] A budget of that enormity meant that managers could scour the western minor leagues for likely prospects and open wide the door for jumpers, or outlaw players. And the camps weren't the only professional teams. The town of Gallup, near the Navajo reservation on the western edge of the territory, had a monthly team salary of $2,500 that year.[83] But Dawson and Gallup were the exception as most of the municipal teams—like those of Las Vegas, Santa Fe and Albuquerque—relied on donations and gate receipts to keep themselves in balls, bats and natty uniforms. Limited funding didn't inhibit the semipro teams, however, and they bounded into an unscheduled season like eager puppies, anxious to take on their paid competition. For a semipro team to win against a professional one symbolized the triumph of moxie over money; to lose was the bitterest of pills and the *Albuquerque Journal* sportswriter seemed to choke on it more than most.

As soon as the northern New Mexican weather improved and teams of every ilk took to their fields in preparation for the official opening of the season, the sportswriter took to his typewriter. In mid–April, the Albuquerque Grays began training amidst either swirling clouds of alkali dust or muddy bogs at their field, Traction Park,[84] the same field that been established in the early 1880s in the center of the fairgrounds race track. Grays Manager Dan Padilla worked the team as furiously as he could in the pre-season, no mean feat given the conditions of their diamond. After one practice, the dismayed sportswriter reported that "Traction Park presented the appearance of being a much better place for ducks than for ball players, in fact three feet behind first base, and a few feet southwest of third, the wading was excellent."[85]

The official opening of baseball season was scheduled for Sunday, May 7, in a game between the Grays and the Santa Fe team. The sportswriter generously described the enemy from the capital as "some of the classiest material in New Mexico wherewith to make the dust fly out of the mauled horsehide and the fans contract frog in the throat."[86] Among the festivities would be baseball exhibitions by the Indian School, varsity and high school teams. A band would provide musical accompaniment. The mayor, drafted to throw out the first pitch, would lead a parade to the field in his 90-horsepower automobile, packed with as many of the city's elite as could be shoehorned into it.[87] Manager Padilla decreed that no one but the players, reporters, scorekeepers and waterboys would be allowed on the field and hired muscle to enforce the rule. These five "special officers" were also given the unenviable task of keeping spectators from swarming the field in the final innings of the game, a moment historically beloved by Grays fans.[88]

The game began in a raw, cold wind that eventually died down, allowing the New Mexican warmth to heat up the festivities. In a two-hour match, the Grays won by a score of 9–5. While an Albuquerque favorite by the name of Rueben Weeks ("the only actual salaried man on the team"[89]) toed the rubber, his younger brother, appropriately called "Young" Weeks, caught him. Ross Salazar at shortstop began what would become a memorable season for him. They were victorious over a Santa Fe team that boasted one alleged former major leaguer, a southpaw from the Pittsburgh Pirates named Frye (sometimes spelled Fry) and Albert Clancy, a local boy covering second who, within a few weeks, would be playing for the St. Louis Browns. While the Grays were a typically New Mexican team, a roughly equal mix of Hispano and Anglo players, the racial makeup of the Santa Fe team offers up the unexpected. "The Santa Fe team is a motley aggregation, numbering among its members Whites, Browns and Blacks. Three Sons of Ham were in the game from the beginning, while the rest of the team was made up of Americans and New Mexicans."[90] (It is curious that, six decades after New Mexico became a territory of the United States, the Anglo press still routinely referred to a Hispano as a "New Mexican" while an Anglo was never anything but an "American.") Two of these African American players were brothers named Anderson, who covered left field and third base, and had been playing for the Santa Fe team since at least 1905, when the *Las Vegas Daily Optic* referred to them as "two chocolate colored gentlemen" while praising their skills.[91]

With the season officially opened, northern New Mexico baseball enthusiasts could now look forward to the next big event, a series of early-season exhibitions between the local town clubs and a touring team of Japanese American players.[92] Despite the sportswriter's description of it as the "Honorable Team from Nippon,"[93] and use of other traditional bits of stereotyping, the players were all resident Californians, representing the Japanese Baseball Association of Los Angeles.[94] Grays manager Dan Padilla attempted to sell a few more tickets by stating that the opposing team's starting pitcher had frequently been compared to the immortal and beloved Christy Mathewson.[95] But the Grays were not intimidated; ace hurler Rube Weeks was hard at work developing a pitch to put the Japanese on alert. As a great fan of Weeks, the sportswriter was gleeful in his reporting of the pitcher's progress while remaining careful to praise the legendary Japanese players. "It is reported that Rube names his new ball the green snake and that it is a wizzeroo. The Jap team is some pumpkins itself. It is reported privately that the Jap pitcher is so fast that the air smells like burnt sandalwood after the ball passes you up."[96] In an effort to goose municipal pride and increase attendance, the sportswriter went further, laying the potential dangers on thick.

> It is reported that they are the fastest folks on bases yet on the diamond, the whole team showing up nearly in Ty Cobb's class. They are good pitchers, having an ability to mix them up to satisfy the most fastidious critic of baseball on the continent, and it is said that the throwing to second of the catcher is up to any of the work of the big league artists.[97]

As the appointed day grew closer, in a moment of complete racial inanity, Albuquerque was plastered with flyers that read, "Peace and Joy between the two countries but battle royal on the diamond."[98] The media hoopla achieved the desired effect and the crowds turned out in force to see the "the little brown men, playing the big American game ... a sight for gods and fans."[99] Sadly, probably neither party found the game that interesting — the sportswriter certainly didn't. "The game was rotten, but perhaps the players are not to blame. The wind was blowing a gale and the sand would engulf both bleachers, grandstand, and players during critical points in the game."[100] In addition to bad weather, the Los Angelenos fell victim to Rube Weeks' infamous green snake, their Japanese Christy Mathewson famously absent from the mound. The Californians did, however, employ a local Native American spitballer named Lockhart who, by the end of the season, would be one of the biggest names in New Mexican baseball.

After one final spring storm (referred to by the sportswriter as a conspiracy on the part of Jupiter Pluvius[101]), the teams and fans of northern New Mexico threw themselves into full-fledged summer with energy and delight and gossip. Rumors had been circulating for some time concerning Roy "Binger" Corhan, a former Albuquerque Gray (and Western League) shortstop who'd recently been signed by the Chicago White Sox. By mid–April, when no newspaper mention could be found of "the festive Binger," as the sportswriter called him,[102] loyal Duke City fans were vexed. In fact, Roy Corhan played in his first big league game on April 20 of that year and, to the delight of the entire city, by June was hitting papers across the country, leading the *Journal* sportswriter to pen the dramatic headline "BINGER CORHAN IS BASEBALL IDOL" which was followed by a subhead reading "Fans Go Bugs Over Way Roy Sprinkles Salt on Sizzlers and Shoos Them to First."[103] Another former Gray, Bert Graham, had recently begun playing with Montgomery Billikens of the Southern Association. He had played seven unremarkable games with the St. Louis

Browns in the previous year; perhaps his most shining moment would come in the Western League in 1919 when he apparently allowed Joe Wilhoit of the Omaha team to reach first safely on a bunt, stretching Wilhoit's hitting streak to sixty-three games in a row.[104] The Duke City wasn't the only town to proudly watch one of its own go the way of the best and the brightest. Santa Fe's Albert Clancy followed in Graham's footsteps to St. Louis in May.

Baseball chatter also included what was happening in the town of Roswell in the southeast corner of the territory. Although Sunday games were officially outlawed in New Mexico, officials in the larger cities had neither the desire nor compulsion to enforce the rule. Not so Judge William H. Pope of Roswell, who let it be known that participants in any Sunday tilt would be arrested forthwith.[105] It was not just in Roswell however. Sheriffs of all the counties in the judge's district — large in area but mercifully small in population — were put on alert to stop any Sunday games, by arrest if need be.[106] The judge was not without likeminded thinkers. A few archconservative citizens sided with him, convinced that baseball was only one sign of the territory's moral degradation. The *Albuquerque Journal*, with barely concealed mirth, had recently run the comments of a local minister, deploring the lack of enough petticoats on the town's ladies and the Duke City's turpitude in allowing a red light district within its boundaries.[107] New Mexico's failings were picked up and carried with sufficiently loony enthusiasm by one anonymous gentleman from Deming who, in a letter to the *Journal*, decreed that baseball in particular was leading the whole country down the road to Hades.[108] Happily, all such silliness, including strictures against Sunday games, was completely ignored by the teams from Albuquerque northward. In the Duke City, the sportswriter, in a bid for more support from the citizenry, pointed to the looming threat from the north, including Las Vegas — called the Meadow City — which "has secured the services of Lochart [sic] the sterling Indian pitcher who made such a sensation here with the Jap team," and Dawson ("...another town not to be considered in the class as metropolitan Albuquerque" but smart enough to believe "in the substantial advertising value of a good baseball team").[109] Everyone had very good reason to fear the all-salaried Coal Diggers of Dawson, as their roster was packed with seasoned players including professionals from the Western, Southern Atlantic and Three-I leagues, along with mining team veterans and one gentleman who had served a three-year hitch with the Boston Bloomer Girls.[110] And the Santa Fe club now enjoyed its own celebrity, local boy Doc Cornish, a former shortstop with the Yale Freshies.[111] At the end of June, these four teams settled down to play in an extremely loose confederation, with games scheduled at the eleventh hour and players routinely transferring loyalties to whichever team offered the greatest amount of coin on a given day.

For all of the sportswriter's dire warnings about the professionals to the north, all the clubs were fairly balanced. Although the Coal Diggers took the first game from Albuquerque, the Grays turned around and won the next from

Dawson, sending the sportswriter into paroxysms of merriment as he explored the deeper significance of the victory saying, "...and all the Albuquerque youngsters, costing nothing a month, and boarding themselves, showed the fifteen hundred dollar beauties just how it was done in the bush leagues...."[112] The joy faded when it was announced that the Grays' invaluable shortstop Ross Salazar had signed with Charleston of the South Atlantic League. (Charleston also took "Noisy" Donovan, Dawson outfielder—"Noisy, as he is called, rather ironically, as he is always quiet, is one of the best fielders and base runners that ever showed at Traction Park."[113]) In addition, the Grays' first baseman Walter Allen left for the mining camp of Santa Rita, New Mexico (birthplace of Hall of Famer Ralph Kiner), which, a decade later, would be fielding highly competitive teams in the Copper League.[114]

Despite player losses, by early July, Albuquerque and Las Vegas had established themselves as the most dangerous of the four teams and went after each other with a vengeance, the newspapers following suit. When the Grays boarded the train to head north, *Journal* readers read the sportswriter's portentous pronouncement over their oatmeal.

> This is the day the Grays and the Maroons of far away Las Vegas meet on the diamond of the latter city, tie into each other in the best known style for the purpose of showing the superiority of one and the inferiority of the other team. It is so.[115]

Team boundaries being rather porous, players from one club would frequently join with an enemy of the day before "to help drag home the scalps." Facing a tight match against the Meadow City, Dan Padilla could often enlist off-duty Santa Fe players to join the Grays on their way to Las Vegas.[116] But even the added manpower couldn't completely eradicate the threat. By mid–July, the Maroons had won nine of their fifteen games, primarily because of Pitcher Lockhart, who, being a Native American, was predictably called "Big Chief." Not only was he a magnificent performer on the mound, but he was leading the Las Vegas club in batting at .387. However, the Grays were doing slightly better in the wins/losses column with an 11–6 record and their ace, Rube Weeks, was batting an impressive .469. But all four teams were not only competing against each other in the "almost-league" but against outside competitors as well and they were including all wins and losses in their team records for the season. "One good thing about the arrangement is that the assumed league is in such a shape that all the teams can lead it at the same time and all be correct," quipped the sportswriter.[117] All were playing well despite the fact that the Las Vegas Maroons had, overnight, been transformed into an all-salaried team[118] (which now included a stellar Native American battery in two brothers named Smith), to the obvious contempt of Albuquerque and Santa Fe. The Grays had performed admirably despite the fact that a month of unusually wet weather had made Traction Park an unnavigable swamp. But Dan Padilla had it drained and improved just in time to host an important series with a crack team from Amarillo, Texas, a thirteen-man club intrepid enough to enter the wilds of the territory. The sportswriter, as usual, did his level best to inspire attendance with descriptions of the Texan horde:

> They are a likely looking bunch. Quiet and soft spoken after the manner of the intense Tehano, and they look, act and walk like ballplayers. They don't talk much. They have brought with them some four stars who expect to materially assist in the lemonizing process. So used have the visitors become to chasing the festive pellet over the sandy slopes of the sun-kissed Panhandle and incidentally chasing every team to the ball timbers that they expect no trouble in doing likewise with Albuquerque.[119]

The game was a complete rout, announced in the sportswriter's funeral subhead "Brawny Texans Hang Crepe on Padilla Braves." Against the powerful Rube Weeks, the Texans put a former Western Leaguer from the Des Moines club on the mound. Pitcher/manager Bill Barngrover came into the game with a broken wrist and still managed to go the distance for a 5–0 victory over the New Mexicans. According to the *Journal*, Barngrover wired home to Amarillo after the game to inform the owner of the day's victorious outcome and the tragic state of his wrist. "Return wire said, 'Pitch Bill again tomorrow if his wrist isn't too sore. P.S. Pitch him anyhow.'"[120] The next day's game was not quite as embarrassing as the first but Amarillo still took it 3–1, in a seventy-minute-long game. Bill Barngrover started — as per orders — only to leave after three and a half innings.[121]

The beginning of August saw a feud beginning to boil between the managers of the Maroons and the Grays, over what the Las Vegas Baseball Association referred to as too much "rag chewing" by manager and fans of the Albuquerque club. Apparently, the number of spectators who routinely took to the playing field to add their two-cents-worth was growing and unduly prolonging the games in the process. The sportswriter, displaying a rare tin ear in regard to the feelings of Dan Padilla and the home team, wrote, "The Las Vegas fans, during the present season, have been forced to listen to some considerable oratory ... and this has made them tired.... Albuquerque lovers of the national game will join with them in their praiseworthy efforts to eliminate the talkfest feature...." The Maroons suggested they would condescend to visit the Duke City for a series if the field were secured from fans and a mutually acceptable umpire appointed.[122] Dan Padilla lashed out in righteous fury the very next day:

> We have never had a complaint from a visiting team ... on the treatment they have received. We are civilized here, we are not cannibals, and we know how to treat people, but one thing is certain, I am not going to allow them to dictate under what conditions my team will play them.[123]

Both teams brooded for weeks, each carefully monitoring the games of the other. Now that Albuquerque's number one enemy had been clearly identified, the sportswriter jubilantly announced that the Raton, New Mexico, team had "hung the green persimmons on the necks of the Las Vegas team"[124] and less enthusiastically told of the Maroons' ensuing revenge on Raton, plus their sweeps of the Dawson and Santa Fe teams. Now, in addition to the unflappable Indian pitchers Smith and Lockhart, Las Vegas was also enjoying the talents of yet another Lockhart, this one named Tommy, who had been hurling successfully for Trinidad until lured by the now-professional Maroons. He was said, rather vaguely, to have at one time "drawn pay from Comiskey."[125] The Grays were still proudly represented by pitcher Rube Weeks who continued to impress, despite some erratic behavior. While warming up before a loss to Santa Fe "...Rube seemed to be seized with the idea that he was going to pitch with his left hand, as he went about his warming-up efforts into that paw. Of course, Manager Dan was standing on his head in the grandstand about this time, beseeching Weeks to do the thing rightly."[126] By the end of the month, the sportswriter noted that Weeks had a record of 187 strikeouts in 16 games, one fielding error for the entire season and a batting average of around .400. It came as no surprise to the fans when Frank Isbell, manager of the Western League's Pueblo club, who had just retired from a lengthy career as a utilityman with the White Sox, sent Rube a contract ("Traction Park Will Know Him No More" mourned the *Journal*).[127] But before Rube could consider the distant spring, his team would again entertain that from Amarillo, whose name had been enigmatically changed from the Longhorns to the Monograms. The real attraction of the Monograms now was a player, who, rumor had it, was seven feet tall. The sportswriter was at the train station to meet the team and described the players:

> [They] began to get larger as they came off until this Jones person, a Choctaw Indian pitcher, began to unload himself. He was so tall that he had to lean down to get out of the car. Then he was so broad across the shoulders he had to climb down sideways.... He took one step and landed clear off the train to the ground just the same as if he had been getting off one small step. When he was introduced to pert little Dan, manager of the locals, he had to lean down to hear what Dan was saying about being glad to meet him, and the it took two minutes for the handshake which began at the shoulder to communicate itself to the small paw of the manager....[128]

Rube Weeks and the Grays took the first game of the series, 8–4, against "Big Chief" Jones and "Old Broken Arm Bill Barngrover" who were unable to pull the Texans from a "slough of despond."[129] The next day's tilt was a pitching duel between Jones and Barney McGrath of the railroad town of San Marcial, having been brought in by Albuquerque especially for the series. (McGrath's claim to fame was once having pitched a full nine-inning game in fifty-eight minutes while with the Western League.[130]) It was Barngrover, in the bottom of the ninth with two strikes against him, who drove in the winning run with a wild swing of the "wagon tongue."[131] The third game ended abruptly in the bottom of the ninth when the Monograms left the field over a disputed call. Cooler heads later prevailed and another match was arranged, with the winner promised all the gate receipts and a one hundred dollar side bet. The Grays won the rainy game, 6–1, happily collecting on the receipts from a record attendance.[132]

With the departure of the Texans, the real day of reckoning arrived. After almost a month of trading subtle barbs, carefully avoiding one another, and each team piling up wins, it was finally decided that the Albuquerque Grays and the Las Vegas Maroons should put aside the backbiting and meet for the series of the season, set to begin September 8 in the Duke City. Dan Padilla was taking no chances. He managed to entice some of the Grays' famous alums, now released for the year, back to Albuquerque to assist in the effort against the hated Maroons, now recognized as the highest paid club in New Mexico.[133] Ross Salazar returned from Charleston, as did former Gray Bugs Nuemeyer, who'd just won 18 of his final 24 games with the Southwest Texas League ("His peculiar grin with which he fools the batters is one of the funniest things seen on the diamond"[134]). Albert Clancy of the St. Louis Browns planned to return in time for the final two games of the series and Bill Barngrover was coming from the Texas Panhandle to lend assistance as well. But the sportswriter wasn't about to let the Grays fans forget what they were up against in Las Vegas's Chief Lockhart and the Smith brothers, writing, "The Indians are the best players on the team. They are all terrific hitters, wonderful base runners, and splendid fielders." So important was this five-game series that arrangements were made to telephone the scores by inning of every game back to anxious fans at home.[135]

The Maroons, apparently unaffected by Bugs Nuemeyer's facial contortions, took the first game, giving Indian Smith the win. As for the second game, "It was awful," wailed the sportswriter. "For ten loathsome innings did the barbarians from the higher altitudes fritter the poor rabbits on the spit, and then in consolation to them came around and said what a good time they had."[136] The score was 13–0. The next three games were held in the barbarians' own bailiwick and, having home court advantage, the Maroons won the first one 10–8, the second 10–5, and the final game 8–1, a decisive rout of the Grays.[137] For the season, the Las Vegas team had played forty-five games, winning thirty-two. The Maroons reveled for a few hours in their new title as the champions of New Mexico, then promptly disbanded for the season.

The Grays' mourning period was, by necessity, brief. For fall was in the air, the cool nights and autumnally bright mornings heralding the New Mexico fair and its storied baseball tournament. No longer a two-bit backwater event in the remote West, the New Mexico Fair baseball tournament had become an opportunity for professionals to earn decent money after the end of the regular season. And so they came, from all over the country, to add clouting and pitching might to the competing rosters of the West — Albuquerque, El Paso, Santa Fe and Dawson. This year's fair had added significance because on August 20, residents of the New Mexico territory had received the joyous news that the United States House of Representatives had passed the Flood-Smith Resolution, decreeing that "New Mexico would ultimately, irrevocably, positively and finally be a sovereign state of the union and a new star would be added to old glory."[138]

Dawson entered the fray with the local talent that they'd used during the season, although they managed to nab Tommy Lockhart, the ace pitcher, late of Trinidad and Las Vegas.[139] Santa Fe not only stuck with some of their own proven players, like the Anderson brothers, but they were also able to obtain Native American hurler L. Smith, pride of the Las Vegas team, and two more pitchers, Faber and Ellis, of the Western League.[140] El Paso, a member of the Texas League, already boasted sound semipro and professional players but hired Dale Gear to play center field.[141] By now somewhat long in the tooth, Gear had played for the 1896 and 1897 Cleveland Spiders, the 1901 Washington Senators, and in 1904 had managed the Kansas City Blues of the Western League. He eventually became the president of the Western League, a position that he held for several years. Not only was he there to help El Paso but to do a bit of scouting as well.[142] El Paso also had Chick Brandon of Kansas City, Louis "Bull" Durham, formerly of the New York Giants and shortstop Tom Downey of the Reds.[143]

But it was Albuquerque that reached into the firmament and plucked the biggest names. At the end of September, the sportswriter appealed to businessman and fan alike for the financial support to hire the best possible men. Fan favorite Bert Graham had returned to town and taken over the captaincy of the fair-bound Grays and he planned to pull in a few heavyweights from some Class A league teams.[144] Dan Padilla, apparently not content with Class A prospects, aimed the highest and wired Ty Cobb with an invitation to come and play for the Albuquerque club. The rather courtly sportswriter seemed to have mixed feelings about an invitation to the Georgia Peach. "He is the especial mark of the bleachers who try to tantalize him with jeers, but he jeers back absolutely unconcerned, and proceeds to pull off some startling play immediately afterward as of to show them the contempt in which he holds the common herd."[145] (There was no mention of a response from Mr. Cobb.) Even without Cobb, two days before the fair was to begin, it seemed as though the Duke City roster was in glorious form. From the regular season there was Kunz, an outfielder, and Rube Weeks. Graham and Padilla pulled off a coup when they managed to land Native American catcher B. Smith and Chief Lockhart.[146] Ross Salazar was at shortstop and Noisy Donovan was added to the burgeoning roster as well. To round out the bullpen, the Grays snagged Bill Bailey, a southpaw from the St. Louis Browns[147] and Pug Cavet[148] from the Tigers who, two years later, would toss Nap Lajoie his 3,000th hit. Tex Jones from the White Sox was brought in to cover first base[149] and Art Phelan, who had led the Southern League in stolen bases for 1911 (after having been sent down by Cincinnati) would be at third.[150] He would return to the Reds in 1912, then spend the three following seasons with the Cubs.

Padilla thought he had landed a failsafe second catcher when Bill Pettus, former player for Albuquerque and Santa Fe, agreed to come. An African

American, Pettus was finishing his second season with the Chicago Giants and would play the next one with the New York Lincoln Giants. In his *Biographical Encyclopedia of the Negro Baseball Leagues,* James Riley says that Pettus was "one of the best batsmen of the deadball era and is one of the most underrated players from black baseball," and goes on to mention a series between Albuquerque and Las Vegas in which Pettus collected an astonishing 15 hits in 18 at bats.[151] To the dismay of every Albuquerque booster, Pettus was injured in a game in St. Louis at the last minute and was unable to return to his stomping grounds for the fair tournament.[152]

The first game of the tournament was played on Monday, September 9, and was a victory for El Paso over Albuquerque, the catchers of each team — Noyes for the Texans and "Indian" Smith for the Grays— leading the batting charge with three hits each. Cavet's pitching couldn't hold up under that of "Young Cy" Young of El Paso.[153] Albuquerque took its second game 17–5 from Santa Fe, behind the pitching of Bill Bailey who, though wild at first, settled down when men were on base. The major leaguers all did some heavy hitting but Santa Fe's catcher Smith and Chief Lockhart, now covering right field, hit well themselves.[154] Dawson fell to El Paso, 12–3. By midweek, Albuquerque and El Paso were tied for the lead in the standings with two wins, one loss each. A fight due to a bad call by the umpire on Thursday saw the game between the Grays and El Paso forfeited to the former in the fourth inning, leaving four thousand fans complaining and even the ever-loyal sportswriter suggesting that a new umpire was in order.[155] But the tournament carried on and at the termination on Saturday, the Grays claimed first money ($1,000) with a 4–1 record. El Paso was on their heels at 3–2 (winning a purse of $400), Santa Fe in third and Dawson trailing sadly with no wins to its credit.[156] On Sunday, an exhibition game was played between the two top winners and the bitterness— perhaps merited — of the Texans spurred them to a 13–6 thrashing of the Grays. And on Monday, the sportswriter contorted himself into a bit of uneasy justification that must have rung hollow in the ears of even the most rabid Grays fan. Relying on local dope and considerable speculation, he concluded that, even if the game had not been forfeited to Albuquerque, they would have won it, given the baserunning and team batting numbers compiled.[157] And he might have been right. But one senses that he — as a journalist and a true fan of the game — was uneasy making that call.

The 1911 New Mexico Fair Baseball Tournament was hailed as an unqualified success. A few major leaguers headed into winter with a bit of extra cash in their pockets. A few local idols received some well-deserved attention and a couple signed minor league contracts, courtesy of El Paso's center fielder and scout, Dale Gear. The sportswriter took this last opportunity to extol the talents of Native American catcher B. Smith, who ranked third in batting (.600) in the contest, and whom Gear had signed to Topeka of the Western League.

> Smith was a star of the first magnitude uncovered by the series and will, one of these days, stand beside the best catchers in big league company.... Smith is a

Cherokee Indian, 22 years of age. He was born and raised in California. He is a blacksmith by trade, a quiet, soft spoken, likeable young man, of sterling habits. His future as a baseball player is assured.[158]

Accompanying B. Smith to Topeka would be Chief Lockhart, whom Gear had also signed.

The sportswriter was correct when, while summing up the tournament, he noted that it was a rare event when so many big leaguers and bush leaguers banded together in the national pastime. Given the racial mindset of the times, it is even more remarkable that so many colors and cultures played together so seamlessly at a fair in 1911 America. But this was a place that, by the eve of statehood, had already learned to tout its tri-cultural history. For three centuries, the different peoples had been forced to learn — and periodically have to relearn the same lesson — that New Mexico's strength lies in her diversity.

* * *

When New Mexicans first took up ball and bat in the nineteenth century, horse and burro were still the primary means of transportation. A generation later, during the 1911 Territorial Fair, New Mexicans squinted into the October sun at the first-ever flight of an airplane in the territory. On Wednesday, after the conclusion of that day's tournament game, "daring sailor of the air" Charlie Walsh sped his Curtiss biplane across the Traction Park baseball field and ascended, "sweeping in wide circles, dipping and soaring, for the first time in the history of the Rio Grande valley ... to the tune of deafening and prolonged applause and at times silence fully as eloquent from the thousands of people who packed the grand stand."[159] The days of the Wild West were over. The Land of Enchantment had entered — or had been invaded by — a brave new world.

3

Picks, Shovels and Bats

For hundreds of years before Coronado entered what would become known as New Mexico, the Ancestral Puebloans were trading a native stone that, in the tiniest chip, reflected the beauty of the world they inhabited. Some turquoise is as deeply blue as a cloudless southwestern sky. Other pieces are blue-green like the sea, with a dark and delicate filigree like sargassum. Still other samples incorporate a range of colors, making the stone resemble the earth from the eye of an astronaut. For the Puebloans, turquoise was a prized trade item and today it is still the state's most recognizable mineral resource, carried home by visitors in the form of concha belts, bracelets and rings. The hills surrounding the village of Cerrillos, located on the aptly named Turquoise Trail, were full of mines, originally exploited by area Natives. The Spaniards, soon after their arrival, noted the native peoples mining turquoise but were not overly impressed with it. They were in search of much greater treasure—and nobler enterprise—than digging for stones that didn't even sparkle.

A long standing legend, one that lived in the heart of every conquistador and every tonsured friar that accompanied him, was of the Seven Cities of Gold. These cities had allegedly been built on an island in the eighth century by seven Portuguese bishops and their parishioners fleeing the Muslim invasion of the Iberian Peninsula. It was said to be not only a utopian paradise for the descendents of the long ago wayfarers but also a place of untold wealth, particularly the cities of Quivira and Cíbola. So widely held was the belief in this island that Christopher Columbus planned to stop there for a respite on his way to Asia.

While the Spanish explorers remained frustrated by the whereabouts of the Seven Cities, they did manage to find a mineral extravaganza in New Spain (Mexico), to the extent that royal mints had to be built in most of the provincial cities.

> They stamped out lustrous pieces of eight, to the value of two billion dollars by the end of the colonial era, and another two billion worth of ingots was exported to Spain. The northern mining city of Zacatecas ... is said to have yielded one-fifth of the world's silver by the close of the eighteenth century.[1]

And despite the centuries-old belief that the Seven Cities were on an island in the Atlantic Ocean, since 1536 rumors (courtesy of a misguided Franciscan) had run rampant through Mexico City suggesting they had been sighted in northern New Spain. Inspired by the scuttlebutt, Francisco Vasquez de Coronado headed north in 1540 with a grand following of men, horses and dogs of war. After many months of exploration and disappointment (along with the brutal subjugation of quite a few Pueblo people), Coronado was encouraged by the words of a cunning plains Indian currently living at the pueblo of Cicuye. El Turco, christened thus by the Spanish because, to them, he resembled a Turk, had an admirable talent for tall tales and he set about telling a whopper for the foreign visitors.

> Through signs he told of a distant kingdom, ruled over by an emperor who slept under a tree festooned with golden bells. In a river six miles wide floated galleons with gold ornaments at the prows, and in the water swam fish bigger than horses. Gold and silver were so plentiful, claimed the Turk, that wagons would be needed to cart it all away.[2]

Convinced that what El Turco described was the golden city of Quivira, the eager Spaniards happily enlisted him to guide them there. And guide them he did, across the Texas panhandle and into Kansas, to the home of the Wichita tribe, where they found nothing but a few grass houses and an aging leader wearing a single copper bauble. They killed El Turco on the spot and now, disabused of their dreams of instant wealth, returned, for a while at least, to Mexico where they would plan for more expeditions into northern New Spain. El Turco, for his part, became a martyr to the cause of Native independence by leading the Spaniards on a wild goose chase far away from his adopted Pueblo. To this day, the Pueblos of New Mexico remember the days of the artless Spanish explorers with wry humor: the casino at the Pojoaque Pueblo is called "Cities of Gold."

Although never the silver capital that Mexico had been, New Mexico would begin to give up silver and other mineral resources in a serious way in the nineteenth century. In the southwest corner, home to the Apache, silver and copper were found early on, the latter in amounts so vast as to make modern day New Mexico the third largest producer of copper in the United States. The area around Carlsbad was for many years the leader in mining potash, primarily used as fertilizer. Taos County in the very north of the state is where one finds molybdenum, a metallic agent used to strengthen alloy steels. New Mexico is ranked second in the United States for uranium reserves. And coal has been mined in the upper third of the state since the mid–1850s. Yes, New Mexico has abundant mineral wealth and a number of its towns began as mining camps, some of the most fecund soil for competitive baseball.

There were many reasons for the long-lived popularity of baseball in the American mining camp, remoteness usually at the top of the list. Camps were typically isolated communities, built as close to the mines as possible. With the company store providing most of the necessities of a miner's life, his need to go outside the camp for goods was lessened if not alleviated altogether. As the camps grew and began to offer amenities such as schools and doctors, entire mining families moved into them. With entertainment options severely limited, baseball became wildly popular, with each camp forming one or more teams. As enjoyable as the sport was for the players, it might have been more so for the fans who loyally followed their teams to other camps and towns along the railroad lines. For the company bosses, baseball served as a multi-purpose panacea: it was a wholesome distraction for the workers and also served as an effective anti-union tool. Mining camp teams engaged in heated sporting rivalries were unlikely to join together to promote the United Mine Workers of America. In addition, a top notch baseball team could be a public relations bonanza for a mining town, attracting and keeping good workers. Gambling on games was of utmost importance but where it might just mean extra beer money for the working man, for the company bigwigs, a winning game could mean thousands of dollars earned in a single afternoon. To this end, mining camps across the country were notorious for putting baseball ringers on the payrolls, allowing them to idle the work week away but expecting them to throw fire from the mound on Sunday. Some ringers were seasoned semipro players from other camps. Others were professional ballplayers, pulled from minor leagues around the nation. Still others were men on their way up or coming back down from the major leagues. And many a red hot hurler or catcher was an outlaw player, banned from the ranks of Organized Baseball for crimes including contract jumping.

New Mexico was no different from any area that drew its fortune from the earth except perhaps for the diversity of mineral resources. From one end of the state to the other, the history of New Mexico's mining baseball teams can be told in the names emblazoned across the shirts of its players: the Carlsbad Potashers, the Dawson Coal Diggers, the Laguna Jackpile Miners. Of all the mining teams in the history of the state, those connected with the infamous outlaw Copper League of the mid–1920s are the best known.

Grant County sits on the Arizona border in the southwest corner of the state. Like many areas of New Mexico, it is semi-arid and mountainous, its lower dun-colored slopes dotted with prickly pear and yucca, its higher elevations thick with ponderosa pines. From a thousand feet above, any flowing body of water—from the smallest stream to the Gila and Mimbres rivers—can be spotted by a ribbon of verdant green created by the thirsty cottonwoods that plant themselves alongside. Hundreds of years ago, the Mogollon people lived in the area and history buffs can find breathtaking evidence of the culture at the Gila cliff dwellings, just across Grant County's northern border with Catron County. Generations after the Mogollon, the Chiricahua Apache claimed the area, as part of their homeland, holding it against incursions by the Spanish, Mexican and American governments and their avaricious civilians. After Geronimo's surrender in 1886, the Chiricahuas were banished from their lands, most ending up in Fort Sill, Oklahoma. When he died there in 1909, Geronimo was still a prisoner of war.

In 1870, a silver strike in the foothills of the Gila Mountains led to the birth of Silver City. By building their village of red brick and employing eastern architectural gewgaws, the founding fathers hoped to present the new township as several notches above a mining camp (or a warren of melted adobes). But Silver City could be as rough and tumble as any camp in the land, with a constant influx of new miners and the trades that catered to them. It lived — hectically and colorfully — until the silver boom of the West turned bust with the repeal of the Sherman Silver Purchase Act during the Panic of 1893. But Grant County's days of mining were far from over; in fact, the mining economy was on its way to a huge resurgence, due to a less coveted, but more essential, metal.

By the very early nineteenth century, copper was being worked at a location a few miles east of what would become Silver City. Called Santa Rita del Cobre (the Spanish word for copper), during the years of Spanish government it was a penal colony, with underground mining carried out by convict labor and Indian slaves. "Collapse of the workings and live burial of the laborers were undoubtedly frequent, as suggested by the artifacts and skeletons found some hundred years later in the open pit mine."[3] In the years of Mexican and American governance of New Mexico, Santa Rita was the site of numerous acts of terror committed by Apaches and miners against one another. By the turn of the century, the mines had passed through countless hands, producing a copper of such low-grade that it was deemed hardly worth the investment of industrialists. But a phenomenon known as open-pit mining was beginning, in which huge amounts of minerals could be harvested by steam shovels, with much less manpower involved. In 1910, the Chino Copper Company began gouging the land around Santa Rita. From the mine, the copper was taken for processing to Hurley, a camp that formed ten miles away. Under the watchful eye of Chino Copper, Santa Rita and Hurley grew into thriving company towns. In 1913, an effusive writer for the *Deming Headlight* praised them both but singled out Hurley as "the prettiest, cleanest, and most charming village I ever saw."[4]

The communities surrounding Santa Rita and Hurley had always supported baseball. Silver City, Deming, Tyrone and the soldiers at Fort Bayard had consistently supported teams since the early days of baseball in the territory. Silver City, in particular, approached the game with nothing short of hilarity. An 1887 game between the Slim Jims and the Fat Fellows serves as illustration. The two teams dressed in uniforms sporting everything from skull and crossbones to porous plaster ads to beer mugs. But it wasn't merely dreams of beer that kept the players going. "An ice wagon was on hand rigged up as an ambulance and stationed at third base with a plentiful supply of beer which the jolly teuton who handles the lines dealt to players who reached that goal."[5] As the beer-awarding umpire was wearing a sidearm, his decisions were never second guessed; the Fats won the tilt 20–6.

Almost inevitably, the strong local teams would begin to require something less haphazard than the occasional pickup game. "For years there had been a great baseball rivalry between the two divisions of the Chino Copper Company — the 'mine' team at Santa Rita and the 'mill' team at Hurley."[6] Joining these two in 1912 were Silver City and Fort Bayard, to form the New Mexico Copper League. In early 1914, a local paper ran a tidbit that was a poor portent to the powerhouse that the league would become within a few years. "The opening of the Copper League season has been indefinitely postponed until Silver City can find out who stole the hose used in watering the diamond."[7] The thief must have been brought to justice and the season officially began. For the next two years, the Copper League was an unremarkable collection of clubs, although the Silver City club (if not all the teams) was paid a salary, a surprising fact for a municipal team.[8] Ringers soon became an expected feature of most games, some even coming over the border from the nearby Arizona mining camps. In a game lost by the Deming Boosters to the Tyrone Miners, the Deming paper attributed the defeat of its boys to the skills of the mining camp pitcher, a former hurling star of Miami and Morenci, two Arizona copper towns. But he wasn't the only reason the Deming players had fared so poorly. "The Boosters were unaccustomed to the diamond, which is situated on the slope of the Burro Mountains, and generously sprinkled with boulders of various sizes, and made a number of costly errors, which lost the game for them."[9]

As the teams of the New Mexico Copper League found their footing in the world of semipro ball, in Arizona a parallel Copper League had formed as early as 1914,[10] the focal point of which was the copper mining town of Ray, which boasted a team featuring a few former major leaguers like Fred Carisch who had spent four seasons with Pittsburgh starting in 1903, and three more with the Cleveland Naps. He would stay in the Copper League until he made one last unsuccessful stab at glory with Detroit in 1923. Also playing for Ray was outfielder Dick Bayless, who'd played nineteen games for the Reds, then five seasons with the Pacific Coast League and one with the Western League. Bayless would stay with the league, dying in a mine explosion at Santa Rita in 1920. Hap Myers was in Ray as well; he played for the Red Sox and the St. Louis Browns but became a star of the Western League in 1912 when he stole 77 bases. Quickly grabbed by the Boston Braves, he stole 57 for them the next season.[11]

By 1917, the New Mexico Copper League had taken a valuable lesson from its identically named counterpart in the next state. Chino Copper Company in particular must have seen a winning team as a good investment. For the next few years, both states' leagues enjoyed a reputation for raiding larger, more important circuits. In January of 1917, the *Sporting News* ran the following headline and subhead

IT'S BACK TO MINES TO STAY IF THEY GO
WARNING TO PLAYERS WHO LISTEN TO COPPER CAJOLING

The article warned that jumpers could find themselves banished from Organized Baseball for good if they gave in to the siren song of the "wild and wooly organizations" of New Mexico and Arizona. Furthermore, the Texas League, which had already lost several good players, was battening down the hatches for a "genuine wholesale raid as the teams report for spring practice."[12] But the initial warning seemed to fall on deaf ears and was repeated with more vehemence a couple of months later:

COPPER COUNTRY IS CALLING THEM AGAIN
THIRD HOUSTON BUFF DESERTS AT OUTLAWS' BIDDING

This time a second, sanctimonious subhead was added: "Everybody Happy Just the Same, for No Man Was Ever So Good His Place Cannot Be Filled."[13] Even Bert Graham, Albuquerque's pride and joy from the 1911 fair tournament, jumped his Waco contract and headed for the outfield in Silver City.[14] And it wasn't only teams from Texas that were waking up to find their players gone. The Pacific Coast League suffered prodigious losses to the Arizona Copper League. One sportswriter tried to see it from the players' point of view. "War or no war, the mines must be kept going, and the miners must have their recreation. They have the money to pay good baseball salaries to get the kind of baseball they want, and they seem to be getting it. Who wouldn't want to be a miner?"[15] At one point, the steady trickle of deserting players stopped short when it was discovered that the new recruits might find themselves entering the camps as baseball-playing scabs, the teams having recently gone out on strike with the miners.[16] When the strike ended, the campaign for players began again. Santa Rita historian Terry Humble says that Chino Copper Company telegraph correspondence shows the company made overtures to many a fine baseball player, including salary offers of up to $250 a month, with work of the lighter kind, naturally, mostly in the engineering office. Also guaranteed were daily wages of up to $5 a day during the offseason.[17]

For the New Mexican Copper League, the 1918 season opened with a bang when the team from Santa Rita took on the Chicago Cubs who were on their way back home from Pasadena, California. The two teams would meet at the sports arena at nearby Camp Cody. (Just outside Deming, Camp Cody was a massive military training facility, named in honor of Buffalo Bill.) This wouldn't be the first time that the miners had engaged the Cubs; a 1917 exhibition game had proved something of a rout with the Cubs winning, 14–6.[18] This tilt, it seemed, might be a repeat performance or worse, as this time the Chicago team would have Grover Cleveland Alexander and Bill Killefer as its battery, along with Max Flack, Les Mann and Dode Paskert in the outfield and Fred Merkle, Pete Kilduff and Charlie Deal playing infield with Charlie Hollocher at short. But the famous team's opponents weren't exactly a gathering of ingénues themselves.

> The Santa Rita team had plenty of big-league know-how in its lineup. Frankie Truesdale had been with the Browns, Yankees, and Red Sox in the American League. "Bunny" Fabrique had played with Brooklyn in 1916–17. John Sheehan

was with the Dodgers later, 1920–21. Larry Pezold had played with the Cleveland Indians in 1914. Bobby Keefe ... was an ex–Cincinnati Red and New York Giant. Bill Burns had been a hurler for the Senators, White Sox, Reds, Phillies, and Tigers.[19]

In a testament to the power of the copper-mining teams, the Santa Rita boys ousted Alexander in the third inning and won the game, 6–5.

The war years took a toll on the rosters of both Copper Leagues. The Arizona version kept up its raiding of minor league teams, one newspaper reporting that forty Pacific Coast League players had signed with them and the copper agents were on their way east to pillage the big leagues.[20] But as this was wartime, the Arizona league found itself attempting to improve the image of the mining camp teams which were commonly accepted as havens for spoiled outlaws, who reaped big financial rewards for little actual work. In doubtful times, it was assured, the mining teams offered security and good wages for the man who was amenable to manual labor in addition to hard play. "Six dollars a day straight wages to copper miners, and the ball players will have to earn the money, working eight honest hours a day; $3 extra to ball players with games Saturday and Sunday."[21] Meanwhile, the New Mexico Copper League was also attempting a public relations tidying-up in the *Sporting News*.

> No prima donna salaries are being paid to ball players to camouflage as workmen by the copper concerns ... but it does offer positions at good pay to men who can do real work and gives them a chance to make neat money on the side playing ball in the Copper league, or copper leagues, since there seem to be more than one of them.[22]

The pedigree of the league, shown in the rosters of the teams, was undeniable, beginning with man who was the voice of Chino Copper Company in that article. Harry "Klondike" Kane was not only an official representative of the company, but was also Hurley's center fielder with four years in the majors under his belt. Playing with him were the state's perennial favorites Bert Graham and pitcher Noisy Donovon of the 1911 territorial fair tournament and Rudy Baerwald, one of the heroes of the tournament of 1903. Behind the plate, Hurley had Jack Roche, probably the same man who had caught for St. Louis in 1914, 1915 and 1917. Santa Rita's roster boasted a homegrown favorite in Rube Weeks (former Albuquerque hurler and father of the famous "green snake" pitch). When he died in 1927, the *Silver City Independent* wrote, "He was for many years the most consistent winner of games in the Copper League.[23] That team also had shortstop Jack Sheehan, who would go on to two seasons with the Brooklyn Robins, and Ray Jansen, who managed to play one game with the St. Louis Browns. The third team in the league was that of Tyrone, an immaculate model camp built by Phelps Dodge a few miles to the southwest of Silver City. Tyrone had managed to lure Fred Carisch and the doomed Dick Bayless from Arizona and one McArdle at shortstop who may have been Roy McArdle, of the San Francisco Seals. (By the end of August, Tyrone had also acquired Paul Meloan, former right fielder with White Sox and pitcher Bill Pertica, fresh from his major league debut with the Red Sox. He would go on to two strong seasons with St. Louis in 1921 and 1923.[24]) The fourth team was Fort Bayard which, at the turn of the century, had ceased to be a military installation and had become a general hospital for the Army. Because it was an all-soldier team, no roster was given and it was considered the "weak sister" of the league.

Certainly part of the reason the mining teams found themselves in the 1918 season the beneficiaries of so many fine professional players was the work or fight order that had been issued in June. "Although motion picture actors and opera singers were specifically exempted, baseball was expressly classed as nonessential."[25] When the major league season was ordered to end early, and its players to find essential jobs immediately thereafter or head for a European foxhole, many found it expedient to make their way to the copper mines.

> The work or fight order has not worried the Copper League for the players of the Copper circuit are workers in the sense that has the War Department's approval. They work in the mines of southwestern New Mexico when they are not playing. The high wages offered by the mining camps has been an attraction to professional players and as the mining camps have been liberal in their support of the game quite a number of former stars of better known leagues have been drawn to the copper belt.[26]

For several years following the close of the war, and subsequent crash in copper prices, the copper mining teams of the Southwest played more quietly. It seemed that the pre-war days of pirating players from established leagues were gone, along with the value of the metal being mined there. The leagues existed but without the same noise and fireworks they had enjoyed in the past. In early 1925, the Copper Leagues of Arizona and New Mexico combined into what would be called the Frontier League for at least one season. It was a geographically large circuit, even though it was made up of only four towns: El Paso, Juarez, Fort Bayard and Douglas. At the initial organizational meetings of the league, it was decided that Douglas might lawfully enlist the managerial services of a single outlawed former major leaguer but this opened the floodgates. By the second half of the 1925 season, what had heretofore been a penny ante outlaw league became a haven for some of the sport's most brilliant and tragic characters. "They are the lost boys of baseball, lashed together, ... in a ship that can never return to harbor."[27] It all started with Hal Chase.

Hal Chase reputedly had been involved in the White Sox scandal of 1919 — forever to be known as the Black Sox — functioning as an intermediary between the gamblers and the various members of the team who were interested in throwing the series. Although Commissioner Landis never formally ousted him from organized baseball, Chase left in 1920. Since his exit, "Prince Hal" had been living along the Arizona-Mexico border, playing baseball and even running a saloon at Agua Prieta, across the border from Douglas.[28] When the league was organized, Chase was handed the reins of the Arizona team, one he knew very well.

Across the border in New Mexico, Fort Bayard, no longer a soldier team, enlisted pitcher Harry Althouse, who had become something of a New Mexican legend since his arrival at the former fort in 1923. The *New Mexican* sang his praises, going so far as to compare him to the "Big Six" Christy Mathewson and talked about his history with the Western League.[29] The gossip that followed him suggested that he had given up professional baseball after hitting a batter and only reluctantly returned to pitching at Fort Bayard.[30] For its part, El Paso had expressed its opposition to the use of outlaw players, only begrudgingly allowing Douglas to use Chase. But in April, Juarez signed Tom Seaton, former Phillie, Cub and Federal League Tip-Top, El Paso expressing its disapproval at the hiring of another "ineligible," but remaining in the league. Like Hal Chase, Seaton had the stink of dishonor about him, the implication being that he gambled on games. He arrived in the southwest after having been "purged" from both the Pacific Coast League and Southern League. One is left to wonder at the extent of El Paso's dismay when, in July, after Douglas fared very poorly in the first half of the season, Hal Chase went shopping for talent and managed to snag two new players: Chick Gandil, allegedly one of the Black Sox ringleaders, and Buck Weaver, who had suffered banishment, not because he'd taken an active role in the chicanery but because he had chosen not to report what he knew.

The league had instituted a split season and Fort Bayard handily took the first half but went south in the second. The pennant race in September, which should have ended in a series between Fort Bayard and the second-half winner (disagreed upon by Juarez and Douglas) was a soap opera of tossed players not staying tossed, individual clubs making decisions that defied those of league officials, and forfeited games. When the smoke cleared, Juarez was deemed the winner and proceeded to sweep Fort Bayard (despite that team's recent acquisition of Chick Gandil who'd jumped from Douglas) for the championship. Historian Lynn E. Bevill suggests that when the Arizona club limped home the loser, a cloud of suspicion hung over manager Chase.

> It again appears as though Chase's reputation affected people's perception.... The only possible criticism of Chase would have to be his on-field playing or managing and never a hint of criticism had or has been found to support this possibility. The unfortunate ending seems to be that a controversy occurred, Chase was a controversial individual, so Chase must have in some way been involved.[31]

Chick Gandil, from his vantage point at Fort Bayard, went to great lengths to defend Hal Chase, or at least his performance on the field. "Hal loafs a little bit now, he elucidated, "but still snatches the ball around that bag. That, you know, was the secret to the gracefulness of Chase. He never caught a ball. He snatched it like a kid grabbing for the ring on a merry-go-round."[32]

The 1926 season saw the league's return to its original name and an expansion in team number. In addition to the previous season's members, two new clubs joined the Copper League, Bisbee (a team which didn't allow banned players) and Chino, which was the combined teams of Santa Rita and Hurley. In addition to the new teams, the league had also added extra star power. Jimmie O'Connell, another outlawed player, joined the Fort Bayard club. He'd been ousted for life after an incident in which, as an outfielder with the New York Giants, he had approached Phillies shortstop Heinie Sand and offered him $500 in exchange for a poor performance. This offer was immediately reported to management and then to Landis. O'Connell, the picture of naïveté, testified that he thought the entire team was aware of the offer and that he'd been ordered to make it because he was well-acquainted with Sand. When he heard about O'Connell's soft landing in Fort Bayard, writer Damon Runyon seemed pleased.

> I think even Judge Kenesaw Mountain Landis feels sorry for O'Connell, and would like to relent in his case. In fact, the judge told me last fall that he had sat down and tried to write out a case that would convince himself justifying the reinstatement of O'Connell but was unable to do so.[33]

O'Connell rewarded Fort Bayard's sympathy and confidence in him by poling a 460-foot, early-season homer, "the longest drive ever seen in the southwest."[34]

There was now pan-circuit approval of outlaw players, except for Bisbee. Even the previous year's holdout, El Paso, was willing to consider looking at an ineligible. In perhaps the most riveting — and then most disappointing — page in Copper League history, El Paso now proved itself so open to the idea of outlaw players that it went into negotiations with perhaps the greatest one of all time, Shoeless Joe Jackson, the most pitiful victim of the 1919 Black Sox and the wrath of Landis. But El Paso balked at Jackson's salary demands and lost its chance. As early as May, when the team was already becoming sluggish, sportswriter Slam Marshall, in his "Slam-Bangs" column in the local *Times*, bemoaned the city's penny-wise/pound-foolish strategy for the team.

> This writer still believes that El Paso made a mistake when it failed to take Joe Jackson at his own figure when the season opened. We have a good ball team, one of the best in the Copper League, but the Shoeless Wonder would make hundreds of dollars worth of difference in the gate receipts if he were cavorting around the El Paso outfield. O'Connell right now is the idol of the fans around the circuit but O'Connell would be dwarfed alongside Jackson.[35]

Meanwhile, Douglas had moved Hal Chase to first base only and brought in Buck Weaver as pilot. Weaver immediately went headhunting and returned with infamous Black Sox pitcher Lefty Williams. Douglas suffered a small mutiny when, within a few weeks, Williams jumped to Fort Bayard, while Chick Gandil accepted the reins of the Chino club. Once there, Gandil ruffled many a league feather with his raiding of the other teams for players. "Gandil states with emphasis that he has made no attempt to take players away from the other clubs, but that he is in the market for ball players any place that he can pick them up."[36]

Juarez took the first half of the season and Fort Bayard the second, its boys ending the year with a 47–19 record. The Bayard boys ran over Juarez in the championship series because the Mexican team had actually been forced to disband several weeks earlier because of finances and was so broke as to be completely unable to hire anyone back for the series. In fact, after the season's official end, and team accountants had pored over the books, it became apparent that the season had taken its toll financially on several of the clubs, with only the Fort Bayard, Chino and Bisbee in the black. But Bisbee had suffered performance-wise, due to its policy of not using banned players.[37] And Douglas had taken a blow when in August, Hal Chase was involved in a car accident and seriously injured, functionally ending his career with the Copper League. He would attempt a brief comeback the next season but without success. After that, he disappeared from Arizona, eventually ending up in California where he died in 1947. In 1961 author Lee Allen wrote of Chase, "You can still find people in such places as Douglas, Arizona, who will show you the hotels at which he stopped and the bars at which he drank. This talented and perverse man became an alcoholic desert drifter, still playing baseball wherever he could find a team that would take him."[38]

If anyone, player or fan, believed that the Copper League was going unnoticed by the larger world of Organized Baseball, they were wrong. At the end of the 1925 season, the *Sporting News* had made note of it.[39] In June 1926, the paper again mentioned the league saying, "The fate of these players, most of whom would still be drawing big league wages but for their shady connections is a sermon in itself for the rising generation of big leaguers to profit by."[40] Other reporters took a less pejorative tone when writing about the circuit. Louis R. Curran, in an International News Service wire story that circulated throughout August and September 1926, wrote rather glowingly about the outlaw league players, likening them to Robin Hoods, and embellished the story by adding Swede Risberg and Hap Felsch to the band of merry men. He reported rather wistfully that Gandil and Weaver were both batting "around .400" (declared by Slam Marshall to be "just a tol'able average in this league"[41]) and quoted a local pitcher who said, "Jimmy O'Connell is packing the fans into the parks because of his sensational hitting. He gets a base hit on nearly every ball thrown him and cracks the pill so hard even the good infielders are scared." Curran also gave the staggering figure of $4,000 as the monthly salaries paid by Chino Copper Company[42] (although a $2,250 cap had actually been put into effect when the league organized in early spring[43]).

But sports reporters hadn't been the only ones taking notice of the Copper League, for Commissioner Landis had fixed a gimlet eye on it as well, especially El Paso, which he obviously considered the weak link in the chain because of its shaky financial state (it had folded and been barely resuscitated in August[44]) and the city's enduring discomfort with the league's outlaw status, its courting of Shoeless Joe Jackson aside. He suggested, winking all the while at the Texans (and at Juarez), that they could and absolutely should belong to an official Class D circuit.[45] Scuttlebutt had El Paso attempting to form a new league but it would have had to entice the anti-outlaw Bisbee to be viable and the Copper League needed the Arizona town too much to let it fly the coop.[46]

Thus, despite the commissioner's persuasive words, the Copper League organized for the 1927 season with Fort Bayard, Chino, Bisbee and, yes, El Paso, which now boasted Tom Seaton on the roster and managing. Douglas was still reeling from the loss of Hal Chase when Buck Weaver left for an Illinois team of the Midwest Semipro Baseball Association in early 1927. (For his part, Chick Gandil was happy to see the last of Weaver, saying, "He double-crossed us at Chicago," in reference to Weaver's support of Swede Risberg's testimony about a doubtful 1917 Chicago/Detroit series.[47]) Chino still had Gandil at the helm and Fort Bayard, like the year before, had its strong triumvirate of Lefty Williams, Jimmy O'Connell and Harry Althouse. It was no surprise when Fort Bayard won the first half of the season, with Jimmie O'Connell hitting .481. Chick Gandil led his Chino team to a second half victory, its 21–10 record standing in stark relief against El Paso's dismal 5–26. Oddly enough, in what should have been a moment of glory near the season's end, instead of piloting his team into a successful championship, Gandil mysteriously resigned and left the area for good. But he'd left a sound team, one that — even without him — took the crown in a difficult championship series against Fort Bayard.

The 1927 Copper League season ended with El Paso and Bisbee having suffered poor attendance and in financial constraints. It would be a while before El Paso fielded another municipal team. Bisbee, on the other hand, immediately hearkened to the call of Organized Baseball and entered the newly formed Arizona State League; as early as April, the mining town was considered the favorite to win the pennant.[48] Unable to function by themselves, the two New Mexico Copper League teams gave up the ghost. The *Sporting News*, in an editorial, welcomed the news of the Copper League's demise.

> Recently backers of baseball clubs in the Arizona "copper country"— real good sportsmen at heart most of them — decided to have done with the brand they been promoting, an outlaw organization into which had been drawn about all the renegades of the game who could still toss a ball (or toss a ball game). They "got wise," these backers of baseball, and becoming so, they put off the old and took on the new, and now Arizona has a league to be recognized by the National Association.[49]

On the other hand, the fans of Grant County, New Mexico, bemoaned the loss of fine baseball to which the area had become accustomed. The outlaws, homeless once again, left in search of the limited opportunities to play elsewhere. Only Jimmie O'Connell stayed in New Mexico, where he was a much-beloved citizen for many years.

* * *

In the spring of 1925, the Central New Mexico League proudly sailed into its maiden year as an official circuit. A formal agreement, making clear the objectives of the league, had been signed by all the parties involved.

To re-establish the good old baseball spirit in New Mexico, it is understood and agreed that this league is formed for the promotion of good amateur baseball in and for the fostering of baseball support in central New Mexico, and the members hereby agree to observe the rules of the game, the rules of good sportsmanship, to be controlled by the rules of the league, and to be governed at all time by the decisions of the officers.

It was further decreed that the league would play a split season, that each team would deposit $100 to ensure it would finish the season no matter its standing, and that absolutely no outlaws or professionals were allowed. The members were exactly what one might expect from a gentlemanly Sunday afternoon league—city teams, Knights of Columbus, small businesses.[50] It probably would have remained an unexceptional and uninteresting circuit but for the fact that in 1928, an element was introduced that would add powerful players, drama and endless rule-bending. That element was mining camp teams.

The mineral deposits of southern Colorado and northern New Mexico had spawned hundreds of camps since the late nineteenth century, attracting mining families from as far away as Asia and Eastern Europe. The most famous of these, or tragically infamous, was the coal camp of Ludlow, Colorado, roughly 35 miles north of the New Mexico border. In 1914, the Colorado National Guard attacked the striking miners of the camp, resulting in the deaths of twenty people, eleven of them children. It was a turning point in the fight for unionization; the images of dead children shocked many Americans away from an entrenched opinion of miners as Bolsheviks and toward the idea that they were deserving of basic human rights.

The rich veins of bituminous coal reached from Colorado into northern New Mexico, an area that was riddled with camps, attracting hordes of the hopeful.

> Each new strike was an unknown quantity; the ores and deposits could eventually sustain a large community of labor and businessmen, or they could be exhausted in a few seasons. Women and children signaled the "maturing of a community, but they would only come with the promise of steady production and steady jobs."[51]

One of these camps was Madrid (pronounced with the stress on the first syllable), located in the Ortiz Mountains south of the capital at Santa Fe. Coal was being mined in small quantities in the area as early as 1835, and the village was in a nascent stage by the 1860s, but large scale mining didn't start until the arrival of the railroad in 1880. Madrid was unique in that its 30-plus square mile fields offered both anthracite (hard) and bituminous (soft) coal, a highly unusual geological occurrence. When the Albuquerque and Cerrillos Coal Company took over the mines in 1906, it turned what had been a shambolic collection of wood huts into a model camp, its approximately 3,000 inhabitants enjoying all the amenities one might expect, including medical care, schools, churches and eventually a "fine baseball park with an electric scoreboard."[52] By 1928, when the Madrid Miners joined the Central New Mexico League, the town that sponsored the team was at its coal-producing peak.

Madrid had begun fielding teams in the early part of the twentieth century, along with other coal camps like Dawson, with its all-salaried team that had competed in the 1911 Territorial Fair tournament. After years of playing when and who they could, in 1928, the latest incarnation of the Madrid team entered the Central New Mexico League, bringing with it Albuquerque and Cerrillos Coal's gritty desire to win. Within two years, the roster was packed with men brought in from Organized Baseball, including a catcher and outfielder from Bisbee, a pitcher from the Arizona State League and, for a few games at least, the famous Harry Althouse, Copper League veteran.[53] While the use of outright outlaws would have shocked the sensibilities of some of the other teams, polished ringers didn't seem to offend anyone; in fact, the other teams that could afford it weren't averse to hiring the occasional professional hurler themselves.[54] Madrid also made use of amateur talent in addition to professional, and if they were good enough, they could name their terms. A former pitcher told the *Santa Fe New Mexican* years later that he'd moved to Madrid just to play ball but refused from the beginning to work underground and, indeed, was never asked to do so.[55] With Madrid's entrance into the league, the "good old baseball spirit" envisioned by the signers of the original league statement was thriving, but the word "amateur," when applied to the league, was now laughably inaccurate.

By spring 1929, the Madrid Miners were a lethal force in the Central New Mexico League, competing against clubs with more limited budgets for talent. One of the reasons they especially caught fire that season was an apparently inexhaustible Native American pitcher — a Potawatomi from Oklahoma — named Emmett Jerome Bowles. Bowles' story is the type that leaves the baseball fan choking back salty tears. Born in 1898, he made it to the big leagues for a single inning with the Chicago White Sox in 1922. In a bit of bitter irony, he debuted against Tris Speaker's Cleveland Indians on September 12. Called in during the ninth inning, he gave up two hits which led to three runs, and walked away with a lifetime major league ERA of 27.00. The Indians won 8–2.[56] By the time he reached Madrid, Bowles had a few years on most of his teammates and as early as 1930, local papers were referring to him as "the old master." [56]

The Miners also had a powerhouse hitter who'd recently played with Jimmie O'Connell's Fort Bayard Veterans. Harry "Pop" Stowers would brilliantly cover third base for the Miners for many years but it was his bat that made him irreplaceable to the team. Pop Stowers was the quintessential mining camp player, so talented that, if not for an early injury, he might have reached the majors. But without regret, he spent his lengthy baseball career in semi-pro circuits of the southwestern mineral fields, committing himself to the support of his young family. His son, Harry Stowers, Jr., is the beneficiary of that paternal devotion. Harry Stowers is also the beneficiary of a coal camp childhood. "Madrid was a great place for the fundamental values of life. I learned to be honest and fair, and to play it straight. I learned there that if your word was no good, neither were you," says Harry from his home in the village of Los Ranchos, New Mexico. The lessons he took from his childhood have served him well. Harry went to the University of New Mexico, then worked his way through law school at Georgetown. He has enjoyed a long distinguished career as a jurist, highlighted by eight years as a New Mexico Supreme Court justice.

Growing up in Madrid also gave Harry a love of baseball and he, a generation after his father, played a season for the Miners, in addition to college ball and in an Albuquerque semipro league. "That's the only game we played in Madrid. No basketball, no football — we played baseball year 'round practically. We all wanted to be major league players," he says. And of course, bearing the genes of a legendary hitter didn't hurt. Pop Stowers was born in Little Rock, Arkansas, in 1905. Harry doesn't know a lot about his father's early years. "I cannot remember any discussion where my mother and my dad and myself discussed how he got to Fort Bayard, but my presumption was that he had a job there." With the talent that was demanded by Copper League clubs, chances are Pop was hired to play baseball and the "job" came second. What is known is that he was scouted and signed by San Francisco during the Copper League's playoffs of 1926.[57] Sadly, that opportunity would come to naught because of an accident shortly after his arrival in California. "In those days," explains Harry, "the circus and carnivals would use the ballparks and in this one, they somehow left a little spike sticking in the ground right by second base. My dad slid into second and his spikes caught on that spike and sort of wrapped his leg around it. That was the end

Harry "Pop" Stowers, veteran of the Fort Bayard team of the Copper League and the Madrid Miners of the Central New Mexico League, helps son Harry learn the ropes in front of their house in the coal camp of Madrid. Harry Stowers, Jr. followed in his father's footstep and played for the Miners in the early 1940s before going to law school (courtesy Harry Stowers).

of his professional career. They said he'd never walk again but my mother said that, very shortly after that happened, he was going around the bases on crutches, practicing." After that, Pop returned to Fort Bayard, where Harry believes he worked at the hospital, like the other members of that Copper League team, including Jimmie O'Connell and Harry Althouse. With the league's demise, it is not surprising that Pop found immediate employment at Madrid, where he became a motorman in the mines.

The place that Harry Stowers describes while reminiscing about Madrid could be a blueprint for company towns from one end of America to the other. "It was a very isolated town about sixty miles from Albuquerque and about thirty from Santa Fe. In those days there were no paved roads. It was a very self-contained little community where everything was owned by the company. They owned all the houses. We had our own monetary system called scrip. If you had a scrip card, your mother would send you down to the office to draw five dollars scrip and it would be deducted from whatever your father was earning." Yet far from some of its woollier, more rowdy counterparts elsewhere, Madrid was an upright, family-oriented place, and a town so consumed with yuletide fervor that every square inch was decorated with lights. Legend holds that airlines diverted flight plans so that passengers could gaze down in amazement on the coal camp wonderland.

The general wholesomeness of town life applied to baseball as well. Harry Stowers states unequivocally that there was no gambling on the games, either by company brass or individuals ("Nobody had any money in those days— people were working for a dollar a day. If something like that were happening, everybody in town would have known it"). He also describes a team of players that, while friendly with one another, left after the games and immediately returned home to their families. The ball players were employees of the coal company but were such valuable assets that none worked underground. Harry says, "I can't remember them all but my recollection is that they had jobs in the machine shop or the garage — above ground employment." And in appreciation of the team's talent for winning, the people of Madrid turned out in full force for every home game. "On Sunday the whole town came to watch the ballgame. When it was going on, if you came in on the other end of town, you wouldn't find anyone until you got to the ballpark." They parked their cars along the foul lines, and every hit or run scored by the home team was met with a symphony of horns.

In 1929, the first year that Pop Stowers played for the Miners, they took the first half of the season, the second half going to the Santa Fe Saints. In a portent of the squabbling that would plague the league, the championship series wasn't played because the two teams couldn't come to an understanding on gate receipts.[58] But the mining team roared into the next season, with Pop hitting a home run out of the park in his first at-bat of the year and Emmett "Chief" Bowles earning himself a 14–8 win. "The Madrid team looks to be a stronger aggregation that that of last season with another lineup of hit-

The Madrid Miners, one of the most feared teams in the Central New Mexico League of the 1930s. In this 1936 championship photograph, the legendary Emmett "Chief" Bowles, Potowatami pitcher, is standing in the back, wearing a jacket. Pop Stowers is third from the left in the front and his brother-in-law, John Garcia, that year's league leader in batting, is in the front, far left (courtesy Harry Stowers).

ters that won for them the name of 'murderers' row.'"[59] The league fell apart in June when the Albuquerque Dukes protested the Miners' use of Chick Rossi for one game, a player that they called an outlaw. Detente was reached in July and play resumed, the Miners taking the first half. Madrid's competitors remained baffled by the almost flawless pitching of Chief Bowles, and obviously hoped that age would eventually catch up with him.

The hard-to-beat Madrid pitcher put to an end all rumors that he was slipping as he limited the Grays to five singles and one earned run. During the first seven innings, Bowles allowed the Grays only one hit. In the eighth they fell on him for four hits and four runs, but he set them down 1–2–3 in the ninth to make the victory a lopsided one.[60]

The championship playoff in September, between the Miners and a sawmill team from Bernalillo, could have provided the plot for any number of sentimental movies, as age and wisdom gave way to youth and talent. The Bernalillo Piners put their regular third baseman, a fifteen-year-old boy named Russell Howes, on the mound for the first game of the three-game series, which he won and returned him for the second game. "He allowed six hits this time instead of four, but he kept them well scattered and but for errors behind him would have been credited with a shut out game." While Chief Bowles pitched in typically stellar fashion, very poor support behind him lost him the game and the Miners the championship.[61]

3. *Picks, Shovels and Bats* 69

The Madrid Miners seated in front of one of the crowds that this champion team always drew in the Central New Mexico League (courtesy Harry Stowers).

The 1931 season saw Madrid winning both halves, the undisputed champions of the Central New Mexico League. It was another brilliant season, with Pop Stowers leading the league in batting[62] and marred only slightly near the end by Chief Bowles accidentally beaning to unconsciousness the captain of the Albuquerque Grays.[63] The league disbanded in 1932 when Albuquerque joined the Cactus League but reorganized for a late start in 1933, with Las Vegas, Bernalillo, Santa Fe and Madrid involved. Again, the almost invincible coal men dominated the season, winning both halves.[64]

From its entry into the league in 1928, the Madrid Miners had proven themselves almost bulletproof. It seemed that no club could conquer them and the only club that could possibly match them — bat for bat, pitch for pitch — would be that of another mining town, Tererro, which entered the league in 1934.

To reach Tererro today, one must begin in the village of Pecos, with its haunting Pueblo and Spanish mission ruins, and travel a circuitous fourteen-mile ascent through the Pecos River canyon. Once in Tererro proper, the traveler can stock up on a few hiking supplies at the general store or book a guided horseback tour of the breathtaking Pecos Wilderness. But if one has gone in search of what was in its day an immense mining operation, one that produced silver, gold, copper, lead and zinc, there will be no trace. For all that's left of the mining town is one bridge near Holy Ghost Canyon. Although the town has disappeared, there is one man who can talk at length — and expertly

—about it, because his family was one of the very first to take up residence in 1926, before the mining town had even been given a name.

Leon McDuff is a genteel man. Talking to him on the telephone, one pictures him in a wingback chair with brandy and pipe, and perhaps a well-loved volume of Gibbon. "I look back on Tererro as having been one of the happiest times of my life," he says and he has written his own book on the topic to keep the memories and history alive. His father was one of the first men hired by American Metal Company of New Mexico and went to work as wooden structures superintendent. He was the one who supervised the building of the aforementioned bridge, the single lonely monument to the vanished town.

Metals had been mined in the area since the 1880s by individuals and various small companies. But in 1925, American Metals purchased the mine and surrounding properties (including a parcel in Dalton Canyon, so named for the Dalton Brothers gang who had hidden out there[65]) and sank two shafts that would eventually go down 1,200 feet. Because they hit the water table, huge pumps had to work steadily, ridding the mine of water at the rate of 1,000 gallons a minute.[66] Adding to the general misery of underground mining, these workers also faced the possibility of pump failure and bitterly cold winter temperatures underground. "Air doors had to be installed ... to prevent cold air currents from freezing the water and air supply lines."[67] The shafts sunk, the operators turned to the difficulty of transporting the raw ore from the mines to a mill. After considering various options, what they finally did was build a fourteen-mile aerial tramline that conveyed the crushed ore down from the mine to the mill and to the tailings site. "It was the longest tramway in the world at that time," says Leon. From 1927, when they swung into full operation, until 1939, when they closed, the mines at Tererro were the largest producers of lead and zinc in the state.

When the McDuff family arrived in 1926, Leon's father, who had come before, welcomed his family with a home built in a two-acre meadow. "We lived in very small houses. My father, being one of the officials in the mine, lived in one of the biggest houses," Leon explains. "The biggest house was 12 feet by 36 feet. There were about four houses that size. Everything else was only 12 by 24. My brother and I slept in a tent. And at that altitude, pretty close to 10,000 feet, during the wintertime, it sometimes got down. The lowest I ever remember my dad saying was 33 below zero." He chuckles at the shock effect of this information. "Just a sheet of canvas between my brother and I and the outside. You just slept under a ton of quilts." While the spartan quality of this lifestyle might give pause, the children enjoyed great rewards in the form of a mountain Eden, abundant with plants and wildlife. As the town attracted miners and their families, it grew into a bustling international community, like mining camps everywhere. And like most camps from the Appalachians to the Rockies, the varied ethnic groups were segregated. Leon says that perhaps seventy percent of Tererro's population was Hispanic and there existed a constant hum of racial tension between them and the Anglo population. But the hostility directed toward the handful of African Americans at Tererro was "open and vociferous,"[68] imparting a lifelong sense of right and wrong to the impressionable young witness.

While Tererro didn't have a company store, there was an independently owned one in the camp[69] and a few in nearby towns. There was also a movie house, built from an old barn on the outskirts of the mine property and named the Dixie Theater. Down the canyon in Pecos, there were clubs like the Casanova and the Nightingale ("with soda fountains and slot machines," Leon says). And for the miner with a few extra dollars to spare, Tererro had its own red light district known as Chihuahuatown.

There were entertainment options more suitable to youth such as golf, although it might be difficult to imagine a course in alpine wilderness. Perhaps even more so than Tererro's record-breaking tramway, the golf course there was a study in Yankee ingenuity. Leon McDuff describes it. "They took the oil that came out of automobiles and mixed it with sand and this is what the greens were. The dairy had cattle that roamed over the golf course. So they had a rake that you used to smooth a path from the ball to the cup. You always had to do that. The sand was such that some places it was very soft and some places it was harder so that gave the golfers a more difficult time. That's where I learned to play golf." Does he think the unusual course made him a better golfer? "Oh yes," he quickly affirms, adding that his brother was the New Mexico state high school champion. (Golf almost spelled Leon's demise when he was hit in the head with a club. In a testament to the creative medical care that mining camps could employ, Leon has a silver quarter in his skull to this day, a competent patch job done by the company doctor.)

The packed sand golf course sat right next to the Tererro baseball diamond which, at 10,000 feet has to have been one of the highest in the history of the national pastime. Teams expected to perform badly there, even those from Santa Fe which sits at 7,000 feet.[70] And, like many a field in mostly mountainous New Mexico, it was hardly level and gave new meaning to the phrase "home field advantage." Leon writes, "The infield was comparatively level, but the left outfield declined toward the golf course about four feet at its furthermost edge and the right field declined ... by about two feet. A hard-hit ground ball into left field gained considerable momentum as a result of this slope. For a return throw to home plate of a ball to deep left, the fielder had to throw uphill about five feet."[71]

What Leon McDuff recalls is a mixed team of Anglos and Hispanos. He is adamant about the company not hiring ringers. "There was a rumor that the mine hired people to work if they were good baseball players. The mine manager's son and I were very good friends and so I asked his father about this after I came to California and was writing my book. 'Did you hire baseball players simply because they were baseball players?' No, they didn't. They hired them because they were good miners and if they were good baseball players, that was an extra advantage. But they never hired them because they were good baseball players."

There are those who take exception to Leon's belief. Authors James and Barbara Sherman do.

> Tererro boasted one of the best baseball teams in the state. The camp sent out notices to entice players to try out for their team. If accepted, a player would be hired as a mucker by the mining company. Jobs were in demand, and miners failing to fill a daily ore quota were fired and immediately replaced by a waiting miner. The baseball players hired as muckers, however, did not have to fill their ore quota and never feared being replaced.[72]

When Tererro entered the Central New Mexico League in 1934, its competitors consisted of two Santa Fe teams, a team from Mountainair (south of Albuquerque on the edge of the Manzano Mountains), a team from the Duke City and the fierce Miners from Madrid. The latter two were the teams to beat from the outset of the season, the Albuquerque Dons boasting a powerhouse pitcher named Charlie Brown and the Miners their ace, Chief Bowles. The Tererro Tigers seemed to begin their season with a philosophy of winning by attrition. No grandiose plays, no stars, just solid play. While the Santa Fe Stationers won the first half of the season, the Tigers were gaining on every team to take the second half pennant. A headline in July conveyed the seriousness of the threat that Tererro was becoming: "Tererro Defeats Madrid by Hitting Chief Bowles Hard."[73] That a Tererro relief hurler, Joe Lucero, could achieve a 9–4 win over the veteran Madrid pitcher was almost unthinkable. By the end of the month, the Santa Fe winners of the first half had their eye on sweeping the season and the mining team from up on the Pecos River seemed the biggest obstacle to it. In discussing the issue with a sportswriter, it was brazenly declared that the management at Tererro was paying big money to win.

> Terrero [sic] is regarded by the Stationers as the team they must beat to win the second half pennant and they are considerably worried about what they call "Terrero's [sic] high priced professional team," which boasts such new stars as Matt Ortiz, an old standby of many an Albuquerque baseball team. In addition they will be bothered no doubt by the hillside playing field and its 11,000 feet elevation.[74]

The complaints about the field sound a bit like a team prophesying and justifying a future loss. The mention of big money, however, certainly must have sparked a degree of ill will in the semipro league. Perhaps that was the real reason behind the Stationers refusal to play a championship series against the Tererro Tigers, who did indeed win the second half, although the Santa Fe team cited their desire to play the entire series at home as the reason for not participating.[75]

The 1935 Central New Mexico League season started with only slight changes to the teams, mostly in the addition of a second team from Albuquerque. Even though the Albuquerque Tigers took the first half of the season, the Tererro team, now called the Sluggers, caught fire in July and by the middle of the month led the league in wins and the Tererro skipper, Mickey Nance, was leading in batting averages with .489. It wasn't just Nance; four other players on the team — Reed, Griego, Valdez and Budzinsky — were joining with their manager to give Tererro "a long lead in the team batting averages," as well.[76] In August, with a perfect record for the second half, the Sluggers took on the Albuquerque Dons and extended their lead with a 15–5 victory. The *Albuquerque Journal* supplied a bit more evidence supporting the mining team's use of ringers. "Steel, imported Tererro pitcher from Oklahoma, was wild, himself, walking four and hitting one, but, with fine support from what looked like the best infield in the league, he was touched for only three safe hits, all singles."[77] Finally, at the end of August, the Sluggers' perfect record was spoiled by the Dons of the Duke City, in a game that almost turned into a free-for-all when Tererro pilot Micky Nance slugged the home plate umpire and the benches cleared, all players with bats in hand. Tempers were assuaged and after an apology to the umpire, the game was allowed to continue.[78] And although their perfect run had been marred by that loss, the Sluggers must have enjoyed it a few days later when they were able to give their previous season's party-pooping nemesis, the Santa Fe Stationers, a 20–5 thrashing.[79] The Sluggers ended the season by winning the second half.

It was agreed by both team managers and the president of the Central New Mexico League that the first game of the championship series would be played at Rio Grande Park in Albuquerque, the second at the perilous Tererro field, and the third, if one were necessary, at Santa Fe.[80] Albuquerque took the first game, 9–8, in a contest described by a *Journal* writer as "sloppy but interesting."[81] The Albuquerque Tigers probably spent the night before the second game racked with nightmares of the terrible Tererro field. It is more than likely that their dreams couldn't hold a candle to just how awful the diamond really was and just how badly it would handicap them. A reporter elaborated on Leon McDuff's description.

> But the blame does not fall entirely with the Tigers. The Tererro diamond, 10,000 feet above sea level, resembles a sea during a good wind storm. It is level from home to first and third, downhill from first to second, and uphill from second to third. The outfield is another mass of billowing hills. Both right and left fielders play in a valley; only the center field is level. Once a ball gets away from the fielders it goes for a home run.[82]

Albuquerque lost the game, 18–5. The deciding game was played at Santa Fe in front of the largest crowd that town had seen in years. In a four-run, ninth-inning rally, the Tererro Sluggers took the crown.[83]

Two glorious seasons were all that the Tererro baseball team would have; in February 1936, the International Union of Mine, Mill and Smelter Workers called a strike at the mineral mines in Tererro, their brethren at the coal mines in Madrid having done so three weeks before. The union sought higher wages, better living conditions (including a sanitary system in camp houses and mines, and an end to the scrip system[84]), and an air circulation system in the mines.[85] It was a fight between labor and owners to rival almost any in Harlan County, Kentucky, with violence committed by both sides. While the Madrid coal strike ended early enough to organize a team for the Central New Mexico League's season, the Tererro strike lasted until mid–May, leaving the camp without baseball except for a couple of sandlot teams[86] and a "ladies team" that formed in late July.[87] Leon McDuff speculates on the mining camp's absence from the Central New Mexico League. "You know, there was a lot of ill feelings between those who struck and those who didn't. They may not have been able to put together a team during those years because of the animosity between the two groups. Some of them might have been strikers and those that didn't strike were called scabs."

Tererro tried to re-enter the league in 1939 but in May, just as the strong New Mexico sun would begin to thaw one of the game's highest ball fields, the American Metals Company closed the mines and began to dismantle the remarkable tramway that had been such a symbol of the mining community. Like many Americans who spent a good part of their lives in mining camps, and then been forced to watch them die, Leon McDuff was eventually struck by the tragedy of it.

> It was only fifty years later that I began to realize the significance of the real world drama that unfolded around me during the thirteen years, three months, and seventeen days that Tererro was my home.... During those years, the population had grown from 192 male employees, two women and four children, to over 850 employees and a bustling community of almost 3,000; in three months, it had withered away to half a dozen...."[88]

The Central New Mexico League carried on without Tererro but interest in the league had begun to suffer, probably due to the fact that Albuquerque had landed a spot in the Arizona-Texas League in 1937 and was doing quite well, winning the league title in '37 and '38, hence drawing local attention. And the now-professional team was attracting scores of regional fans. As for the Central New Mexico circuit's remaining mining team, Madrid still had Pop Stowers on the roster although he never again competed for a batting title. He and his family soon moved to Santa Rita where he still had some good years left at third base.

Harry Stowers says that, as a young player, Pop had been hit with a ball hard enough to cause a depression in his skull but he'd always assured his family that doctors had put a silver plate in to protect him. When Pop fell from a tree at age 56, x-rays showed that there was no such plate. He died a few days later of a brain hemorrhage. Harry wonders if that early baseball injury had anything to do with it.

The aging Chief Bowles was not mentioned after 1938. The appellation "chief" would soon be applied to another Native American force, a Potowatamie named Marcell Littlehorse, who would float between the Duke City's professional team and the rising Albuquerque Indian All-Stars, who joined the Central New Mexico League that year.

After the league disbanded in 1939, various baseball teams from Madrid continued to play in sandlot leagues. Harry played for the Miners in the early '40s. What he didn't know, but might have sensed, was that Madrid, like Tererro before it, was headed for extinction.

* * *

On Interstate 40, about half way between Albuquerque and Grants, an ancient assortment of adobe structures surrounding a white Spanish mission church hugs a northern hillside. One can stop at an overlook and peer "across a narrow wash, and seeming vaster gulf of time," as esteemed historian/photographer David Grant Noble once wrote of the village of Old Laguna.[89] Old Laguna is the first and foremost of the six villages that make up Laguna, the largest of the Keresan-speaking Pueblos of New Mexico, with an enrollment of over seven thousand members. As with many of the Pueblos, there is disagreement between the beliefs that sustain the people and those that compel science. The latter say the ancestors of today's inhabitants arrived there a few centuries ago. Many of those who inhabit the land will say that they have been there for eons, having migrated from a northern homeland. Until the 1950s, they lived the way that most of the region's Natives did, mostly as small-scale agriculturalists raising sheep and a few cows. And, like many of the other tribes, they loved baseball to distraction.

As early as the 1930s, the Laguna teams began making the sports page of the *Albuquerque Journal*, and the Pueblo's position as mover and shaker in the world of Indian baseball was cemented in 1935 when it hosted the debut All-Indian tournament, "believed to be the first ... in the United States."[90] Throughout the following decades, Laguna remained a force. In the early '50s, however, change came to the Pueblo, one that would alter the lives—personal, professional, athletic—of every member of the tribe. It would enrich them beyond their wildest dreams and would also damage them in profound ways.

Laguna is located in what is called the Grants Uranium Belt which stretches across the lower edge of the San Juan Basin. Uranium was first discovered on the Navajo reservation in 1950 by a tribal member. The ore was considered to be of such a high grade that deeper investigation of the surrounding area began immediately and thus began a uranium boom with the town of Grants as the geographic center. One newspaper described the carnival (and dangerously naïve) atmosphere of the era and the place. "Prospectors, with Geiger counters in hand, swarm over the region in ever increasing numbers, especially on weekends. They often gather in the hotel lobbies in the evenings, dump yellowish rocks on the floor and compare them for size, color and radio-activity."[91]

When the hot rock was discovered at Laguna Pueblo shortly thereafter, Anaconda Copper Company acquired a lease on nearly 5,000 acres within two years and mining began in 1953, including both open pit and underground. What would become the world's largest open pit uranium mine—the Jack-

The village of Old Laguna at Laguna Pueblo. From the 1950s until the mid–1980s, Laguna was the site of one of the world's largest uranium mines. A strong baseball presence in the state since the mid–1930s when it started the annual All-Indian Tournament, the Pueblo became even more of a powerhouse in the '50s with two mining-company-backed clubs (Belinda Winn).

pile — was begun perilously close to the edge of the Pueblo's village of Paguate. A mill was built at Bluewater, to the west of the mines; there the complicated process of extraction began, eventually producing yellowcake, which was sold to the Atomic Energy Commission. In 1955 the mines and mill were fully operational and many tribal members found work with Anaconda, the majority of them being paid $350 to $400 a month.[92] By that same year, the constant blasting, particularly in Paguate around the Jackpile mine, was already taking a toll on the village residents and their homes.

> Although Anaconda officials insist that blasting has been maintained at one-tenth of the impact necessary to sustain damage, residents complain of cracked homes, noise and dust. The ancient, delicate stone dwellings which comprise much of the village were built before man and machines could manipulate the earth. Many were built without mortar or a foundation."[93]

Uranium mining didn't interrupt the baseball life at Laguna; in fact, it broadened it. Historically, most of the Pueblo's multiple villages fielded teams, meaning that in any sandlot or semipro circuit, the tribe was usually represented by at least two clubs. Two of them — the Merchants and the Braves — graduated to the semipro Albuquerque City-County League in the early '50s from sandlot leagues before the war. In 1955, the Laguna Anaconda team arrived on the scene, the first mining team in the area since the glory days of the Madrid Miners. Following within two years was the Jackpile Miners, named for the vast pit that was growing larger by the tune of 3,200 tons of earth removed every day.[94]

Al and Jean Riley Green, both from Paguate, recall baseball during the active mining years. Jean says, "When the team initially started out in Old Laguna they were called the Laguna Merchants until Anaconda sponsored and took over. 'Anaconda' became their team name thereafter." She proudly talks about her brothers, Roger and Emerson Riley, who were two of Laguna's most memorable players in those days. If one attempted to chalk her enthusiasm up to a sisterly bias, the local newspapers would back her with the Riley brothers' impressive stats. "My brother Emerson, who played for the Merchants, who later became Anaconda, was the best shortstop I can remember. My other brother Roger played first base for the Laguna Braves and he was the best until I saw my husband play. He was long-legged and could stretch out and catch that ball like nobody else." When asked about company-backed mining teams, she nods. "They were quite well provided for. The other teams didn't have all that. They lacked uniforms—some of them just wore their Levis," she says. Jean's husband Al, who played for Paguate, joins in, saying, "The Anaconda and Jackpile teams were composed of a conglomerate of different villages because everyone worked at the mine then. Our teams, we supported ourselves but Anaconda and Jackpile, they always had new uniforms every year. They were always well-equipped. For us, we donated our own money." In addition to uniforms and equipment, Anaconda also helped to maintain and improve the Laguna field. Unlike most mining team stories, however, neither Al nor Jean remembers Anaconda players receiving more money or lighter work. Nor, says Al, does he remember ever seeing any Anaconda brass attending the games. Anaconda's support of baseball at Laguna seems to have been less personal than the old days of mining camps and companies, where officials were deeply involved in the day-to-day workings of the ball clubs. But whatever the company's involvement, the money spent on the Anaconda team was not wasted, even if the effect was simply a psychological one, born of new uniforms and equipment and a field that was the envy of Indian teams from New Mexico to California. The Anaconda team won the Laguna All-Indian tournament the first three years they competed.[95]

There was so much baseball enthusiasm in the Pueblo in the 1950s that the *Albuquerque Journal* wrote a piece with the headline "What's This??? Move the Dukes!! Laguna Becomes Baseball-Mad."[96] Just a few years later, another article appeared, comparing the typical Laguna crowds of 2,000–3,000 fans to the paltry 1,500 that a Dukes game might draw.[97]

"In the 50s, that's when baseball was the biggest thing on the reservation," says Paully Kiro of Mesita, one of Laguna's six villages. "It was one of the biggest shows around. They had vendors and everything." He is an animated talker with a booming voice that announces his arrival while he is still outside. He has brought his sons to see their grandparents, Ann and Paul Kiro, at their home in Mesita. The elder Paul, born in 1930, was a star baseball player in his own right and a fine all-around athlete. Living there to help care for their parents is Paully's brother Terence, whose quiet demeanor is a stark contrast to his brother's garrulousness.

At age 50, Paully's memories of Laguna baseball begin in the 1960s, with his entrance into Little League, but he knows the stories of the glory days because they are still told around the Pueblo. Those stories generally start with Laguna teams entering the remarkably long-lived Albuquerque City-County League that began in the post-war years. Defying the national trend of losing momentum in the 1950s, it continued to play throughout that decade and into the 1960s. Laguna consistently entered two or more teams throughout the life of the league. The Jackpile Miners competed in it until they folded in 1964 and Laguna Anaconda continued playing in it until 1969. But in the '70s, as interest in local semipro baseball died out, so did the league and the uranium-sponsored teams from Laguna.

But the Laguna people's interest never waned and there were still six villages left at home full of baseball-loving boys and men. To fill the need, a league was formed, comprised of teams from the six villages there. "When we had our own league," says Paully, "we had games Mondays, Wednesdays, Fridays and Sundays. All the villages had one or more teams and usually Isleta had one in it too. The league was still very strong in the '80s. We had a lot of teams when I was playing for my dad's team, the Laguna Redskins. I played second base, my brother Terence was a catcher. The big baseball families were the Marianos and the Rileys; from grandfathers to grandsons, all had athletic ability, mainly in baseball. So they didn't have to recruit. And once you finished Little League, you were playing semipro right away." (As is common in baseball everywhere, the word "semipro" can have broad definitions. In this case, Paully refers to the Laguna village league.)

Growing up to work in the mines, in addition to spending his life playing ball, Paully is intrigued by the issue of those company-supported baseball teams of years past. He believes that, in Anaconda's heyday, the teams not sponsored by uranium had to apply to the Pueblo council if they need financial help. The teams representing Anaconda would have had no need to do that. "If a team was going to be funded by tribal money, the council would have to approve. But Anaconda, being their own company, could do whatever they wanted to with their money without having to go through the council." Like others, he knows that the Anaconda team always had good uniforms and equipment but that the other teams were on their own. If they couldn't come up with the money needed to cover expenses, "they'd have had to go to the council to get it."

The arrival of Anaconda in the 1950s put an end to what had been high unemployment rates at Laguna. Paully Kiro went to work for the mines after two years in the Navy. "I was gonna enlist in the four-year program but, golly, all the classmates that I had in school here, instead of going into the service or college, they went right into the mines. And when I came home for leave, they were all driving Camaros or new Trans Ams because it was big money paid for even unskilled. I came home driving a little Volkswagon bug and thought, 'Man, they're all making so much money here.'" For a seventeen-year-old father, that kind of income was irresistible and he went to work for Anaconda, staying there until the mines closed. "I worked underground. I worked at P-13 and at that time it was the deepest underground shaft in the world. When we were shutting down, we were hitting the highest concentration of pure grade ore. I was in ore that we'd blast out and it would be black as coffee, it was that pure. I'd out it on a Geiger counter and it'd go off the counter ten times — there was no way to register how high it was. At that time, we didn't have any respirators and I'd be in high-grade ore, knee deep, all day long." He talks about the older generation of miners, the Lagunas that started with Anaconda when the company first leased the land. "A lot of these guys are finally getting compensated that worked from 1970 back — they've started to award them some money. Regardless of whether they've got any long-term residual effect or not, everybody who worked then is eligible for money. At that time, they hadn't even hit any of the high level uranium, so they're very fortunate to have gotten that. It seems like the generation from 1970 to 1984, nobody's been compensated for working in the mines. Just the old-timers." Terence adds, "After the mines came, people all got sick." And that's not surprising, given the fact that, during the 1970s, the EPA determined that both the surface and groundwater at Laguna was contaminated. Also, Anaconda had used radioactive ore to pave the Pueblo's roads and build public buildings and housing.[98] The radioactive dust, particularly coming from the Jackpile mine, routinely blanketed the village of Paguate. When asked about his own health, Paully admits that years of blasting have cost him some hearing. He adds, "I've always been in pretty good shape but it seems like in the last couple of years, if I get sick, I don't recover like I used to." In the early '80s, Anaconda sold its interests to ARCO which closed the mines in 1984. "ARCO took over the last two years but we weren't actively mining because they were getting ready for the reclamation," Paully explains.

Looking back on the last sixty years at his home, Al Green has grave misgivings about decisions his people made in the past and those that could be foisted on them from the outside in the future. "I think we thought it was good at the beginning when Laguna was bringing in the money," he says. "However, I think that's changed because of the number of people that have been affected by the mines — negatively affected. Quite a few people have passed on as a result of working at the mines. Right now, there's a division between the Anglo and the Mexican [Hispano] population in and around Laguna because those people want to start up the mines again. Laguna is against it. They're allied with Acoma and Navajo don't want anymore mining done. Just recently, they wanted to open up mines around the Mount Taylor area. The Pueblos — Zuni, Laguna, Acoma — and the Navajo, they consider that mountain sacred and they're totally against any mining being done up there."[99]

Supporting Al's argument, Author Ward Churchill points out what Anaconda brought to the Pueblo and what it left behind.

> Only a few years ago [i.e. 1977], Laguna had the highest per capita income and lowest unemployment of any reservation in North America. Then the uranium played out, and with it went the jobs and royalties which had made Laguna "prosper." Now the corporate sugar daddy is gone, the water is radioactively contaminated, and so are the foundations of homes and community buildings, the roadbeds and the farmland. The old economy of Laguna cannot be reconstructed, the new economy is bust, and the chances are that the people will not even be able to remain on their homeland because of the contamination.[100]

As for Paully Kiro, he doesn't dwell on those things. He is chipper and optimistic, a busy single father with a young generation to keep inspired. "My older son played and I've got two little boys who are in Little League now." And he has never stopped playing baseball since he began Little League in 1966. In this season's opener of the All-Indian Men's League at Laguna, packed with much younger men, he did very well for himself. "The first time up at bat I hit a home run over the left center fence on the third pitch. It's not something to brag about — it was a lucky stroke. I'm fifty years old and they couldn't believe it." Still, Paully thinks back sadly to the circuit he played in, the one made up of Laguna village teams. "It seems like our league started deteriorating, not by people not wanting to play but because, when our director of recreation — he was a good ball player — couldn't play anymore, he let it all go downhill. The young guys are still playing ball out here but it's not as organized as our league was. Now they don't even play at the Old Laguna ball field. They play at the Old Laguna high school field."

Terence asks, "Have you been to the Laguna field?" The two brothers shake their heads, Paully saying, "It's a wasteland now."

To this day, most of the Laguna people maintain their fondness for baseball and it is still a source of tribal pride. The government office boasts a trophy case, crowded with the proof of the Pueblo's prowess. Families like the Rileys, the Greens and the Kiros still cherish faded photographs of men in uniforms. For multiple generations, nothing has the power to diminish Laguna's love of the game.

* * *

With its vast mineral resources, mining has always been one of the underpinnings of the New Mexico economy. Today, the area around Silver City is pleasant to visit, filled with Old West charm and dramatic scenery. The inhabitants of the area are a convivial and history-minded lot, happy to acquaint the visitor with interesting tidbits and good places to visit. And most truly love to talk about the Copper League. When it disbanded after 1927, the Arizona and Texas teams went on to long lives in professional baseball. Fort Bayard continued its life as a medical facility and today is known simply as Bayard, a satellite community of Silver City. It was the only one of the towns to hang on to an adopted outlaw son. Jimmie O'Connell married there and remained immensely popular; one regional paper even ran a photo of Mr. and Mrs. O'Connell happily washing dishes together.[101] As for the mining teams of the New Mexico Copper League, they died with the towns that had supported them. The model camp of Tyrone sat deserted for forty-five years, then fell victim to strip mining. A new Tyrone was built a few miles away. Hurley still exists as a retirement community. As for Santa Rita, the open pit copper mine that had once sat on the edge of the camp kept expanding until the camp was consumed by its voracious appetite. What it left was the third-largest open pit mine in the United States, a gaping maw almost 1,500 feet deep and one and a half miles wide.

Tererro, New Mexico, consists today of a general store and riding stables and the wooden truss bridge that Leon McDuff's father built all those years ago. Otherwise, the Pecos wilderness has reclaimed it, smothering any evidence of town or ball field or cunningly-constructed golf course. From the village of Pecos, a county road will lead one past a farrier and the local dump to the lonely, almost otherworldly, remains of the mill. A concrete foundation spreads out like a vast stage while behind it, what looks like a giant's staircase ascends the steep hillside. It gives an effect that's oddly evocative of a Mayan ruin, some mythic jungle city lost to the ages.

Madrid very nearly became a ghost town. In fact, in 1954, the entire town was put up for sale for $250,000.

ENTIRE TOWN
200 HOUSES, GRADE AND HIGH SCHOOL
POWER HOUSE, GENERAL STORE, TAVERN,
MACHINE SHOP, MINERAL RIGHTS
9,000 ACRES, EXCELLENT CLIMATE,
FINE INDUSTRIAL LOCATION[102]

Although no one deemed the town worthy of that investment of money, it came back to life on its own in the 1970s, by virtue of the transplants who relocated there. Artists, mostly, and counter-culturalists introduced a relaxed, bohemian atmosphere to the former mining town. Today, Madrid is completely revived and a visit to it means a remarkably colorful trip to the past, as much a celebration of the hippie era as the mining one. In 2001, the New Mexico Preservation Alliance listed the 75-year-old ballpark as "endangered," leading concerned citizens from around the state to rally to its rescue.[103]

Laguna Pueblo remains where its founders built it eons ago. The church of San Jose still faces the rising sun as it has for centuries. The savaged landscape has undergone reclamation, the scars smoothed over and covered with fast-growing plants. In Paguate, the houses no longer strain under the man-made tremors caused by blasting and digging. It is a village of ordinary people, leading ordinary lives. But some of the roads of the Pueblo were built from the detritus of uranium mining, as were some of the houses. In those houses, how much of the dust — the kind that lies in hard-to-reach corners or on the top shelf of a pantry — could be left over from what was carried home on a miner's clothes, the kind that would cause a halogen counter to erupt in ominous tocking? And how safe are the people of the Pueblo from what may lurk in their water? The parents and grandparents may look back on the recent past and wonder about the legacy left to them and future generations by the mines. The children, however, do not. They think of nothing but baseball as they grab their mitts and race into the dust and heat and hard brilliance of summer.

4

Doing Time: The Penitentiary Players

On a Saturday in March 1923, Warden John McManus of the New Mexico State Penitentiary was informed that a prisoner, whose sentence had just been commuted by the governor, refused to leave the prison. Instead of joyfully departing, prisoner Steve Heinrich was squatting in his cell, determined not to budge. Warden McManus received a negative reply when he asked the prison doctor if any malady ailed prisoner Heinrich. The warden then sent for the prisoner and asked pointblank what kept him there. It seemed that Heinrich simply wanted to delay his departure for a short period and for a very good reason. The opening game for the prison baseball team was scheduled for the next day and, as last season's star hurler, he intended to be on the mound for it. So, he was granted permission to stay in his cell for one more night, and the next day "with his old time speed and unusual control, Heinrich once again brought home the bacon for the 'alma mater.'" Once the game was over, he changed from stripes into civilian clothes and walked through the gates, a free man.[1]

The New Mexico Territorial Penitentiary opened in 1885, and so relieved were the citizens to finally have a safe place to deposit their criminals, they celebrated the opening with a grand ball. The upper crust of the territory descended on the imposing structure to dance merrily in a space that would soon be given over to much grimmer pastimes. Within two years of its auspicious opening, charges of malfeasance and calls for reform were flying like ack-ack,[2] and an 1891 article hotly stated that "incompetency, immorality, dishonesty and lack of discipline reign supremely in that badly managed institution."[3] Those charges— along with cronyism and nepotism — were repeated with regularity throughout the ensuing decades. The mismanagement ran the gamut, from brutal control of the inmates to almost no control of them at all.[4] Along with chronic overcrowding and underfeeding, there were countless escapes and incidents of violence. In 1922, at the command of Warden Jaramillo, guards in the towers opened fire on inmates in the yard who were protesting lack of food, killing one and wounding five. (In a moment of black comedy, an employee and witness stated that the killing of the one prisoner had to have been an accident, due to the poor marksmanship of the guards.

"He said that the guards had target practice every week and were unable to 'hit the target.'"[5])

In its day, the austere structure housed a catholic mix of inmates, from run-of-the-mill miscreants to regional and national celebrities. Prisoner Number 1262, otherwise known as "Bronco Bill," was considered "one of the most notorious bad men, gun fighters, train robbers, murderers and all around outlaws that ever terrorized New Mexico," yet was a model prisoner until his escape in 1911.[6] Silver City murderess Ada Hulmes, who in 1889 killed her married lover in a fit of jealousy, was lodged there in luxury after her conviction, as was Albert Bacon Fall, one-time United States senator from New Mexico and Secretary of the Interior in the Harding administration. Fall is undoubtedly best known for his role in the Teapot Dome scandal, which earned him a prison term that began in 1931.[7] For both Hulmes and Fall, life at the penitentiary was hardly grueling. In fact, local citizens indignantly derided the warden for pampering the fallen woman and Albert Fall could never be credited with having done "hard time," having spent his entire tenure in the prison hospital. But for other inmates of the penitentiary—from its earliest days until the present—conditions haven't been quite so pleasant. Like countless convicts in countless prisons throughout this country, the only relief to be found—from the loneliness, the fear, the boredom, the rage—has been baseball. And many a prison team has been formed and played well against the outside world. What makes the New Mexico State Penitentiary different is that its club was a mainstay of two city leagues for many years.

By the time Albert Fall arrived at the penitentiary in 1931 and was tucked into his infirmary cot to ruminate on his many sins, the New Mexico State Penitentiary had boasted fine teams for several years. It was certainly not unique. Harold Seymour discussed the introduction of the sport in young men's reformatories as early as the nineteenth century,[8] and it gained credence until eventually "in the 1920s and 1930s baseball ripened into a full-fledged feature of prison life reaching the full season of its maturity."[9] It is entirely possible that the sport was introduced to the prisoners of the New Mexico State Penitentiary in the early twentieth century by Santa Fe baseball club manager Billy Martin, who served in a variety of positions at the prison, including that of assistant superintendent.[10] In 1918, a newspaper article on the prison mentioned that, although overcrowding was a problem, inmates found recreation not only in moving pictures and lectures but in baseball as well. Indeed, accompanying the article was a photograph of a game in the prison yard.[11] By the early '20s, the prison team—featuring future reluctant parolee Steve Heinrich—was routinely engaging some of the Santa Fe municipal teams and boasting some highly talented personnel. Gallant bandit Harry Davis was considered by many to be the finest catcher in the state. British by birth, Davis only learned to play baseball after his incarceration. Having completed his sentence in November 1924, he was released, only to immediately rob a bank in Des Moines, New Mexico, where he was referred to as "the most gentlemanly hold-up artist they ever knew in their rather limited acquaintance with members of that profession." In lieu of a trial, he pled guilty to the offense and "so got back to the institution in time for spring training, receiving a hearty welcome from the manager and players and fans of the penitentiary ball team."[12]

By the early '30s, the prison team had expanded its list of competitors to include regional high schools, colleges, WPA and American Legion teams as well those from various mining camps, and hot stove chatter always included speculation on the convict teams.

> "This year finds us with an unusually large number of likely prospects," writes the manager of the state penitentiary baseball club, which last season won 19 out of 24 games played. He does not say why the district judges supplied so many classy rookies, but declares that the prison team wants to meet the best baseball aggregations in the state, and feels well able to cope with any of them. The pen team plays strictly "inside baseball," all games being on the prison diamond.[13]

By the advent of World War II, the team had a name — the Grays — as did their prison yard diamond, jokingly referred to by one and all as "McManus Stadium," in honor of the long-serving warden. Sadly, despite the serious competition offered by the incarcerated athletes, jest often played too large a role in newspaper coverage of them. In 1942, for instance, the team was allowed to play the very first away game in its history when it traveled to the Albuquerque Air Base to play a benefit against the soldier team there, the Colin Kellys. It was to be an important event, not only in that it was to raise money for the Army Emergency Relief Fund, but also because of some of the people invited. War hero Kelly's widow was first on the list, of course, but the real draw would undoubtedly be the "Big Train," Walter Johnson, the august pitcher who by this time had seen fifty-five summers. He was invited to watch his son, who was stationed in Albuquerque, toe the rubber in a Kelly uniform.[14] Newspaper coverage of the upcoming event was thorough but the writers were at first unable to afford the penitentiary players the barest semblance of respect as athletes. It required the testimony of a couple of the Kellys, who had played against the prisoners before and knew how tough they could be, to make at least one reporter treat the tilt as more than simply the equivalent of a donkey baseball game. Sportswriter Paul Weeks mentioned the pen team in his July 4 column, passing along what he'd heard about the prison battery.

> They say this pitcher whiffs 'em right and left, and if it weren't for a short outfield due to the position of the walls, he'd do even better. The other half of the battery is also a sensation. One soldier told me the other day: "Say, if you're on first base, you might as well stay there. If you start to steal, it's much shorter to go back to first and a heck of a lot safer. That catcher has a peg like nobody's business."

Weeks added that he fully intended to go to the pen "one of these days" to see a game.[15]

The Penitentiary Grays lost that game; a triple hit by their third baseman would have been likely insurance for a win if he'd been more accurate in touching first. An enthusiastic wartime crowd of three thousand, if disappointed that Walter Johnson, Jr. pitched only three innings, enjoyed other diversions, including swing music and a demonstration of jitterbugging at home plate. One of the convicts, in his prison stripes, kept the crowds in stitches with a comedic routine that involved threatening players with a fake razor. It was an afternoon of high hilarity, good baseball and patriotism on the part of every fan and player. And yet, when the story came out the next day, not a single prisoner was identified by name. Although the lack of names had been a request of the warden, the newspaper only enhanced the marginalization of the men by repeating the prison puns ad nauseam. Even in the box score — where each man's name should have been — there were only inmate identification numbers.[16]

After the war, the prison acquired a new chaplain and the Grays a new manager, all in the person of Father Eusebius, who protected and pushed his flock of players. Father Eusebius (the name itself evokes a Spencer Tracy–type, in biretta and cassock, supervising batting practice) had no reluctance in going to the press when his team needed games or publicity. In March 1946, while the rest of an exhausted populace tried to recover from the last several years, Father Eusebius was whipping his team into shape while attempting to get the local teams moving to provide his boys with games.[17] When one plea in the newspaper wasn't enough, he contacted a local sports editor, throwing in a subtle yet irresistible taunt to ambitious clubs:

> In the three games to date, the Grays have scored 49 runs, allowing the opposition but 14. The batting order carries a punch which stems from being able to balance right- and left-handed batsmen against the opposing hurlers. The Grays also boast a snappy infield, fast outfield and a brace of first-rate chuckers.[18]

At one point, when the team faced a long stretch of unbooked Sunday afternoons, Father Eusebius contacted the Albuquerque Chamber of Commerce to demand their assistance in finding willing teams. That body, like everyone else, was unable to resist him and ran a plea in the newspaper, which included a request for local club managers to send in their pertinent information so that the good father would no longer have to go to such lengths to secure games.[19]

It was under the watch of Father Eusebius that rules for visiting teams were first printed in a newspaper. They included exactly what one might expect of visitors to a penitentiary — rigid timetables, maximum number of persons admitted — until it came to age limits, where they took a curious turn: "No spectators under the age of 18 years will be admitted to the grounds. (This excludes babies.) No person under the age of 10 who is connected with the team will be admitted unless he is a playing member of the team."[20]

As the Penitentiary Grays played out of the '40s and into the '50s, cementing an already sound reputation, the prison that housed them was going through more than the usual upheavals with food riots, gang fights, hostage taking and murder becoming more frequent. In 1950, the building complex itself was sixty-five years old and located in what had once been an outlier section of Santa Fe but was now in the midst of the growing town. Even twenty years earlier, it had been apparent that the comfort level of the citizenry at having a prison in the middle of their homes, schools and churches was decidedly diminishing. Additionally, it simply wasn't suitable for the charming tourist Mecca known as "the City Different."

> Concentration of prisoners in Santa Fe in some respects is a menace to the city and does not fit in with the capital city's idea of "the city different," its preservation of quaintness, historic interest and artistic atmosphere. There is no local pride in penitentiaries and in this instance, with its hazards of outbreaks, Santa Fe would probably have no serious objection to removal of part of its prison population to some other place.[21]

Even a local sportswriter noted the grim conditions in which the Grays and their visiting competition played — "the barren, dusty prison yard, the ancient blackened brick kilns and the dreary buildings" — and suggested that more school children should be forced to tour the facility in order to deter them from any romantic ideas of the criminal life.[22]

In 1956, the city heaved a sigh of relief when the old prison was razed and all of its tenants moved to a new eight million dollar facility located several miles from downtown Santa Fe on a flat plain, punctuated only by cholla cactus and chamisa. With mountains only distantly placed, it stood unprotected from the high, cold winds of winter and the brutal summer sun. The advantage for the team members was a new ball field. Surrounded by steel fences and guard towers, and pocked by prairie dog holes, it was still an improvement over what they had been playing on at the old pen. In the christening of this new park, the penitentiary team achieved a historic first and another was on the way.

In 1961, Father Eusebius was long gone, but he would undoubtedly have swelled with pride when it was announced that the penitentiary team was to join the Greater Albuquerque League, a National Baseball Congress–sanctioned semipro circuit.

> Ray Dumont, National Baseball Congress president, said in Wichita, Kan., that the New Mexico chapter of the national organization definitely scored a "first" in permitting the Grays to join the league. Dumont also verified another "first" for the Grays. They're the only team in NBC history that ever played all their games at "home."[23]

The league would comprise almost thirty teams in five divisions and the penitentiary team would be one of four (including the Fire Department, Camilio's Insulating Service and Simons Department Store) representing the Manzano Division.

At this time, the team officially changed its name to the Penitentiary Rocks, eventually naming its prison yard field Rockland Park. For the inmates, it must have meant a proud change in status, and certainly the batteries were now named in game reporting. But however accepted the team was by other members of the league and local sportswriters, there were still condescending reports from outside the area. The Associated Press ran a brief attempt at humor, with the headline "Batter Up" in 1963.

> The boys are getting ready for spring training, but not one is counting on a trip to a Florida camp. A recent purchasing order received by the New Mexico Purchasing Office called for two sets of baseball baseball [sic] bases, assorted baseball shoes and socks, fielder's gloves and 10 dozen baseballs. All will be shipped to the New Mexico Penitentiary.[24]

The Rocks played in the Greater Albuquerque League for many years, well into the 1970s, without great success as a team, although, beginning in 1963, a number of their players were invited to take part in league all-star games. The coach of the 1970 state semipro champions (and seventh in NBC national standings that year) welcomed the inmate all-stars. "That's a fine baseball team they have up there," said Ray Hernandez, manager of the Metro Greater Albuquerque Division champion Roberson Homes team. "The only loss we've suffered in league play was to the State Penitentiary. They have outstanding players and I think the fans should see a few of them play."[25]

In the mid-sixties, a Rocks softball team was formed as well, and, like their hardball counterparts, joined a municipal league. They however were eventually allowed to play away games. And it wasn't just diamond games that appealed to the prisoners. By the end of the decade, they were routinely involved in both varsity and intramural sports at the facility, including basketball, flag football, handball and tennis. In addition, the penitentiary inmates had become the hosts of an annual sports banquet, an event attended by athletic directors, coaches and sports reporters from around the state. In 1969, a prison awards ceremony was begun in order to fete the best inmate athletes in every sport at the institution. In an article on the celebration, the recreation supervisor proudly stated that, out of a prison population of roughly 850, more than 600 of the inmates were involved in athletics of some sort. A poignant photograph showed the best all-around athlete accepting a trophy for his many feats, his face awash with joy.[26]

In 1977, an *Albuquerque Journal* writer named Bart Ripp did a complete story on the Rocks, accompanied by photos—group portraits, action shots, and the diamond with its crown of razor wire. In it he introduced the inmates to the reading public—without jest or smugness—as men and as athletes. He allowed several of the Rocks to talk about baseball and what it meant to them. The words of each man, given along with his crime and sentence, are deeply moving, but none more so than that of Rocks catcher Richard Sisk, who was serving his third stint at the penitentiary. Although he admitted to having trouble adjusting to life on the outside (and a certain sense of security at being back on the inside), he was looking forward to parole in two months.

> If I ever get my head straight, I want to play ball, just play ball. If I hook on with some team, that would be far out. I'll do anything to play ball. As soon as I get out, I'm going to pick up my old lady and take her to a ballgame. I'd love that more than anything in the world.[27]

A month later, Ripp — in an obvious mix of fondness, sadness and exasperation — reported that Sisk, just weeks away from his parole, had escaped, only to be meekly recaptured in Colorado. The additional charge of escape would probably net him another ten to fifty years at the pen. His place on the ball team would be assured.[28]

Images of an almost wholesome environment at the penitentiary played into one that had, within the last year, been painted by one local newspaper. After decades of bad press for the penitentiary, the *Santa Fe New Mexican* had run a three-part series on it, exploring its modern philosophy of rehabilitation over pure punishment. Not only was the recreation program touted but the educational programs as well. Inmates had access to basic education classes or college and vocational courses. The industry system within the walls of the "plant" provided on-the-job training that would guarantee employment opportunities in the outside world.[29] "Good nutrition provided through the food services system and a modern hospital facility insure that the inmate will leave the institution in good health, usually better than when he come."[30] New training for correctional officers meant that every prisoner's rights were understood and respected.[31] The warden questioned whether the New Mexico State Penitentiary wasn't the "best facility in the country."[32]

As enlightened as that sounded on paper, it was hardly the case in actuality. In a report on the physical conditions of the prison, a reporter from another newspaper said, "The cramped quarters will give one a first hand look at a human zoo."[33] A closer inspection of the institution revealed that it was far worse than most zoos. Author Roger Morris, in his disturbing and revealing book *The Devil's Butchershop: The New Mexico Prison Uprising*, attempts to convey just how bad conditions in the pen had become when Richard Sisk was incarcerated there.

> By the mid-seventies, the New Mexico penitentiary was a physical as well as a psychological horror. Rats and roaches infested the building. Poor ventilation made it stifling by summer. Inadequate heating left the cell blocks sickly chill in winter. Drinking and waste-water systems were cross-connected, spewing sewage into sinks.[34]

But it was the human activity that went on inside the increasingly derelict structure that would result in one of the worst catastrophes in American penal history.

> Pervasive nepotism not only fostered incompetence, but it also spawned ... a chaos in inmate discipline in which each newly empowered commander ruled the cell blocks and houses his own way.... Finally, and perhaps most characteristic, the Santa Fe pen was a community constituted in treason. In its inherent weakness, the administration became incessantly dependent on inmate informers for the most rudimentary intelligence and security. And, in turn, it passed along its preoccupation with treachery, like some lethal contagion, into the vulnerable bloodstream of its convict society.[35]

Since 1885, the New Mexico Penitentiary had been a hotbed of abuse, neglect, lies, encouraged snitching, gang wars, food riots, rape and murder. With every lurid detail that emerged, calls for reform grew. As late as 1977, a Santa Fe grand jury returned fifty-three indictments against the facility, including overcrowding, poor food and, in a prescient moment, the dormitory system of housing which they felt would be dangerous even if there were a manageable number of inmates, let alone the throngs that clogged the pen.[36] Then in 1980, every black deed ever committed within those walls by prisoner, administrator or guard rose up in a conflagration that would leave America shocked and shuddering. In the early hours of February 2, the overpowering of one guard by two inmates would set off a chain reaction. More hostages were taken and snitches hunted down for retribution. The violence grew in fury, engulfing every prisoner and guard. Talks began, then broke down in confusion. On the cold morning of February 3, terrified prisoners escaped the confines of the buildings and made it to the baseball field, their own Rockland Park, where they huddled in misery. By mid-afternoon of February 3, thirty-six hours after it had started, the riot was over. National guardsmen and prison employees entered the building, only to emerge with horrific tales of what they'd found inside: incontrovertible evidence of torture and murder.

When it was over, after a slapdash evacuation of the prison, the death toll sat at thirty-three, although the savagery of the murders—the almost complete obliteration of the bodies—suggests that the toll could actually be higher. Two hundred inmates were injured and twelve guards taken hostage, seven injured. It was an event that stunned the nation and one from which the City of Holy Faith has never fully recovered.

* * *

"I wish I would never have seen it," says Anthony Martinez, describing what he found when he surveyed the pen shortly after the 1980 carnage had ended. "I was one of the first ones to come in and—let me tell you—what a big mistake. I slept with the lights on for a very, very long time. I was scared to fall asleep in the dark."

Anthony is a reserved man with almost military bearing. Although almost painfully polite, he obviously doesn't suffer fools gladly. Straining to hear his soft voice, one is rewarded with the lilting accent that identifies the native New Mexican speaker of both English and Spanish. He grew up playing baseball in the village of Pecos, twenty-odd miles outside of Santa Fe. His employment in the New Mexico correctional system began right after graduation from high school. "In 1974, there were hardly any jobs in this entire state, "he explains. "The only jobs available were with the Department of Corrections. I had friends in there who really encouraged me. I just went in and did my job. I never had any problems with the inmates." When asked if he had been nervous as a greenhorn guard, he replies unhesitatingly. "Of course I was, yeah. A lot of people say they weren't but I was. Yeah." By 1980, he had been promoted to accounting supervisor, a position he filled in the dark days before and after the riot. Today, Anthony is the Auditing Compliance Manager for the Santa Fe County Correctional Department. He has always held positions of respect in the New Mexico penal system but, arguably, his most important — and least heralded — job was as recreation supervisor, rebuilding the tattered sports programs and repairing the prison's gruesome post-riot image. It was a challenge that would take a commitment few else could muster.

In the late summer of 1979, the Penitentiary Rocks baseball team still played but had been absent from the Greater Albuquerque League for three years, the result of a crackdown after a small uprising, what Anthony calls a "mini riot." Now limited to playing only other prisoners, and any outside team courageous enough to visit, they finished the season, looking forward to the next year. But by next year's baseball season, and for years to come, the penitentiary was convulsed with violence, distrust and general mayhem. It took the federal courts to institute the most basic of changes to relieve some of the ills that had caused the riot, including improved training and pay for guards, new procedures for discipline and security, a thinned-out inmate population with high risk prisoners separated from the least dangerous. Despite the improvements, the state pen remained a terrifying place to live or work.

Happily, none of the Rocks was among the official list of dead from the riot but the baseball program was moribund, with play limited to nothing more than the occasional scrimmage, says Anthony. Becoming the pen's recreational supervisor in 1996, he decided to reorganize the sports programs and reintroduce the Rocks — both the baseball and basketball teams — to the outside world. And the best way to do that was to get them back into municipal leagues. He set his sights on the city baseball league of Santa Fe and decided to approach anyone that would listen to him, inviting them to the penitentiary. "I wanted to bring in as many outside teams as possible so they would know what type of program we had. After the 1980 prison riot, everybody had the impression that those folks behind bars were a bunch of animals and that just wasn't the case." He admits it wasn't an easy sell and most of the people he talked to balked initially, but the undeterred recreation director took his campaign straight to the top of the league. "I requested that the chairman talk to the captains of the league, tell them that it was safe to go into the prison, that the program had improved. I said, 'I can guarantee you that if you go in, you'll want to come back again. Give me a chance. *Give me a chance.* I have an excellent program inside — it's well-structured, well-organized and we have by-laws for the inmates to go by.' Then I would meet with the captain or the coach and explain what our program was all about to make them feel comfortable. If there were concerns from other ball club members I would meet with them too."

When the first teams began signing up, Anthony had his hands full with the joy and anxiousness of the Penitentiary Rocks. Slight delays in processing at the prison gates might make a visiting team a few minutes late, to the distress of the inmate team. "They'd say, 'Martinez, they're not coming, they're not coming!' and they'd only be five or six minutes late." When a handful of teams found the courage to play at the penitentiary and were pleased with the visit, Anthony promptly recruited them to address the concerns of others. "I would tell those teams, 'You know what? I need help with this. Why don't you talk to this individual and tell him what kind of program we have? Because I don't think they're gonna show up next week and I really want them to because the players here are waiting.' So they would be my recruiters to go out and say, 'We just got back from the prison and they really have a good program.'" And while his team of recruiters was out encouraging other teams, Anthony was cementing the rules of behavior for his own boys, lectures interspersed with pep talks and advice on not taking the game, or themselves, too seriously. "What I used to tell them was, 'Win or lose, we win or lose as a team. We're not out here to fight or argue. We're out here to have fun simply because, if we were that great, we'd be playing in the American League or the National League. But we're not. We're just out here to have fun.'"

To keep everyone involved safe, Anthony imposed strict regulations, thoroughly explained to visitors and insiders "so they knew what my expectations were," he says. Metal detectors were used on the incoming team and complete inventories taken of the equipment before and after the games. For safety's sake, no outside fans were allowed at the games. He also had to check the backgrounds of any potential competitors. "I'd have a roster of every player coming into the facility. Sure enough, we got some good teams in." During the first year of visiting competition, he allowed only the players to come out into the field. "Later, I started allowing the population [of inmates] to go out after talking to them and telling them, 'This is what's going on and this is how I want you guys to act.' I never had any problems. There were times I would have up to five hundred inmates out in the baseball field. And I only had two other officers out there with me. They were out supporting the players and also the other teams. It was a combination of both. It was nice to see that." As more and more of the league teams agreed to play at the pen, the relationship formed between them and their incarcerated opponents was a healthy one. "There was respect on both ends. Both teams were out having a

Anthony Martinez, who restored the New Mexico State Penitentiary's athletic program after the 1980 riot. He not only built an intramural program inside the prison but got his Penitentiary Rocks into a Santa Fe municipal league (Belinda Winn).

good time," Anthony maintains. (One aspect of playing at the pen really did ensure a good time for the visitors: lunch. Harry Stowers recalls accompanying the Madrid Miners there in the 1930s and enjoying his first strawberries. Al Green of Laguna Pueblo says, "The food was good — it was always a special trip when we went up there. We really ate good, like steaks and stuff.")

It wasn't long before the New Mexico State Penitentiary found itself hosting Santa Fe city league tournaments, a tremendous red-tape and public relations challenge for Anthony. "This wasn't planned overnight — I'd start four months before," he says. "It's a lot of work. It's not something where you just say, 'I'm gonna put together a tournament.' It's about convincing the administration, it's about selling the idea to our community, and then putting an ad in the paper and see how many teams respond, and then from there go out and meet with the athletic director of the Santa Fe Recreation Department, get names and numbers of coaches and players, then convince them. It was a lot of work. It wasn't just ideas. I'd be out in the field talking." The tournaments not only lifted the spirits of the inmates but, with Anthony's expertise in numbers, they became a financial boon as well. "A tournament would generate so much money. With that I was able to pay my officials, which were inmates. I would pay them a dollar, two dollars a game. Now, of course, I would have to have quite a few officials. I'd pay my scorekeepers too." With sixteen municipal teams entering a tournament and each putting up $100, Anthony could pay his host expenses and be left with a balance of up to $500 which would be returned to the Rocks' coffers to pay for uniforms and equipment. In addition to tournament profits, the sports program was funded by an inmate commissary, where a five percent tax was levied on each item. These funds also helped Anthony expand the recreation department to include other non-sports programs such as hobbies like wood and leather working, self-help programs, and self-esteem groups for the various ethnic populations in the pen. Many of these groups hosted their own fundraisers, the profits going to local charities.

For every natural baseball talent, there are ten who lack what it takes. Like all good coaches, Anthony understood this. "I didn't want to discourage any people who wanted to be a part of the team. For the people who didn't make it in the tryouts, I had an intramural program in the prison. So I could have up to eight, nine teams playing and they'd compete with each other. The ones that would officiate were my original team, the ones that played against outside teams." He cannot hide the pride he feels in that inclusive program, saying, "That worked out just beautiful, that intramural program. That was about thirty percent of the population out there playing and the rest were their buddies, other prisoners that weren't playing. At the end, we would reward everybody with maybe a cheeseburger and a coke. They were happy. They didn't want to mess up the program, they really didn't." Anthony always made sure that the games ended in a bit of shared glory for hard work, pointing out that what might seems trifling to a person on the outside means quite a lot to an incarcerated man. "What I used to do, I'd award my players a little commissary sometimes, or maybe at the end of a tournament we'd have a pizza 'out.' You know, that's an incentive for the inmates, to have pizza and soda from the outside, any kind of food items from the outside. They would just love that." Perhaps a day of baseball followed by one of these events of Anthony's—burrito nights, ice cream night, movies and popcorn night—made the inmates under his watch feel, momentarily anyway, a little more human.

Anthony Martinez seems to have been keenly aware of the power of sports and the positive effect they could have on prisoners. "In regard to sports in prison settings, it tends to make them understand that it's a group effort, not an individual effort. They're not out there alone. After the game, they'd go back to their cells as a group, as one unit. They would discuss the game, what they needed to improve and how they needed to work as a whole team. So to see them talk about that, and organize and be able to talk to the rest of the [prison] population, not only was it good for them but it was good for the entire prison. The way that I see things in a prison is if you have inmates just wandering around being idle, they have 24/7 to think. But if they're preoccupied in some sort of organized sport, they go out and recruit others to be part of it, to be involved in the program."

With a mixture of respect and compassion, Anthony Martinez not only built an excellent sports program, but he attempted to teach the outside world about the humanity of his athletes. "Like I tell people, we all make mistakes. Some have not been caught, others have. These folks have already been judged and tried and they're doing their time. So we, as correctional officers or administrators, are not here to judge nobody at all. And that's what I used to tell the inmates too." But his ballplayers understood that his kindness to them would always be tempered with a healthy warning about their behavior while under his watch. "I would say, 'You know what? My job is to make sure that you walk in to this facility and walk out the same. I don't want to push you out in a wheelchair or take you out in a body bag. So if you're sentenced to three years, do your three years and get out.'"

Retiring from the penitentiary in 2000, Anthony has watched with sadness as many of the programs he built have been done away with. "I used to volunteer a lot of my time because I really saw that it was something good for the entire population, not only the inmates but the administration. We had less problems, we had a better-run facility. Of course everybody's going to have problems but we didn't have as many as we had before." He laughs as he says that he runs into some of his former wards from time to time in Santa Fe. "I see some of the old-timers—you'd be surprised. My wife says, 'Where do you know that guy from?' 'Oh, I know him from the prison.' 'It looks like you've know each other for a long time.' 'Well,' I tell her, 'we had respect for each other.'"

The New Mexico State Penitentiary moved to a new facility in 1997. The old building still stands on its unfortified plain, an object of ghoulish curiosity to ghost hunters and lovers of the sensational, of revulsion to those who remember the events of 1980. By its nature, a prison is the most brutal of places, with wars and battles, large and small, waged constantly. It is the temporary or permanent home of people who seem to be either irredeemably wicked or foolishly, often recklessly, misguided. Respect is earned primarily through brutality, whether wielded by inmate or guard. So where does the man in the cage find respect for himself? And where, in this toxic bog, lies his hope for redemption?

Anthony — and Father Eusebius before him — believed that both could be found, however briefly, on a Sunday afternoon in a dusty prison yard, even with its nimbus of razor wire. And both could be found in the heart of a player, who, for a few exquisite hours, felt free. Respect and redemption. In baseball, Anthony Martinez saw both.

5

A League, a Town, a Legend

In the southwestern corner of the Great Plains is the Llano Estacado, a semiarid grassland that stretches from the Texas Panhandle across that state's western border into New Mexico. The exact origin of the name is debated but it is often rendered in English as "staked plain," alluding to a theorized Spanish habit of staking the ground to avoid getting lost in the thousands of square miles of unremarkable flatland. A more exact translation is "palisaded" or "stockaded" plain, courtesy of Francisco de Coronado when he viewed the escarpment of the 32,000-square-mile mesa. It is a place of big skies and very large winds, a staging ground for towering summer thunderheads and devastating twisters. A storm chaser's paradise, the level, almost treeless tableland provides easy observation of careening funnel clouds. But this very flatness is deceptive, for these are the High Plains, and every square acre is hundreds of feet above sea level.

From 1938 until 1955, this area was the location of the West Texas–New Mexico League, a loop that often played in the most extreme conditions—sizzling summer temperatures, grassless diamonds and undulating dust devils that could send most of the infield swirling heavenward. But some of the same impediments also helped the West Texas–New Mexico circuit earn itself a reputation in baseball history, that of a notorious hitter's league. High altitude and dry conditions added up to a game where the defense was forced to stand in mute amazement as balls sailed over the fences, only to delight in the same action from their own bats. The league was even referred to once by no less than the *Sporting News* as "the happy home of the home run."[1]

During the lifetime of the West Texas–New Mexico League, as with any other circuit, franchises shifted, clubs expired and new ones came to life. But one of the stalwarts was Clovis, New Mexico, and its team, the Pioneers, a member for fifteen of the loop's sixteen years. The westernmost point in a geographical triangle with Lubbock and Amarillo, Texas, Clovis now has a population of just over 42,000. The population of Curry County, of which Clovis is the seat, is just over 45,000. The town was established in 1907 by the Atchison, Topeka and Santa Fe Railroad. Its original name of Riley's Switch was changed to Clovis allegedly on the suggestion of the local stationmaster's daughter who was studying French history at the time. The town boasts two important claims to fame, first for having given an important Paleo-Indian culture its name. Any first-year student of North American archaeology can identify the fluted spear tip known as the Clovis point, first discovered in the late 1930s near the town. Zooming ahead several thousand years, the town achieved rock and roll notoriety as the place where, in 1957, Buddy Holly and the Crickets recorded such hits as "That'll Be the Day" and "Peggy Sue."

A lesser-known claim to fame is Clovis' long history in professional baseball. In fact, with the exception of Albuquerque — which has always been many times its size — Clovis can claim the greatest number of professional teams in the state. But there have been others as well. Partially due to their close proximity to Texas (and its many leagues), several middling-sized towns in the southeast quadrant of New Mexico have hosted lower level professional baseball clubs. Albuquerque, recognized as an important player in the sport today, began its professional life, along with Las Cruces, in the short-lived Class D Rio Grande Association in 1915, a venture which lasted only until the middle of July. The Artesia Giants were in the Class D Sophomore League from 1958 until 1961, as was Carlsbad with its team, the Potashers. Hobbs played in the first two seasons of the West Texas–New Mexico League, disappeared for two decades, then reappeared in the Southwestern and the Sophomore leagues, where it existed as a farm club of the St. Louis Cardinals and then the Pittsburgh Pirates. The Sophomore League would also provide a home for the Roswell Rockets for seven years, and one of their own would set an important record, which has just recently been broken. But Clovis really led the charge in professional baseball, entering the first West Texas League in the early '20s as the Buzzers, under the tutelage of Dutch Wetzel, who'd just finished two seasons in the outfield with the St. Louis Browns. In 1923, as the Cubs, Clovis joined the Pecos Valley–Panhandle League, which survived for just one season.

Indeed, Clovis was a great little burg for baseball. But its successes rarely matched its enthusiasm for the game. From its entry into the West Texas–New Mexico League in 1938 until the league's demise after the 1955 season, Clovis was in or near the cellar for all but six of those years. Those half-dozen victorious seasons came by virtue of one man, Grover Seitz. Just as it had for the Clovis Pioneers, the West Texas–New Mexico League provided a fifteen-season roost for Seitz, one of the most vivid personalities ever found in Organized Baseball. And for six of those seasons, he entertained the crowds as the Pioneer pilot.

Commonly called "the wild Bull of the Pampans" by reporters, Seitz nurtured a reputation as the circuit's bad boy and lovable clown. And early on, sportswriters within a two-hundred-mile radius learned that no one in the sport could work their literary muscles more, or have them racing to the thesaurus more often for an alternative to the word "colorful." Whether they loved him or hated him, for the men who covered baseball, Grover was, quite simply, a goldmine.

The West Texas–New Mexico League came into being as a Class D circuit in 1937 with four teams from Texas (the Wink Spudders, Monahans Trojans, Odessa Oilers, and the Midland Cardinals) and two from New Mexico (the Hobbs Drillers and the Roswell Sunshiners). Roswell's entry fees had been posted by the Beaumont (Texas) Exporters,[2] an affiliate of the Detroit Tigers (the Exporters had served a couple of years earlier as a stepping stone for Hank Greenberg and Schoolboy Rowe[3]). All the clubs except for Midland were new to Organized Baseball, and the president and vice-president were tyros as well.[4] Any new league is not without its fits and starts and the West Texas–New Mexico certainly had its own. Midland and Odessa both withdrew by July. The circuit reduced to four teams, it is not surprising that both clubs from New Mexico made it to the playoffs, and Roswell to the championship series, only to be swept by the Spudders from Wink. In 1938, the league reorganized with four Texas clubs, Midland and Wink returning and Lubbock and Big Spring coming on board, and New Mexico again represented by two teams. The Hobbs Boosters, still under the auspices of the Tigers, were back but Roswell was gone, replaced by the newly minted Clovis Pioneers. It was the town's first foray into professional baseball since 1923 and there was much ado. The preseason festivities began when the local venue, Bell Park, played host to a match between the Pittsburgh Pirates, on their way east from spring training in California, and the Phillips 66, a tough semipro team out of Texas. Sportswriter Dee Blythe of the *Clovis News-Journal* echoed the sentiments of town boosters when he wrote, "It should pave the way for a successful debut for this city in the West Texas–New Mexico League, for it won't take until mid-season to steam up the fans. This one game tomorrow should turn the trick."[5] Five thousand fans were expected to show up for the game and were indirectly encouraged by the same paper to gather at the train station to welcome the professionals who would arrive in three special railroad cars. "A dozen cars, furnished by local fans, will be lined up to dash the Pirates to their headquarters at Hotel Clovis. State and city police will clear the way with their sirens."[6]

The Pittsburgh roster for that game couldn't have helped but stop the breath of the ambitious 66ers, peppered as it was with future Hall of Famers. Brothers Lloyd and Paul Waner would be patrolling the outfield while fellow Cooperstown-bound star Arky Vaughan would be at shortstop and Pie Traynor directing from the dugout. And the immortal Honus Wagner was along for the ride.

The day started in glorious New Mexico fashion, cloudless and bright. But a genuine norther howled in by game time, giving Traynor no small amount of worry, but the audience a boon. "The fierce north wind, bearing with it clouds of dust and stinging sand, was especially dangerous to the pitchers' tricky flippers, but to partially offset this Traynor used a fresh pitcher each inning. This gave the fans a chance to see no less than five Pirate pitchers in action...."[7] For the Phillips 66 team, longtime residents of the windswept Texas prairie, the storm might have been uncomfortable but was not out of the ordinary and they wrested a 2–1 victory from the Pirates. For Clovis, it was a red letter baseball day; the sportsman who had promoted the event lost less than $100 on it[8] and the local citizens basked in the glow of Honus Wagner, who regaled them at a Kiwanis luncheon with tales of the old days.[9] For the town, it was as dramatic a splash into professional baseball as could have been hoped for.

With the *Clovis News-Journal* encouraging the public to support its new team, the Pioneers began their maiden season and did quite well, winning the league opener against the Lubbock Hubbers and even scoring the first run of the West Texas–New Mexico season. But by mid–May, they were in the cellar and their fans were patently not "steamed up," showing up in numbers of around a hundred at the most. Pioneer officials, along with the newspaper, berated the populace and issued dire warnings. And, in a rare instance of successful chastising, the crowds began to increase. A sign campaign was launched, in which seemingly every square inch of the town was festooned. Home games were announced with ads on taxi cabs and neon signs in business windows. It worked so well that the city was able to make a down payment on lights for Bell Park.[10] Not only did Clovis make it to the final championship series in September (falling to Lubbock) and win the team batting average with .307,[11] but actually ended the season in the black.[12]

When spring rolled around, the West Texas–New Mexico League began its plans for the season with the ringing news that Grover Seitz, Texas boy and former Big Spring outfielder, had returned from his tour of several minor league clubs. The big news was that he was now part-owner and pilot of the Pampa club and he would enter it in the West Texas–New Mexico League. Born in 1907 near Miami, Texas, in the high plains of the Panhandle, Seitz became a star athlete in high school. He began playing semipro ball in nearby Pampa, and eventually turned professional in 1929 with Wichita Falls of the West Texas League. Bought by St. Louis, he began the time-honored waltz through the minors, beginning with Houston. "From Houston, Seitz was transferred to Springfield, Missouri, where he paced the league in runs scored, doubles, triples and stolen bases. He hit .317 that year, pulling up short of a full campaign when he broke a leg three days before the finish."[13] The following years found him with the Rochester Redwings and at Elmira of the Class A Eastern League, where he handled the outfield with Johnny Mize and Buster Mills. After a "tryout stretch with the Pittsburgh Pirates,"[14] and two seasons with the Western League, Seitz disappeared from the world of Organized Ball, only to resurface in 1939 with the two-year-old West Texas–New Mexico loop.[15]

Seitz, at age 31, was still one of the most threatening sluggers and baserunners in the minor leagues, a fact bemoaned by one Texas sportswriter of a competing town's newspaper. "He's still fast enough to beat out many an infield roller. His speed was brought into evidence Saturday night when he scored from third on a pop fly back of third. Seitz managed four bingles in seven trips, including a triple, in two games here."[16] But he was also a danger in his managerial abilities and his gift for sniffing out good available talent for his roster. His secret weapon in 1939 was outfielder Gordon Nell, who by early June was the bane of pitchers the league over. *Abilene Reporter-News* columnist Howard Green spoke for some of the frustrated pitchers in the West Texas–New Mexico League in a column headlined "GORDON NELL TOO POTENT FOR CLASS D HURLERS."

> They can't see why youngsters attempting to break into Class D ball have to face a clouter who over a 1-year period has a batting mark in excess of .340. From the time he broke into organized ball with Pensacola in the Southeastern league in 1929 up to the present day Gordon "Our Girl" Nell has been one of the most feared hitters in the country. Never has he failed to bat over .300 and his baseball ramblings include two years of Class A and a season of AA.

Green elaborated on Nell's career, which had included a stint with the White Sox ("Nell failed to stick in the big show, not because he couldn't hit major league pitching, but because he was too slow to field like a big time outfielder should") and a place on the roster of the all-star team of the 1937 National Semipro Baseball Congress.[17] Nell easily won the batting title of the first half of the season with an unapproachable .406[18] and helped Grover Seitz propel the team toward what must have been taken for granted as being a victorious season's end.

What Grover Seitz had probably not expected was the distinctly diva-like stance assumed by his star hitter. While the Pampa Oilers finished the season in second place behind the Lubbock Hubbers, the crown lay in the playoffs, and to Pampa fans' horror, their team entered those games without the services of its golden bat, Nell, who in a fit of pique had left the club.

> Gordon, who reputedly played during the season at a salary a Class A-1 players would have been glad to have received, quit the club when he discovered he was to be given no part of the playoff's gate receipts, retiring to his farm near Hollis, Oklahoma....[19]

And his absence took its toll. Lubbock won the championship in a five-game series with Pampa. But Gordon Nell left an astonishing mark in the 1939 season of the West Texas–New Mexico League. He led in batting (.389), total hits (207), runs scored (152), total bases (413), doubles (60), home runs (44) and RBIs (189).[20]

In 1940 Grover was still at the helm of the Pampa Oilers and Gordon Nell had come off the farm to pilot the Borger Gassers, a team and fan base so hard to handle that their first manager lasted just thirteen days.[21] The former colleagues split the rewards at season's end, the Oilers finishing the regular season in first place and the Gassers winning the championship. Both managers fared well on the field; Nell led the league in home runs and RBIs and Seitz in runs with 163 of them. Grover also batted .356, had 36 doubles and managed to steal 32 bases.[22] But the real star of the show turned out to be a right-handed pitcher named Bob Crues, who began the season with Lamesa, Texas, and ended with Nell's Gassers and a 20–5 record. Boston bought his contract and he disappeared from the league, only to resurface years later and win himself even more laurels.

Clovis, meanwhile had had two dreadful seasons, ending 1939 in sixth place and 1940 in seventh. They did manage to whitewash the Albuquerque Dukes (of the Arizona-Texas League) in an end-of-season exhibition game to claim the New Mexico professional baseball title for 1940.[23] But 1941 would see the Pioneers' fortunes rise, beginning with the surprise acquisition of Grover Seitz as manager at the beginning of June. He had sold his Pampa interests and allegedly retired from baseball after the 1940 season, but it was soon rumored that he had bought into the Clovis team or at least into the park.[24] The afternoon that his hiring was announced, a torrential rain hit Clovis and fans waded through flooded streets to city hall to hear any good news about their cellar-dwelling Pioneers. Seitz didn't mince words. "I've got one of the toughest jobs ahead of me that was ever put in a man's lap, and I'm going to be in there trying every minute, and all my players are going to do the same."[25] And he was true to his word. By the first week of July, the new pilot had pulled the team from last to seventh, a significant improvement. Writer J. H. Nail of the *Clovis News-Journal* described the progress that Seitz had made with a team of green players that until that point had been manhandled by other clubs in the league.

Grover Seitz, the West Texas–New Mexico League's irrepressible wag. This portrait was taken during one of his many tenures as pilot of the Pampa, Texas, Oilers (courtesy Panhandle Sports Hall of Fame, Amarillo, Texas).

> He's stopped that and put the Pioneers on their toes—told them that they can play ball, and that they had to play ball—and they're doing it too. One instance, the other night I heard Seitz telling a pitcher that if he dusted off one of our batters that he was going to see that he was taken care of—well, that pitcher, knowing Seitz, tossed that ball in decently all through the contest. That's the type of stuff that makes the players appreciate their manager.[26]

Indeed, he could be very paternal with young players. It was said of him that once, while at bat, he dropped the bat and caught a fastball with his bare hand just to ease his young players' fears of an opposing pitcher.[27] But while Grover Seitz was protecting his striplings, he was pushing them as well. By the beginning of August, the Pioneers were holding down third place in the league. He was also earning a reputation as a hothead, a man with a temper that could blow in as swiftly and dangerously as a high plains prairie fire. Still, at moments of extreme tension, he was able to rein in his anger, replacing it with an almost vaudevillian humor to diffuse the situation. At a game in Big Springs in early August, he tangled verbally with the Texas fans. Jack Douglas of the *Big Spring Daily Herald* obviously enjoyed describing the brouhaha.

> Grover Seitz, Clovis Pioneer Skipper, is a slick one on the give and take business with the wolves. At the close of the Friday evening game, Brother Seitz indicated that he would not find it disagreeable if one of the more vocal fans would discuss the situation with him. For a minute or two, it appeared that there might be a bit of a scuffle, but Seitz brought in the old comic touch when he whipped off his cap, subjected his bald pate to the evening breezes, and, in an injured tone inquired, "Now you wouldn't jump old Grover Seitz, would you?" Now we don't know how pert Old Man Seitz is with his hands, but, sizing up those logs he calls arms, we figure it would take a fair amount of jumping to make him say "uncle."[28]

As the playoffs approached, one writer from Texas had begun to refer to the Clovis team as "giant killers." "In the past, Big Springs has been able to take the Pioneers measure without too much ado, but of late there has been a tendency in the Clovis camp to wallop the opposition when they are least expecting it."[29] And while the Pioneers finished third in the regular season standings, behind the Big Spring Bombers and Gordon Nell's Borger Gassers, Grover Seitz—from his post in center field—steered them into the playoffs where they took the championship from Big Spring, four games to three.

The following January, Grover Seitz assured the stockholders of the Clovis ball club that the team would be in the top division of the league in the upcoming season.[30] To guarantee this, he re-signed two of his best pitchers from the previous season, right-hander Bill Hewitt and lefty Ken Wyatt. The Pioneers won the season opener against the Albuquerque Dukes, victims of the recent demise of the Arizona-Texas League. Managing those same Dukes was former University of Alabama running back Dixie Howell. Just a week into the season, a wire service article went country-wide, telling the tale of a mighty set-to between Howell, Seitz, and an overzealous fan with a steel chair. An *Albuquerque Journal* sportswriter gave his take on the battle.

> It is said that there was bad blood between the managers before Friday, but the argument this time got hot enough to translate thoughts and words into fistic gestures. It was mostly "in" fighting, with no haymakers visible from the ringside—er, grandstand. They finally fell to the ground, and it was while they were rolling around that the chair was supposed to have descended on Dixie's headpiece.[31]

As it happened, however, the fan had been aiming for Grover's head and apologized profusely to Howell for the errant clout as the police led him away. Clovis won the game, 11–9.

While Grover Seitz emerged from that incident with only a few drops of shed blood, on May 31, his actions would wound him far more deeply. In the midst of what would become a fourteen-game winning streak (broken by the Dukes and his arch-enemy Dixie Howell), the hot-tempered manager had a meltdown over strike rulings made by umpire Red Norman. In a game at Lubbock, following a rain of verbal abuse by Seitz on the head of Norman, the Clovis skipper then ripped the umpire's chest protector away, tearing the shoulder straps, then tore off Norman's face mask and threw it at his feet. So bitter was the assault that Texas Rangers were called in to remove Seitz from the field. An immediate fine of $50 was levied on him but worse punishment would be delayed until after league president Milton Price bumped the case up to W. G. Bramham, president of the National Association of Professional Baseball Leagues. From his office in Durham, Bramham lowered the boom on Grover Seitz: a 90-day suspension, which would automatically include the rest of the 1942 season and some of the next. The normally effusive Seitz had nothing to say except, "I'm gonna write Judge Bramham a letter and give him my side of the story."[32] And he may have, for what little good it would have done him. He was replaced as manager and forced to fume in the stands, excommunicate, while his team continued what was turning into an absolute assault on the pennant, due primarily to the pitching of his holdovers from the year before. At the beginning of July, lefty Ken Wyatt, formerly of the House of David,[33] was headed for his seventeenth straight win of the season and right-hander Bill Hewitt his thirteenth victory against four losses. Even with Grover in the stands, nothing could stop the Pioneers—except for a world war.

Albuquerque had entered the West Texas–New Mexico League because of the decision of the Arizona-Texas circuit to not even attempt to operate in 1942. It had fallen victim to what would claim dozens of minor leagues beginning that year. Not only were they losing men to the war but they were losing crowds as well. And on July 5, the West Texas–New Mexico League ceased to exist. It didn't come as a surprise; all the teams were suffering financially. The death knell came when the higher-ups in Clovis took dramatic action to insure that, headed as they were into dark times, they wouldn't go into them in debt.

> Sale of the league's two best pitchers pried loose the keystone which finally brought the whole league tumbling. Clovis sold Ken Wyatt and Bill Hewitt to Beaumont of the Texas League and although the Pioneers were running far ahead of the race, announced the team was withdrawing because of "lagging interest and gate receipts."[34]

Within forty-eight hours, the six-year-old West Texas–New Mexico League had been cannibalized by the Texas League for its best players. As for Clovis, it had ended what should have been another triumphant season with a sweep of Borger in a doubleheader.

And Grover Seitz? When the curtailed season's stats were released, they showed that the fiery Clovis pilot had hit a remarkable — and sadly aborted — .395.[35]

* * *

The decimated minor leagues were given new life in the spring of 1946 and the West Texas–New Mexico League took up where it had been forced to leave off in 1942, albeit with several changes. Most importantly, it had been raised a notch to Class C where it would remain for the next nine years. One team, the Abilene Blue Sox, became a farm club for the Brooklyn Dodgers. And Grover Seitz returned to Pampa, where he stayed until mid-season 1951. During his five-year tenure with the Texas club, Pampa finished the season in first place twice and made it to the playoffs three times, winning the championship series in 1946. For its part, Clovis, although it enjoyed the 1946 season affiliated with the Cleveland Indians, faced a lean five years, perennially finishing at or near the bottom of the heap.

But in that immediate post-war period, the West Texas–New Mexico circuit earned itself a reputation that it still boasts, that of a hitter's league. In his funny and informative essay for *The Hardball Times*, Steve Treder writes, "Some combination of altitude, heat, and outmoded bandbox ballparks worked together in wicked conspiracy to break pitchers' hearts."[36] In fact, typical of the times was a 1947 bit in the *Sporting News*.

> Home runs are still flying in wholesale numbers over the short fences of the West Texas–New Mexico League, and Bill Chick, statistician of the circuit, wearily reports that the eight clubs hit 445 circuit clouts in the first 250 of 560 scheduled games. Last season, 888 round-trippers were hit in the loop, and at the current pace this season, the total will reach 997.[37]

One of the minor league power hitters born of that era was Stubby Greer, who managed the Abilene Blue Sox, and played shortstop in 1946 and 1947. In '46, his Texas nine finished first in the league with an incredible 97–40 record, only to fall in the first round of the playoffs (Grover Seitz and his Oilers won the championship). Greer also had 202 hits, 23 home runs, 39 doubles, 8 triples and 131 RBIs in 135 games. He was fifth in batting with .358 (and also led the league in stolen bases with 38). The league leader in home runs that season was a phenom named Joe Bauman who would later make a name for himself in the history books while playing for Roswell, New Mexico. A star of the 1947 circuit was Bill Serena, shortstop for the champion Lubbock Hubbers, who hit 57 homers and 190 RBIs. In the playoffs and in a Class C Texas championship series, he hit another 13 home runs for an even 70 for the year.[38] In 1949, Serena went to the Chicago Cubs where he stayed until 1954.

The managing center fielder of the Albuquerque Dukes in 1948 was Hershel Martin, who'd played for the Phillies from '37 to '40 (and was a National League all-star in 1938) and the Yankees from '44 to '45. He snagged the West Texas–New Mexico League batting title with a .425 average and led the league with 61 doubles. But he didn't captivate the crowds quite so much as Amarillo center fielder, Bob Crues, who returned to the league to tie Joe Hauser's 1933 Organized Baseball record with 69 home runs. Harry Gilstrap of the *Amarillo Globe* wrote that, for all intents and purposes, Crues had broken it.

> And it may be recalled ruefully that he was cheated out of one homer this year which would have given him the all-time record. That was at Abilene on June 30,

when he bounced a "triple" off the scoreboard. Umpire Frank Secory thought it had struck the fence below the scoreboard, and ruled it so. But the Abilene outfielders and the scoreboard boy all reported later it had been a legitimate home run.[39]

While tardy reporting on the part of actual witnesses cost Crues dearly, when the final game of the season rolled around, the natural generosity of baseball players shone through. In front of a record crowd of 4,851 paying customers, the Lubbock Hubbers pitching staff intentionally eased up, walking Crues' teammates when need be to make sure he got to bat as often as possible.

> Bob didn't do it. In eight trips to the plate he had four singles (one of which caromed off the left field fence and probably would have been No. 70 if it hadn't lined into an inblowing wind), a base on balls, struck out once, grounded out once and popped up once. Also he hoisted a couple which were over the wall but foul.[40]

In addition to wearing the home run crown, Crues ended that season leading the league with 185 runs and a staggering 254 RBIs.

In December of that year—after a season in which Crues hit his 69 homers, his team hit 214 and the league hit 1,217 to set records—the National Association decided that a ball of "uniform resiliency" was to be introduced in the minors and its usage made mandatory for 1949. Besides high altitude and small parks providing advantages for the West Texas–New Mexico League, it was thought that perhaps the teams there were using an unusually rabbity type of ball.[41] But even after a season's use, the West Texas–New Mexico League's 1949 batting king, Roberto Fernandez of Abilene, hit a healthy .408 and Pud Miller of Lamesa managed 52 homers. What the National Association hadn't understood was the science involved. If the officials of the organization had sent five identical baseballs to Boston, Tampa Bay, San Francisco, Seattle and Albuquerque, and then tracked them, they would have discovered that the last one would have begun to dry, shrink and harden the moment it arrived in New Mexico. After a day there, it would have been a daunting task for the best hurler to put spin on it. It would have become, in effect, the anticurve ball.

The hits just kept on coming. In 1950 Grover Seitz's Pampa right fielder Joe Fortin was in the limelight. He had the most hits (236) and the most RBIs (171) but lost the batting title by an eyebrow-lifting "breakage of percentages," to Harry Bright of Clovis, who had hit .413.

> Minor league rules say that a batting champion has to play in two-thirds of his team's games and Bright, who doubled between shortstop and catcher, participated in 95 contests. Two-thirds of Clovis' 143 games would be 95.33, the fraction being less than one-half and giving Bright the chance. Late-season rainouts kept him from playing in more. Otherwise, Joe Fortin, Pampa veteran, would have taken the crown with a respectable .401 mark.[42]

Environmental conditions, coupled with unarguable league talent, yielded astounding results in batting for the West Texas–New Mexico League. The mean league batting average from the years 1946 through 1951 was an impressive .2993. As Steve Treder aptly puts it, "This warn't no league for namby-pamby 'low-scoring' games. This was a league for serious hitters playing hardball in the hot sun."[43]

Meanwhile, as the circuit was building a name for itself with its fearsome hitting, Grover Seitz was attempting to become a less fearsome figure. The *Sporting News* painted a rather cuddly picture of him in 1946. "Grover, who owns a Pampa pool hall, has settled down this year, however, and has lost his former aggressiveness and tendency toward umpire baiting."[44] Perhaps. But when it came to winning, he was certainly not beyond actions that were, at the very least, underhanded. In September 1946, when up against the formidable Bob Crues at bat, with bases loaded in the seventh, Grover decided to call for a reliever.

> Stalling for time so Warren Hacker could get warmed up, Grover took the box for warm-up throws, then, when he decided Hacker was ready, started to return to left field. After a lengthy argument, however, Umpire Craig compelled him to pitch to Crues. He served up a single pitchout, then ran back to left field while the Pampa fans cheered.[45]

Not only did his behavior delight the Pampa fans, but drew large crowds for its away games as well. Sports columnist Putt Powell of the *Amarillo Globe* wrote

> Seitz is a real showman as well as the most successful manager in the history of the West Texas–New Mexico League. The fans fill the stands every time he comes here just to see him put on his famous diamond antics. He usually stops the game several times to "talk the situation over" with the umpires—and, in general, pleases the crowd.[46]

Other sportswriters were less enamored of Grover. Harry Gilstrap of the *Amarillo Daily News* described the aftermath of his team's victory over Pampa. It had been such an unexpected win that the Amarillo fans, in joy, threw all of their seat cushions on to the field, "...an unfortunate action which caused Grover Seitz, Pampa's embittered manager, to deliver them a lecture on sportsmanship. Sietz, always the sportsman himself, then turned and shouted obscenities at the press box."[47] But even as much as some might disapprove of him in his darker moods, most of the regional sportswriters appreciated his wit. Joe Kelly of the *Lubbock Avalanche Journal* shared his favorite Grover Seitz story, which took place in the all-star game of 1948 (Grover Seitz played or managed in every all-star game during his tenure with the league).

> The players from Abilene, Lubbock, Lamesa and Pampa gathered around him for the customary talk before the game began. Grover looked at them. "Hell, you all know why you're here. I don't have anything to say. When you get on the bases you're on your own. No, I take that back. We'll use Pampa signals—you all know them anyway."[48]

After drawing yet another suspension for assaulting an umpire in 1949, the owner of the Pampa Oilers fired Grover in early 1950, only to elicit a flood of stories and reminiscences from reporters as if they were at a wake. Every writer for 300 miles shared his favorite, and outdid each other in celebrations of Seitz's traits, including the physical, one suggesting that Grover's bald head gleamed "like a New Englander's skillet" when under the bright lights of the ball field.[49] When the Pampa club was sold shortly thereafter, and the new owners hired Grover back within a day of buying it, it only enhanced his image as a sort of devilish phoenix.

But as much as Grover Seitz was selling himself in his personal sideshows, he was also selling the game. Because he understood that dull games lost fans, he'd do whatever it took to keep them lively. In a late May game in 1950, his team was mired in a sleeper against Lubbock.

> Then just as the fans were beginning to read the advertisements in their scorecard programs, Grover went into his act. It all started when the umpire called a strike on a Pampa batsman. Now, there wasn't anything remarkable about that, particularly since it wasn't even a third strike. But Grover Seitz is a man who recognizes a draggy ball game when he meets it face to face, and who knows how to remedy the situation. So he came storming out of the dugout like a Yank doughboy wading ashore at Normandy on D-Day.... Grover's stormy session was as short and sweet as a 10-cent soda, but it achieved its purpose. By the time Seitz simmered down, everyone else in the ball park was boiling like a coffee pot at breakfastime.[50]

Seitz and the press clearly enjoyed a symbiotic relationship; he delighted in the attention paid him by writers and they, in turn, enjoyed the stories he supplied. But not everyone was amused. After an early August tantrum of Grover's, a column on the editorial page of a Lubbock paper blasted both parties, Grover for his outbursts and the press for winking at them. "After a dozen years of Seitz rowdyism, it is time for the disseminators of the league's news to begin calling a spade a shovel, instead of chuckling so much about good, old Grover and his antics."[51] Unfortunately for the editorialist, his words more than likely fell on deaf ears; that morning, a competing paper had printed the standings of the West Texas–New Mexico League which showed Grover Seitz's Pampa Oilers in first place at 86–42.[52] With the help of Joe Fortin and his astounding performance that season, the Oilers cruised home with a 92–53 record, the league leaders. As Grover himself put it, "If that isn't a Class B ball club, I'll walk down Broadway, or whatever the main street is, nekkid!"[53] Unfortunately, they lost in the first round of the playoffs.

Having seen some of the initial Pampa workouts the following March, there was little doubt in anyone's mind that Grover Seitz would field another powerful team for the 1951 season. One Texas writer stated his belief that the volatile manager could find ball players in the Sahara Desert if need be and fully expected the Oilers to make it to the playoffs.[54] He went on to say, "Although we saw only the seven players ... this reporter is ready to convey the intelligence that the Pampa Oilers will be a pretty tough team this year.

Because Manager Seitz said, quote 'We will be a pretty tough team this year.'" But unexpectedly, by mid–June, the Oilers were in fifth place and the grumbling was becoming audible. Attendance at home games was "exceptionally poor,"[55] which drew attention to the fact that the previous season's attendance had been down as well. Seitz himself admitted that he had probably overstayed his welcome and resigned. "The fans are tired," he said, "of seeing me out there and maybe some new faces will bring more fans out to Oiler Park."[56] Once again, the area sportswriters threw themselves into frenzy of mourning, and the high plains readership was hit with a new wave of favorite Grover stories. Tales were told of the time that, in angry protest over a call, Grover picked up dirt and rubbed it on his head, only to make the painful discovery that he'd rubbed lime into his scalp as well.[57] And there was this regional favorite:

> ... and the night when, having argued with Bob Seeds that the field was too muddy for play, he met Seeds and the umpires at the plate for pre-game ground-rules discussion ... and, reaching into his hip pocket, produced a small mud-turtle and solemnly presented it to Seeds.[58]

* * *

Over in eastern New Mexico, the Clovis Pioneers had endured a dramatic and miserable five years of their own, never ending any higher than sixth place in league standings. Like a wallflower at the ball, the team had barely even put toe on the dance floor. In the fall of 1948, the Clovis Baseball Association had run an ad in the *Sporting News* offering the team for sale ("With purchase, you receive all equipment, player's contracts, bus in good condition, and lease on a fine baseball plant").[59] And in this dark hour, who should ride up to the rescue but a pair of white knights, in the form of Paul "Daffy" Dean and his brother, Dizzy. The famous siblings "bought" the club by taking over its debts which were estimated at $17,000.[60] It was Paul who would be the hands-on manager (and do a little pitching) while Diz would be more of a silent partner, visiting only occasionally to toss a few balls. Paul Dean promised the frustrated Clovis citizenry "a hustling, scrappy Pioneer baseball club" that would finish in the first division "not in 1950, not in 1951, not five years from now — but this season of 1949."[61] The *Clovis News-Journal* sports editor Bern Gantner attempted to stir up some local jubilation with the headline: "Baseball on Way, Paul Dean Coming."[62]

Dean entered into the relationship with a lot of enthusiasm and some big ideas. He scheduled a baseball school and tryout camp for the first week in April and Gantner played it for all it was worth, informing his readers that several major league scouts would attend to get a good first look at the new Pioneers.[63] But when the camp was finished, the depressed populace took one look at the roster of recently-acquired novitiates and settled in for another bad season. By the end of April, they clucked resignedly at the team's 1–4 standing. By the beginning of June, they shook their heads when their boys established themselves firmly in the cellar at 13–28. The ever-optimistic Bern Gantner labored like a serf to keep the collective chin up with reassurances that the playoffs were still within Pioneer grasp. But depressed fans stayed away in droves. It would take nothing less than drastic action to get them fired up and back in the park. It would take Dizzy.

> Dizzy Dean, former National League pitching star, made an appearance here the night of July 8 for the first time since he and his brother, Paul, purchased the local club last December. Paul and the Pioneers had been on the road and when they arrived home Dizzy was on hand to meet them, and some 2,400 fans, largest crowd in the history of the local club, were present to meet Dizzy. The game was delayed 20 minutes because the crowd was still filing into the park. Dizzy was signed on a five-day "look" by Paul, but it took him only one night to give the fans a show.[64]

Clovis won that game, one of the 52 they took that year. But they lost 87, ending the season 31 games behind the leading Albuquerque Dukes.

In January of the next year, Clovis fans learned that Paul Dean had landed a working agreement with the Chicago Cubs. And when it was announced that the opening game for the league would be played at Clovis — for the first time in the Pioneer's history — Bern Gantner, the *News-Journal*'s easy going sports editor encouraged fan attendance in numbers that would set West Texas–New Mexico records.[65] And they obliged him — by setting the record for the lowest turnout for an opening game in the loop's history.[66] To add insult to injury, in front of the meager crowds, skipper Dean was ejected in the sixth inning. As bleak as the attendance was on opening day, it got worse, falling to a degree that was alarming to Paul Dean and on May 22, he announced that he was putting the club up for sale. Within two weeks, Clovis Baseball Inc. (a group of local businessmen) bought the fifth-place Pioneers and the town's brief and unsatisfactory flirtation with the Dean brothers ended. The team went through three more managers before the season mercifully ended, with the Pioneers in seventh place.

By mid–April 1951, the Clovis Pioneers had lost four of the five exhibition games they had played; two months later they were 27½ games out of first place and in the damp of the cellar. When word came of the resignation of Grover Seitz from the Pampa Oilers, "the fever spread like wild fire."[67] From Texas, he stormed westward into New Mexico. He signed a contract with Clovis Baseball, Inc. on the morning of June 22 and was in uniform that night.[68] The regional press chuckled at the swift dis- and re-appearance of Grover Seitz, one writer saying, "…this is HIS league, and nobody was surprised to learn that he was staying with and in it."[69]

Unfortunately, Grover didn't get to build the club; he inherited it and found it woefully short in many departments, particularly in slugging power and in pitching, which was "spotty and unpredictable."[70] By the time he took the reins, the shattered sportswriters at the *Clovis News-Journal* were so desperate for even the most minor of breaks that one used the word "spectacular" to refer to a three-game winning streak.[71] Stalwart Bern Gantner kept attempting to rally the troops' excitement but knew better from long, sad experience to shoot for the moon. "It must be admitted that hopes can't be elevated too highly.... After all, overcoming a 17 game bulge isn't any easy undertaking, but it can be done...."[72]

Pep talks were all well and good in their place but Grover Seitz had a more effective method for rousing the fans, and he put it to use almost immediately, as was reported in this headline: "Fireworks Shatter Calm, Grover Ejected by Umpire Negri." Yes, he was back and in fine form — swearing, gesticulating and kicking dirt on the umpire's shoes, all followed by the receipt of a hefty fine.[73] And he spent the entire season engaged in the type of volatile displays that had made him a legend in the grasslands. But he had arrived too late and even his histrionics and deft maneuvering of players couldn't save the 1951 Pioneers who finished the season dead last. And it was cold comfort to learn, when the league's official standings were released, that Clovis led in at least one category: the Pioneer shortstop led in the bobble department with 86, a league record.[74] Still, Clovis Baseball, Inc. remembered 1941 and had faith that Grover Seitz was the only man to lead them to better days and signed him to a two-year contract.[75] In addition, they gave him their financial blessing to go shopping for talent if he knew where to look and, as usual, he did.[76] Despite losing their affiliation with the Cubs,[77] Grover put together a team for 1952, including "the best catcher in the league," Frank Benites, and "a couple of front-line fast ball pitchers," Bill Hair and Red Dial, a player who had loyally followed Seitz from Pampa.[78] Grover assured the Clovis baseball establishment, "If this team doesn't finish in the first division it will be the best second division ball club ever seen in the league. And if we don't finish in the top bracket, you can kick me in the rear."[79]

Grover Seitz "officially opened" the West Texas–New Mexico season in the third game by getting fined. As the season progressed, it became evident that he wouldn't be the only one misbehaving; he was giving at least tacit encouragement to his players to act out as well[80] although Collier Parris of the *Abilene Reporter-News* found room to forgive some of the team's umpire baiting. He pointed to the "new crop of umpires, liberally sprinkled this season with undried, inexperienced rookies."[81] But Grover still led the Pioneers in bad behavior. In June, with the team in first place, Grover left the field arm-in-arm with a Texas policeman after an ejection, only to be joined by his first baseman Virgil Richardson, who'd thrown a bat after popping up.[82] Despite, or maybe because of, the tantrums and expulsions, the Pioneers were playing spectacular baseball, to the good-natured resignation of some managers whose teams were losing to them.

> One rival manager has observed, without rancor, that the Pioneers seem to be having an inordinate amount of good luck. He added amiably that they have had so much bad luck in other years that the good luck has heaped up and isn't likely to run out for awhile. But good luck isn't the only answer. They have the players

too, and they have Grover Seitz, who has great ability to get the most out of Class C ball players and who will outsmart you, too, if you ever try to take forty winks during a game...."[83]

And yet, for all the victories and substantial publicity that was being earned by the Pioneers, the team was in financial distress, mostly because of poor weather affecting attendance. Grover's poetic response to this was, "It could be the bad weather, but methinks the fans are so astonished at watching a winner after seeing a cellar-dweller that they're overcome and afraid the balloon might burst in their faces."[84] In the second half of the season, the club and the fans managed to right their listing financial ship to the point that they were able to reward their captain with a brand new Mercury and expensive luggage.[85] From its 1951 record of 47–94, 42 games behind the league leader, to 1952 and a notable reverse of 94–47, Grover Seitz had once again rewarded Clovis for its faith in him. Although they fell in the playoffs, their triumph was padded with pitcher Red Dial's 27 wins.

Grover Seitz leading the Clovis Pioneers. He was the only manager able to make the Pioneers a contending team during their years in the West Texas–New Mexico League (courtesy Panhandle Sports Hall of Fame, Amarillo, Texas).

Grover Seitz stayed with the Clovis Pioneers for another two years. They finished second in the league in both with Red Dial setting a league record in 1953 with 28 wins (one of the top four minor league hurlers that year[86]), and then repeating it, to the number, the next year. In both years they made it to the playoffs. Seitz's pyrotechnic reputation continued to dominate the sports pages although there was less comedic schtick these days and more outright abuse. More than ever, he seemed to inspire the same sometimes violent behavior in his players, particularly Virgil Richardson, who continued to accrue fines and Red Dial who, according to one sportswriter, modeled himself on his beloved boss.[87] Although Seitz had given Clovis a verbal promise to return in the spring of 1955, he went back to the Pampa Oilers in January of that year, citing the lack of gate support he received in New Mexico.[88] When he wanted to take his protégé,

Dial, with him, Clovis demanded $2,000 for the contract. As Dial fumed, saying he would play in Pampa or not at all, Seitz reached a deal with his former team: he would put the $2,000 toward the $3,000 still owed him by the club.[89]

Back on his home turf, Grover was more irascible than ever, drawing down the first fine of the season in early April for "overripe language."[90] Then, in June, he was involved in an incident which effectively dammed the seemingly endless flow of goodwill from the press. In a doubleheader against his old team, Clovis, Grover was ejected in the first tilt, yet refused to leave the field and the game was forfeited to the Pioneers. During the second game, he tangled yet again with the umpire, this time racing to the dugout for a bat at which point he had to be restrained by his own players. He received an immediate suspension.[91] That began a descent into paranoia, Grover telling anyone that would listen that the league wanted to get rid of him[92] and, beyond that, the umpires were in a conspiracy to get him.[93] When the league president, Hal Sayles, lifted the June suspension early and levied no fine on the Wild Bull, the newspapers fumed, pointing out that, not only had Seitz turned into an overweening bully, he was also bringing adverse publicity to the league which was now struggling at the Class B level. "The West Texas–New Mexico League has built up a long list of ills that make major league executives glance elsewhere when talk of working agreements is mentioned. It added another malady to the ledger the past week in the case of Grover Seitz," wrote J. D. Kailer, sports editor for the *Albuquerque Journal*.

> That Seitz is colorful and a gate attraction is recognized. That his teams are always contenders is not denied. That Sayles missed an excellent opportunity to prove who's boss in the WT–NM is obvious.... A $250 fine would have helped the WT–NM office, indicated Sayles was squarely behind his officials and silenced parties who thrive on umpire baiting.[94]

In Clovis, where the outrage had occurred, former Seitz booster, the *Clovis News-Journal*, concurred with Kailer. In a new column called "Sports Outbursts," Jack Mayfield turned his attention to the league president. "So, Mr. Sayles, we believe that you have missed one, but we won't stand around and stomp our feet and mouth off at you for it, but we will take the next punishment meted out with tongue in cheek."[95]

All the protestations were to no avail. In August, a first baseman for the Amarillo Gold Sox accused Seitz of hitting him in the back of the neck with his fist, then hitting him three more times as Pampa Oilers held the infielder.[96] And in a possible no-mean-feat first for the national pastime, Seitz was ejected and fined in September for using what the umpire described as "the worst language I've ever heard on a ball field."[97] Despite these distractions, the Oilers finished the regular season in third place, and won the playoffs for the crown against Amarillo.

Over the winter, it was decided to combine the West Texas–New Mexico League with the Longhorn and Big State leagues to form the largest loop in the minors at that time, a Class B, 10-teamer called the Southwestern. The Texas teams included Pampa, with Seitz at the helm (and Red Dial at his side), El Paso, Lamesa, Midland, Plainview and San Angelo. New Mexico had additional entries in this loop with Hobbs, Carlsbad and Roswell. And, as it had since 1938, Clovis had its Pioneers. As the team leaders engaged in the spring scramble for players, Grover showed that he hadn't learned humility from any of the last season's disapprobation. He boasted to the media that he "could take one infielder and one outfielder and open the Southwestern League tomorrow."[98] But his Oilers got off to a very poor start and wallowed at the bottom of the league until May 30, when Grover Seitz suffered the ultimate outrage: Pampa officials booted him up to the position of general manager — a desk job. He watched as his replacement, Allen Cross, took the team from last place to third in under two months[99] where it finished the season. "Old Grover suffered his final humiliation in the playoff. Cross broke his leg in the opening game of the series with El Paso. So, Seitz took over the managership and despite all the sagacity he could command his Oilers lost the next three in a row to El Paso, and were eliminated."[100] He may have been down but everyone knew better than to count him out. On February 1, 1957, he took the first step toward his comeback when he signed on to pilot the Plainview Ponies of the Southwestern League. But that night — a moonless one — he, his wife and two others were killed when their car rammed an eastbound Rock Island freight train on the dark plains outside Amarillo. The impact was such that the car's engine was hurled some thirty feet. Grover Seitz was 50 years old.

Suddenly, it was like the old days, when Grover — temporarily resigned or suspended — was the source of endless stories swapped by sportswriters. Except that many of the ones that had known him when he was more clown than menace were gone, moved to other newspapers (like the prim and gentle Bern Gantner who'd accepted the helm of a newspaper in Farmington) or perhaps they had retired from the business of news altogether. But for a week or so after his death, those that remained trotted out the old war stories of the once-lovable rogue. There was the time that Grover, when given an allotted amount of time to leave the field, threw the umpire's watch over the grandstand.[101] Later, more details emerged concerning that famous scene. "Seitz was hit with a $100 fine, so he sent a few clubhouse boys out to look for the watch since he figured he paid for it. They found the watch, but it was of the cheap $5 variety. Seitz was 'fit to be tied.'"[102] And then there was the time when he and another manager decided to stir up fan interest by staging a fake fight during an exhibition, only for Seitz to be royally thrashed when it escalated into an actual brawl.[103] One writer ended his eulogy by saying, "Seitz never lived long enough to become an umpire, which perhaps is just as well. He's probably got it made now, however, provided he didn't start an argument with the caretaker on his way through Valhalla."[104] Harry Gilstrap, whose feelings for Grover had always vacillated between amusement and irritation, was profoundly moved by his death and penned this lamentation for the fans who would never get the chance to see him in action. "I can answer only, you missed something. There will never be another Grover Seitz. They won't feel it in Ebbets Field or Comiskey Park, but something has gone out of baseball."[105]

As for Clovis, the Pioneers had played in the Southwestern League in 1956 and started the next season with a new name — the Redlegs — in keeping with their working agreement with the Cincinnati Reds. It must have broken the curse because they caught fire and took a commanding lead early in the season. By mid-June, they had a win-loss record of 33–12. And then they quit. As in many a small town, fans were otherwise occupied and barely trickled into Bell Park. At a meeting of the league, they returned the franchise to officials. At roughly the same time, Pampa folded as well, along with El Paso and San Angelo. The league hobbled to season's end with four teams and then disbanded.

In his musings on the recent decease of professional baseball in Clovis, Eddie Mullens of the *Amarillo Globe-Times* paid a final tribute to the man whose shadow still hung over the High Plains ball parks.

> An odd twist to the Clovis incident, to this department anyway, was this is the first contending ball club the eastern New Mexico city had there without the services of the late Grover Seitz. Until this year, only Grover had ever fielded a first place ball club there but the team this year had the earmarks of outdoing Grover's 1952 team which finished the season with a 17½ game lead over second place Albuquerque.[106]

All of the juicy rhubarbs and comedic displays aside, none could deny that Grover Seitz was perhaps the finest manager ever seen in the West Texas–New Mexico League, his teams reaching the playoffs in 15 out of 16 seasons. Perhaps the best tribute to his abilities came from a column written several years earlier by Harry Gilstrap.

> But the old boy is quite a manager for Class C at that ... with remarkable talent for assembling a sound ball club at minimum investment in player purchases ... and great talent also at getting the utmost out of his young men ... perhaps partly because, like most old ballplayers, he has sympathy for the player and treats him right.... He has had his squabbles with his athletes, as have all other managers, but few of those who have worked for him would have a hard word to say for him now.[107]

What he gave to baseball is only partly quantifiable. The stats, certainly, are there for the reading. What he gave the fans in sheer delight is an unknowable, but his gargantuan presence promised new stories with every opening day and he filled many a bleak panhandle winter with much hot stove pleasure. None enjoyed those stories more than the small-town reporters who doggedly followed the buses of the West Texas–New Mexico League teams as they hurtled through the barren southwestern landscapes. Sports reporting can be a thudding and thankless job for some, given its narrow guidelines—the literalness of numbers, the prosaic play-by-plays. Grover Seitz had demanded nothing less of the regional sportswriters than a fitting account of his Bunyanesque personality and exploits, and, in humoring him, a few of them were exercised almost to poetry.

6

The Flying Kellys

In the decades since World War II, the pivotal role New Mexico played in that conflict has been clarified. No state in the union could claim greater contributions and none sacrificed more. The memorials to its efforts dot the landscape, some officially recognized and frequently visited, while others require some searching and perhaps a willing local to point the way. Still other important landmarks are forgotten by all but the people who are old enough to bear witness to a proud and painful chapter in their state's history.

The world is well-acquainted with the story of Fat Man and Little Boy but, if there are any gaps in one's complete understanding, a visit to the Bradbury Museum in Los Alamos will fill them. Perched on a mesa in the Jemez Mountains, the city looks like any suburb, its uninspired architecture starkly contrasting with the breathtaking vistas surrounding it. On the outskirts of the town, however, it is impossible to miss the signs of an edgy military presence; warning signs, high chain link fences and armed guards attest to the fact that the city is still one of the major players on the global nuclear stage. But one can touch the atomic past without leaving the environs of downtown Santa Fe, for in a tiny, humble courtyard amid the tinseled trappings of the City Different, are a couple of rooms, the former "first portal" for the Manhattan Project. It was there that scientists and military personnel, under a veil of secrecy, first stopped on their way toward the Manhattan Project and history. Dorothy McKibbin, who ran the office for twenty years, later revealed some of the orders she'd been given, particularly those regarding what she said to and the questions she asked of the incoming scientists. And if one desires a more tangible connection to the atomic age, there is always Trinity Site, where the first atom bomb was tested. Located on what is now the White Sands Missile Range, a few hours' drive to the south of Santa Fe, it is open to the public only twice a year. While the official website for White Sands stresses that levels of radiation there are low, it is subtly suggested that pregnant women and children might want to enjoy an outing elsewhere.[1]

Starting in 1942, New Mexico housed German and Italian prisoners of war at camps across the state. Because of the labor shortage, they were put to work at local farms. In the Mesilla Valley, Italian soldiers picked cotton for the "prevailing wage" of 27.5 cents an hour.[2] Unfortunately, the state was also used in the forced relocation and internment of thousands of Japanese Americans. At Camp Lordsburg in Hidalgo County, a U.S. Army facility where up to 1,500 people were held, two elderly and infirm Japanese American men were shot to death by a camp guard who was acquitted in the incident. Near Ruidoso, at Fort Stanton, the Department of Justice operated a detention camp for Axis prisoners including fifty-eight Japanese considered to be "incorrigible agitators." And in what is now a quiet residential neighborhood less than a mile west of the Santa Fe plaza, a shopping center (which, curiously, houses a sushi restaurant) sits on the remains of an internment camp that held over 2,000 Japanese Americans as well as Japanese men from Alaska, Hawaii and Peru. Some 350 renunciants (those who'd renounced American citizenship) who'd been transferred from the Tule Lake relocation center in Nevada started a riot there in March 1945 in which they "bombarded the administration building with rocks and defied tear gas bombs tossed among them by guards."[3]

As far as American military efforts, it is acknowledged by most students of history that the Marines would not have been able to win the war in the Pacific had it not been for the Navajo Code Talkers. The 382nd Platoon of the United States Marine Corps was formed of young men from Arizona and New Mexico who were able to create an unbreakable code from the combined complexities of their native language and English. But the Native Americans of New Mexico — Navajo, Pueblo, Apache — weren't limited to outwitting the Japanese with uncrackable communications. They were also in the trenches, and medals for valor gleamed on their chests or the coffins that carried them home. One of Albuquerque's most beloved adopted sons, Ernie Pyle, wrote movingly of meeting some Navajo soldiers from the Duke City as they prepared for the invasion of Okinawa.

> Before the convoy left the far south tropical island where the Navajos had been training since the last campaign, the boys put on a ceremonial dance. The Red Cross furnished some colored cloth and paint to stain their faces. They made up the rest of their Indian costumes from chicken feathers, sea shells, coconuts, empty ration cans and rifle cartridges. Then they did their own native ceremonial chants out there under the tropical palm trees with several thousand Marines as a grave audience. In their chant they asked the great gods in the sky to sap the Japanese of their strength for this blitz. They put the finger of weakness on the Japs. And then they ended their ceremonial chant by singing the Marine Corps song in Navajo.[4]

Indeed, the first American soldier to fire against the Japanese after Pearl Harbor was from Cochiti Pueblo. Just hours after the bombing of the Hawaiian base, Juan Manuel Chavez took to his gun against the initial air attack on Clark Field Air Force Base on Luzon in the Philippines. He was a member of the 200th Coast Artillery, formerly the 111th Cavalry of the New Mexico National Guard, a mixed contingent of troops — Hispano, Anglo and Indian. The next day, the 200th was split to form the 515th Anti-aircraft battalion which was sent to Manila. With their Filipino counterparts, they made up a roughly 75,000-troop force that defended the Bataan Peninsula for four months, with outdated equipment, dwindling food supplies and increasing illnesses, until their unavoidable surrender on April 8, 1942, still the largest in American military history. On April 9 began what would become known as the Bataan Death March, a 65-mile nightmare for those that endured it. Those that survived the march were put into prison camps; those that survived the camps were sent to other destinations in Asia to perform slave labor. As the Bataan Memorial in Albuquerque points out, "New Mexico earned the tragic distinction of having the highest prisoner-of-war population per capita of any state in the Union." More than 1,800 New Mexicans were part of that ordeal and fewer than half of them made it home, where more died of health complications.

With America's entry into the war, the United States Army Air Force built airfields, or took control of existing ones, all over New Mexico and used them to train bomber and fighter crews. Their geoglyph targets, from bulls eyes to swastikas, are still visible from overhead. The Albuquerque Army Air Base, built near the municipal airport, was one of the earliest. "The summer of 1941 saw the arrival of the first troop train, loaded with 500 base support personnel, as well as the arrival of the 19th Bombardment Group ... Business on the new airfield really began to boom with the arrival of 2,195 pilots, bombardiers, and navigator trainees for the new B-17 'Flying Fortress.'"[5]

In late winter of 1942, the athletic officer of what was now called Kirtland Army Air Field announced ambitious plans for a baseball program there. His idea called for a post team to play local semipro and professional teams in the area, as well as teams from other regional air fields. The *Albuquerque Journal* wrote, "There are plenty of former pro and collegiate stars on which to build a team of high caliber, the athletic director believes." For men that couldn't make the post team, there would be an intra-mural league, one that the director believed would be large enough to call for two divisions.[6] Within two weeks came the announcement of the official formation of the post team, to be called the Colin Kellys, in honor of the B-17 pilot who was the first to be shot down in combat. (While Kelly is commonly referred to as the first American hero of World War II, the aforementioned Pueblo soldier Juan Manuel Chavez could certainly vie for the same title.)

The Kellys began their season against the Albuquerque Dukes in a tilt to benefit the men who were suffering on Bataan. Those ill-fated Dukes were as new a team to the city as the soldiers were, having just been organized as part of the Class D West Texas–New Mexico League (their inglorious life would be short, lasting only until June of that year). Having had just two weeks of spring training, the Kellys fell to their professional competition, but by a respectable score of 9–6.[7]

Like any other management body in the national pastime, the brass at Kirtland wanted a winning team and did all that was necessary to get it. Early on they appointed Sgt. Danny Pavlovic, "former fence-busting outfielder in the Texas League," as manager of the team. "Cowboy" Foster Thornton, formerly of Macon in the South Atlantic League, had been recruited for mound duty[8] and later, Danny Matthews of Trenton of the Interstate League. Behind the plate, the Kellys boasted Rudy "Pop" Voyles, veteran of the San Francisco Seals. At shortstop was John Melago from Little Rock of the Southern Association and at third, Lem Hale from the Sally loop.[9] In May, Ted Shipkey, the head football coach at the University of New Mexico, was sworn in as an Army Air Corps captain[10] and, almost immediately, and very conveniently, put in charge of "physical training" at the base.[11] He would take the reins of the newly-minted team.

But perhaps what made the team stand out from any other team of ringers was the manner in which they traveled to their away games. It didn't take long for the Colin Kellys of Kirtland Field to be called the "Flying Kellys" as they became known for roaring into the competition's turf in the bombers in which they trained. In early June, the *Sporting News* published a picture of the team (and touted its 7–1 record), preparing to board a Consolidated B-24 Bomber on their way to a game in Denver.[12]

By the third week of June, the Kellys had beaten the Biggs Field, El Paso, airmen team twice and a few days later notched their thirteenth win with a no-hitter against a powerful mainstay of Albuquerque semipro baseball, the Armijo Yanks. The lopsided 19–0 win wasn't just the product of perfect hurling by Ray Morton and new reliever Harry Micewski, but an offensive win as well. Former Duke Troy "Cotton" Gann started the hitting and was abetted by Pavlovic, who showed what had made him a Texas star by going 4 for 5.[13] At that point in the season, seven Kellys were hitting over .300.[14] Their triumphant run was finally broken at El Paso in the regional semipro tournament with an 8–4 loss.[15]

The baseball fans of Albuquerque, having lost their professional team in June, became enthusiastic supporters of the air field players and a huge crowd was expected for a benefit game scheduled for mid–July between the Kellys and the Penitentiary Grays from the prison in Santa Fe. But probably more intriguing even than seeing soldiers play prisoners was the moundsman slated for the Kellys. Twenty-seven-year-old bombardier cadet Walter Johnson, Jr. was given special permission to start. Johnson had been in organized ball until 1937 when he played with the outlaw Carolina League and various army teams before ending up at Kirtland. He expressed a mournful wish to the *Albuquerque Journal* that his father would be able to attend the game.[16] Sadly, the "Big Train" didn't attend and Walter Jr. lasted for only three innings although the Kellys won the game.[17]

Capt. Ted Shipkey got an able right-hand man in July when Lieut. Ted Wright was named his assistant and coach, as well as an outfielder. Like his superior, Wright had made a name for himself in football. "In 1932, he led the ball carriers of the nation's gridirons with 117 points while totin' for North Texas Teachers. He was named Little All-American quarterback. Following that were three years in the Washington Redskins' pro backfield and two more as a coach for them."[18]

An early August game against the Lubbock flying school was a 3–2 win for the Kellys when shortstop Melago blasted a home run over the 385-foot left field fence in the thirteenth inning[19] and put the team in the proper frame of mind to take on the Northrop Bombers of California. This airplane-building nine were on their way to the National Semipro Baseball Tournament in Wichita for the second year in a row, having finished in fourth place the year before.[20] When they flew into Albuquerque, they would be bringing their estimable record of 35–2. They, too, had a few notable ringers on their team, including Sam Arico who had played with Bisbee in the old Arizona-Texas League and a couple of former major leaguers to boot. John Miljus, known in his early career with the Pirates and the Dodgers as "the Big Serb," was the team manager. As a Pirate reliever, Miljus had been called from the bullpen in the seventh inning of the last game in the Yankees' four-game sweep of the 1927 World Series. After performing well in the seventh and eighth innings, in the ninth, with no outs, Miljus intentionally walked Babe Ruth to fill the bases. He managed to strike out the next two batters—Lou Gehrig and Bob Meusel—but then threw wild to Tony Lazzeri, scoring Earl Combs. He became the goat of the 1927 World Series and just another notch in the belt for the "Murderer's Row."

Miljus' coach for the Northrop team was reported to be Otis Crandall, famously christened "Doc" by Damon Runyon who called him "the physician of the pitching emergency" because of his excellence in relief. "Doc Crandall is generally regarded as the premier relief specialist of the Deadball Era."[21] Doc Crandall's major league career lasted from 1908 until 1918, and comprised stints with the Giants, the Cardinals and the St. Louis Terriers of the Federal League. According to historian R. J. Lesch, Crandall spent the 1937 and '38 seasons coaching for the Pacific Coast League, retiring from baseball in California. It is a testament to the Kellys that, even with this kind of seasoned leadership, the Northrop Bombers won the game by only one run.

As August wound down, the Kellys finished their season with jaunts to Lowry Field in Denver where they lost to the Colorado airmen, 10–9, but came home to enjoy an 8–2 victory over the Madrid Miners. A rematch with the flyboys from Lubbock had the bespectacled Kellys pitcher "Professor" Morton throwing two-hit ball but with errors behind him. Despite whiffing ten, Morton lost to the Texans' submarine hurler, but won a post-game throwing contest with a 397-foot bullet.[22] Their season ended, some of the Kellys banded with airmen from other fields to form an all-star team to take on a local semi-pro team, Giomi Brothers, the only New Mexican nine to have beaten the Kellys that summer.[23] The civilian team coyly hinted that they had procured the services of a former Philadelphia Athletics pitcher for the game, but wouldn't name him. Despite wildness and many a base on balls, the mysterious hurler, by the name of Bordamis, led Giomi Brothers to a 5–3 victory over the Air Base All-Stars, the Kellys' almost-perfect season of 26 wins to 4 losses[24] tarnished by ignominious defeat.[25]

6. The Flying Kellys

* * *

The national pastime during World War II was an entirely different animal than it had been up until then, its ranks decimated by the Selective Service and Training Act of 1940. "By 1943, over 100 major league players were in uniform and over 1,400 minor-leaguers. A year later the figures were 500 and 5,000."[26] The major leagues were playing with much older and much younger men, and the minor leagues had folded like paper fans. Legendary sportswriter Hugh Fullerton, in an April 1943 column, included a bit of verse to summarize the game's mournful state and entitled it "Fan's Lament."

> Sonny's on the pitcher's mound;
> Grandpa guards first base;
> Uncle Joe is fat and slow;
> But still he has his place.
> You'd never know our slugger's row;
> To call it that is treason.
> We ain't got what we used to have
> To start the baseball season.
> We don't need what we used to have
> As long as there's a war on,
> If you don't think we miss those guys,
> Pally, you're a moron.[27]

For the service ball teams of the American military, however, the upcoming season was rich with possibility, stocked as they were with former professional players. With the vast presence of the Army Air Force in New Mexico and its preponderance of fields and bases, baseball seemed to be on a solid footing there. In April 1943, it was announced that Ted Shipkey would pilot a new southwestern air base league, formed of Army Air Force teams from Kirtland, Camp Luna at Las Vegas, Hobbs, Carlsbad, Alamogordo, Clovis, Fort Sumner, Roswell and Deming.[28]

Uncle Sam had substantially aided the efforts of Kirtland Air Force Base by stationing a few more nimble players there. Added to the roster of returning stars (Cowboy Thornton, John Melago, Danny Matthews and Lem Hale and Troy Gann) would be pitcher Clarence Beers, an Albuquerque native, who had assisted the Sacramento Solons to the Pacific Coast League pennant in 1942. Another addition was Hank Weaver who had pitched with Anniston, Alabama, in the Southeastern League the year before and a man with baseball in his genes. He was the nephew (and "spittin' image"[29]) of "the Arkansas Hummingbird," Lonnie Warneke, right-handed Cub, who in 1932 led the National League with 22 wins and an ERA of 2.37, in addition to helping his team to the pennant. At shortstop they had Bill Haddican who came from Denver of the Western League and John Bottarini "catcher and understudy to Gabby Hartnet in 1937–38 with the Chicago Cubs."[30]

The Flying Kellys began their season with an outside-the-league bang, playing host to the nine from the Santa Ana, California, Air Base and their illustrious outfielder Joe DiMaggio. Two games were scheduled and the New Mexico boys won the first.

> The game, ending 3 to 2 in favor of the Flying Kellys, drew a crowd of 7,000 fans and those who came to see the great "DiMag" perform were not disappointed. Joe, who used to smash that apple for the Yankees, collected two doubles and a single, batting in one run and scoring the other Santa Ana tally.[31]

The Kellys sent the California air men home with a second loss after an 11-inning, 14–13 tangle in which Joltin' Joe managed only two singles.[32] Within a few weeks, however, they suffered their first defeat of the season at the hands of the Mustangs of Davis-Monthan Air Force Base in Arizona. Striking out 15 Kellys in 10 innings was Bill Clemenson, former Pirate hurler.[33] Lt. Ted Wright said of the loss, "Unquestionably the Mustangs were the hottest baseball team we've run into—and I'm not making any exception of Joe DiMaggio and his Santa Ana gang."[34] The Kellys redeemed themselves in another week, taking both games of a doubleheader against those same Mustangs.[35]

The official opening of the Southwestern Air Forces Baseball League was slated for mid–May and by that time, their performance against Santa Ana had impressed observers enough to pick the Flying Kellys as the logical candidates for the pennant.[36] They cemented their status by winning the opener against Carlsbad Air Base, 19–4, with Beers hurling, allowing only four hits through the seventh inning.[37] In addition to Beers' performance, every Kelly got a hit and all but one had an RBI in that game.[38] By the end of the month, they'd won nine of their first ten games, with Beers victorious in four and Weaver taking three.[39] Ted Wright, never reluctant to brag a little, told reporters, "We don't have the pitching staff in size that a professional team has, but we have the quality, I believe."[40]

In a June doubleheader, they met California's Long Beach Ferry Command, led by future Hall of Famer Red Ruffing. "Worried because they had been too good for nearly all the opposition available, the Flying Kellys of Kirtland Field rekindled their high spirits."[41] On game day, Ruffing took the mound in, rather remarkably, his old Yankees uniform, as the team's uniforms had been "lost in a flood"[42] (there was no mention of what the other players wore). The old uniform didn't offer Ruffing any protection against the heat nor the blizzard of cottonwood fluff that blew across the field. To his credit, Ruffing pitched his innings under stifling conditions and with a bit of the white stuff in his eye. Regardless of the difficulties, the *Albuquerque Journal* reported that he looked as though "he were not extending himself at all in limiting Skipper Ted Wright's boys to exactly one hit an inning except the fifth chapter." [43] It was a 7–2 defeat for the Kellys but they were up against a stellar lineup of competitors. Ruffing had brought along versatile Boston Brave Nanny Fernandez, New York Giants catcher Harry "The Horse" Danning and Chuck Stevens, one of the very few major leaguers produced by the state of New Mexico. (Born in the coal camp of Van Houton, Stevens would play first base for the St. Louis Browns in 1941, 1946 and 1948.[44]) The second game was a tense one, the score tied in the tenth, when Ruffing (who had played right field in that one) doubled, inspiring a "seven-run outburst that won the game 18–11."[45]

Those losses to Long Beach gave the Kellys what one sportswriter referred to as "the jitters,"[46] and although they swept a series with the Las Vegas, Nevada, Gunnery School,[47] their infield fell apart against the Winged Commandos of Lubbock. It was Hank Weaver's first loss of the season.[48] But they regrouped and recovered and flew down to El Paso to win the Texas–New Mexico Semipro Tournament, hence a berth in the National Semipro Tournament in Wichita, Kansas. The Kellys also won themselves a nickname—the Crying Kellys—and a few enemies when they protested an El Paso pitcher's windup, calling it a balk. This tickled Ted Wright who said, "They didn't like us; there wasn't a man in the stands pulling for us, but we sure drew the crowds in. Among other names they called us was 'big leaguers.'"[49]

Wright wasn't joking when he said that his pitching staff was one of professional quality. Going into July, Cowboy Thornton sat at 5–1, Danny Matthews 4–1, Hank Weaver 6–2, and Clarence Beers 5–2.[50] With this rotation, the Kellys boarded their chariot and headed for California to once again tangle with Santa Ana Air Base and the Long Beach Ferry Command. While Hank Weaver was able to hold DiMaggio to two singles, the Kellys fell to Santa Ana 9–8 in eleven innings.[51] And Long Beach handed them an 11–4 loss.[52] To make matters worse, stopping in Arizona on the return flight, they were manhandled by the Williams Field Flyers, another team from the Southwest that would be playing at the tournament in Wichita.[53]

Back at Kirtland, the Kellys prepared for a return engagement by Santa Ana. This series was a decided improvement over what they'd been playing lately. Clarence Beers held Santa Ana's star slugger hitless in a 7–6 win for the New Mexicans and was proclaimed "the only pitcher ever bold enough to say he'd make a 'batting practice hitter' out of Joe DiMaggio."[54] As a sort of consolation prize, Albuquerque City Commissioner Clyde Tingley presented DiMaggio with a six-week-old burro, which was promptly named the new Santa Ana mascot. In front of five thousand fans for the second game, DiMaggio went 2 for 4 but the Kellys won 6–5, with Danny Pavlovic blasting a 425-foot home run in the eighth.[55]

As the regular season wore down, the Flying Kellys headed for Wichita where, after winning the opener, they lost to the Enidair Army Flying School and then were eliminated by the Beech Flyers of Wichita.[56] When they returned to New Mexico, they finished their season against Camp Luna, a game in which Ted Wright managed two homers in one inning. Their record for 1943 was 30–15, a far cry from the 26–4 of 1942.

That fall, a travel restriction was announced by the Army Air Forces Training Command that would affect all athletics on the bases. All sporting teams were henceforth limited to a maximum 25-mile travel distance for events. This effectively grounded the Flying Kellys, who looked to the 1944 season with limited ambitions. Even when the ban was lifted in April, the Kellys would still be required to seek permission from the Western Flying Training Command to travel.[57] They decided to make the best of being grounded. Kirtland was divided into several teams (with big league names like the Cardinals, the Yankees, the Pirates, etc) for intramural competition and every one entered into an "all–G.I." league with a Navy team from the University of New Mexico. At the same time, officials of the regional air bases went ahead with plans for a league but with far fewer tilts (this was probably due in part to an announcement of the ratcheting up of training at Kirtland which would limit the number of appearances by the Kellys during the season).[58] The team would never again enjoy the same freedom of the skies that it had just a year before.

It is a cheerless image, this once mighty team — with all of the same famous names— reduced to mostly intramural play. Then, in late May, Danny Pavlovic, one of the original Kellys— was transferred.[59] So it must have been a morale booster for everyone involved when a game was scheduled with the Camp Luna team of Las Vegas, New Mexico, and their very famous second baseman, future Hall of Famer Joe "Flash" Gordon, who had been drafted just a month before.[60] Two years earlier, as a Yankee, Gordon had been named American League MVP and by that point had played in five of his eventual nine All-Star Games. Past and present Kirtland stars competed for the chance to play against the Camp Luna team and the eagerly awaited tilt rewarded both the Kellys and Albuquerque at large.

> Pvt. Joe Gordon, the "flash" of Yankee Stadium, for many seasons, fielded 11 chances perfectly and poled out one of his famous home runs for 4000 delighted customers at Tingley Park here Wednesday night, but his Camp Luna team from Las Vegas went down 13–5 before the Flying Kellys of Kirtland Field.[61]

After that triumph, it was back to the G. I. League where the Yanks won the first half of the season, partially due to the fact that the many of the Navy players of the University team were granted leaves at that time. The second half of the season saw the Kellys taking to the air more often as they engaged bases all the way from Amarillo to their old enemies at Williams Field in Arizona. And they seem to have regained some of their former invincibility because by the end of August, they had a 12–1 record for the air base league, their one defeat courtesy of Deming and Warren "Pop" Bridgens, a former Southern Association pitcher.[62] For the Kellys, accustomed as they were to darting around the Southwest to tilt with major league names, it must have been a disappointing year for baseball. And it ended in a particularly picayune manner: the Kirtland Pirates defeated the Kirtland Yankees for the Kirtland Army Air Field championship.

In April 1945, everything about the Flying Kellys was different, starting with the name. They were now the 29ers (or the Twenty-Niners), "after the airships that occupy the players' serious moments."[63] They were also a completely different team, all the originals transferred or finally off on their daring missions overseas. There was one element of the 29ers that boded very well for Kirtland and that was the new pilot, former Chicago White Sox pitcher Jess Dobernic.[64] And, they were now in the Southern Division of the Second Air Force League, with teams spread out across the West. Although they lost the opener to Clovis,[65] by the beginning of June they were second in their division behind El Paso's Biggs Field[66] and leading with a 9–1 record by the end of the month.[67]

With the war in Europe ended, bases were losing men. Yet, despite the loss of solid batters,[68] the 29ers maintained the league lead throughout the rest of the season. In late August, they won the division championship against Peterson Field of Colorado Springs and turned their attention to the Sioux Falls Maurauders, the winners of the Northern Division. In a three-game series, the 29ers won two to become champions of the Second Air Force. It was understood that their pilot was the inspiration for the rest of the team. "The team boasts a star in Jess Dobernic, the property of the Chicago White Sox. He virtually pitched the 29ers to the 2nd Air Force title single handed."[69] When the 29ers defeated the Camp Pinedale Interceptors of California, champions of the Fourth Air Force,[70] they donned the crown of all the Army Air Force teams west of the Mississippi River.

But it was 1945. The boys were straggling home, Rosies around the country were laying down their rivet guns, and an odiferous billy goat in the stands at Wrigley Field was about to become the focus of a curse that apparently still holds. As a war-weary country mourned its dead, it also engaged in a wild celebration of the living and the post-war present. All hopes were turned to the delicious promise of spring training 1946. There was little attention left for the nine of Kirtland Army Air Field, one of the finest service ball teams of the long war.

7

Soldiers, Cowboys and Baseball Players: African Americans in New Mexico

In 1536, four bedraggled men lurched into a Spanish settlement in northern Mexico. Three of them were Spanish, including the leader Cabeza de Vaca, and one man was of African descent. His name was Estevanico and he was the slave of one of the others. The people who crowded around the wanderers were enthralled when the men identified themselves as the only survivors of a 1528 expedition to colonize Florida. For eight grueling years they had wandered westward. "It was a harrowing odyssey that carried them — the first Europeans — through the interior wilds of the North American continent."[1] It was the tales of this journey, particularly the descriptions of Pueblo cities to the north, which excited the imagination of the Viceroy of New Spain. The next year, Estevanico found himself again traveling across Arizona and into New Mexico, this time as a scout and interpreter for the party of Fray Marcos de Niza. When the Zuni Pueblo was spotted, Estevanico was sent ahead to investigate, at which point, for reasons unknown, he was killed by the inhabitants. Had he survived and de Niza's party been welcomed, the entire history of the American Southwest might have turned out differently. But, as it stood, when he heard of the slave's murder, Fray de Niza hightailed it back to Mexico without getting a closer look at the Zuni village. Had he done so, he would have discovered that what appeared to be a city made of gold was in fact one built of mud and stone and timber, awash in the bewitching illumination of a New Mexico sunset. His tales of Cíbola turned the tide of Spanish exploration in northern New Spain.

As brutally as Estevanico's New Mexican odyssey ended, he is still considered one of the first and most important explorers of the American West. He would be the first but not the last person whose veins ran with the blood of Africa to seek opportunity in New Mexico. While the numbers of African Americans in the state have historically been small and remain so (the 2007 percentage was less than three percent of the total population), the role that they have played in the state has been a dramatic one.

Certainly one of the most recognizable instances of an important black

7. Soldiers, Cowboys and Baseball Players

Buffalo Soldiers of Troop L, Ninth Cavalry, at Fort Wingate, New Mexico, ready to do battle on the baseball diamond in 1899. Instrumental in the taming of the West, these men were also well known for their skills on the diamond (Palace of the Governors Photo Archives [NMHM/DCA], negative number 098374).

presence in the territory was that of the famous Buffalo Soldiers. In 1866, legislation was passed in Washington creating six African American regiments in the United States Army. Two, the 9th and the 10th, were cavalry and four were infantry, those later merging into two units, the 24th and 25th. One explanation for the nickname given these troops is that it came from the Cheyenne, who were duly impressed by the soldiers' bravery. Another is that the Native Americans were fascinated by the soldiers' hair, the thickness and curl they thought comparable to that of buffalo. The task of the soldiers was a thankless one, as they set about trying to settle the Wild West for people who naturally considered them second-class citizens. They protected civilians against outlaws, assisted in the capture of Geronimo and Victorio (author William Katz sympathetically points out that the African American soldiers were tools used to enforce the government will on Native Americans, the original casualties of racism[2]), and fought off the incursions of Pancho Villa. Buffalo Soldier units were in Cuba with Teddy Roosevelt and fought in both world wars.

Throughout their long and impressive history, the Buffalo Soldiers shouldered a massive military burden (and with fewer resources than most white soldiers), while under the withering gaze of the very people they were sent to protect, and they managed it with stubborn grace. In 1879, a Las Cruces newspaper that had fallen victim to scathing—and utterly erroneous—reports of black soldiers' behavior in a particular battle, summed up local desire for the

9th to be replaced by white troops. "Disbanded, they might contribute to the nation's wealth as pickers of cotton and hoers of corn, or to its amusement as a traveling minstrel troupe. As soldiers on the western frontier, they are worse than useless—they are a fraud and a nuisance."[3] A week later, when it was reported just how valiantly the 9th had acted in said battle, the same newspaper, in a jolly elbow-in-the-ribs sort of delivery, admitted its error and trusted that all its slander would be forgiven.[4] For the white officers who served with the Buffalo Soldiers, the reality was always far different from the chatter that emanated from the mouths of those who never saw the men in action. Captain William Thornton Parker, who'd served at Fort Cummings, New Mexico, with the 125th infantry (an established regiment since 1865), dedicated a book about his adventures to the black soldiers he served with, "whose faithful and gallant service ... won the respect of their Indian foes and the admiration of their friend, the author."[5]

It was not just soldiers who represented African Americans in the territory of New Mexico. The decades following the Civil War saw a massive migration westward of former slaves. In the forty years between 1870 and 1910, the black population of New Mexico, along with other mountain states of the West, increased thirteen-fold.[6] Of the opportunities available to intrepid migrants, one called for particular strength and endurance and, for a while at least, paid huge dividends of respect and freedom, heretofore unknown among men accustomed to bondage. The black cowboy was an integral, yet frequently overlooked, character in the American West. The thousands of black cowboys who rode the legendary cattle trails enjoyed an unprecedented amount of camaraderie with their white colleagues on the range. The rough-and-tumble fraternity of hard-living cowpokes suited many of them, at least until towns began to encroach on the range (and brought with them the women that white machismo felt compelled to protect).

There had been a black presence in the New Mexico territory since the 1860s. And, because there were only twenty-one slaves there at the beginning of the Civil War,[7] African Americans as a people were not viewed solely through the lens of slavery as they often were in the East (and almost always were in the South). Thus, their image there was, for the most part, a professional one—that of soldier and cowboy. While they certainly hadn't found a paradise of racial tolerance, they had marshaled at least a begrudging respect from the Anglos, Hispanics and Native Americans who witnessed them at work. Perhaps it was not so irregular, then, that turn-of-the-century Santa Fe and Albuquerque—always the most cosmopolitan of New Mexican towns—would have baseball teams that included black players, even after African Americans had been officially cast out by Organized Baseball. As has been mentioned, Bill Pettus was the hero of the Albuquerque club from 1902 until 1906 and then played for Santa Fe for two years after that. After leaving New Mexico, Pettus took his prodigious talent to the Negro Leagues, where he played for fourteen years.

Playing with many of the top teams, he was always hitting in the heart of the batting order, yet he demonstrated an ability to steal bases when the game situation dictated a need. A versatile player afield, he could play any position, and was a catcher early in his career, but played more at first base as the years passed.[8]

In 1911, Santa Fe, which seemed to be the most broadminded of New Mexico towns, thought nothing of its town team boasting a lineup that was one-third African American.[9] The Anderson brothers, at third base and left field, were just two of three black players that season.

Santa Fe, Albuquerque and the coal camp of Madrid all relied for a few seasons on the pitching of one of New Mexico's most genuinely talented athletes, Bazz Owen Smaulding. From a black pioneer family in the northeastern corner of the state, Smaulding attended Albuquerque High School from 1915 until 1919, where he excelled in numerous sports, setting records and earning fifteen varsity letters.[10] Receiving a college scholarship to the University of Washington in Seattle, he continued to distinguish himself, then signed with the all-black Queen City Stars baseball team of that city in 1923. In 1928 he advanced to the Negro Leagues, where he pitched for the Kansas City Monarchs, Chicago American Giants and the Gilkerson Giants. After leaving the last club, Smaulding stayed in Chicago and, in his own words, "rehabilitated the Palmer House Baseball Club (as secretary and general manager)" until the team dissolved in 1951 when most of its players were drafted.[11] Unlike many cities that have been home to astounding black athletes and forgotten them, Albuquerque fully understood what it had had in its star. When Smaulding died, one local sportswriter referred to him as, "the most durable and remarkable athlete in Albuquerque High School history."[12] *Albuquerque Tribune* sports editor Carlos Salazar went one further, calling him "one of the greatest athletes who ever stepped on an athletic field in New Mexico."[13]

As the century wore on, even in the broadminded City Different of Santa Fe there were fewer references to black players on white teams, although the town team did employ an African American catcher for at least three of the seasons that it was in the Central New Mexico League.[14] Mr. Hamilton, who sometimes covered right field, was a hitter of some power. When league batting numbers were released for the first half of the 1936 season, he was eighth at .378, just three places behind the legendary Pop Stowers who had hit .417.[15]

After that year, mention of integrated teams was virtually nonexistent until 1951 when two clubs in the West Texas–New Mexico League announced that they were seeking promising black players. Lamesa (Texas) Lobos owner Jay Haney rather bravely asserted that, after playing with African Americans in the service, he'd overcome any lingering opposition to the idea. He even went so far as to announce the first "all–Negro tryout camp"[16] because of the volume of inquiries he'd received from black players after he'd agreed to look at "a pair of Cuban Negroes."[17] During the camp, Haney himself would be on the field with the men, as would Reuben Jones, a local favorite[18] and an aging veteran of many Negro Leagues teams, including the Birmingham Black

Barons, Memphis Red Sox and the Chicago American Giants.[19] (Haney said he'd written to Jackie Robinson to ask about prospects but it seemed more likely that he was seeking a very public plug from the legendary Dodger.)

Besides the obvious playing qualities that could make a player invaluable to his team, that of being a "gentlemen" was as high as any on the list. The white players of the West Texas–New Mexico League, as evidenced particularly by Grover Seitz and some of his unmanageable thugs, were allowed to misbehave with abandon. But, as was the case with Jackie Robinson, the aspiring African American players of the league would be held to much higher, much stricter standards of behavior, on and off the field.

The first exclusively African American tryout in Texas yielded shortstop J. W. Wingate, from Beaumont (who'd played professional baseball in Canada[20]), and Connie Heard from Texas City, but they were released almost immediately. As one newspaper put it, "Both displayed qualities of talent and gentlemaness [sic], but were outshone by other members of the club."[21] But just as the 23-year-old Wingate was packing his kit, Haney called him back. He did very well for the first few weeks of the season, particularly in defensive plays. In one game, he was involved in three double plays and managed an unassisted one and showed hitting promise as well. But he soon entered a slump and was released for good after twenty-seven games.[22] Author Bruce Adelson suggests that, while Wingate was undoubtedly a good enough Class C player, manager Haney realized that he would have to have been almost superhuman to be accepted by the West Texas crowds.

> Many believed, and with some justification, that white fans, already discomfited by the prospect of watching blacks and whites playing interracial baseball, would have their angst salved only by the opportunity to watch the best African American athletes available, making the act of purchasing tickets to integrated games easier to swallow.[23]

Although there were doubtless a few contented sighs upon the dismissal of the state's first black player, one columnist, Collier Parris of the *Abilene Reporter-News*, was disgusted.

> Maybe we're a bit strong for the ex–Lamesa shortstop because he showed great form here in his games against the Blue Sox.... Lamesa fans, being sturdy, southern hometowners to whom Negroes mean cotton pickers, shine boys and car-washers, never did give Wingate a chance. Even refused to attend the home games because of his presence in the lineup.... In other towns in the league, Wingate was accepted as another ball player. He happened to shine like a comet in the Abilene park.[24]

Over in New Mexico, Albuquerque Dukes owner Cy Fausett had been the other West Texas–New Mexico owner to run the integration banner up the flag pole. But he didn't sign Albuquerque's first black player until June 1952 when he acquired first baseman Herbert Simpson from Spokane of the Western International League (Simpson's thirty-year career had included seasons with the Homestead Grays and Chicago American Giants). Unlike the fanfare accompanying J. W. Wingate, the announcement of Simpson's signing was kept very low key. His entrance on the playing field was anything but. "Simpson made a single in his first appearance against Borger, June 20, and blasted seven hits in 15 trips to spark the seventh-place Dukes to threes straight wins,"[25] and hit .383 for the season.[26] His spectacular first efforts were the kind that might have saved J. W. Wingate a year before. It certainly set the stage for further progress: the Dukes signed a second African American in July, Joe Wiley, a former top hitter with the Birmingham Black Barons.[27] A year later, the West Texas–New Mexico circuit boasted sixteen African American players.[28] But the lesson of J. W. Wingate, that one had to be quieter and play better than anyone else, was not lost on that first generation of black players in Organized Baseball. In early 1953, Roy Lozan, a Dukes right fielder, kept a seriously sore arm a secret throughout spring training, only informing the manager of it when he was informed of his imminent release due to a poor performance. He was promptly reinstated.[29]

From the turn of the century until 1952, a few African American baseball players in New Mexico had managed to successfully step over the color line to play on white teams. But most sandlot and semipro players joined all-black teams. A 1922 announcement of the formation of the Albuquerque Monarchs shows that they were already organizing, the obvious inference being that even truly talented players were not finding adequate opportunities on white teams. In those early years, one advantage for black clubs like the Monarchs was the availability of men who had a lot of baseball experience under their belts. "It is likely that Neal and Boggs will be the battery, the former being a southpaw from the 24th infantry."[30] Yes, like their white counterparts at forts across the territory and state, the cavalry and infantry units of the Buffalo Soldiers played a good bit of baseball in their well-earned off hours. Obviously, some of those men had settled in New Mexico and were putting their diamond experience to good use.

As white leagues formed, African American ones did as well, their member clubs often adopting the names of the white teams of the same cities, only with the word "black" inserted. A virtual shadow league of the West Texas–New Mexico League played, with teams like the Lubbock Black Hubbers, the Lamesa Black Lobos and the Clovis Black Pioneers. As with towns across the country, the black and white teams of one town rarely played each other except in exhibition, but frequently used the same diamonds. One of these teams — and a long-lived one — was the Tigers, from the eastern New Mexico town of Hobbs.

Situated within a few miles of the Texas border, in the southwestern section of the Llano Estacado, Hobbs is a young town, certainly by New Mexico standards. Established in 1907 by pioneers, it remained a sleepy, virtually empty backwater until 1928 when oil was discovered there. During World War II, Hobbs was just one of a number of southeastern New Mexico towns, including Roswell, Alamogordo and Clovis, to have air fields built just outside them.

In 1942, a field in Hobbs was built for the Air Force Pilot Training Program. Between oil and war, it was a boom time for the town and that part of the state. Among the people arriving in search of new lives were African Americans, escaping the dreadful realities of the Jim Crow South. Indeed, New Mexico as a whole saw its African American population double during the Depression, from a 1930 total of 1,768 adults to 3,156 in 1940.[31] Their migration into the southeastern region means that today, in a state with a black population of less than three percent, some of the cities that hosted the air force—like Clovis, Alamogordo and Hobbs—boast larger percentages.

"A lot of people came from different places—Oklahoma, Louisiana, Arkansas, south Texas," says Zeak Williams, Jr., a lifelong resident of Hobbs. "A lot of them migrated here because there *were* jobs in Hobbs. Most of them were working on farms and heard things were booming around here. Someone would come here and they'd call a relative. They'd pack up whatever they had and come on." Williams is the beneficiary of his family's migration, which began in Louisiana, landed them for several years of sharecropping in the Texas Panhandle town of Quitaque (pronounced kwitta kway), and ultimately in Hobbs. Williams, when asked how this journey began, says, "Well, my great-grandfather was run out of Louisiana and went to Texas. He had nine children. My grandfather left Quitaque and went to Hobbs to work at the airbase. They told him to load everybody up, there was plenty of jobs over here, so he got a Model A Ford and they came over to Hobbs to go to work."

Baseball was a generational pastime for the Williams family, going back to the days when Zeak's grandfather, John Henry, Jr., played for a sharecropping team in Louisiana and, once in Texas, he taught his son Zeak (born in 1921) how to handle a ball. "My grandfather was a pitcher and he taught my daddy," Zeak Jr. says. "When my father was twelve years old he was playing on a baseball team. He started pitching with the men when he was twelve. *At twelve.* And sometimes he'd pitch doubleheaders. He just threw his arm away by the time he got to 21 or 22. But that's what them old folks used to talk about. When we were little, playing baseball, they used to tell us about how good he was." This young right-hander was poised enough that he could attract the attention of at least one barnstorming team, one that might have been the St. Louis Stars. "My daddy, at eighteen, one of the St. Louis teams wanted him to come tryout. My grandfather wouldn't let him go. He thought he'd get up there and get lost." But there was an even more practical element to the decision for Zeak Sr. not to go, as his son explains. "You gotta understand sharecropping. Everybody had to work. He had to do his share. You see, my father and his brother and my granddaddy would pick a thousand pounds of cotton a day. You had to pick a certain amount before you could get to your own crop. That's just what they had to do to make a living."

New Mexico, with the beginning of the boom years, offered opportunities not found before, one of which was the chance to leave sharecropping behind and settle in a place where workers were needed. "In the late '30s," Zeak explains, "the oilfields was just getting started and there wasn't a whole lot to do in this part of the country other than farm. But when World War II started, they built the airbase. New Mexico is sparsely populated, especially in this part. So if you could get to New Mexico, you could get a job. Wherever they were, whether they were black or white, they'd tell you the same story: they came here to get a job. In New Mexico, you could come and get started and do whatever you wanted to do. They didn't care about the color of your skin as long as you were a hard worker." And in addition to work, what the Williams family found in Hobbs was a proud and growing African American neighborhood which was, as Zeak describes it, "a city within a city." "Well, it was segregated but we had a cleaners, two plumbers, two electricians, three homebuilders, four grocery stores. You really didn't go any farther than the neighborhood because you really didn't have any need to."

As with African American teams countrywide, Zeak's Quitaque team had been forced to roam far and wide to find quality competitors, sometimes driving as far as Arkansas. So this baseball-loving family was delighted to arrive in Hobbs to find, not only an African American team already in existence, but playing in a loosely organized league that, although crossing into west Texas, still had much smaller borders than what they had been accustomed to in Texas. Zeak isn't certain when the Hobbs Tigers first came into being but when he knew the team, it was made up of oilfield workers, airbase workers, all men who, like Zeak Sr. had come from the East and South in search of opportunity.

One of the driving forces behind the team was an African American orchestra leader by the name of Sunshine Butler. Butler and his Rays of Rhythm were well-known throughout the region, not only because of a half-hour radio show that was broadcast out of Big Spring, Texas, but also because of the Sunshine Club, located in the black neighborhood of Hobbs. No humble hole-in-the-wall, it attracted some of the biggest acts in post-war African American music. "When I was little, B. B. King, Fats Domino, Little Richard and Ray Charles would come through here and play in the club," explains Zeak Williams. "They'd make a tour — go through Houston, Dallas, Lubbock, Hobbs, Clovis, Albuquerque, Phoenix and on to California. I can remember Fats Domino's long bus — a lot of dominoes on the side. Mama would always take us and let us see." He chuckles as his memories return to him. "I remember Ray Charles in a brown suit, someone leading him around. I wasn't but about five or six." The Sunshine Butlers of the world were often a critical part of African American community baseball. As a local figure of prominence, his patronage of a team could yield substantial benefits, not the least of which was the publicity he could generate through his business, an essential as newspapers in that era gave limited coverage to their games.

His pitching arm used up in his youth, the majority of Zeak Sr.'s career as a Tiger was spent at first base and in right field. When asked about his father's physical stature, his son says, "He was probably about 5' 6" or 5' 7" but he was pretty quick." He could still, on occasion, be called in to start or close

The Hobbs Tigers around 1950. Mostly oil workers who'd migrated from the East, the Hobbs Tigers were part of an African American league that shadowed the West Texas–New Mexico League. Rear, left to right, name unknown, Joe Lester, Chester Smith, Robert Whitmore, Willie Norris, Calvin Harris, Odel Crow, James Laster. Front: Oscar Butler, Zeak Williams, Sr., Allen Smith, Frank Spencer, Charles Mitchell, Bill Richardson, S. J. Jackson (courtesy Zeak Williams, Jr.).

an especially important game and had the unflappable calm needed for the task.

The hardworking men of the Hobbs Tigers played on the weekends, mostly Sundays, rarely able to fit in an evening's practice because of their lengthy work days. The seasons were unscheduled but games could be arranged a few days in advance. Even with limited practice, it appears that the Tigers could be a force as evidenced by the fact that in 1952, they were the team that added the only loss to the Big Spring Black Giants 19-win season.[32] The whole team was highly competitive and brooked no silliness from the next generation of youthful baseball players coming up in Hobbs. Zeak laughs and says, "We played against them when I got a little older and they didn't give us any slack. *Oh no.* You got in a man's place, you had to play like a man — that's what they told us. You want to play against us, you have to take what we dish out." Did the young players ever win against the Hobbs Tigers? "Nah." But by the time those boys had grown to adulthood, their fathers, the Hobbs Tigers, had stopped playing. "They just got old," says Zeak.

Asked if, as a child, Zeak Jr. had idolized his father, the baseball player, he says fondly, "He was just my daddy." And a very good one, too, apparently. "It was hard work to make my daddy mad. I never saw my father angry in my whole life. He was just an even-tempered person. He was a hard-working person, an honest person. When he told you something, he meant it — there wasn't no going back on it. You could count on that." At the end of the conversation, Zeak suddenly interjects, "I want to tell you one last thing about my daddy. When I was in high school, I was the third fastest man in the Southwest and my daddy could still outrun me. That's the kind of athlete he was. He was in his early 50s and he was still that good." (No mean feat, as Zeak Williams, Jr., was a New Mexico track star in the early '60s and is still referred to as "the Streak" by sportswriters who remember his prodigious talent. His record of 9.5 seconds in the 100-yard dash still holds.)

For the nineteenth and twentieth century transplant to New Mexico, the untamed attitudes of the place could mean that everyone started out on an almost equal footing. For the African American, this must have been a tantalizing lure. Buffalo Soldiers, black cowboys, men of color on early baseball teams, and the Hobbs Tigers—they'd all come from unjust elsewheres to the vast and unforgiving landscape of the desert Southwest, where proving oneself could be its own reward.

8

The King (No Asterisk)

It was Sunday of the long Labor Day weekend of 1954 and around the state, New Mexicans were idling away the final bittersweet days of summer vacation. Scattered clouds throughout most of the state gave relief from the intense September sun, making it a perfect day for picnicking, swimming and leisurely hikes. It was a day of rest and relaxation for everyone in the state — except for one town's baseball fans and several frantic newspapermen. In Artesia, at the local baseball diamond, flashbulbs popped and palms sweated. Behind the chicken-wire backstop of NuMexer Park, amidst the other 2,600 fans, stood a phalanx of journalists and photographers, from publications as mighty as *Life* and *Sports Illustrated*. All were waiting for history to be made. After having tied the record, two days earlier, for the most home runs hit in one season in Organized Baseball, Joe Bauman of the Roswell Rockets was now intent on setting a new one.

It had taken years of hard slog to reach this point. Born in Oklahoma, the 32-year-old, 6 foot 5 inch, left-handed first baseman had begun his professional baseball career in Little Rock (Southern Association) in 1941, only to have it interrupted by World War II. After three years of playing in the Navy, he returned home to be farmed out by Little Rock to Amarillo of the West Texas–New Mexico League, where he led the league in homers with 48 in 1946 and had 38 the next season. Sold to the Boston Braves, that club sent Bauman to Milwaukee, then Hartford, at which point he began to chafe under the penurious salary he was receiving. He and his wife Dorothy returned to Oklahoma, where he ran a gas station and played for a semipro team in Elk City, his home town. He stayed there even when Boston offered him a position with Atlanta. It was while playing for Elk City that Joe was invited to move to Artesia, New Mexico, to play with the Class C Longhorn League (Artesia NuMexers, Carlsbad Potashers, Roswell Rockets, San Angelo Colts, Odessa Oilers, Midland Indians, Sweetwater Spudders, and Big Spring Broncs). In 1952, Bauman's first season with Artesia, he led the league with 50 home runs and followed the next year with 53. But Joe, always practical in matters of making a living, wanted more financial security than was offered in the minor leagues and he certainly knew the service station business. Forty miles north of Artesia was Roswell, a town he'd always liked. Moving there would afford him the opportunity to buy a service station and play baseball with the Rockets of the same league. He bought his release from Artesia for $250 and he and Dorothy headed north where he donned a Rockets uniform. "Although Joe was a self-professed slow starter, the home runs were soon pouring in 1954. And he wasn't simply hitting baseballs. He was punishing them. No one ever measured the distance, but folklore soon began describing 500-foot arcs."[1]

Three people who watched Joe's ascending star in 1954 are still around to talk about it. Supporting him from the sidelines throughout his entire baseball career was Dorothy, his wife of sixty-two years. Now his widow, she still lives in the modest house he bought for them in Roswell. Several blocks off the city's main drag, the neighborhood might be a quiet one except for the din created by the great-tailed grackles that fill the surrounding trees, making it sound like a rainforest. Dorothy shares her house with a couple of wantonly affectionate cats and the memories of the man she was married to for sixty-two years. "A fine man," she says softly, as she seats herself on the edge of Joe's big chair in her living room. Married in 1942, theirs was a real love story, one that began in high school and lasts to this day. Far from begrudging her talented husband his lengthy career in the bush leagues, Dorothy seems to have been well-suited to the semi-itinerant lifestyle of a minor-leaguer's wife. With an uncle who pitched in exhibition games against the likes of Ruth and Gehrig, she was born a fan. "I just loved the game. I went to every home game and I'd listen to most of the games away from home on the radio because Amarillo broadcast them." When she talks about Joe thumbing his nose at the Boston Braves, there is real pride in her voice. "In those days players were treated like cattle. Joe said he could make more money selling shoestrings on the street. And he was right." When asked if she was as swept away as everyone else back in 1954, she shrugs saying, "As his wife, I knew he had the talent."

In his capacity as sports editor of the *Roswell Daily Record* that year, Buck Lanier was overworked and understaffed in 1954 and Bauman's legendary season almost took him by surprise. "I was too busy. I had professional baseball to cover, I had the high school, New Mexico Military Institute which also had a high school section.... I wrote the column 'Riding Herd on Sports.' I had to do it all." But he adds, "We started looking at the numbers and said, 'Joe's hitting a lot of home runs.'" These days, Lanier—who is 85—still leads the kind of hectic, hell-for-leather lifestyle he did in Roswell. He remains an old-style newspaperman at heart, frequently spelling out words in the course of a conversation, just to make certain the listener gets them right. When a colleague dies, Buck refers to him as "having left the newsroom." Although no longer spending feverish days working toward a deadline, he is still the busiest man in Long Beach, California, having retired from that city's *Press-Telegram* after 31 years. He has covered everything from sports to the Vietnam War, been to Antarctica more than once and believes he holds the world record for number for mule rides down the steep walls of the Grand Canyon (27). Doug Krikorkian, a writer at his former paper, affectionately called him "a Renaissance Man who delved into myriad pursuits, a journalistic critic given to leaving lengthy critiques on the voice mail of local columnists, a character not meek about conveying compelling opinions on any subject."[2]

In 1954, Buck says, it took until the second half of the season to realize where Joe Bauman was headed. After all, almost-atomic blasts across the fence were everyday fare in the High Plains. It was Bob Crues of the 1948 Amarillo Gold Sox, who tied Joe Hauser's 1933 record of 69 homers hit in one season. But when July rolled around, the local sportswriters, including Buck, began to sit up and take notice. Bauman had hit 45 homers in the first 89 games of the season. Furthermore, he was at or near the top of the league in total bases, doubles, runs scored and percentage, and had been since the beginning of the season. While not mentioning his growing home run numbers, one sportswriter suggested that Joe would easily take the crown for RBIs that season. "The Longhorn League record for RBI's is 180, set by Tom Jordan, then of Roswell, in 1950. The latest averages show Bauman with 117, with less than half of the season completed."[3] Several days later, Robert Green of the *Albuquerque Journal* frankly broached the subject of records. "Folks are beginning to wonder if Joe Bauman is going to break the minor league home run record this year. Some say he will. Some say he won't. Asked about it, Bauman said: 'Good God!'" Joe went on to tell Green that he wasn't consciously doing anything differently than he ever had. "I'm not hitting for the fences any more than usual,' the big first sacker said. 'In fact, I'm playing it just about as I usually do. No changes in swing. No changes in stance. Just no change.'"[4]

Joe Bauman is congratulated by his teammates following his record-setting seventy-second home run in 1954, when he played for Roswell, New Mexico, in the Long Horn League (courtesy Dorothy Bauman).

Perhaps not, but opposing managers were desperately pulling in any portsider they could find every time Bauman came to bat, going so far as to draft them from other positions.[5] The streak continued. In the third week of August, he broke his own record of 53 set in 1953 while with Artesia, and on Joe Bauman Night, near the end of the month, he belted number 64.[6] Asked if the Rockets began to draw capacity crowds as Bauman edged closer to the record, Buck says no. "Oh they knew Joe because the year before he had hit the 53 home runs. But it wasn't a surge of everybody in the ballpark talking about the Rockets. It didn't get really interesting until the last two weeks. You've got to remember, all of this happened over a very short period of time — that last week in August up through the time the record was broken." But this didn't mean that Buck wasn't fully aware of the importance of the moment, not only for Joe Bauman but for the town as well. In his September 2 column for the *Daily Record*, the day after

Joe Bauman, surrounded by fans. Bauman still holds the minor league record for number of home runs in a season. Many believe he holds the same record in Organized Baseball at large (courtesy Dorothy Bau-

Joe hit numbers 65, 66, 67 and 68 (and doubled for good measure), Buck wrote, "The eyes of the United States are on Roswell at present. It isn't too often that the activities of a Class C league are pegged on the national Associated Press trunk wires as prime material.... If Joe does break it, pictures of him will be the sports pages of every paper in the U.S...."[7] Yes, the little New Mexico town, up to that point known only for a 1947 close encounter with aliens, was about to go big time.

On September 3, the last home game for the Rockets, in an eighth-inning at-bat against Midland, Texas, with two men on base, Joe sent one over the right-field wall for number 69, an event he compared to getting a piano off his back.[8] Buck Lanier described the event. "When his bat swung on the first pitch to him the stands rose as one to watch the ball sail over the wall. For about five minutes the fans roared their approval as Joe received handclasps and backslaps from his charged up teammates."[9] He went homerless in two games against Big Spring. Then on Sunday, September 5 — the final day of the season — the Rockets headed to Artesia for a doubleheader. Buck Lanier tells about his day at the ball park. "I went over and stood outside near the area around home plate where I could see the pitcher and catcher. Jerry Brown, my man from Carlsbad, was holding an open line on a pay phone about 50 or 60 feet away. He had Robert Green on the line in Albuquerque (where the Associated Press had their headquarters) waiting to get what happened on Joe's first at-bat. As soon as Joe swung his bat that first inning, I said, 'It's gone!'" Buck can't help but chuckle at this point, saying, "Back then, we got a scoop on United Press which wasn't that good in that part of the world. So we got a scoop. The radio station from Artesia did and so did the Roswell station and so did the Albuquerque station as far as I know. How 'bout that?"

Joe Bauman saved his final two home runs for the second game in the doubleheader. His total for 1954 was 72, a record that held until 2001. But it wasn't only his home run record as author Robert Obojski points out.

Bauman's statistics for 1954 are eye-popping:

G	AB	R	H	2B	3B	HR	TB	RBI	Pct.
138	498	188	199	35	3	72	456	224	.400

He walked 150 times and compiled a stratospheric slugging average of .916. Babe Ruth's highest slugging average, compiled in 1920, was only a measly .847.[10]

After his record-setting home run — his fists stuffed with money — Joe Bauman pauses for a congratulatory kiss from wife Dorothy (courtesy Dorothy Bauman).

The following week, the Rockets were eliminated from the playoffs. Asked if Joe was considered a hero around Roswell, Buck says no, but that his filling station was quite busy for a while and that Joe ran an ad in the paper, thanking the locals for their support. "Bauman didn't even get a raise from his $300-per-month salary the next season, his last in pro baseball. He 'slumped' to 46 home runs and 132 RBIs in 1955, then retired."[11] The record-setting slugger and the sportswriter who covered his greatest year became good friends and stayed that way until Joe's death.

Another longtime friend and former teammate of Joe's is Jim Waldrip. "Most of the stories say that a doctor in Artesia was the one that brought him out here. The man who really talked him into coming out here was Earl Perry," he says. Jim is a tall man with piercing blue eyes, a sort of James Whitmore type only better looking. He has come to Dorothy's house, as many still do, out of love and respect for the widow and her late husband. There is also a lot of playfulness in their sixty-year-friendship as well. He calls her "Do-Bau," because that was what his daughter called her as a child.

Jim and Joe met playing against each other in Oklahoma. Earl Perry's history with Joe went back even further — they'd played with and against each other during the war. "Earl was a heckuva minor league manager and put teams together. Back in those days they had 47 minor leagues and then with TV coming, why, you couldn't draw flies. But Earl Perry put together the Artesia Drillers. He was known for straw hats and Hawaiian shirts. He wasn't the biggest guy but he was a scrapper." And Perry fully knew what kind of force he was getting in Bauman. As he once told journalist Toby Smith, "You can't teach power. You just watch it, amazed, and hope your teeth don't fall out."[12]

Of course, Jim Waldrip had been Bauman's friend from way back in Oklahoma. Jim is a retired science teacher and it shows. Like his friend Buck Lanier's emphasis on correct spelling, Jim will quiz you on facts he thinks everyone ought to know. And one will almost never leave a conversation without having learned something. He still lives in Roswell and has a room devoted to baseball mementos. He's also fond of golf and is justly proud of the fact that, when he was teaching, he put a young Nancy Lopez on his high school boys' golf team.

Jim was a right-handed pitcher who grew up in a tiny Oklahoma town whose high school didn't offer baseball. "In fact, during the war, my brother came back from Guam and took his mustering-out pay and bought us some baseballs and bats. Then he took us to a high school tournament up at Oklahoma University and that's when the OU coach saw me. I ended up at OU and we won the national championship at Omaha in 1951." He sheepishly admits that he still holds the record in Omaha for the most walks in a game. "Yeah, I hate to admit it. I pitched a 2-hitter and walked 15 men but we won 7–1." He signed with the Giants system but ended up in Korea instead. Returning from the war, Jim was encouraged by pals Earl Perry and Joe Bauman to come play baseball in New Mexico.

"Those were pretty good days," says Jim. They were lean years of traveling the Longhorn circuit in battered station wagons and making do with what one had, including baseball's famous sanitary hose. "There was a right fielder that was a tough guy — in Patton's army. You know how socks do—they wear out at the toe. This guy would just cut the end off and fold it over. He kept cutting it off and it got shorter and shorter until the white was down like a foot stocking. But you didn't make much money in those days." And equipment wasn't free, which meant that sometimes Joe Bauman's hitting in a home game could be costly. "We have a rodeo arena outside of the park, now called Joe Bauman Stadium. In those days you had to retrieve the balls—they didn't have unlimited budgets. So sometimes those that Joe hit into the rodeo grounds weren't playable. Especially if it had rained a little bit."

With Joe Bauman as a teammate instead of as a competitor, Jim was able to watch him and could now write the primer on the legendary clouter's style. "Basically what he did, he used a 35-inch Vern Stephens model. In minor league and some pro ball, we'd say he 'cowtailed' it—like getting hold of a cow and just swinging it over the fence. He was a left-handed hitter and rather than have the knob exposed, he held it with the palm of his right hand. That was rather unusual and of course he developed a callous. He kind of used a golf swing. If you were a right-hander and threw anything below his belt, you could kiss it goodbye. In other words, he lofted the ball. I'd call it an 'uppercut' swing. And he could foul off the high pitches and wait until someone made a mistake and got it in his good zone. He could hit with power to all fields. I saw him hit three home runs out here one night—one to left, one to center, and one to right—all out of the park. When his eyes were good, he could see the ball come off the bat. So many people, like in golf, pull their head up and take their eye off the ball. But he had his head down." Sure enough, any photo of Bauman in full swing shows his chin down, his eye following the escaping orb. But his wrists are telling a story as well. Until this moment, Jim has been speaking as a baseball player. Now the golf-playing science teacher emerges. "You know what pronation and supination is? Or did you take biology? Do you play golf? If you hold your hand out palm up, it's supination. If it's rolled over it's pronation. If you watch a golfer, say a left-handed golfer, when they finish their swing, if they don't roll that wrist over, they leave the club face open. Joe's left hand was coming over the top. There's similarities between a golf swing and a baseball swing."

Jim recalls that, as the season progressed and Joe was headed toward the record books, Roswell was inextricably drawn into the excitement. "We had a local packing plant and for every home run he'd hit at home, they'd give him a ham. He kept a lot of us other players in food." As for the fans, they too supplemented Bauman's income and often rather handsomely. A 1954 photo in *Life*

Jim Waldrip, a teammate of Joe Bauman in 1954 (Belinda Winn).

Magazine shows Joe at the backstop, looking abashed but happy, awkwardly trying to fit bills into a fist already stuffed with them as fans cram more through the wire fence.[13] Jim Waldrip remembers those instances well. "I helped collect money for Joe one night. Sometimes he'd hit his home run with two outs and they'd try to stall the next guy coming up. They'd say, 'Get some dirt in your hands and slow the pitcher down so Joe can collect his money.' But then, if this guy made an out, Joe had to go out to first base. When I went back out [of the dugout], it would look like lettuce sticking in the screen wire. We'd take a ball cap and go around. Oftentimes he'd make maybe $200 hitting a home run, which was more than a guy made all month."

For all of the angst of the race to the record, Joe Bauman, Jim Waldrip and the players in the Longhorn League could still have a good time. Jim still has a ball, autographed by a barnstorming team they played, made up of the likes of Jim Bunning, Tom Brewer, Gus Triandos, Bill Tuttle, Milt and Frank Bolling, Jim Lemon and Roy Sievers. "Back then," he recalls, "the minimum salary for major leaguers for a year was $4,000. These guys, in order to make extra money, would get a team up and they'd contact towns that had little minor league fields. They'd say, 'We'll come in and take 50% of the gate or a $500 guarantee' (I'm just making up numbers) and we'd get some of the locals — the wannabes or the has-beens — and play a nine-inning game. The lights were bad and there were gopher holes in the outfield. Those guys were taking a real chance of ruining their careers but they wanted to make a buck. But pros don't like to get beat. We stuck with them for a while and they didn't lay down on us. But we had a pretty good little game and afterward we had a few sarsaparillas with them. You know what sarsaparillas are, don't you?"

Jim can also add to Joe Bauman's mythical status by telling a story about Jackie Price, one of the three Clown Princes of Baseball. "He had some sort of bazooka or compressed air cylinder and he'd put balls down it. Price would rev this thing up and shoot it straight up in the air. You'd be out there in the infield or the outfield and see that thing come down and it just seemed to explode on you. A lot of people don't realize that if you shoot a rifle on New Year's Eve, that bullet will come back down with the same velocity as when it went up. Joe was the only one I ever saw catch one of those balls. If he'd missed, it would have broken his wrist."

Jim Waldrip was with Joe Bauman when the record holder decided to retire in 1956. "It was down at Carlsbad and there was a pitcher that'd been sent down from the Texas League which was Triple A. This kid could throw it and he threw three right into Joe's power. Driving back he said, 'Jim, I'm gonna hang 'em up. I just can't see the ball.'" For a slugger who'd once claimed the "the damn ball was big as a cantaloupe," this was a sad turn of events.

For the next 49 years, Joe Bauman lived in comfortable semi-obscurity in Roswell. Buck Lanier says his friend "took part in civic activities, was just a good citizen." Of course, the periodic baseball fan called him on the phone or showed up at his door, but for the most part, Joe's celebrity was limited to the region. Then came 2001 and the floodgates opened. As the day grew closer when it seemed inevitable that his record would be broken, more people wanted to know how he would feel about it. When it finally happened, every one else seemed to take it much harder than Joe did. His response to the Associated Press was textbook Bauman — humble. "I was watching on TV when Barry Bonds hit that last one. It didn't bother me or anything. I just thought, 'There goes my record.'"[14]

Once the fuss had died down, his record again grew dusty. It was New Mexico Governor Bill Richardson, one-time pitcher and lifelong fan, who turned the limelight on him for the last time. In October 2003, when in Roswell on an official visit, the governor proclaimed it Joe Bauman Day. The next year, Fair Park Stadium was renamed to honor the town's biggest hero. Buck Lanier says, "The city of Roswell was twenty years late in doing this for him. That's just my comments. It should have been done sooner." At the ceremony, the 83-year-old Bauman collapsed on the stage, breaking his pelvis. He wouldn't allow himself to be taken immediately to the hospital but stuck it out through the remainder of the event. He died in the hospital a month later.

The people that knew him well still love to tell stories about him. Buck describes him as "very nice" and adds, "You didn't have to worry about any back alley talk with him." Jim says, "Joe was really laid back. Everyone liked him but he didn't promote himself." With a chuckle he adds, "And the strongest thing he ever did was drink Miller High Life." For her part, Dorothy likes what their family doctor said, pointing out that while steroids might have been a factor in breaking the famous record, Joe had used meat and potatoes to set it. "I thought that was cute," she chuckles.

Dorothy Bauman, wife of long-time home run record holder Joe Bauman (Belinda Winn).

Joe Bauman's death left many sad people, from baseball historians to buddies to former teammates. Most of them have done their grieving and recovered, but not his widow. She is loved and respected by both Buck and Jim and the legions of others who knew them when they were Joe and Dorothy. But now she is just Dorothy, a tiny woman who carries on under the interminable weight of her grief. She spends a lot of time on her back porch, listening to the doves that compete softly with the raucous grackles. She says that the doves seem to be saying, "Come back to stay, come back to stay." She laughs as she says this but her eyes are sad. But she's tough, too, and talking to her, one gets the impression that it was she who bore most of the weight of Joe's famous 1954 "piano," that Joe Bauman could never have done what he did without this woman at his side. And she is regarded by Joe's old friends almost like the widowed consort of a beloved king.

These days, Buck Lanier is still the busiest (former) newspaperman in the United States. One is lucky to find him at home. When Buck Lanier visits New Mexico, Dorothy's home is one of his first stops. Jim Waldrip, who lives fairly close by, drops by more frequently; he and Do-Bau share a sense of humor and six decades of memories. Jim still teaches astronomy in Roswell and is happy to impart a few facts about the stars.

Dorothy Bauman carries on with her daily routine, which occasionally includes fielding inquiries about her husband who, for many a fan of baseball, remains the unequivocal owner of one of its biggest records.

9

The Connie Mack World Series

Farmington, New Mexico, is an unassuming little city in the Four Corners region of the United States, the only spot in the country where four states meet in one geometric point. The area is home to some of the most iconic western landscapes to be found. The Navajo reservation, which borders Farmington, spreads westward into Arizona and Utah. To the north are the Ute Mountain Ute and Southern Ute reservations and Mesa Verde. Its Ancestral Puebloan Cliff Palace is so perfectly preserved one almost senses the imminent return of its long departed inhabitants. Straddling the Continental Divide to the east of Farmington is the one-million-acre Jicarilla Apache reservation; it also marks an unofficial divide between the arid desert of the West and the ponderosa pine, high-mountain environs of the southern Rockies. To the south lies the Chaco Culture National Historic Park, with ruins to rival any others, and the eldritch wilderness of the Bisti Badlands.

Situated at the confluence of the Animas, La Plata and San Juan rivers, Farmington was an ideal site for settlement and, indeed, the number of Ancestral Puebloan sites proves that people started taking advantage of the surroundings early on. Later, it became home to the Navajo, Ute and Apache, with a handful of Spanish settlers arriving in the early 1800s. By the late nineteenth century, Anglo settlers had come and recognized its potential for farming, particularly apple orchards. Farmington was incorporated in 1901, and remained a quiet agricultural community, unknown outside the region. It briefly hit the national stage in 1950 when an estimated eighty-five percent of its population watched as "perfect replicas of a dinner table plate," the size of bombers, hovered over the town for twenty minutes before zipping away.[1] But it was discoveries of vast reserves of oil and natural gas that really pricked attention. "These discoveries combined to stimulate serious interest in Four Corners oil and gas exploration among the nation's top petroleum producers—Gulf Oil, Standard Oil of California, Sinclair Oil, Shell, Phillips Petroleum, and Atlantic Richfield."[2] At that point, Farmington entered its boom years, going from a population of a little over thirty-five hundred in 1950 to almost twenty-four thousand a decade later. As the populations of the western states increased, and the wealth of bituminous coal underground became irresistible, a behemoth of a coal-fired power plant was built on the Navajo reservation in nearby Fruitland. When the oil and gas boom ended, Farming-

9. The Connie Mack World Series

ton cleverly reinvented itself as a regional retail hub, a role it serves today. From all the states that constitute the Four Corners, shoppers make the drive to Farmington to spend the day in its malls and restaurants. An orderly community, it prides itself on its climate, unlimited outdoor activities and friendliness.

An unremarkable place at first glance, perhaps, but in a world filled with "baseball crazy" towns, Farmington may just be the unlikely capital. There is no other town of its size that, fueled only by gritty self-confidence and elbow grease, could win for itself not only the most prestigious tournament in amateur baseball, but the organization that sponsors it as well.

Established in 1935, the American Amateur Baseball Congress is the largest amateur baseball organization in the United States and, according to its official handbook, is "the only amateur baseball program that provides progressive and continuous organized competition — sub-teens through adults — at World Series levels." It has seven different age divisions, each named after a superstar of the game, all operating in a system of regions throughout the United States, Canada and Puerto Rico. Teams are joined into leagues, the winners of league play going to state then regional tournaments, culminating in a World Series for each division.

The President Emeritus of the AABC is Joe Cooper, who began as a player in the organization in Kalamazoo after World War II and eventually climbed in the administrative ranks. He served as president for many years and today is still in charge of Michigan and the North Central region. He is also quite active in the RBI program (Reviving Baseball in Inner Cities). In his early years with the Congress, there was only the Stan Musial Division, an unlimited age group. Cooper helped establish the Connie Mack Division of the Congress, for boys eighteen and younger, eventually whittled down to the sixteen to eighteen year range. The first two Connie Mack World Series were held in Missouri in 1959 and 1960. "The Connie Mack World Series was in St. Joseph, Missouri, for two years. It was just not doing the job that we expected or they expected," remembers Cooper. "So there was the common idea that we should move. So we went to Springfield, Illinois, and had fair success there. And Springfield wanted it back." Little did the host city know but, rising in the desert Southwest, was a movement that would come on like a thunderhead, wresting this prized sports/tourism boon out from under the nose of the Illinois capital.

In 1963, Farmington stepped into the amateur baseball spotlight by pulling off a Babe Ruth World Series that was one for the record books. To begin with, the series organizers had pulled in a Who's Who of ageing baseball personalities, including a still-grieving Mrs. Babe Ruth, Lefty Gomez, Vernon Kennedy, Pepper Martin (the "Wild Horse of the Osage"), Paul Dean and Bob Feller (who had pitched in the very first AABC World Series in 1935). As feted as those luminaries were, they didn't receive any better treatment than the visiting teams did. All were greeted with wild enthusiasm when they arrived in Farmington. The team from Frankfurt, Germany, was greeted at the Albuquerque airport by the Greater Albuquerque Chamber of Commerce, the Farmington Evening Lion's Club and the business manager of the Albuquerque Dukes. The boys were then escorted the almost two hundred miles to Farmington by the New Mexico state police.[3] Once there, all of the teams and honored guests were kissed by comely princesses and honored with a parade of seventy-five floats (each team had its own) and an estimated twenty thousand animated spectators lined the route, all with an eye to promoting not only Farmington but San Juan County.[4] A banquet for twelve hundred was held before the opening game and when the official first pitch was thrown, the 1963 Babe Ruth World Series began. When it was over and the dust had settled, the team from Tulsa wasn't the only victor. The games had been attended by over fifty thousand fans and the little oil town of Farmington was ambitiously eyeing a big future in amateur baseball.

The outrageous success of the 1963 Babe Ruth World Series didn't just happen but was the result of the determination of two men in particular; they, along with several others, would be pivotal in Farmington's next big gamble. One of these men was managing editor of the *Farmington Daily Times*, Bern Gantner (former sports editor of the *Clovis News-Journal*). "He has organized, promoted and coaxed the area into action. As general chairman, he has shoe-horned World Series committee meetings in between and around his editorial duties," wrote the *Albuquerque Tribune*.[5] But a larger personality, one of hurricane force, was overseeing one of the most important aspects of the endeavor. J. W. "Doc" Jones (referred to in the same article as a "chunky and cigar chomping baseball enthusiast") was the man who, by hook or by crook, enlisted almost the entire population in creating the best possible venue for Farmington's important debut. "It was El Paso that employed Doc Jones. He was their safety engineer. He was the one who really, really, really pushed hard to get the park built," says Carol May, who is the Assistant Director of Recreation for the City of Farmington Parks, Recreation, and Cultural Affairs Department, and an instrumental figure in the administration of the World Series these days. She explains that El Paso Natural Gas Company, one of the largest employers of the day, had always fielded fine baseball and softball teams. "A lot of oil field workers played on company teams. In fact, some were recruited just because they could play ball and then given a job later," she says. When it came time to build a first-rate baseball field, Doc Jones leaned on whoever he thought could help. "He got local companies to donate materials and the El Paso welders to donate their time." When Doc wasn't sending gas company workers to build the stadium, he was raiding the city jail for free labor.[6] Other companies donated man hours and materials as well, including Justis Supply Company who built the bleachers.

> In fact, sometimes the owners and managers would filch supplies from their own companies to help the project along, some of the people who helped with the effort admit with a wink and a nod. Though much of the pipe was surplus, or

9. The Connie Mack World Series

wire cut or victimized by electrolysis, and therefore destined for the scrap heap anyway, some materials were inventoried for another job on paper but sent directly to Fairgrounds Road.[7]

Perhaps the best way to illustrate how much a labor of love the original Ricketts Park (it was christened such in honor of Orval Ricketts, publisher of the *Farmington Daily News*) was is to consider what it would have cost to build anywhere else, which was estimated at $100,000. Farmington spent less than $3,500 on it.[8] Jones had increased seating to hold five thousand spectators (Danny Carpenter says the figure of 7,000, which was commonly stated at that time, was an exaggeration), and the fact that the park was sold out for every game of that 1963 Babe Ruth World Series had impressed everyone, especially the AABC. In 1964, Farmington reprised its 1963 success and hosted a well-orchestrated Connie Mack Regional Southwest Tournament. With those successes under their belts, the town's boosters set their sights on larger prey.

In November 1964, after two unparalleled successes with the Babe Ruth and Connie Mack Regional tournaments, a coalition of seven local citizens, mostly businessmen and politicians, traveled to Chicago for the annual AABC meeting with the purpose of winning the Connie Mack World Series away from Springfield. "I'll never forget it," laughs Joe Cooper, who was vice-president of the Congress at that time. "It was a team, the original committee was. They had the assets of the Navajo world well-represented (one of their chief officers), they had the mayor, they had a person representing the various civic clubs. They had every influential aspect of their community involved. And they didn't just represent the 'quote' upper classes. They represented everybody." Once there, Joe says, the Farmington delegation lost no time trying to win over the Congress. "The meeting turned into quite a political scene, one group trying to hang on and the other trying to get in. I'd say that political maneuvers were great on the part of both parties. But the Farmington group was so well organized and right away, you could read nothing but dedication. They were very convincing of what they could do, they were very convincing with the dollars that could be generated for the Congress and for Farmington. And they were convinced that Farmington was sort of the hospitality capital of the West."

At that time, each state in the congress had one vote and certainly there were some that voiced serious doubts about the logic of having the World Series in the middle of — what they perceived to be — nowhere. Joe Cooper could understand that. He says that the first time he visited the Four Corners, there were five stops between the Denver airport and Farmington. Carol May can also sympathize. "Still, transportation to Farmington is dicey on a good day. Because our airport is on a mesa, we couldn't land very big jets." But one of the town's delegates, Paul Almquist, had expected qualms. Employed by Frontier Airlines, he put together travel packages, with every detail and every travel misgiving addressed. Still, Joe says, a lot of people remained unconvinced. "It was down to the last minute. The Farmington boys were politicians—I use this word in a very positive manner. It indicated how great they really were, how great their community was and how solid they were." He slyly adds, "And they set their eyes on the one person they knew they could convert and they worked pretty hard on him." It paid off. When the final vote was tallied, Farmington had won the Series—by one vote.

The 1965 Connie Mack World Series in Farmington was an unqualified success. The visiting teams received a slightly smaller, but no less tumultuous, reception than had the Beatles at Shea Stadium a few days before. Future Hall of Fame slugger Ted Williams spoke at the opening ceremonies and conducted clinics for the young players. The host team, the Farmington Hummers, welcomed teams from Long Beach, Nashville, El Paso, Toledo, Chicago, Long Island and Portland. The highlight of the Series occurred when Greg Lebeck of Portland pitched a no-hitter. His team eventually won the championship, the final game drawing six thousand spectators. When it had all ended, in stark contrast to the 10,000 attendees at the last Series held in Springfield, 42,600 fans had turned out to watch the fourteen games in Farmington. Other New Mexico cities marveled at what the isolated Four Corners town had been able to accomplish. At least one, the capital city, was left wondering why it suffered a shortsightedness that the much smaller town lacked. "It's a great credit to the city itself that it visioned [sic] such possibilities from a ball and bat. The economy factor alone is enough. World Series games bring in people from all parts of the country, they spend money and without a doubt it has influenced many to live in New Mexico."[9]

The net profit for the Series was over ten thousand dollars; Springfield's last Series had netted them three hundred.[10] Thus, in that year, the ABCC received a much heftier chunk of money than it had seen from any other Series. The World Series was indeed paying off, for both parties, and Farmington's future as the host city was secured. Joe Cooper explains that, in the split in net profits, the larger share goes to Farmington because they do most of the work. Because of the income generated by the now-lucrative Series, the AABC, after a couple of years, was able to help the teams with transportation costs. Then they assumed the full burden for transportation, leaving Farmington responsible for room and board for the visiting teams. It is in this responsibility that is found the enduring charm of the Farmington Connie Mack World Series.

Back in 1964, one of the foremost organizers in helping to win the Series from Illinois was Danny Carpenter, a local businessman and politician. Upon first meeting, Danny speaks very deliberately but as he warms up, a funny, cantankerous character emerges. A transplant from Colorado, Carpenter had come to northwest New Mexico in 1950. "When I came to Farmington, the town was three thousand. There was one paved street. Being raised in Denver, I thought it was the end of the world," he recalls. But then the oil began to flow, attracting hundreds of transient workers; soon there were ten thousand trailers parked in the city limits. After almost sixty years of living in

9. The Connie Mack World Series

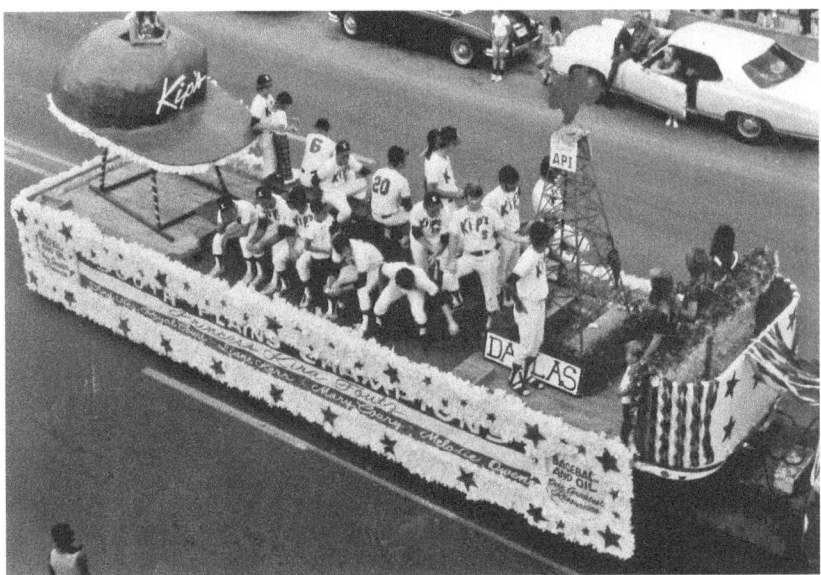

One of the most important elements of the Connie Mack World Series held in Farmington, New Mexico, is the parade, a young player's first taste of the spotlight. Named for a chain of hamburger restaurants, the Kips of Dallas, Texas, enjoy the parade from the vantage point of their float, complete with accompanying princesses. The Kips won the series in 1971 and 1972 (courtesy Farmington Museum, *Farmington Daily Times* Collection).

Farmington, Carpenter is one of the town's most enthusiastic boosters. "It's one of the greatest places to raise a family and I'll tell you why. I don't care what your children want to do, they'll have a program for it." He adds that newcomers to the community seem delighted to get involved themselves with all that Farmington offers their children. In addition, the Four Corners region is enticing. "We have a good climate. Many years ago, when I snow skied, I could go snow skiing one day and play golf the next. You can drive seventy-five miles and see some of the worst desert, then drive another seventy-five and see some of the prettiest scenery." Carpenter twice served as general chairman of the Series, as a regional director for the AABC, and coordinated construction of yet another ball field, Justis Park. It was built in the same fashion as Ricketts Park, with labor contributed by oil field and gas workers and volunteers from the community. Danny laughs, "On Easter Sunday or Father's Day, we invited all the dads to come pick rocks up off the field." He still serves on the advisory committee for the Series, and the games he has missed can be counted on one hand. But his most important contribution to the success of the Connie Mack World Series is undoubtedly the foster parent program. "Without the foster parent program, we wouldn't have the tournament today," he insists and the rest of the world seems to agree.

Even with the Congress helping with transportation costs, many teams were finding the financial strain of attending the Series a daunting one. In 1975, after ten years as host city, Carpenter approached the president of the AABC with the idea of the "host family." He had employed it successfully during the 1963 Babe Ruth World Series and knew that, along with all of its other advantages, it would mean tremendous savings for everyone involved, including the AABC. But it is not simply a matter of room and board. The host families of San Juan County literally adopt the boys for eight days, providing everything that they would have at home, including affection in generous doses. The families feed them, drive them everywhere they need to go, show them around the region and attend every game, creating an immediate fan base for boys who are far away from familiar voices cheering them on from the stands. And the program has recruited countless new baseball fans over the years, as community-minded families, who perhaps had no interest in the sport before, now find themselves attending every game to support their temporary sons. The iron bonds forged between visiting players and their foster families are profound and permanent. Foster families proudly add their boys' Christmas cards and wedding announcements to scrapbooks they have built over the years.

Of the boys who have played at the Series in Farmington, roughly two hundred of them have gone on to the big leagues. Manny Ramirez maintains a relationship with the family that hosted him in 1990. "Those people — quite, quite often — attend a major league baseball game where Manny is playing and have sort of a reunion," says Joe Cooper. And a locally famous 1986 photograph shows a touchingly youthful Ken Griffey, Jr., and his teammate from the Midland Redskins of Cincinnati; they are on a picnic with their foster siblings. Besides four kids obviously having a great time together, the photograph is unique in that, while the players are black, their foster family is white, illustrating one of the best aspects of the Farmington foster parent program: it is completely colorblind. When asked if players are placed according to their race, Danny Carpenter is almost indignant. "No, no. We don't do that. We don't do that at all. There are no color barriers — never have been." What is remarkable is that, since 1975 — a year in which, while Frank Robinson was named the first African American manager in major league baseball, enforced busing caused black students to suffer abuse at the hands of white Bostonians — Farmington has quietly, proudly, and fully integrated for one week every year. And when Farmington isn't doing its part to combat America's fractious race relations, it is forging international bonds, although sometimes in unorthodox ways. One of Danny's three sons, Kirk, served as batboy for the Puerto Rican team during one tournament. The coach, spotting a bat lying on the field, picked it up to throw it toward the dugout. Ricocheting off a fence, it hit Kirk in the mouth, knocking two teeth loose. "His other brothers were a little envious and wanted to do the same thing," Danny laughs, "because Kirk got presents from Puerto Rico for two years." The coach, the

9. The Connie Mack World Series

team and the country continued to demonstrate their remorse to Kirk and to Danny as well. "I used to go to the national meetings. I'll never forget—the year after this happened, I came back to my room and there was a case of rum there. I had a helluva time getting that home."

Of all the Carpenters involved in the Connie Mack World Series—and baseball at large—the quietest and perhaps the most hardworking is Danny's wife Maureen, known as Mo. She has dedicated much of her life to baseball, serving in a variety of capacities. For two years she served as president of the Farmington AABC and of the Umpire's Association and she slogged away for countless seasons as a member of the Homerunners Club, the organization that handles concessions. Asked about her tenure with the AABC, she gives a lively response. "How did I get it? By being plumb stupid and getting into something I shouldn't have." Running the concessions stands gave Mo an intimate look at the inner workings of the league. When she'd happen upon something that irked her, she didn't hesitate to say so aloud. "Finally, a friend—this big Okey—said, 'Why don't you run for president?'" She did and won. "I had to have another phone line put in the house and at one o'clock in the morning I'd be talking to some coach gone off on a tournament who'd run out of money or something like that. I didn't go to bed 'til late at night—I'd get all these phone calls, coaches arguing and carrying on." She adds thoughtfully, "And I was nice to them. Now I'm not too nice. Now I'd take a bat to them I think." Her entrance into the Umpire's Association was the result of much the same disapproval of shoddy practices. "One of our head umpires was goofing up on the job, not writing the checks to the kids (of course we used a lot of young umpires) and the books were getting into such a mess. So I went down to the club and picked the books up and brought them home. I had to start calling and scheduling all the umps—that wasn't too much fun," she chuckles. Danny interjects, "The umpires didn't mess with her. The coaches didn't mess with her. They did what she said."

Danny Carpenter can't say enough about the Homerunners Club and the role that women play in the success of the Series. He talks about his days as a regional director, traveling over several states to help get teams and leagues established. "When we'd set up meetings I'd say, 'I want the mothers there. Dads can show up, but I want the mothers.' Because if you want to get something done, you get them involved. Dads mainly get involved just so they can coach a team." The Homerunners Club is tightly organized and the amount of work that it does—not to mention the revenue it brings in through concessions—could never be pooh-poohed.

> In 1999, the Homerunners stocked the concession stand for Connie Mack week with 7,800 Frito pies, 1,146 pounds of nacho cheese, 1,440 burritos, and 60 gallons of jalapeños. For the less spicy-minded, they provided 5,000 hot dogs, 192 pounds of popcorn, 1,152 Snickers bars, and 1,936 dill pickles.[11]

The year 2001 brought a complete renovation of Ricketts Park, most of the funds coming from the state of New Mexico. Danny estimates the price tag at about a million and a half dollars. With backs for all the seats, new bleachers, press box, bathrooms, and seating for over six thousand, it is ostensibly a brand new park. He explains the need. "We could provide more seats than what we had. We have a waiting list. Our reserve seats are sold — period. You can't buy reserve seats unless someone doesn't want them, then they're put out at auction. I wanted to do more but the city stopped us. When you stop to think about it, we're talking about an event that lasts eight days of the year and that's the only time we have a seating problem. You spend millions of dollars trying to provide more, well, a person who's not a baseball fan — and there are a lot of them — might question it."

But for all the celebration over the new and improved Ricketts Park, there are those that grieve over the loss of the old one which was a true Western original. Myles Schrag, onetime Farmington resident, is the sorrowful lead mourner. In his thoroughly entertaining book, *Diamond in the Desert*, which was released shortly before the renovation began, Schrag called Ricketts Park "the symbolic and literal hub of Farmington" [12] and went on to clarify:

> You will find more attractive baseball venues than Ricketts Park, and you will find bigger ones. Most definitely you will find more comfortable parks. What you will not find is a baseball stadium more indelibly linked to its community by its history and appearance. The stadium how known as Ricketts Park is in place because Farmington and San Juan County residents willed it.[13]

In the renovation, all the details that illustrated Farmington's past as an oil boomtown were lost. Gone was the evidence of Doc Jones' skillful finagling — and Justis Supply's donation — of materials and the careful construction by the roughnecks. Gone was Ricketts Park's visual connection to its historic beginnings. In an e-mail, Schrag elaborated on his sadness at losing an important baseball landmark. "My feeling is that the CMWS leaders in town became enamored with the greater number of seats and state money that they got to upgrade the park, and they didn't think through how unique the old park was. I realize they couldn't have upgraded without making significant changes.... It now is spacious, but has no character." His fondness for the community and the Connie Mack organizers is such that he readily gives them credit for looking out for the best interests of the Series, but regrets they didn't take into consideration the fact that what was lost is irretrievable.

> It is accurate to say Ricketts Park was built by non-professionals, but they were only amateurs in the realm of stadium building. The workmanship was totally professional; a glance underneath the bleachers at the precise seams in the welding is proof. Yards and yards of backbreaking steel, forged together by the finest of welders: Ricketts Park, like Anasazi stone architecture a millennium old spread throughout The Four Corners, was built to last.[14]

* * *

The Connie Mack World Series means a lot of different things to different people. For teenage aspirants to the big leagues, it is an invaluable glimpse into the rarified air of the majors; every player is treated like he's already in pinstripes. And they play their hearts out. As Mo Carpenter says, "It's kind of shocking sometimes—they're *that* good." The tournament is fertile hunting ground for the majors and every year the stands are filled with big league scouts. Visitors to the tournament have the joy of witnessing (and the players the joy of hitting) what would normally be a double go sailing for a home run through the thin air. For the citizens of Farmington, it is a social event, a chance to catch up on events of the past year, and to bask in the continuing triumph of a gamble taken forty-three years ago. Perhaps there is no other small city that could have done what this one has so well and for so long. But what was it, in the beginning, that made a little town, isolated by vast expanses of desert badlands, aspire to such a goal? Carol May's first answer is a fairly simple one. "We love our diamond sports here. Maybe we're a small enough town that we don't have a lot of the other distractions of the big city. We have baseball." But, upon reflection, she adds dimension to her initial response, saying, "I think that because we grew so fast, we were trying to find an identity, to say, 'This is it!' You know, boomtowns generally don't have a long history, where they've been around for two hundred years. They can point back to a lot of history. We didn't have that."

Short on a lengthy municipal history, what Farmington does have is eight August nights, every year, to make clear to the world how much one little city can love baseball. Joe Cooper, who has never missed a Series, says that each year, as he packs his bags for Farmington, he thinks, "Here we go again for another great time. And it always is."

10

The Rio Abajo

The urban centers of New Mexico are everything a melting pot should be, filled with people of all ethnic backgrounds. As in other American cities, the state's Hispano population is thriving, adding its own unique vitality to the cultural mix. The cities offer an abundance of restaurants, bars, and retail establishments with distinctly Latin flavor. Hispanos fill countless government positions, elected and appointed, and no community is without its movers and shakers whose ancestors often include some of this country's first colonists. They are an integral part of twenty-first century New Mexico. But drive the back roads, deep into the mountains or along the state's few waterways and one will find the roots of this contemporary culture. For the old enclaves still exist, where the Spanish that is spoken (and it is the primary tongue) is still flecked with bits of medieval Iberia. There, tidy adobe houses are watched over by cherished saints, or *santos*. Women still make tortillas by hand and elderly men in straw cowboy hats lovingly tend gardens of chiles, beans and tomatoes. *Quinceañera*, or the celebration of a girl's fifteenth birthday, is still a huge familial occasion. In these places, Christmas is a time of understated magic as entire villages decorate with *farolitos* (brown paper bags lit with a single candle). Here the traditional arts can be found: delicate *colcha* embroidery, religious images like *bultos*, the carved statues of saints, and *retablos*, or wood paintings of the same. Family weavers in the Sangre de Cristo Mountains practice age-old techniques, like shearing and spinning their own wool from Churro sheep (a breed that the first settlers brought from Spain) and making their own dyes. In Chimayo particularly, the traditional weaving style creates exquisite and functional pieces, from housewares to clothing. In these communities, mass is faithfully attended at least once a week, for nowhere is there a more devout Catholic presence and the state is filled with picturesque churches. A drive up the high road to Taos will take one past the village of Las Trampas, with its own church of San José de Gracia. No basilica in Rome, no gothic cathedral in France can surpass this structure in dignity or poignancy. Yes, far away from the teeming Nob Hill of Albuquerque or the busy bistros of Santa Fe, old New Mexico still exists. One just has to look for it.

Among all the misconceptions about New Mexico, one of the most enduring is that regarding its Hispanic people. Beginning with the American government in 1846, the Spanish-speaking populace was assigned the heading "Mexican." Legally speaking, they were Mexican at the time of the invasion, but had been so for only twenty-five years, just since the war for Mexican independence. But it was a convenient term and one that completely ignored their long history on this continent as proud children of Spain.

That Americans would regard the Hispanos of New Mexico with no small amount of disdain was apparent as early as the 1840s when Josiah Gregg's *Commerce of the Prairies* was published. In it, he summed up what he believed to be the Hispanic character.

> Being of highly imaginative temperament and rather accommodating moral principles ... their conversation frequently exhibits ... a false glare of talent, eminently calculated to mislead and impose. They have no stability except in artifice; no profundity except for intrigue: qualities for which they have acquired an unenviable celebrity. Systematically cringing and subservient while out of power, as soon as the august mantel of authority falls upon their shoulders, there are but little bounds to their vindictiveness of spirit."[1]

Far into the twentieth century, the misleading term "Mexican" continued to be applied to the Hispanic people, just as the word "Indian" was given to all the diverse languages spoken by the state's Native American tribes, inferring no possibility that there was any difference among them. This complete disregard of cultural history—both Hispano and Native American—was carried over into the campaign for tourism that was waged in the first forty years of the century. Author William Tydeman describes a lantern-slide show, presented several times a week for fifteen years at La Fonda in Santa Fe, which was then a Harvey House. It was used to encourage tourists to sign up for the Indian Detours program. Not only did the slides present on off-balance look at Native Americans, presenting some as "good Indians" (Pueblo) and others as definitely not so good (Apache), they ignored Hispanic people altogether while flaunting that people's art and customs.

> However, to promote effectively the fifty miles surrounding Santa Fe, other Hispanic images had to be included: churches, archaeological sites, and homes festooned with chili peppers and ristras. There were photographs of wood wagons and the standard imagery of the wood-bearing burro, but never ... a Hispanic face. While this avoidance of Hispanic people may be surprising, it is not exceptional. The same stereotyping and racism are found in the conventional written sources of the period.[2]

Even today, the average tourist's search for Hispano culture will often be limited to cuisine. Hispanics of New Mexico have become somewhat used to their place down the list of tourism priorities but it can be a hard pill to swallow. Rita Padilla-Gutiérrez is one that believes that what is presented to the first-time visitor as "must sees" is controlled by slick advertising firms and wealthy galleries which tend to focus more on Anglo and Indian attractions. "There are still those tightly knit 'art folk' who come out of Santa Fe and Taos who dominate how art and culture are defined," she says. "That has been taken away from us. Sometimes there are attempts—very weak attempts—to portray our culture. All over the state, there's dominance in who runs art and culture in New Mexico. And it's not the Indians and it's not the Hispanics. We have Indian Market and Spanish Market every year and those are big deals. But it's that whole other process—what goes on with the media—I don't know how it's done but it doesn't feel like *we* have a hold on it."

Rita was born in Tomé, a tiny village in an agricultural belt that follows the Rio Grande River and she can speak with some expertise on the history of Hispano settlements in the northern part of the state. "There are two things in New Mexico history: the Rio Arriba, everything north, including (in some people's eyes) Santa Fe and above, and the Rio Abajo, which encompasses Isleta all the way to Socorro. That's what we consider the corridor of the Rio Abajo, 'the river below.' It's an agricultural, land-based existence that we have here. The beautiful Rio Grande has been our lifeline in the Rio Abajo." From its origins in southern Colorado, the Rio Grande bisects New Mexico and, flowing in a southeasterly direction, creates a natural boundary between Texas and Mexico before it empties into the Gulf, although that only occurs in a wet year these days. In the high desert, the only agricultural pursuits of any size will be found along water and the Rio Grande has sustained and nurtured New Mexico's people for centuries, as is attested by the number of Pueblos along its banks. It has also been a source of life for the state's Hispanos since the 1600s. Spanish settlers planted crops that could be irrigated from an *acequia*, or ditch. In fact, to this day, every small Hispanic (and most Pueblo) agricultural village has a communal artery of water, called the *acequia madre*, or "mother ditch," from which individual farmers water their crops. With water the most precious commodity, there is a *mayordomo* to see that no one uses more than his fair share and to monitor the condition of the acequias. A time-honored tradition is the yearly cleaning of the ditch, a task that used to involve every member of the village.

Rita's family, the Padillas, was one of the earliest to arrive in the Rio Abajo and settled in Tomé. "Oh gosh, we trace them back to at least the 1600s here," she says of her ancestors. "Tomé was established in 1739 but the history goes even further back to pre-revolution days—the days of the Indian revolt [1680]. All the areas around us—Peralta, Valencia—they were here at least during the Pueblo Revolt days. When the Indians moved us out, some of our people went as far as El Paso, them came back later to re-establish Tomé and then in 1739 it officially became a land grant patent." The issue of land grants in New Mexico is one that still resonates profoundly with its Hispanic sons and daughters. When the king of Spain awarded a community land grant, it served his interests (settlers meant not only defense in unstable areas but a tax base as well) along with those of the colonists. For them, it meant individual plots of land that each family would farm (and eventually own) and a large communal parcel for grazing livestock and finding needed resources. The Treaty of Guadalupe-Hidalgo, which made New Mexico a part of the United States, said that these grants would be respected. Unfortunately, when convenient, the United States government felt fairly comfortable in not recognizing many, and the lands were overrun by wealthy ranchers in the nineteenth century and developers in the twentieth century.

An intangible of the land grant system was the bond that its heirs shared as families that had inhabited the land for three centuries or more. Their roots were sunk so deep that the words "family" and "land" were fundamentally inseparable. And because so much of the land was communally held, all the settlers were obliged to work together to maintain the health of the property and its waters. This centuries-old need for cooperation wove the families together into an entity as tight and as durable as a Chimayo rug.

When the communities of the Rio Abajo began playing baseball in the nineteenth century, the sport appealed to every member of the close-knit communities. By the mid-twentieth, the area was filled with teams ranging from those made up of war veterans to hard-hitting young women. Rita Padilla-Gutiérrez knows a good bit about the subject. First, she was one of those family members whose world revolved around the Sunday afternoon games of her youth. She is also the creator of a pictorial exhibit on the topic for Raíces del Río Abajo, an organization that celebrates the area's proud history. In an introduction to the show she wrote, "It was a time when baseball was a passion; it was a time when older brothers, uncles, and fathers taught and practiced with their children; it was a time when Sunday was devoted to any given field, and it was a time when baseball was played in its purest form."

Beginning in the late nineteenth century, a string of Rio Abajo villages across three counties — Bernalillo, Valencia and Socorro — began competing. These villages begin with Isleta Pueblo in the north, followed by Los Lunas and tiny agricultural hamlets like Peralta, Valencia, Los Chaves, Tomé and Adelino. The important railroad town of Belén sits on the path as well and then the Rio Abajo ends informally with Socorro, Luis Lopez and San Antonio, to the south. Rita says that the towns of Socorro (which always had a strong team from the School of Mining) and Luis Lopez really started the furor, primarily because they had the powerful railroad teams from nearby San Marcial to compete against. The other towns of the Rio Abajo soon joined in and played against each other informally for decades. Small perhaps, but some of these towns were able to pull off a few highly impressive coups through the years. For instance, Rube Waddell represented Socorro in a 9–0 victory in the 1909 territorial fair against the Albuquerque Grays, which included ever-popular native sons Ross Salazar, Binger Corhan and Bill Pettus.[3] And Los Lunas was able to draft Christy Mathewson to pitch for them once.[4] Later, that same village would become a mainstay in Albuquerque semipro circuits and its neighbor to the south, Belén, was one of the early members of the respected Central New Mexico League.

Rita says, "The tradition was well under way when most of the guys came back from the war. There were really no jobs. Some of them were doing their family farms, that kind of thing. In essence they had time to be in this kind of a league, all those guys that were born in the '20s and '30s." In 1958, several of the villages banded together to form a circuit called the Mid Rio Grande League, which, with the sanction of the National Baseball Congress, became New Mexico's sixth semipro franchise. It was comprised of two teams each from Belén and Los Lunas, one each from Los Chavez, Los Trujillos, Bosque Farms and the combined townships of Tomé and Adelino.[5] These are the days that Rita remembers so well. "Coming from a large family — I have nine brothers and seven sisters — we had few resources to partake in organized anything, much less things that required a fee or any kind of money exchange. We just couldn't afford to. Baseball is the poor man's game. All you needed was a bat and ball and a few gloves and there you went. It was quick and dirty," she laughs. Her father didn't play but loved the game. "He took us to games that were there in the community. If they didn't play in Tomé they played in Adelino. If we had to travel to Socorro, that was a treat. It was a treat to drive to Isleta. From Tomé to Adelino was like a five-minute drive but to us kids it was a different world because you actually had to get in the car and travel. It was all very connected geographically. You didn't have to go very far to get entertained on a Sunday afternoon. The children that were in my age bracket grew up watching the guys play. We were there as moral support, sort of a motley crew of cheerleaders. All of us who were at least five would gather in the car and my father would take us." Once there, the children were expected to behave and watch the game. "It was a very organized, very serious business," she says. There were no concessions and no facilities. "You had to be well-prepared to not need the restroom or not ask a lot of questions. You got on top of your car or backed up your truck by any little tree that offered shade and pulled the tailgate down.[6] You knew what everybody in the community drove so if you spotted different cars coming in, well, that would have been the opposing team's caravan coming to watch their team. It was a nice display of communities coming together."

Libby Sanchez was a young mother during those years and knew what it was like to cart her five kids to the games to watch their father Ernesto, who played shortstop for Los Trujillos. She spent a good part of the game in the back seat changing diapers or doling out sips of Kool-Aid. "I would tell the neighbor who was in the truck next to my car to tell me when Ernesto came up to bat so I could honk the horn. He looked forward to me honking the horn, so I had to know when he was up at bat." Libby can attest to the poverty endured by the families of the Rio Abajo and the ingenuity that was employed to get around it, often with the help of the women in the village of Belén. "When Ernesto was young, they couldn't afford to buy balls so they would take the strings from flour sacks and wind them into a ball. Then he'd collect a penny from each of the players to buy tape to cover it." Libby also grew up in Belén, where she and Ernesto were childhood sweethearts. She was an only child and claims now to have been quite spoiled. But she was married at 17, got pregnant right away, then watched as her husband was sent overseas to fight in World War II. Her first child, a son, was three years old before he met his dad. "It really unspoiled me quick," she sighs. Life improved dramatically with the end of the war. She recalls the late '40s and early '50s as happy times, filled with families and baseball. Ernesto had to give up the game at around age 30, when he slid into first and tore cartilage. Libby says she missed the fellowship with the other wives but was just as happy to put the sport behind her. "Actually, baseball didn't interest me at all. I was just there to honk the horn."

As to the brand of ball that was played, Rita Padilla-Gutiérrez feels like there was an enormous amount of talent in those little villages and considers money one of the main obstacles between some of the

Baseball was truly a family affair in the Rio Abajo, with every member attending games if they weren't playing in them. Ernesto Sanchez (right), a shortstop for Los Trujillos, holds daughter Sylvia. His wife Libby (left) holds Audrey as Neddie stands in front (courtesy Libby Sanchez).

players and the professional ranks. She rather proudly points to the Tomé-Adelino team as one of the best in the league. Its rivalry with a team from Isleta Pueblo was notorious. "Those were some of the more exciting games to watch because of the quality of players on those teams. They had Pablo Abeita who was *the* person to go see. He was a helluva ballplayer. He was a catcher — a big tall guy, kind of stocky, built like all catchers are built. He was fun to watch because he was a great athlete. There were a lot of good athletes at Isleta and playing them was a big deal. They were very competitive and very territorial."

One of the hometown players of whom she is understandably proud is her brother Matthew Padilla, who played for Tomé-Adelino, beginning at age 13 in 1960. Matthew is retired from the University of New Mexico where he was Director of Education (Rita is retired from the same institution where she was Director of Scholarships. Of the seventeen children in their family, fifteen of them attended college, Matthew being the first). By the time he started playing for Tomé-Adelino, the Mid Rio Grande League had expanded its number of teams. "It depended on the years, but most of the time there were twelve to fifteen teams." Apparently the Mid Rio Grande League put the "pro" in semipro. He says that some of the players actually got paid, depending on the sponsor. "Yeah, there was a team out of Albuquerque and they had players that they hired to work. But they didn't *work*." As each of the league's communities was relatively poor, the players themselves tended the fields. "We had ours and we maintained it. We dragged it and put the lines down and watered it down. It didn't have grass." As with most small community parks, the seating was meager to nonexistent. Just as his sister maintained, most spectators watched from their cars which were parked along the foul lines. Without the hint of a boast, Matthew dryly sums up the competition. "There were some teams in the league that weren't that good and we just beat the hell out of them because there wasn't much there. Then there were better teams and between those there was a fierce rivalry." There was no split season and no playoffs at the season's end. Matthew says that the pennant was determined simply by the team with the most wins. More often than not, Tomé-Adelino was that team. The league championship automatically meant a berth in the state semipro tournament. He says that ringers were often brought in for that all-important National Baseball Congress semipro tournament, particularly from New Mexico Highlands University in Las Vegas which had one of the best college baseball programs in the country at that time.

Matthew Padilla played mostly in the outfield but was known to occasionally serve as pitcher. In that role, he had the opportunity to partner with the remarkable Isleta catcher Pablo Abeita, who was usually the only member of the team who was not a hometown boy. It is a testament to the quality of the Tomé-Adelino team that they were able to snag him because he remains a towering figure in baseball, not only in the Rio Abajo but throughout the region, among players of every ilk. As Rita pointed out, he was the single player that everyone wanted to see in action. An element of Abeita's mythic status is his penchant for brawling. When asked if that part of his reputation was merited, Matthew Padilla sounds mildly surprised. "No, he wasn't a brawler — he just played baseball really, really hard." Then he rather happily adds, "Of course, if he was going into second base and you were turning a double play, he would spike you."

A player who remembers Matthew Padilla well is Nick Martinez, who played third base for Valencia and El Cerro, among others. "Matthew Padilla? I used to kill him. I used to beat the heck outta him. We used to get Matthew mad 'cause he's a hot-tempered son of a gun. I'd tell the players and the fans, 'I bet this guy's fastball isn't fast enough to get me!' and he'd throw one straight down the middle and BANGO! Goodbye! Because that was what I had wanted. That was my ball. Oh man, I loved it."

Nick cuts quite a dashing figure at 73. He is fit and lively with a distinguished moustache. He becomes extremely animated when talking baseball in the Rio Abajo. He grew up in a tiny village called San Fernandez which he estimates had, at most, ten houses. "But I would say that, at that time, it had thirty boys all within three years of me. I started playing catcher when I was nine years old—without a mask. No mask, no knee guards, no nothing. With a glove my mother made out of the cover of a mattress with the mattress filling inside, that's what I used to catch with." He played in high school, where his team not only won the state championship one year but Nick was named all-state top fielder. "I could catch like Willie Mays—it was nothing to me." He says that he was offered a Fulbright Scholarship to Highlands University in baseball (and was encouraged by a coach to try for the University of Arizona as well), but he decided against both. "The main reason was we were very poor and my daddy was really sick. I was the oldest one in the house and I didn't want my brothers and sisters to suffer what I did in high school. Because I was so poor, I didn't have a suit to go to the prom, I didn't have a car, I had to borrow a little sport jacket for my graduation. I didn't have a penny in my pocket in high school—not one penny. I wanted to quit school but my daddy wouldn't let me. Later I went to work to support my mother and everybody to make sure they had good clothes and the things they needed in school. That's the reason I didn't go. Because I wasn't dumb. I wasn't slow. It was so that that my brothers and sisters wouldn't go through hard times. The whole community here was very poor. They were barely making it. I dug cesspools to buy my class ring—it cost me $22."

While still in high school, Nick joined a team of men in their twenties ("the machos—you know, the big boys"), that included his pitching older brother, whom he credits with making him a good catcher, but in a rather brutal way. "My brother used to criticize me for every little mistake I made. Anger made me improve and that's what made me good—to show him that I could be better than him or anybody else. It gave me the strength and the motivation to become what I became." He talks about the difficulty in catching for his brother. "I didn't really give him any signs because he just threw what the hell he wanted." His brother also inspired Nick when it came to batting. "They put me in as a pinch-hitter to bunt and I'd never bunted before. So I hit the ball and they got the guy out at home. My brother kicked me and told me, 'Godammit, you're not worth a darn.' After that, I decided that I was going to be a bunter. And in practice I'm bunting, I'm bunting, I'm bunting—every time. In high school games, that was my duty. I was second batter. Usually the first batter would get on first and I knew automatically I had to bunt. I made it to first seventy to eighty percent of the time. I was such a perfectionist in bunting—I could place that ball where I wanted it."

After high school, Nick started playing third base for the Valencia team of the Mid Rio Grande League, eventually playing for the crack Tomé-Adelino team as well. Also playing in the league at that time, for Socorro, was Max Gonzales, a former right-handed pitcher for the Class B Albuquerque Dukes. Getting one off of him is one of Nick's proudest memories. "I sent one over

400 feet. I banged that ball and that's how I got a reputation as a heavy hitter. I had power. I only weighed 145 pounds but I used to bang the hell outta that ball."

Nick and his team were headed to the semipro finals in 1958 when he was drafted into the Army. He played service ball in Germany during his first year and would have been back for a second but was called home to be with his dying father. He's proud of his service-ball stint because most of his teammates were former professionals. "That team was equal to the Dukes *right now* (referring to the Albuquerque Isotopes which is the Dodgers' Triple A team). For the second season, they were going to get some major league scouts from the Milwaukee Braves and they picked out 26 players to be scouted by them and I was one. But like I said, I came home because my daddy was real sick. So I never got the chance to be scouted by the pros."

Nick says he never played on a good field until he went into the Army. When he came out, it was back to the hardscrabble world of the New Mexico semipros. "Rough parks. Rocks in the field. Sometimes it was just pasture grass. Sometimes they were sandy and sometimes so hard that you could slide and rip half your leg." All of the Rio Abajo teams struggled for money. "We had to buy equipment ourselves or the coach would by it. We had broken bats. We had to tape them to keep batting with them." But even then, life in the semipros had its rewards ("There were a lot of young girls who wanted to go out with us or had a crush on us. We had ten to fifteen girls who would come to see us play") with a good performance on the field coming in very handy with New Mexico's pesky blue laws. "All the bartenders liked me because they had seen me play. We played on Sundays and they would sell me liquor for the same price they'd sell it during the week, then give me a couple of beers or wine on the

Cousins Candido Montoya (batting) and Rufie Montoya at play in their civvies in San Antonio, New Mexico, in the 1950s (courtesy Stanley Montoya).

side." Nick can name an extraordinary number of bars in different towns that the team frequented. "So we'd buy about six cases. After the game, the players would drink beer and argue."

Although the Mid Rio Grande League had no end-of-season championship game, he says that there was always a Fourth of July tournament between the two top teams at that point. That was the most important game of the season, Nick says, because the momentum of winning that one would almost always allow the winner to coast victoriously to the pennant.

Nick Martinez spins a good yarn but none is better than his memories of the infamous Pablo Abeita. Along with Pablo, the Tomé-Adelino team used to employ another Isleta as pitcher. Together they made a powerful battery and had the advantage of a shared Native language that no one else could understand. This not only did away with the need for signs, it also meant that Pablo could give his pitcher a thorough rundown on the batter, his strengths and weaknesses, as the man was standing in the box. Nick says, "Let me tell you a little story about Pablo," and settles down to tell a good one, complete with dialogue. "He was a catcher — a helluva good catcher and a helluva batter. I was batting one game when he was catching and there was an Indian pitcher. I swung at a high ball and Pablo said something to him and I knew exactly what he told him. I mean, I didn't understand what he was saying but I knew what he meant." Here Nick's voice takes on a baritone growl and with a slightly demonic chuckle, he speaks for Pablo, saying, "'He's a sucker for a high ball.'" Nick's own voice returns as the story builds. "So he threw another high ball and I banged that ball about 400 feet!" When his laughter subsides, Nick begins another tale. "I was playing against Abeita and I hit a ball really hard and tried to make a homer out of it and it would have been if we'd had fences. But they retrieved it and when I was running to third, I looked back and the second baseman already had it and threw it to Abeita. So I went running home and he got in front of the plate and I banged him — POOM! I butted him with my shoulders and he fell way back there but got me out because he still had the

After a 1947 game, Avilio "Lefty" Otero relaxes with his mother Josefita and nephew Manuel Otero. Otero's nickname came as much from his career as a boxer as pitcher (courtesy Avilio Otero).

ball. His face mask and everything went flying." Nick again assumes the menacing growl. "He said, 'Grrrrrr, Nick, you hurt me! Goddam, you're rough Nick!' I said, 'You get in my way and I'm gonna bang you buddy.' We played rough. We were rivals and we meant business."

Was Pablo Abeita really as good as everyone in the Rio Abajo remembers? It seems appropriate to ask the man himself. Although he laughs (and, indeed, there is a slight growl there) when he's told he is a legend in the Rio Abajo, he doesn't seem to think his status is unmerited. "To everyone in Tomé, I was like a god in baseball. I was like a Babe Ruth. I hit balls that they still talk about." And his talent would have come naturally. Pablo is descended from some of New Mexico's finest Native American baseball men; if they aren't remembered for their skill on the diamond, they are remembered for their managerial talents, all since the turn of the century. Pablo's athletic ability was already highly regarded in his high school years. In fact, several schools competed for him. The St. Mary's coach, a renowned Albuquerque sports figure named Babe Parenti, along with future United States Senator Pete Domenici, convinced the boy to go there and, indeed, Parenti paid the $1.25 monthly tuition. In his high school baseball years, Pablo played shortstop. He didn't start catching until he was in the service. When asked about the weight of responsibility that position entails, he answers, "Yes, but I liked it." Drafted into the Army right out of high school, he began playing on a Fort Polk Special Services ball club right away. When he returned home, he married a woman from Tomé. His marital affiliation with that village was the reason for his joining the Tomé-Adelino team. "All those guys in that league were good friends of mine," he says. "We had a pretty good league." As for the Tomé-Adelino club, he says that it won the league pennant seven years in a row, then the state semipro tournament for six. In all, Pablo says he played on the Mid Rio Grande League for roughly seven seasons.

While Pablo was playing for Tomé-Adelino, the athletes from his Pueblo were competing not only against each other, but playing in the huge Albuquerque semipro City-County League, often with more than one team. And Pablo had certainly played for a few of them on and off, from high school onward. Early on, his father had drafted him to catch for a tough team of Isleta war veterans. When they acquired the sponsorship of an Albuquerque restaurant, they became the Isleta Pollys. And, from time to time, an Isleta team would enter the Mid Rio Grande League, always with Pablo catching. But for the most part, and for the longest amount of time, Pablo played as usually the only Native American on a Hispanic team in that purely Hispanic league. "I never played for Isleta too much except when my dad was managing. It seems like I had a bigger fan base with the Spanish people than I did at Isleta. I think the Isleta players were a little bit intimidated by my style of play." He considers this for a moment and says, "I was probably treated with more respect in the Rio Abajo because of my ability." He tells a story about being with his grandson recently when they met up with another veteran of the Rio Abajo, a pitcher. "He kept saying to my grandson, 'I remember striking out your grandfather once. Yes, one time I struck him out.' I finally said, 'Yeah, Billy, but how many times did I get a hit off of you?' He said, 'I don't know, but I do remember striking you out that time.'"

Now that Pablo has been asked how good he was, it's time to ask about his reputation for ferocity. He candidly says, "I loved to fight. I don't know — that's just how I played ball." He is tickled by the memories this topic conjures. "I play to win," he growls. "All those years that I played, I only wore shin guards and a mask. I never wore a chest protector. And my fingers aren't broken or twisted or anything." And with that, Pablo Abeita adds just a bit more mortar to the legend that he has become.

The baseball teams of the Rio Abajo weren't limited exclusively to those made up of men. Just a few miles south of Socorro is tiny village, where for many years, young women were as integral a part of community baseball. San Antonio is famous on two counts: it is the birthplace of Conrad Hilton and it is home to the Owl Bar and Café. Rowena Baca is the proprietor of the Owl, which enjoys an international reputation for its green chile cheeseburger. After the Wednesday lunch rush has subsided, she relaxes long enough to talk about her years as the stalwart first baseman for the San Antonio Angels, one of the two teams sponsored by the restaurant.

In 1939, Rowena's grandfather, Jose Miera (who grew up and worked with Hilton), built a small grocery store with five attached cabins which, during the final months of World War II, housed scientists of the Manhattan Project. Rowena says that, as Trinity Sites was only thirty-five miles away, "they had to have a place to go when they came out of the desert." In fact, the warm relationship formed between her grandfather and the scientists meant that they gave him a heads up before the bomb was tested on July 16, 1945. In the early morning hours of that day, Jose stood outside his grocery store and watched as the sky was shocked into blinding white and a roar rolled over the surrounding countryside like a rogue wave. Rowena, who was a tiny child at the time, says, "My grandma pushed me and my little cousin under the bed because she thought the world was coming to an end." She chuckles, "I don't know how she thought the bed was going to help us." When the war ended and Rowena's father Frank Chavez returned, he turned the grocery store into a restaurant and bar and christened it "The Owl."

For many years, the Owl sponsored two local baseball teams, one for men (managed by Frank) and one for young women, with Dee Chavez, Rowena's mother, at the helm. (Surprisingly, the distaff club was one of many in the Socorro area at that time.) Rowena describes her mother as an even-tempered coach who loved all her young players. "But she had us real disciplined. We couldn't slack off, we had to be there for practice." The Angels' practice schedule was a grueling six-day-a-week one. They would play other girls' teams as close by as those in Socorro, which was just a few miles away, or travel as far as Carrizozo or Ancho, more than fifty miles away. For transportation, the players were divided with some going in the back of a pickup truck while their more fortunate teammates were ferried in style in Dee's chartreuse and black late-model convertible ("She was very trendy," Rowena says, in marked understatement, of her mother).

Rowena spent her baseball life at first. "I always liked it. There was a lot of action there." She was a natural athlete and grew up playing every sport that was available to her. "I played football, basketball, baseball, softball — everything. I was raised with my mostly boy cousins (my grandma raised all of us) and all the guys from San Antonio would come play with us because we had the biggest yard. So I was a tomboy right there with the rest of them." And there were more good players on the roster than just Rowena. She insists that the Angels were not a team to be taken for granted. "I think we were tough. We did a lot of sliding. And I was good hitter. I had strong arms." She says that the men's and women's teams often shared doubleheaders and, on the rare occasion that the Angels were unable to find another girls team to tilt with, they'd engage their Owl-sponsored male counterparts. Did they ever win? "I don't *think* so," she admits, dragging the words out slowly.

The San Antonio Angels baseball team, in the 1950s. This was just one of many teams, male and female, sponsored by the legendary Owl Bar and Café. Standing in rear: Lupe Montoya, Christy Chavez, Petra Rivera and Josie Padilla. Kneeling in the middle are Flora Chavez, Dee Chavez (manager) and Rosa Lucero. Seated in front are Mabel Ramirez, Isabel Montoya, Rowena Eaton (Baca) and Celia Martinez (courtesy Rowena Baca).

As was typical of the times and of the Rio Abajo, the fan base was enthusiastic and for both of the Owl teams. "All the people would come out 'cause that was our entertainment. The whole town would show up." She laughs at the memory of the horn-honking, chattering spectators and suddenly bursts out with a boisterous, "Batter, batter, batter, batter!" Rowena says that she played for the Angels for over twenty years, and on a few Socorro teams as well. "There for awhile, baseball was my whole life. We didn't have nothing else to do — no TV, no nothing else. We looked forward to the games, excited all the time about them. And we played to win."

Her golden baseball team of the 1950s dissolved in the most unlikely fashion, at the hands of some military personnel from the Stallion Site of the White Sands Missile Range, just twelve miles from San Antonio. "They'd send all those soldiers from the Stallion Site and they just came in and took all the girls away," she chuckles but with the barest hint of lingering indignation. The majority of her teammates, still with good playing years ahead of them, were spirited away from baseball and into marriage.

The Owl continued to support baseball teams for years but now, since San Antonio was bypassed by a major highway in the late 1960s, the population has decreased and there are no teams anymore, not even Little League as the kids are sent to Socorro after the fifth grade. But even the rerouting of a major travel artery hasn't slowed business at the Owl, which only becomes more famous with the passing years. "I've got people in here from all over the world. I've had delegations from China, Japan, Russia. They'd be touring the country and would stop here. I was always kind of scared they wouldn't like green chile[7] but they love it." And patrons of the restaurant often leave testimonials in the form of dollar bills, tacked to one of the interior walls. Once a year, Rowena allows her clientele to vote on which charities will receive the money. As the owner, she is not above a bit of rule bending. "I always make sure that St. Jude's gets the most votes, even if I have to pad the ballot box," she freely admits.

These days, Rowena Baca is a bigger fan of football (she can name all the Dallas Cowboys) than baseball, the result of many years of supporting her son in the sport. But she keeps an eye on the Albuquerque Isotopes. "I was there Sunday, yelling with everybody else and singing and trying to catch foul balls." One almost pities the surrounding ball-snagging hopefuls with this dynamic former first-sacker in their midst. Because one suspects that, to this day, just as she did with the Angels long ago, Rowena plays to win.

* * *

In the Rio Abajo, the final generation of men to play semipro baseball witnessed the demise of the Mid Rio Grande League in the late 1960s. One of those players is Tony Moya, who at 64 followed in the footsteps of men like Nick and Pablo, although he played for one season with Pablo for Tomé-Adelino. Tony's childhood memories include the last idyllic years of the purely pastoral, impoverished and baseball-loving Rio Abajo. Growing up in Adelino, he was an avid fan of the Tomé-Adelino team and would hike from home to the games. "Baseball was more popular in those days because there was nothing else to do. I would go across the ditch banks and fields and sneak in the back so they wouldn't charge me the dime or whatever they charged. If they saw me, I'd tell them I would shag foul balls and that way they'd let me in free."

Tony was a fifteen-year-old right-handed pitcher in high school when the team spotted him, and already building an impressive record (as a junior, he was the starter in a game against the University of New Mexico freshman team, which the high school team won 22–0). Tomé-Adelino's manager, Junior Silva, actually came to Tony's house, asking him to sign. "It was like real professional ball," Tony says. "They had a commissioner of the Mid Rio Grande League and officers, so they had to sign me up if I was going to play with them." And he did play one year for the seasoned team of older men. But the next season saw a second Tomé team spring to life, one formed from boys much closer to Tony in age. "So I wanted to know if I could get out of the Tomé-Adelino team and they gave me a hard time." He laughs as he remembers that one of the fiercest arguments against his release came from none other than Pablo Abeita who suggested that blacklisting was a good idea for a jumper. "He said, 'If he doesn't want to play with us then don't let him play at all.' But the other guys knew me and knew my family and said, 'Aw, he wants to play with his friends,' so they finally let me out of the agreement." The youthful Tomé team joined the Mid Rio Grande League and Tony recalls the first time that they went up against the older team he had left behind. "All the old men were saying, 'Aw, you're just a bunch of punks. You think you're grown up. Wait 'til you meet up with real men.' We beat 'em," Tony says smiling, "that was a good game."

After graduating from high school, Tony went to work to help support his mother and siblings, his father having died when the boy was seven. In doing so, he was forced to turn down a baseball scholarship to the University of New Mexico (a benefit of his victory over the freshman team years before). But he enjoyed his years in the Mid Rio Grande League, although getting money for uniforms and equipment was still the struggle it had been a decade earlier. "But you were just glad to play. I was. I had to play somewhere — anywhere." The fields were much the same as they had been in decades past although with a few improvements. As for Tomé-Adelino, there was now an enclosed field, dugouts and a concession stand. "They still parked along the foul lines. People would sit in the cars or on the hoods. Occasionally a foul ball would break a windshield," says Tony.

In 1967 he landed a tryout with the Double A Albuquerque Dukes, at that time a Dodgers affiliate. At the helm of the team that year was the legendary Duke Snider.[8] Tony went to the park and was directed to the locker room to don a Dukes uniform. He was told he'd be throwing pre-game batting practice but under strict guidelines. "I had to tell them what I was going to throw every time. I guess they were afraid I would hit somebody or something," Tony says. "So, I'd tell the batter what I was going to throw and he'd be waiting for it. And he would hit it. It was disappointing because I couldn't throw what I wanted." At one point, the young man rebelled and threw one without calling it, immediately getting a dressing-down from the catcher. But his performance caught the eye of the manager. "Duke Snider talked to me and told me to get into real good shape and then in February, at the beginning of spring training, he wanted me to go to Spokane." And Tony planned to do just that. But that Thanksgiving, an accident with a jammed rifle left him without the index finger on his throwing hand. "And that was the end of my baseball career. I tried pitching after that but I'd lost speed. I'd lost control. I played some softball but I didn't play baseball anymore."

Tony has told this entire story with mixed tones of disappointment and confusion. It's not the loss of his finger that seems to vex him so much as that long ago tryout. From the point of view of the young hurler that he was, being forced to call his pitches had left him feeling hobbled and like the tryout had been a failure. "I was used to overpowering batters with my fast ball and breaking stuff. And then you go there and they clobber you." He readily admits that as an intelligent pitcher, he loved and needed the strategizing, as much as velocity and control, to feel like he'd given his best on the mound. The lack of this threw him badly, leading him to completely misread the audition. And there is another important aspect to his lingering disappointment and it is based on a simple error that he carried onto the Dukes' field that day. Tony was a country boy, without money for baseball cards or newspapers that explained the labyrinthine farm systems of major league teams. He was a young man who knew very little about the foreign world of professional ball. Tony went into that tryout believing that the 1967 Dukes were the Dodgers' Triple A farm club and Spokane the Double A, when it was actually the reverse. He misunderstood what had happened, thinking he hadn't qualified for Triple A, and was being, in effect, "sent down." In fact, Duke Snider had seen talent enough in Tony to push him higher, to that place where the demi-gods of baseball played just a step away from "The Show." When this ancient mistake is pointed out to him, he is profoundly surprised. Forty-two years after the fact, Tony Moya has found out just how good he really was.

These days, the former players and fans of the Rio Abajo stay remarkably busy. Pablo Abeita is an active member of the Isleta Pueblo community. His hands may be in remarkably good shape for a catcher, but he's had one knee replaced and is scheduled for shoulder surgery in a couple of months, both a direct result of baseball.

Nick Martinez is still an athlete. In fact, he is a Senior Olympian in track and basketball. He snorts contemptuously when asked if softball has replaced baseball for him. "It's a sissy game for me. I call it that." He looks back fondly on his childhood, when his father nurtured in him a love of baseball that would last a lifetime. He paints a picture of simpler days along the Rio Abajo. "My daddy would lay a mattress in the back of the wagon and take us to Otero to see the team play on Sunday. Those *compadres* there would all go to the game, the people would get together. Baseball was a big part of their lives. But by the 1950s things had changed. We lost a lot."

Tony Moya eventually did get his college degree and was a successful businessman, now retired. He still has land in Tomé. "Yeah, there are still a lot of small farmers—like where I live. I have five acres in alfalfa and I have my horses. That's what I do." Now, there is only high school baseball left in the area. The days of grown men playing sometimes brutal semipro ball are long gone. He remembers watching the Mid Rio Grande League dissolve. "I think it was the expense," he says. "That's what the commissioner said. And I think there was a loss of interest too." He admits that by the '60s, the communities were losing people to the larger cities like Belén and Albuquerque. But his memories of the earlier days are still strong. "It was so much fun in those days. You looked forward all week to playing baseball on Sunday, you know? I guess it's just a sign of the times."

Rita Padilla-Gutiérrez believes that the Rio Abajo is a more fractured place without the sport. "Most definitely we've lost something," she says sadly. To her, the loss of baseball in her hometown goes hand-in-hand, on a symbolic level, with the first talk of selling the Tomé land grant, the two events roughly coinciding in the late '50s and early '60s. "Some people who were heirs were not getting anything out of it because they didn't graze cattle there. It became a huge, huge battle — we're talking about 47,000 acres of land, deeded by the king of Spain. And now we, as a community, were at odds as to what to do with it." The wounds to the community were deep and beyond healing, affecting relations on every level. "Before, baseball was this great competition — meet on Sundays, get to see friends and neighbors and other communities, too. I would say that the impact of the sale of the land grant had something to do with losing baseball." After many years of disagreements, the land grant was sold in 1968 to a company from out of the state which immediately began to develop it and sell off lots. Today, through the hard work of Rita and other heirs, the Tomé land grant has been "reconstituted," meaning that it is once again "a unit of government, a political subdivision." While the land that once belonged to the village has long since been divvied up into faux-adobe houses and parking lots, the land grant heirs hope to see justice in the form of National Forest land in the nearby Manzano Mountains. Part of the original grant of 100,000 acres, a poorly conducted 1871 survey neglected to include that portion located in the mountains. Rita and her fellow activists hope to win back 30,000 acres. "But I miss that sense of camaraderie that brought communities together," she continues, "even if it was in competition. For me, it was some of the most exciting times of my growing up, to be able to see those guys play."

In 1932, Willie Trujillo, member of a Hispano team of the Rio Abajo, was fatally beaten during a racially charged game with an Anglo team from Belén. His assailants included the manager of the Belén team, two of its players and their father (courtesy Joseph Torres).

She seems suddenly very sad. "It has died and I don't know if it can ever be the same. The nuance and dynamic of the times made it more special. Because of the lack of resources, everything was a struggle for the teams—to get sponsors, to get uniforms, to get equipment. But even with what they had, they were able to bring a lot of old-fashioned, clean entertainment to the community. I'm sort of at a loss for words as to what it meant to me."

The history of the United States is frequently told without reference to the multi-generational Hispanic people of New Mexico, even though they were some of the first settlers. Too often, the story of their ancestors stops at the northern border of Chihuahua and frequently doesn't get very much further than rehashings of the Black Legend. No one denies that the first century of the Spanish presence was a dark and deadly period in Native American history. This is the terrible truth of military invasion and occupation. The Spanish people of New Mexico would join their Indian neighbors in tribulation beginning in 1846, with arrival of the United States' military.

Today's descendents of those early American colonists faithfully preserve their time-honored traditions, especially in the remaining Hispano strongholds. In a place like the Rio Abajo, where Hispanics for four centuries have drawn their livelihood from the soil, people over fifty share a memory of want and community struggle. But the fact that they are still a profound presence is proof of an enviable resilience, good-humor and deep religious faith. For many years, every person in the Rio Abajo also had faith in baseball, knowing that, no matter how difficult the grind, the Sunday game would always come. And for a blissful few hours, life would be easy.

11
Making the Ball Sing

Throughout the years of New Mexico's fascination with baseball, no one has played the game with more devotion than the state's Native Americans. Pueblo, Navajo and Apache athletes have played passionately since well before the territory became the state. The Pueblos, in particular, have played in dynastic style, the great grandsons of prominent baseball men carrying family names onto twenty-first-century diamonds. In light of that tradition, it is fitting that perhaps the earliest reference to baseball in New Mexico involves these original inhabitants of the state. No less an authority than Stewart Culin, in his *Games of the North American Indians*, states that the Navajo learned the game as prisoners, by watching Anglo soldiers play it at the desolate Bosque Redondo[1] between 1864 and 1868. The Indians were there at the pleasure of the United States government, captives in a nightmarish experiment in Christianization and Americanization. Forced from their beloved homeland in a scorched-earth campaign carried out by the legendary Kit Carson, thousands of starving Diné were marched nearly four hundred miles to a forty-square-mile tract on the Pecos River near Fort Sumner called Bosque Redondo and forced into cohabitation with their mortal enemies, the Apaches. There, it was thought, both tribes could be transformed into docile agriculturalists, no longer a threat to the good citizens of the territory. Those that survived the march found a prison camp, where the bitter, alkaline water of the Pecos sickened them, the nearest firewood was a day's walk away and the crops that they nurtured with their sweat were destroyed year after year by insect or tempest. Most of the Apaches escaped the Bosque in 1865 but the Navajo remained until 1868, when the government quietly conceded its mistake and they were finally allowed to return to Dinetah from sorrowful exile. Ragged and physically depleted from their ordeal, they returned to their land with little but a bit of food, a few sheep, their unquenchable pride and the curious benefit of an understanding of baseball. They took what they had learned from the soldiers and incorporated it into a game they called *aqejólyedi* or "run around ball," complete with ball, bat and four bases.[2]

Within a few years, New Mexico's youngest Native Americans would find themselves immersed in the sport, once again as unwilling guests of the government, this time at federal boarding schools. Despite the gross failure of the Bosque Redondo, the United States continued its campaign to assimilate its native population into mainstream America and what better way to do this than through the enforced education of the children? But the efficacy of this plan would require separation from their tribes, hence off-reservation boarding schools, and complete immersion in that rigidly structured way of life. Although boarding schools for native students were not unheard of before, in 1870 the federal government took bold steps to assume responsibility for the education of all Indian children and within thirty years, well over one hundred boarding schools existed, on the reservations and off. This was not elective education, but mandatory, with Indian agents complicit in the outright snatching of children from their shocked parents. (An Indian agent transporting Apache children to the Albuquerque Indian School just after it opened was asked if the parents liked sending their children to the government schools. "I hardly think they do, but it is not a matter of choice. The government has given orders that the children are to be educated whether the parents are willing or not."[3])

Once at the boarding school, the children were subject to complete indoctrination. But their roles weren't limited exclusively to that of obedient students. "They also served as hostages to ensure the peaceful behavior of Indian adults."[4] Indeed, parents soon learned that if they rebelled against the wishes of Washington, the Indian agencies were instructed to cut back all material support including food, clothing and money.[5] At school, the children were forced to abandon their languages and traditions under threat of severe punishment. Boys' hair was cut and they were often required to do military drills when they weren't laboring for a pittance in an extreme type of work-study program. Girls were made to wear the constricting garments of American womanhood and study the gentle arts of homemaking, or better put, domestic servant training. All students were given Anglo names. And in the Catholic mission schools, which received funding from the U.S. government, many hours of every day were devoted to strict religious studies. In all the schools, the students lived on a diet of alien and carelessly-prepared foods which, combined with overcrowding and filthy living conditions, made the institutions cesspools of disease, thus particularly dangerous to the Native child already vulnerable from the ravages of homesickness.

As with the infamous Bosque Redondo, eventually the federal government was forced to admit that many mistakes had been made in the planning and execution of the Indian education policy. After the turn of the century, attempts were made to improve conditions at the institutions but it took the Meriam Report of 1928 to evoke real change. Requested by then Secretary of the Interior Hubert Work, it covered the generally abysmal state of America's first inhabitants on their respective reservations but also addressed the horrors of the boarding schools— the inadequate diets, the overcrowding and disease, child labor that would have been illegal in many a state, poor teachers and draconian discipline. By this point, many schools were closing and reforms enacted at the existing ones provided for a markedly improved boarding school

The 1911 team from the Albuquerque Indian School. The photograph was sent to Superintendent Perry of the Indian School on November 24 of that year by one of the young athletes pictured. The sender, named Leo, referred to himself and the others as a "mad looking bunch," after winning a game against another government boarding school (courtesy National Archives and Records Administration, Rocky Mountain Region. The image is from RG 75 Records of the Bureau of Indian Affairs, Pueblo Entry 29, Albuquerque Indian School, General Correspondence, 1917–1936, Box 38).

experience for some students although the legacy of the pre–Meriam Report boarding schools is predominantly negative.

If there was a positive element to life at the boarding schools, it was athletics which were taken very seriously. "All of the schools encouraged boys to play sports, and at one time the Indian schools had some of the best college teams in the nation."[6] Captain Richard Henry Pratt, founder of the Carlisle School in Pennsylvania and coiner of the infamous phrase "Kill the Indian and save the man," was a true believer in sports, particularly football, for assimilation. He thought that a disciplined and successful team of Indian athletes might eventually compete against white athletes, a sound first step toward blending into the American way of life.

> Pratt also believed that football was a powerful tool for acculturating Indians to the American value system. From football Indians would learn the value of precision, teamwork, order, discipline, obedience, efficiency, and how all these interconnected in the business of "winning."[7]

This philosophy was a boon to white America in that it provided some of the finest athletes of the era. Jim Thorpe (Fox and Sac) attended both the Carlisle School and the Haskell Institute in Lawrence, Kansas. Another alumnus of Carlisle was baseball Hall of Famer Albert Bender (Ojibwe), Connie Mack's "money pitcher." Pittsburgh Pirate right-hander Moses Yellow Horse (Pawnee) was a graduate of Chilocco, located on the Oklahoma/Kansas border and is considered by many to be the first full-blooded Native American to play professional baseball. In 1907, the *New York Times* praised the skills of the Indian athlete, especially as a football player: "Stolid and determined, rugged and powerful, fleet and apparently untiring, he appeared to be the ideal physical athlete to make the best of the great game. The essentials he lacked he has in a measure made up for by his keen cunning."[8] As for baseball, it was felt that the boarding school experience had done nothing but help the Native athlete.

> Baseball enthusiasts will remember the advent of Sockalexis, the Indian outfielder of Patsy Tebeau's great Cleveland team, and the furor he created. Since his day the Indian has entered the professional baseball ranks, backed by a schooling that has made him a power. There are few better pitchers in the game to-day than the great Bender of the once champion Athletics, and Jude of Cleveland, Le Roy of the Highlanders, Roy of Philadelphia, and Nephew of Detroit are others who have distinctly made good, while there have been many minor leaguers who have ranked well.[9]

New Mexico had its own off-reservation boarding schools including the Albuquerque Indian School which opened in 1884, St. Catherine's Indian School, a mission school opened by the recently-canonized Katharine Drexel and her Sisters of the Blessed Sacrament in 1887, and the Santa Fe Indian School, established in 1890. Having absorbed the Albuquerque school in the 1970s, the Santa Fe Indian School is still thriving, now under the jurisdiction of the nineteen Pueblos of New Mexico. Its sprawling campus is situated a stone's throw from downtown on the city's main drag, Cerrillos Road. It proudly calls itself the "home of the Braves," the moniker of its successful sports teams.

Once New Mexico's Indian schools opened, it took very little time for baseball to establish itself as a highly popular game and there was rarely an event of any significance that wasn't highlighted by a tilt. In 1890, a wedding was held for two students of the Mescalero reservation boarding school. It was the Fourth of July, and the nuptials were almost overshadowed by a baseball game, patriotic flag-waving and the baptism into the Catholic faith of Geronimo's wife, who allegedly requested it.[10]

While Catholic mission schools like St. Catherine's were more inclined to rigorous religious study than sports, the Albuquerque and Santa Fe Indian schools each had competitive baseball teams from the turn of the century onward. So singular were some of the Native pitchers that it was not unheard of for one to hire out as a ringer for other teams. The coal camp team of Swastika in northern New Mexico at least once relied on one of the Albuquerque school's players, an ace hurler named Oliver, for an important game.[11] In addition, the number of Native American players from tribes across the country, employed as ringers by coal camp and municipal teams throughout New Mexico in the first four decades of the twentieth century, is unexpectedly large (a Haskell graduate of unknown tribal affiliation pitched for Las

Cruces against El Paso in 1906,[12] the Cherokee Smith brothers and pitcher Lockhart were stars of the 1911 season, Jones of the visiting 1911 Amarillo team was Choctaw, and Emmett Bowles and Marcell Littlehorse, both Potawatomie, played in the Central New Mexico League). This suggests the possibility of an efficient "ringer's" grapevine running through the government schools nationwide.

Like school baseball teams everywhere, the student players of the territory's institutions of education had an early and abbreviated season. By mid–April, they were well into their schedules. In the Duke City, for the varsity clubs of the local colleges, the Menaul School or any local high school teams, it was a matter of completing a required number of games before being released to the joys of summer. For the players of the Albuquerque Indian School, however, one of the best of the territory's boarding school teams, it meant playing as fast and as hard as they could before heading for the beet and melon fields of southern Colorado, where they were sent to work during the summer months.

The *Albuquerque Journal*'s engaging sportswriter of 1911 openly admired the local Indian School team, and never lost an opportunity to point out what a quality aggregation it was. In April of that year, he told the entire embarrassing tale of a recent 24–4 rout of one young club with the headline "INDIANS DEFEAT BOY SCOUT TEAM BY A REALLY CRUEL SCORE."[13] He also took great delight in a meeting between the college varsity team and those same Native Americans. The game was slightly delayed as the Indian School scrambled for a pitcher. Their usual starter had been given leave to visit ailing parents at a nearby reservation and hadn't shown up by game time.

> The wait however was short, for in a little while Platero showed up on horseback, having ridden from his residence since 5 in the morning. Only taking time to get into his baseball togs, without a bite to eat from breakfast time, he went into the game and pitching in great form, he struck out ten of the batters who faced him…. While his support at times was ragged, he deserved by his very nerve to win his game.[14]

By the end of May, the Albuquerque Indian School team hadn't lost a game and it was announced that they would take on Dan Padilla's Albuquerque Grays on the upcoming Decoration Day. Padilla and the Indian School Superintendent, Mr. Perry, had gone to great lengths to arrange the tilt, having had to obtain permission from the local Indian labor agent to delay the boys' departure for their summer in the fields. Obviously delighted by the prospect of the match, the sportswriter encouraged all Duke City baseball fans to turn out. He described the Indian club, giving its pitcher the highest praise an Albuquerque baseball writer could, by favorably comparing the hurler to a certain local legend. "The team plays elegant, fast ball, being especially good on fielding, while the pitching of Platero is almost as good as the article put up by the author of the 'green snake,' Rube Weeks."[15] When Memorial Day arrived, attendance was poor for what the sportswriter later called "the fastest and most satisfying game of baseball played on Traction Park grounds during this season."[16] While the Grays won the game, 4–2, they did it by the skin of their teeth:

> In getting the larger end of the game the Grays had to play better ball than they have yet shown, while the Indian School players covered themselves in glory.... The Indian infield was the most effective ever seen here, their system of signaling being simple and accurate, and that it was deadly the fact that six men died by it well shows.... All during the game the smack of the bat on the ball resounded over the grounds, but to no avail. Every time the ball fell there was an Indian to get it.

After their defeat, the young Native Americans boarded a train for the hard labor of Colorado. It would be another year before they'd again don the uniforms of the Albuquerque Indian School. As for the Grays, they'd been rattled by the boarding school boys who were now knee-deep in beets. Immediately after that squeaker, the team started meeting every day and working harder than it ever had "...practicing with the willow, getting down under flies, picking up grounders, and learning to hit 'em where they ain't."[17] It seemed to take a team of schoolboys to goad the Grays into taking their practice seriously.

Happily, by that time, New Mexico's Native American teams were no longer strictly limited to those at the schools. Village teams were beginning to form, particularly in the Pueblos that surrounded the Duke City. The Pueblos certainly didn't find America's pastime too foreign a concept. After all, they had traditionally played shinny (comparable to lacrosse) as a celebratory end to the annual rite of cleaning their irrigation ditches, the teams being divided according to clan.[18] With their close proximity to the metropolitan area, the southern Pueblos began competing with local sandlot and semipro teams. One was the standard bearer, fielding strong teams early and throughout the twentieth century. A headline and subhead from a 1911 *Albuquerque Journal* aptly begins the history.

HANG INDIAN SIGN ON LOS LUNAS
This Is No Joke; Isleta Team Wallops Alfalfa
Aggregation by Terrific Score of 24 to 4

Yes, the Isleta team was already a force and its John McGraw was Pablo Abeita, who when asked about the carnage his team had wrought blithely pronounced himself "well pleased with the showing." Playing that day was another important name in Isleta baseball history: "John Jojola, the Albuquerque Indian whirlwind, made two homeruns and carried off the fielding honors by making a sensational one-handed catch over second base."[19] The names Abeita and Jojola — although not all who bear the names are related — are to this day synonymous with baseball at Isleta.

In the July 3, 1929, edition of the *Albuquerque Journal*, there was an ad for a dance to be held at Isleta Pueblo. Not just your average terpsichorean get-together this; no, it would feature a three-piece orchestra and was a fundraiser for the Isleta baseball club. Although Isleta baseball had begun decades earlier, it wasn't until the 1930s that it began to reach its prime, still under the nurturing hands of the Abeitas and Jojolas. The Pueblo began the decade as an eager sandlot team, taking on opponents in the Albuquerque metro area like the San Jose Sluggers, the Las Lomas Tigers and the Albuquerque Indian School Employees (surely familiar faces to the young players, most of whom had attended the school). One of the strongest early batteries was Mariano Jojola on the mound and a relative, Sam Jojola, also a solid hitter, behind the plate. Later, the pitching staff was greatly enhanced with the addition of Joe M. Abeita, who is still respectfully referred to, years after his decease, as Joe the Umpire. Born in 1905, Joe played at St. Catherine's Indian School, and later for Winslow, Arizona, where he developed a reputation for a red-hot fastball. By the time he took the reins of the Isleta team around 1934, his arm was seasoned and he had the control of a veteran. In 1935, he threw a 13-inning no-hitter against Albuquerque's Armijo Yanks, one of the area's dominant teams.[20]

A team from Isleta Pueblo around 1900. Isleta was perhaps the first Pueblo to field competitive baseball teams, setting the stage for Native American participation in the sport locally. Jimmy Abeita says, "Isleta members felt they were born to play baseball and also felt like they were more skilled at it than any other Pueblo." Standing, left to right, are Felipe Padilla, Domingo Jojola, Manager Pablo Abeita, Paul Shattuck, Frank Anzara. Seated are Tony Abeita, Lazaro Abeita (Jimmy's uncle), John T. Jojola, Marcelino Abeita and Juan Rey Abeita (courtesy Jimmy Abeita).

In 1935 the first annual Indian tournament was also played at Laguna Pueblo, "believed to be the first All-Indian baseball tournament in the United States,"[21] an event that was proudly continued for several decades. Laguna had surfaced in the regional baseball world at roughly the same time as Isleta although it took longer to build up a comparable playing reputation. What Laguna did was to make itself an invaluable focal point for Native American baseball by beginning the tradition of hosting the yearly tournament during the September celebration of its patron saint, San Jose. Along with traditional dances and feasting, the celebrations at the Pueblo included the finest Native teams from New Mexico and Arizona duking it out for the crown. While it began humbly, with just three teams—Isleta, Laguna and a team from Winslow, Arizona—it would grow into an enormous Southwestern competition, eventually pulling in Native American teams from as far as California.

In 1936, Joe M. Abeita was able to focus exclusively on the mound when he turned over the managership of the Isleta sandlot team to another Abeita, although unrelated. A firebrand by nature, Buster Abeita would leave his mark, an indelible one, in New Mexico baseball, primarily by building a crack all–Indian team and getting it into an established and highly respected regional semipro league. Although it seems that Buster took over the sandlot Braves mid-season, he was able to steer them to their second All-Indian championship in as many years that September when they defeated the host team at Laguna.[22] The next season of sandlot ball was another winning one, with Isleta taking 14 out of 19 scheduled games, the indefatigable Buster Abeita even taking the field to successfully pinch-hit in the sixth inning of one game with the bases loaded.[23]

When the 1938 season opened, substantial changes had been made to regional Indian baseball. The players of the Isleta sandlot team were fundamentally the same, with Sam Jojola and Joe M. Abeita still masterful, the latter striking out 11 and giving up only 7 hits in the season opener against Laguna. But Sam was now the man in charge of the team because Buster Abeita had resigned to form a new semipro team: the Albuquerque Indian All-Stars.

> Composed of representatives of 11 tribes, the all-star team added two new men this week, Abeita said. Marcell Littlehouse [sic] ... is the fifth man on Abeita's hurling staff. Littlehorse is a Potawatomie Indian, who was an athlete at Haskell Institute. Nelson Hendrix, a Cherokee, who also attended Haskell, has been signed to play....[24]

Besides a Native American team being given an unusually large amount of press coverage, the most riveting aspect of the story was Buster's announcement that the Indian All-Stars might be joining the Central New Mexico League during the second half of the season. True to his word, in early July, Buster Abeita's Indian All-Stars replaced the Albuquerque Pirates in a league composed of some of the best athletes in the state at that time, including the league-leading Madrid Miners (with Pop Stowers and famous Potawatomie pitcher Emmett Bowles) and teams from Santa Fe, Albuquerque, Las Vegas and Mountainair. In the All-Stars debut effort, infielder Lallo Abeita and left fielder Nevins Eckerman each hit over .500.[25] Unfortunately, just as the second half of the season began, Marcell Littlehorse was poached by the Albuquerque Cardinals of the Class D Arizona-Texas League. For a few weeks, the All-Stars found themselves roughed up by the big dogs but got a boost when the Cardinals released Littlehorse and he returned to the bosom of his former team.[26] By the end of July, Buster's pitching brother Andy was leading the team in batting at .438.[27] At the end of August, the All-Stars were battling Santa Fe for second place in the league, behind the fearsome Madrid Miners in first.

Although they didn't win the second-half title, no one could quibble with the All-Stars debut in the league. Buster Abeita capped off his first season managing the semipro club by taking the reins of the Isleta Braves, still the Pueblo's sandlot team, for the annual Laguna tourney in September. Even with the notable absence of pitcher Joe M. Abeita, due to a broken rib received at the hands of the Socorro club, the Braves muscled their way to the trophy for the third consecutive year.[28]

March brought good news for Isleta baseball fans as the Albuquerque Indian All-Stars had been cordially invited back to the Central New Mexico League and were to begin practice immediately. Buster had gotten an early start in search of players, including beating the bushes of the federal Indian schools, as always a rich source.

> The local team will be composed of last year's lineup, plus three new men. Leroy Allman, southpaw first baseman for Phoenix, will sign, along with Lee Anderson of Chillocco [sic], and Lee Gustbrach of Haskell. The Indians manager has invited all local Indian boys to appear at the field for a tryout Saturday.[29]

The true details lost to history, it is puzzling to consider where Buster was netting all these fine Indian athletes. Was it indeed a grapevine that ran throughout the government boarding schools across the country? As for local talent, it is tempting to think that Buster Abeita was building his own farm system. After all, his Indian All-Stars practiced on the grounds of the Albuquerque Indian School, so he was there on a daily basis. The excellent young school players that he saw there would have been easy pickings to send to Joe M. Abeita and his Isleta sandlot team, the team that Buster piloted in the annual Laguna tournament. After a season honing his skills in a municipal sandlot league, a talented young player might have been "called up" by Buster to the Albuquerque Indian All-Stars.

Whether or not Buster Abeita was Isleta Pueblo's answer to Branch Ricky, he started the '39 season with a team "bolstered this year by players from all over the country."[30] This year he would be benefiting from the state's all-around college athletes, as he brought aboard, among others, two University of New Mexico star freshmen (and regional ringers), George Gustovich and Ray Tanner, the latter having been offered a contract with the St. Louis Browns when he graduated from Albuquerque High School.[31] As fine as the college athletes might be at baseball, Buster had certainly adulterated his pool of Native American talent with some decidedly Anglo players. One *Albuquerque Journal* sportswriter referred to the team as "the heterogeneous lineup of baseball players who go under the moniker of 'Indian All-Stars.'"[32] For the season opener, Buster chose the reliable Marcell Littlehorse to toe the rubber; Littlehorse fanned 11 Tererro Miners and allowed only 5 hits for a 13–3 victory.[33] But even with all of the additional muscle, the season ended badly for Buster, the Indian All-Stars claiming ownership of the cellar.

Meanwhile in sandlot territory, a team from Laguna Pueblo joined an

11. Making the Ball Sing 183

Albuquerque sandlot loop in 1939 and made a bold run for it, losing the pennant by a hair's breadth. The driving force behind the excellent maiden showing was Abel Paisano, who would not only urge his amateur team onward but would take over the illustrious annual All-Indian Tournament at his Pueblo. With their shared borders, Isleta and Laguna were natural rivals in general and particularly for the tournament trophy. Permanent possession of the cup was awarded to a team that won two years in a row. Having won in 1937 and '38, Buster Abeita and the Isleta players owned theirs. Paisano and the young Laguna team wanted one of their own, and after a two-day slog in the '39 tournament, they got it. It must have been particularly galling for Buster to see the Laguna team win, particularly as its victory came on the heels of his dreadful season.

Sadly, for Buster Abeita and the Albuquerque Indian All-Stars, the Central New Mexico League folded after the '39 season. While Joe M. Abeita, Sam Jojola and a new generation of Isleta players continued to thrive, Buster's role in local baseball diminished. But Abel Paisano's profile was increasing and his Laguna teams were still running neck-and-neck with their Isleta competitors when the war clouds that had been building moved inexorably over two oceans toward the United States.

* * *

In April 1940, the sandlot Isleta team joined an amateur circuit of the greater Albuquerque area—the Coronado League—and the homeboys welcomed some of the orphans from Buster Abeita's All-Stars, like Andy Abeita, Buster's brother and hurling ace. The Laguna Indians entered the same league with Abel Paisano as manager. The loop with its diverse teams—Hispano, Anglo and Native American—had become a mainstay of local Sunday entertainment, even drawing some crowds away from the local Organized Baseball clubs.[34] Isleta and Laguna fared well for themselves that year, both making it to the semifinals, where dancers from the latter performed the haunting Eagle Dance before a game played against the other.[35] Laguna went on to win the All-Indian tournament in September, for the second year in a row, thereby taking permanent possession of the coveted trophy.[36] The next year, the Santa Fe Indian Council team won the trophy in front of a crowd of over 2,000 who had journeyed to Laguna from the far reaches to watch the event. That tourney drew a more diverse group of teams including ones from Hopi and Zuni, Santa Clara and San Juan from the Eight Northern Pueblos, the Santa Fe Indian School and even an Indian jewelry store, Maisel's, on Route 66.[37]

In 1942, there is very little mention of either Isleta or Laguna Pueblos and baseball. Joe M. Abeita pitched for the San Jose Victory Club of the Rio Grande Semipro League, until the team folded in July because of loss of men. Of course sandlot leagues, like their professional counterparts, were also losing teams at a brisk clip, the "Tigers" and "Sluggers" of past years suddenly replaced with names like the Ninth Materiel Squadron Ramblers or the Third Air Base. Those teams that survived had a decidedly military aura.

The New Mexico Pueblos seemed to have given up baseball for a United Pueblos Agency scrap metal drive that collected over 50,000 pounds; Laguna, in a separate drive, collected over 4,000. In June, the Laguna Pueblo Council voted to abstain from tribal participation in the New Mexico state fair. One of the councilmen was Abel Paisano, who announced that Pueblo officials felt that the money used transporting the people, livestock and produce of Laguna to Albuquerque would be better spent on war bonds.[38] This was in addition to the $3,000 of community money the tribe had spent on war bonds three months earlier.[39] Among Native Americans, this kind of patriotic sacrifice was the rule, not the exception. Author Kenneth Townsend writes:

> In the weeks and months following Pearl Harbor, American Indians increasingly melded into the war effort. The enlistment of Indian men into the nation's armed services skyrocketed. Reservations marshaled their resources and offered their lands for the military's wartime use. Tribes freely directed their appropriations to war agencies, and Indians purchased millions of dollars in defense bonds. Communities also set aside for the duration all outstanding claims against the federal government. Such direct, tangible contributions to the war effort aided the United States materially and financially.[40]

As for enlistment, he says, within the first three months of conscription, more than 4,500 Navajos registered, along with most of the Puebloans and Apaches.[41] There were no more passionate patriots than these nations, the original sons and daughters of New Mexico and Arizona. This is all the more compelling in light of the fact that, even though all Native Americans were officially recognized as American citizens in 1924, those in New Mexico would be denied the right to vote until 1948. The state had manufactured a device — unconstitutional but very effective — to disenfranchise its Indian population. It said that reservation residents could be denied the vote because of the tax-free status of their land, utterly disregarding the fact that they paid taxes on virtually everything else. It took a World War II veteran of the Marine Corps, an Isleta Indian named Miguel Trujillo, to challenge this in federal court in 1948 and win, giving a voice to all the indigenous New Mexicans who paid in blood and treasure.

* * *

Like all the young men who had survived the war, the Native American baseball players of New Mexico returned to joyfully begin playing the beloved game. Teams from Isleta and Laguna Pueblos returned to the metropolitan amateur and semipro leagues of Albuquerque. The All-Indian Tournament at Laguna became bigger, more popular — and more competitive — than ever. It had started as a friendly end-of-season celebration, a by-product of the September 19 feast day. Now, it carried far more weight and invited sometimes rancorous disputes between teams. A 1947 feud developed when Andy Abeita and his 1946 champion Isleta team claimed that they had been excluded from the 1947 tourney; instead, the Isleta B team (called, appropriately, the Bees), had been invited to defend last season's crown, a charge denied by the sponsor. Abeita refused to return the trophy to the tournament saying that, "the trophy and champions of last year's tournament are inseparable, according to good sportsmanship." At the same time, he plead for a "better spirit" and formal rules among the Indian teams so that "mistake[s] such as substituting one team to defend the championship title of another," could be avoided.[42] By the next year, many more clubs from the northern Pueblos and Navajo country were involved, lending color and competitiveness to the gathering.

The early 1950s brought the final golden years of semipro and minor league baseball across the country. In Albuquerque, the City-County semipro league was established and many teams, including the nearby Pueblos, found enduring homes in it. These players were the babies of the late Depression; most too young to have served in World War II but some just old enough to be sent to Korea. It was a generation hovering between the last years at the Indian schools and release into the larger world.

One of those former players is Jimmy Abeita (no relation to Buster), who left Isleta as a young man for a professional life that took him around the world and then home again. These days, he can be found golfing (conveniently, Isleta has a 27-hole course), gardening, painting local landscapes or attempting to master a BlackBerry. He and his wife Debbie are loyal followers of the Lobos, the University of New Mexico's basketball team. In e-mails, telephone calls and visits, Jimmy talks about baseball and what it has meant to Isleta Pueblo for decades.

Jimmy's baseball years began as a student at the Albuquerque Indian School, an experience that he adamantly defends as a positive one. He talks about a recent alumni reunion and says, "All of us expressed an appreciation of our teachers and the educational system. We all talked about what a great period of time that was for us at the boarding school. It was nothing like the accounts that you've probably read about boarding schools throughout the country. There were isolated experiences—I could tell you about of some negative experiences in my life—but overall, we all said that, if we could do it over again, we would." As it regards one of the most culturally destructive errors charged to the government schools, he is determined to set the record straight, at least according to his experience. "Despite what you hear, we were not prohibited from speaking our language. None of us—*none of us*—ever lost our Tiwa language or our Tewa language or Zuni, whatever—we spoke it. Now our teachers always tried very hard to make sure we learned English but we never lost our mother tongue. We came home and that's all we spoke, or at places on campus where we'd gather, that's what we spoke. If we knew our language before we went there, we never forgot it. We still speak it today—most of the time I speak Tiwa." Jimmy is a man of conviction and when the topic is of utmost importance, as is that of indigenous languages, he freely speaks his mind. "It's a way of continuing to blame some else rather than accept responsibility. Now, our elders are concerned that a lot of our children aren't learning the language. Well, take the responsibility to *teach them*. There's nothing wrong with speaking the Tiwa language at home. If parents aren't speaking it, the children aren't going to be very good at it."

Jimmy's description of his youth is enlightening. He addresses the phenomenon of the Indian school and the segregation of races, even in a place like New Mexico, oft-touted for its multi-cultural character. "We lived in a very isolated world. We went from the reservation elementary school into the boarding school, isolated on a campus from the rest of the world. Our interaction with the non–Indian community was in sports— that was it. I never entered a white person's house until I was out of high school. I saw the whole world from the edge of the campus." Even off the campus, this separate-ness was a way of life. "Of course, I'd go to town [Albuquerque] shopping with my mom but predominantly in the Hispanic community so we had very little contact, except for our teachers, with the white world. And I'm talking about just recently— not back in the early 1900s."

Of the faculty at the Albuquerque Indian School, Jimmy's favorite was Coach Ken Freberg, who made a large and lasting impression on him. "He was a life mentor. He taught us values," says Jimmy. "In my mind, nobody can compare. But he pushed. He pushed hard enough to get the best out of you. He was a friend, meaning that, even when you weren't playing for him, he never failed to recognize you, never failed to acknowledge you— on campus, anywhere. He made every attempt to know just a little bit more which was difficult because most of us didn't talk about our families. Most of the time, they didn't know who our families were." One of Freberg's first tasks was to convince the Pueblo boys, who were small in stature, that they could be contenders in any sport. "Coach Freberg taught us that, despite our size (or lack of size), that we could win. And that's exactly what we did. When you talk about basketball players that are probably 5'5"— and if you look at the Albuquerque Indian School basketball winning record— you see how well-coached we were, how he used the skills we had— nothing but speed and shooting, that was it — but he utilized those." Jimmy maintains that he wasn't very athletic. "Coach Freberg told me maybe I should go out for sports. I went out for track and didn't have *anything* I could contribute," he laughs. "He sug-

Jimmy Abeita represented Isleta on high school and semi-pro teams (Belinda Winn).

gested — he didn't tell me I didn't have it — but just kind of suggested I ought to consider baseball." Jimmy started in the outfield. "I didn't have the arm. Couldn't throw to home. Third base and shortstop were the same way. I had the instinct, I had the glove, I just didn't have the arm." He eventually landed at second base, a position which suited him far better. "I didn't have natural ability but what I found out was that I had the instinct which is the reason I loved playing baseball. Because I could actually anticipate. I remember being able to determine approximately where the ball was going to be by where the pitch was and watching the batter. That's the instinct I had." Second base worked well for a kid without a laser of a throwing arm. "At second base, you're going to first with it ninety percent of the time and you're actually able to flip the ball underhand rather than throw overhand. I covered my territory."

On a bright and windy spring afternoon, there is a gathering of old friends at Jimmy and Debbie's house at Isleta. They are experts on the topic of local Indian baseball in the '50s and '60s. Former players and one of their greatest fans, they are all roughly the same age and all linked by ties of blood, clan, marriage, teams, Indian school memories or simply those of enduring friendship. They are Emil Jojola (the son of the legendary Sam Jojola) from Isleta and Al and Jean Riley Green who are from Laguna. Jimmy, Jean and Emil were classmates at the Albuquerque Indian School. The latter two are seated side-by-side on the sofa, darting joyful, curious looks at each other, as neither has seen the other since school days. Al attended St. Catherine's Indian School in Santa Fe. "It was a small school, run by the Sisters of the Blessed Sacrament. I always thought the nuns were kind of mean but there were a few that I liked," he says. His story of Native language matches Jimmy's; he says that the sisters never made an issue of the students speaking their first language. He chuckles gently as he recalls his general unhappiness at the school and his one great escape. "I ran away one time and my parents brought me back the same day." Most of Al's brothers played baseball, as did his father at the Albuquerque Indian School.

Jimmy describes their Albuquerque Indian School days. "There was tribalism — Navajos, Lagunas, Zunis, Isletas. The Isletas and Apaches were *the worst of the bunch*. But the Isletas were basically like a wolf pack — don't touch one because the rest of the pack will come after you." And the boys of Isleta and Laguna dominated the Albuquerque Indian School teams of the '50s and '60s. Jimmy recalls an immense advantage the Isleta boys had in high school, one that they put to especially good use in the semipros. "We gave our signals in the Tiwa language. We basically didn't have to use hand signals. We'd call out certain signals or our players would get the signals from the coach and yell them out in Tiwa." Emil laughs aloud at the memory. They then tell of the sometimes testy relations, which often led to fights, between the various students at the Albuquerque Indian School. One of the most contentious rivalries would carry over, as it had since the 1930s, into the wilder world of semipro ball, and that was the one between Laguna and Isleta.

At its peak, that rivalry was represented by men like Buster Abeita of Isleta and Abel Paisano of Laguna and some of the important players those men attracted. Emil remembers Buster fairly well although he was just a lad in the elder man's baseball days. "Oh he was very, very friendly," Emil maintains. "He knew a lot of people in Albuquerque, outside the reservation. He bought the uniforms and equipment for the teams back in those years." And where did he find all of his Native American ringers? Emil is intrigued by these questions and responds quickly, "That was going to be my question too. How was it that Buster knew about the people he recruited? How did he get the information about these pitchers? Why did they come here?" And did Buster really create a farm system for the Albuquerque Indian All-Stars back in the '30s? Emil is ready to believe that he might have. "Because Buster was all out for baseball and Paisano was the same way. They were really competitive."

Naturally, when talking about the old days, Emil's father Sam Jojola's name is one of the first mentioned. Sam not only made a name for himself behind the plate, but he devoted many years after that to coaching Isleta youth. "He bought the balls and bats—we didn't have any sponsors. We had old uniforms that somebody would give us and he'd go and gather them. When we'd travel to other Pueblos, he'd pay for our lunches and soda pop and gas. Most of the kids that he took care of, either the parents were separated or the father was unemployed—kids that didn't have a chance."

Al and Jean recall something of a Laguna secret weapon on the mound from times past—a priest. "I remember when I was a little kid, my mom and dad used to go to the games. At that time they were called Merchants," Al says. "Even a priest played for them, a priest by the name of Fr. Kenneth. And he was a good player." Jean nods in agreement. Al continues, "He was the pastor for all of Laguna so he had seven masses to do on Sunday." Fr. Kenneth, they explain, was so devoted to Laguna Pueblo that he asked to be buried there in traditional Laguna fashion, a request that the people gladly granted.

The friends begin to talk about their own playing days and home games, where they received thunderous support from their respective communities. The ambition of Abel Paisano and the Laguna teams had helped build a singular ball

Emil Jojola tried out as pitcher for the Pittsburgh Pirates in Albuquerque and spent a year at Haskell (Belinda Winn).

field, one with which few other teams could compete. The quality of the park was only enhanced when uranium brought more disposable income to the Pueblo; it boasted bleachers (in 1961, a Laguna recreational official suggested that it was not uncommon for a doubleheader to draw 2,000 to 3,000 fans[43]), chain-link fencing, a public address system and booth and a concession stand. At Isleta, the situation was slightly different. Jimmy describes it. "Our field was dirt which we dragged before every game in an attempt to level it. We also had to clear the field of rocks and pebbles. The left-field fence was barbed wire, there was no center field fence, and the elementary school chain link was the right-field fence. The backstop was chicken wire nailed to wood poles. If you were lucky enough to own a vehicle, you watched the game from the comfort of the back of a pickup truck under a makeshift tarp or umbrellas." In addition to their spectacular field, the uranium-era Laguna teams were always well-outfitted in fine uniforms. The Isleta teams, says Jimmy, had to make do. "We always had uniforms albeit we begged, borrowed and maybe even 'midnight requisitioned' them. I do recall that they were pretty beat up with endless miles of stitches and colorful patches."

Al remarks on the amount of horn-blowing that filled that air at the games and Jimmy adds that a good amount of noise also came from the women fans. "They made up probably fifty percent of the crowd and could be more boisterous than their male counterparts. They could be nasty to opposing players, not mincing words or names. But, even egged on by their male companions, they mostly stayed with name-calling." While she doesn't mention name-calling, Jean, who was a gifted softball player herself, describes her life as a fan. "My father didn't play but he loved to watch baseball. He and I would go hand-in-hand down the dirt road to the baseball field. I was a happy little child, going to the game with my father. It was a family affair. The whole community went and the bleachers were always full." In her teen years, it took on added significance. "The most important thing in my life at that moment was baseball. It was exciting, an emotional high. I like to believe that it was just as exciting for the majority of people at Laguna." In fact, she and Al met because of the game. "It was after a game —" she begins and Al laughs, "It was after I hit a home run!" She smiles at him and continues, "I was thirteen years old. He was leaning up against a fence post and I told my girlfriend that that was the man I was going to marry."

Of all of that generation's kids playing at the Indian School in Albuquerque, Emil Jojola was one of the greats. He excelled in all sports, including basketball, track and field, and could handle any position on the baseball diamond. For the most part, however, he pitched. He could also hit, leading the Duke City high school baseball field in 1956 with .571 batting average.[44] (Jean attests to his talent saying, "When I was in boarding school, this guy was the best athlete there, one of many who were very good athletes.") Now, at 71, Emil still carries himself like an athlete — he moves around a room with a natural fluidity and grace. He credits his lifelong love of and skill at baseball to growing up as Sam Jojola's son. "We just sort of took after him and wanted to be like him," he says of himself and his passel of brothers, most of whom ended up pitching (Jimmy says that his best recollections of Pueblo baseball are "the hot Sunday afternoons watching the Jojola brothers play"). Emil says, "I don't actually remember anybody really teaching me or coaching me about my pitching. I just sort of picked it up on my own, just looked at the players and their stances and remembered where they had hit before. But you know what I did I my younger days? I'd go out to the dump and set up bottles on the wall and just throw rocks at them. Then, in the ditches, I'd throw bottles into the water and try to break them. I'd just chase them down until I got them. I did that all the time." When asked about his favorite pitch, he says, "I had two pitches that I really liked to throw, a slider and what they call a knuckleball only it was more like a forkball." He demonstrates. "I'd put it between my two fingers and it would *float* in there and you wouldn't know which way it was going to go. Hardly anybody in this area pitched that, so I really liked to use it because everyone was used to fastballs and curves and I'd sneak that one in. A few guys told me, 'Boy, it took forever for that ball to get to the plate!'" He chuckles, "I used to have fun with that pitch." And about a hitting prowess that kept him well over the .400 mark throughout high school, he says that, as a child, when he didn't have a bat to practice with as a kid, he'd use a two-by-four. "I guess it was my two-by-four and my instinct with a bat."

In his youth, Emil tried out for the Pittsburgh Pirates in Albuquerque. "I had pitched the night before and my arm was sore. So I tried out for shortstop. They selected a few of us for a second tryout at Santa Fe but I didn't have a ride there," he shrugs. He spent one year at Haskell, where he played on that storied school's team. "I was the smallest pitcher there 'cause you know those other Indians from the Dakotas and all are really big and were kind of laughing at me. So I didn't pitch until the fourth game. We had been losing all the games but we won that one. I won all the games for Haskell that year except the last one. We were playing Forbes Air Base and there were scouts for the Kansas City Athletics and that's the only game I lost. They interviewed me after the game and said they were going to come back next year to see me pitch but by then I had gone to San Francisco for college." This story could shake the most jaded to their toes—to come so close and lose it so easily. When asked if he had been heartbroken by the lost opportunities, Emil looks rather surprised. "No, I wasn't heartbroken," he says. "I never focused on playing major league baseball. I just didn't think about it—we didn't at that time. I guess we weren't thinking like white folks think. We just thought about having a good time. I just wanted to play."

At this point, Jimmy makes an interesting observation. "I think we were aware of some physical limitations. Even in Emil's case, he wasn't the biggest guy even among some of the Natives at Haskell. I think we understood that. For us, baseball was nothing more than the moment—whatever happens. In

Native American philosophy, in Pueblo philosophy, *right now* is more important than the future. In Tiwa we basically say, 'This—*this*—is it. Tomorrow isn't as important as right now.'"

Emil nods and continues. "Our folks, going way back, never thought of us, their children, getting into professional sports. The way that white people think and Indians think is two different things. The moment a little white kid starts playing baseball, the parents are thinking, 'Professional. Scholarships.' Our parents never thought, 'My kid is going to be a professional baseball player. One day he's gonna bring in some money.' I never thought of my accomplishments, never kept records. I just played to play." He is quiet for a moment, his face a study in contemplation. And then, as though suddenly the weight of missed opportunities has landed squarely on him, he says, "But if we had had parents that pushed us to a higher level, we could have accomplished something. Now I tell my Little Leaguers, 'Don't just play to play, because other people are out there playing for the future.'"

A youthful Emil Jojola leans against his friend Jimmy Abeita's 1954 Mercury Sun Valley. Emil was a natural athlete, excelling in a variety of sports throughout his days at the Albuquerque Indian School and later at Haskell (courtesy Emil Jojola).

As for Al, he regards the topic with more equanimity. When asked if he hadn't dreamt of a major league career as a kid, he smiles sweetly and says, "No, not particularly. For one thing, I wasn't good enough." He played first base for a team called the Warriors, from the Laguna village of Paguate. "Of course I played that position in high school and it just carried on when we started the team at Paguate. There's a lot of action at first base and I liked the activity." As for batting, he says, "I wasn't an excellent hitter but I got on base most of the time." The Paguate Warriors belonged to the same Greater Albuquerque City-County League as many of the other Laguna teams, plus all the Isleta clubs. When they weren't dueling with another Duke City team, the Warriors could count on some stiff competition closer to home. "Of course the Laguna Braves were on top all the time. We never beat them but we got close," Al says. "That was the main thing that was available for us to do. It was a sport that everybody enjoyed and knew about. I think it was the focus of the population that kept it going strong."

The league that all the Isleta and Laguna teams belonged to was the largest and most diverse league in Albuquerque history. From brick makers to car dealerships to a prison team, it played inexhaustibly for years. "I have no idea why the Albuquerque league called itself 'semipro' although we liked to boast that we were one notch better than sandlot," says Jimmy. "There were no attendance fees although a hat was passed to help defray ball-field rental expenses and, later on, lights." Was there ever any kind of monetary reward given to fine players or teams? He says, "The only thing we ever got was a picnic lunch or a beer after the game. We probably consumed our fair share of beer." Eventually, another purely Indian team joined the league, the Albuquerque Braves. Jimmy describes the team as a mix of many different Pueblos and other tribes. "Albuquerque had a great advantage since they could recruit the best of the metro Indian players while we limited ourselves to the best of the Pueblo players." He played for the Braves for one season and still golfs with a few of them.

During these years, Isleta developed a reputation for being the orneriest players around, but limited its bad behavior to other Native teams. "I recall many a fistfight occurring at those games. Isleta had a notorious reputation for fighting, all instigated by the young Pablo Abeita and his brother Richard. In fact, Isleta was once banned from the Laguna tournament for starting a fight," says Jimmy, who is not related to those two Abeita brothers. (In fact, they were the sons of Andy, nephews of Buster.) Emil concurs. "Oh yeah. There were a few brawlers. They weren't very good sports. Pablo, boy, he'd tackle people. Even if they were safe he'd knock them down." Al joins in, saying, "I remember one instance, during one of the tournaments, one of his own team members made some kind of mistake—couldn't hit or kept losing the ball—and he jumped the guy. They had to pull him off! It was a big to-do for a few minutes." Pablo was undoubtedly the impetus for one of the funnier memories shared by Emil and Jimmy, which the latter refers to as "the Mescalero Incident." It took place in the late 1950s at the Mescalero Apache reservation. It was July 4, the annual celebration of the tribe's maidens. As was tradition, there was a baseball tournament. "The fight began on the ball field," writes Jimmy in an e-mail, "and continued that night when respective members confronted each other at the bonfire celebration. We were able to regroup and consider a counterattack until someone informed us that the Mescaleros had guns. I recall us running down a dirt road away from the celebration grounds and bullets whizzing over our heads. Looking back now, I contend they did not intend to hit us (or they didn't know how short we were). After losing the Apaches in the dark, five or six of us took refuge in Pablo Abeita's car until daybreak, when we decided that a trip to Juarez was better than facing mad Apaches at the afternoon game. After realizing that one of our members was missing, and finding out he was in jail, we stopped in Mescalero on our way back from Juarez to bail him out. Needless to say, we never went back to Mescalero during the remainder of my playing days." Emil adds his own chapter to the saga. "On the way to Juarez, it started raining really hard and Pablo's windshield wipers were broken. We had strings tied to the wipers and had the window rolled down, with one guy on one side and one on the other, working those wipers." (The infamous Pablo Abeita has his own take on the Incident. "Yeah, we had a riot down there. That was my first year back form the service in '58. I don't know how it started but it was a heckuva brawl. We went to Juarez to get away because we heard that they were making gangs from Alamogordo, Carrizozo, and all those guys, getting ready to get us so we took off and came back the next day to play the game." This differs from what Jimmy and Emil said about hightailing it home without playing the second tilt. "Oh yeah, we went back and beat 'em. We really clobbered them." And, ending the story in a fashion that one quickly comes to associate with Pablo, he says, "They were probably good brawlers but they weren't a good baseball team so we just beat 'em, got our trophy and went home.")

Al Green played first base for the Paguate Warriors of the Greater Albuquerque City County league in the 1950s (Belinda Winn).

And while teams from one Pueblo could feud vociferously with one another (or with other non–Pueblo nations), the fiercest rivalry was still between Isleta and Laguna. Jimmy explains. "The intra-tribal rivalry was for boasting rights. Now the inter-tribal competition was intense and sometimes bloody. Isleta members felt they were born to play baseball and also felt like they were more skilled at it than any other Pueblo. But Laguna was equally good, if not better, in some years, which heated up the intensity, often leading to fights." While Jimmy sees it as occasional all-out warfare, Emil considers there to have been a good bit of humor to it. "They kind of argued. They'd say, 'you Isleta chile-eaters!' or 'you Laguna sheepherders.' It was all teasing-like. It wasn't serious. But every time we played one another we packed the stadium."

This intensity of feeling helped feed the anticipation of the annual Laguna All-Indian Tournament. Al says that the double elimination competition would start about a week before the feast day of September 19. "By the time the feast day came, then they'd play for the championship," he explains. Emil enjoyed every tournament he ever played there saying, "They were fun and high pressure because they had the top teams at Laguna, Jackpile and Anaconda, because they were sponsored by the uranium companies. They had the best players." Jimmy claims that playing in the Laguna tournament was like going to the World Series for the Indian teams. "It was awaited with such anticipation because it coincided with the feast which was always a reunion of sorts. It was festive. It might be a chance to see some of your schoolmates. But it was also a chance to renew the old rivalries. To win the tournament was the pinnacle of every baseball team's dreams. And it was an opportunity to be seen by very knowledgeable baseball fans. There was a team in almost every village at Laguna so you knew you were drawing all these people who knew their players, from the time they were little. They knew who their families were. The rivalry between Laguna and Isleta was so intense, I don't know if I ever felt a greater fan dislike that when we went to the tournament. There was nothing that those guys—Laguna, Mesita, Paguate—would rather do than beat Isleta."

In 1961, the locals were handed a much larger list of competitors. Since the early 1950s, while Al, Emil and Jimmy were still in high school, an All-Indian league had been playing to the north of Santa Fe. It featured teams from the Northern Pueblos of New Mexico (the Eight Northern Pueblos are those found to the north of Santa Fe, including Nambe, Picuris, Pojoaque, San Ildefonso, San Juan, Santa Clara, Taos and Tesuque), a few Pueblos to the south of the capital and, from time to time, a team representing the Jicarilla Apaches. At least one sportswriter had given the league some attention, even if his columns were infused with the condescending lingo of the day. Bill Bailey of the *Santa Fe New Mexican*, in his column "Inside Stuff," pronounced himself delighted with Native Americans taking up "paleface sports," and actually wagged a finger at the federal government for at least one of its outdated policies. "It's a shame that more Indians cannot attend the public schools instead of being segregated in this state. Some of the most brilliant students and athletes at Santa Fe High School are Indians."[45] And to prove that his interest in the league wasn't simply token attention given to local tribes, the *New Mexican* consistently covered affairs of the circuit, giving special coverage to the championships, which were held at the Santa Fe Indian School. In 1954, in fact, Bailey wrote a lengthy piece entitled "First Americans Experts at America's National Pastime," in which he extolled what he believed were Natives' natural gifts for the game.

> Like the Japanese, the Indians excel at fielding and base running, but the Redskins add batting skill to their game. Keen eyesight, powerful wrists and shoulders enable the Indians to whack a baseball with authority and for distance.... The ability to stay loose comes as naturally to the Indian ball players as breathing. Few of them ever tighten up at a critical moment and they move with an easy grace after grounders and flyballs in the field.[46]

11. Making the Ball Sing

Not content to stop with praise, however, Bailey went on to suggest that Native Americans were "natural schemers," which made them wily pitchers.

This league enjoyed a large and enthusiastic fan base, the championship games attracting crowds in the thousands. Like the Jojola and Abeita families of Isleta and the Rileys of Laguna, through the years each Pueblo seemed to be dominated by a family name — the Samuels of Pojoaque, the Vigils of Tesuque, the Arqueros of Cochiti. In 1961 it was announced by Sam Arquero, former coach at the Santa Fe Indian School, that a new All-Indian loop had been formed that would include all nineteen of New Mexico's Pueblos, with two divisions, northern and southern. The winner of the league championship would go on to the tournament at Laguna. Jimmy, who was picked for the southern division all-star team twice, says that most Pueblo players really preferred, over any other circuit, to represent their villages in the All-Indian League. And, he does a bit of crowing when talking about Isleta's dominance of its division. "We had Santo Domingo [now Kewa], San Felipe, Cochiti — we just beat them up on the ball field."

As the '60s proceeded, the boys of the Albuquerque Indian School, those famous names from Laguna and Isleta, became men, with responsibilities that limited the amount of time they could spend on a diamond. The rest of the country was getting older too, with children and Little League, television and drive-in movies. The minor league and semipro teams began to go the way of the dinosaur. For most American communities, this was a loss. For the Pueblo communities of New Mexico, it was a blow.

Al and Jean moved away from the area for many years and when they returned, Laguna baseball had taken a hard hit. Al describes the confusion he felt — and feels — at returning to find the Pueblo's love of baseball so altered. "I'm not sure what happened. I think the media opened up — TV and so forth — and people got interested in other areas. Baseball just fizzled." Jean says, "My aunts — there were three of them — told me to ask the *mayordomos* and the councilmen to please bring back baseball. They said, 'We don't have anything to do, there's nowhere to go. We'd love to sit on the bleachers again and watch baseball.'" For a moment, she gets a faraway look, then continues, "It's like losing our tradition." And Emil agrees.

The wind that has been howling around the eaves of the Abeita house now whips up into a virtual simoom. Outside, young trees bend dramatically. Inside, papers fly and doors slam shut. As conversation slows, Debbie brings in the year books from the Albuquerque Indian School and talk of baseball gives way to hoots of laughter from the former classmates, now huddling over the pictures. The group breaks up into smaller units still — some stay in the living room, others migrate to the kitchen from whence floats an aromatic cloud of Debbie's green chile sauce and tortillas. Jean shows Al pictures from the yearbook. Emil idly tosses a baseball. Jimmy tells a story about the church at Isleta, its foundation dating back to 1612. Before a particularly insensitive priest slathered it with actual stucco in the mid-twentieth century, the people of the village used to gather on a yearly basis to re-mud it, a physically grueling but emotionally gratifying exercise for a New Mexican village, whether Native American or Spanish. He compares the loss of baseball to the loss of that annual tribal activity. "The kind of relationship we had then, it was more than family. It was community. The community was all involved. Baseball was a Sunday outlet for everybody. Today, I don't even know who's playing. I think the community has lost a very strong part of its fabric. The good old days, right? We'll never get them back."

* * *

A late spring afternoon finds Paul Kiro seated on a bench outside his house in the Laguna village of Mesita. The day is mild and beautiful and he is basking in the warmth. But as the car pulls up, he leaps to his feet and barrels toward us with arms outstretched in welcome. He is slight of build, made slighter by stiffness and pain, the legacy of a stroke suffered last year. Paul is an unusually hospitable person, possibly made more so because this visit will be devoted to talking baseball.

Inside, Paul's wife of fifty-seven years, Ann, enters the living room, walking gingerly with a cane. Ann is what is called in some parlances "a pistol," directing activity in the house with authority, humor and just the slightest impatience. The Kiro home is crowded with family memorabilia — trophies, photos, drawings, stuffed animals. A gargantuan snapping turtle named Ben watches impartially from a tank on the kitchen floor. Ann frets about the tight quarters. "These houses are built so small," she says, then adds with a wry laugh, "Seems like they always build things small for Indians. It's like a museum now — I don't know where to put anything." She and Paul seat themselves on the sofa, side-by-side, and she reaches for his hand. She, quite obviously, adores her husband. She speaks for him because, after his stroke, he has difficulty finding the words he wants. While he may not be conversant, Paul is still a powerful and abiding presence in the room. An hour spent with him and the visitor leaves feeling like they have really come to know him, perhaps in a deeper way than if he had talked the entire time. And as far as the topic of baseball, his wife can speak with eloquence about it — like so many

Clara Jean Riley Green says the decline of semipro baseball in the 1960s was "like losing our tradition" (Belinda Winn).

Pueblo people, it is in her blood to do so. Her love of baseball was instilled in her by her father.

The description of Ann's father's life could be the blueprint for countless Native Americans. "My father was Tony Toya and he was born at Jemez Pueblo in 1904. A long time ago he was going to St. Catherine's Indian School in Santa Fe. They were taking children from the reservation to the boarding school. They were all little 8-year-old kids and they stayed there for four years without coming home. Everybody went as far as the eighth grade." When his school years ended, Tony (and his wife, a Laguna woman from Mesita, who he met at the Indian school) headed for Winslow, Arizona. There lived a community of Pueblo people, mostly Laguna, who had migrated there to work for the Santa Fe Railroad. Tony was 17 when he signed on with the railroad; it would turn out to be a 45-year hitch.

Ann describes the community in which she grew up. The story of this railroad camp is a mix of construction ingenuity, bottom-line practicality and a clear racial bias. But Ann remembers it idyllically. "After awhile, they lined up fifty boxcars—those orange boxes—and made them into houses for us. Ten in a row. They planted trees, we had a big public bathroom. They had things going on, like Indian dances. We had to walk five miles to school and had to carry our bologna sandwiches (we'd trade our bologna sandwiches for the Spanish kids' bean sandwiches). We got used to the boxcars. The Japs lived in a big two-story building—they were working for the railroad too. They had a big platform where they could dance—you could hear them dance at night in their costumes. In the back they had gardens with tulips and vegetables. They raised rabbits. We had all sorts of things there. Later on when the Japs got taken away to the concentration camps [note: She is speaking, of course, of the relocation camps of which Arizona had two; the Japanese workers from her community probably ended up in one of these], they let some of us Lagunas move over to their luxury place. There was an upstairs and a swimming pool inside that place."

It was in Winslow that Tony Toya started a baseball team. "They played other teams out there like Spanish teams and other Indian teams that were in the vicinity, like the Hopi. My father didn't play, he was the manager. They won the All-Indian tournament six or seven times." Tony was one of the instigators of league which proved wildly popular. "Pretty soon it got big," says Ann, "All of a sudden my dad had teams coming to play against him from Flagstaff and Holbrook, from all around the surrounding area. Arizona teams."

Meanwhile, Ann had met young Paul Kiro, who was also Laguna. One time was all it took. "I met him again at a dance in 1949. He had an Army uniform on and was with a girl. I thought, 'Well, I've got no chance with Paul now.'" But before he shipped out to Japan, he sent Ann a ring and despite some familial friction they married three years later. "An old married lady at 18," Ann chuckles.

Paul had played for the Isleta Pollys, one of that Pueblo's teams in the

Tony Toya's Winslow Redskins around 1960. Toya is holding the trophy; to the left of him is his son Benny and to the right, his son Wilfred. All of these players were Laguna, residents of that Pueblo enclave in Arizona (courtesy Paul and Ann Kiro).

Albuquerque semipro league. After he and Ann married and he came out of the service, they moved to Winslow where Tony helped him find work with the railroad. He joined his father-in-law's team, the Winslow Redskins, and played for him for eight years. "He loved shortstop," Ann says, then pauses while Paul explains that that was the position he enjoyed most but he could play any of them. "He was small and could slide under players—no one could catch him. He was an all-around ballplayer. My dad's team competed at the All-Indian tournament in Phoenix and they beat the Cotton Kings once."[47] Paul rendered his services as a ringer when Navajo Harold Foster, a former Code Talker, took his Fort Defiance team to the Salt River All-Indian tournament near Scottsdale. It was there that Paul was named MVP. Paul, who until this point has remained quiet, says, "I had a real good chance at the majors in Winslow." Ann nods, saying that he was scouted by a major league team but was deemed too small to play. Neither can recall which team it was.

Ann speaks fondly of those years. "I loved baseball. The whole family loved baseball. My youngest son was a newborn baby and I'd put him in a bassinette under the counter at the concession stand. We'd sell hotdogs and pop just so we could buy Dad's uniforms." Eventually, the Kiros left Winslow for California, and then settled in Shiprock where they both worked for the Navajo government, Paul in maintenance and Ann as an audiometric technician. When they finally returned to Laguna to stay, the Pueblo had become a uranium mining capital. "We came home and a lot of our people were already working for Anaconda," Ann says.

11. Making the Ball Sing   199

At this point in the conversation, Ann and Paul's two sons, Paully and Terence enter, along with Paully's sons Wilfred, Antonio and Zalin, and the house become frantic with activity. Wilfred, who is grown, immediately takes it upon himself to rummage through closets in search of photographs of his grandfather; he emerges every few minutes with another stack. Antonio and Zalin, who are little, race in and out of the house with the fury of youth. Terence and Paully, who also played, settle in to talk about their dad, of whom they are understandably proud. As Paully is recounting his father's baseball history, Paul pulls himself off the sofa to stretch his cramped legs and arms, waving off everybody's solicitous attempts to assist him. He makes a circuit of the room and then, with painfully sad clarity, moans, "I wish I could play baseball," and goes outside.

Paul Kiro in Winslow. He was in Winslow representing an Albuquerque team, playing against his former teammates, the Redskins. Behind him is the building that housed Japanese railroad workers before World War II. The child is Ann Kiro's niece, one of the many "boxcar babies" born in the Laguna colony (courtesy Paul and Ann Kiro).

Paully talks about his father playing in Shiprock. "When I was a little boy, he'd take me to all the tournaments with him. I was his sidekick." He remembers going to the All-Indian tournament at the Salt River Indian reservation at which his father was named MVP. "I used to ask the older guys — just to be sure — how good a ballplayer my dad was. They all say he was the best there ever was out here." Terence agrees, pointing around the room. "My father was the best — these are just a very few of the trophies he's won." When asked about the time his father was scouted, Paully attempts to fill in the gaps. It was a St. Louis scout who watched Paul play, he says, and even though they had doubts about a man of his size, they were more than willing to give him a try (Paully says he has the letter attesting to this). "It wasn't because he was too *small* that he didn't go. It's because he was *drafted*," he says with a slightly exasperated look at his mother.

In the 1980s, Terence and Paully both played for the Laguna Redskins, a team organized and managed by their father. It was part of the league of Laguna villages, which Paully says was still a very strong, competitive league well into that decade. As they are discussing the team, delighted yelps float through the

Three generations of Kiro baseball. In the rear are Terence and Paully, seated are Ann and Paul and Zalin, in front is Antonio. Both boys are actively involved in Little League. Zalin is holding a photograph of the Winslow Redskins, organized and managed by his great-grandfather Tony Toya, his grandfather Paul played on the team for many years as well (Belinda Winn).

open window from the outside. Paul, who moments before was the picture of pain and frustration, has just sprinted quite a distance, in front of onlookers, who are impressed with his speed. Back inside, his family members smile and take it in stride, having lived their lives around this indefatigable athlete. Until the stroke, Paul was a regular competitor in Senior Olympics, excelling in everything from long jump to discus to horseshoes on the state and national levels. But it is his medals for archery that he most enjoyed winning and once took his skill with bow and arrow to the World Masters Games in Melbourne, Australia.

The Kiro family agrees to pose for a portrait and all instinctively group themselves around Paul, the patriarch, like planets orbiting a sun. Although his suffering is apparent, his dignity is intact. Although the constant war with words frustrates him, his silence only reveals his power. And although he grieves for baseball, he can still do a 20-yard dash in a time that surprises no one who ever saw him steal second base.

* * *

At the end of the baseball season in 1951, the *Albuquerque Tribune* published an article entitled "Isleta Indians' Success Mostly a Family Affair." The focus of the piece was Joe M. Abeita, sterling semipro and sandlot pitcher since the 1920s, who at 47 was still a force on local mounds. Not only was he still toeing the rubber but managing, and very adeptly; the year before, he had steered his Isleta Indians to a 14–3 record, beating out 17 other teams for the City-County League championship. By the publication date of the article, the Indians had won their division and were headed to the tournament yet again. Assisting in that victorious season had been his son, Joseph, whose recent induction into the Army was a deeply felt loss for the team. "The Junior Abeita would finish up games started by his father while his father would complete others started by his son." Fortunately, Joe M. Abeita had another trustworthy son, Johnnie, at shortstop, so he was still able to count on sound familial defense.[48]

A decade later, writer Ben Moffett of the *Albuquerque Journal* did a piece on the senior Abeita, now commonly called "Joe the Umpire" by everyone in the Albuquerque community who'd ever heard of baseball. "Joe started umpiring because he 'got too old to play, and loved the game too much to quit.'"[49] By the time Joe the Umpire died in 1998, he was one of the most beloved figures of Isleta Pueblo and the surrounding environs. He was considered the fairest and shrewdest of all local umpires and, in his old age, was honored at a ceremony attended by no less than New Mexico Senator Pete Domenici. As a youth playing for a Catholic school (he later spent a season with the Albuquerque Dukes), Domenici had fallen many a time to Joe's wicked fastball.

Crowded around the kitchen table of their comfortable home at Isleta Pueblo, Joseph Abeita and his wife Francis talk about his father, Joe the Umpire, and about Joseph's own career. Jimmy Abeita (who is unrelated) is there as well; not only did his father Bartolo play with Joe the Umpire in the 1930s, but Joe called many a game in which Jimmy played. Francis, the unofficial historian of the family, has piled high the table with innumerable photographs and trophies of the man she affectionately calls "Tata," a Tiwa term of respect for an elder. She is proud of her father-in-law and her husband who both made reputations for themselves on the mound and both ended their careers calling games.

Born in 1905, Jose (Anglicized to Joseph) Manuel Abeita and his six siblings (the four boys were all named "Jose" but with differing middle names) were orphaned at an early age and "sent here and there," says Joseph. Joe was raised in Winslow, Arizona, in the Pueblo Indian boxcar community there. He came to Isleta in his teens to live with an uncle and attend St. Catherine's Indian School in Santa Fe, where he pitched for the baseball team. Returning to Winslow after school, he broke into semipro ball with the Winslow Redskins team in 1920 and played there until 1928 when he returned to Isleta for good.[50] He must have been delighted to find a thriving baseball culture there. "Baseball was always popular here because even his father played, probably even his grandfather," says Joseph. "I imagine he probably started playing here when he came back in his 20s." Joe began pitching for Buster Abeita's Isleta

The 1942 San Jose Victory Club. Although this semipro team consisted mostly of Hispanic players, it employed Joe M. Abeita, "Joe the Umpire," as pitcher until its early demise that season due to loss of players. He is seated on the far left (courtesy Joseph and Francis Abeita).

Braves in the mid–1930s, backed up by Emil Jojola's father, Sam, behind the plate. This battery was essential to the two consecutive Isleta wins in the annual tournament at Laguna in 1935 and '36. Joe was famous for going the distance, even in extra-innings, and keeping hits to a minimum. In 1935, he pitched a 13-inning no-hitter.[51] Three years later, he led his team to victory in the season opener in which he struck out 11 men and allowed only 7 hits, again for an entire 13-inning game.[52] When Buster formed the Albuquerque Indian All-Stars, Joe took the reins of the sandlot Braves as playing manager and kept it going throughout the war years. After the war, his Isleta Bees (with son Joseph now on the pitching staff) entered the Albuquerque semipro league. "He spent his entire life playing baseball," says Francis. "That was his first love."

Joe continued to successfully steer his Isleta team through several more seasons, and a variety of names, until the late '50s, at which point he began to umpire. As well known as he had been on the mound, it was Joe's reputation for calling games that dominated his baseball career. "He was real friendly," says Joseph, "and got along with everybody and anybody." He was also multi-lingual, having mastered a few of the Native languages and Spanish as well. This made him a much-sought-after umpire throughout the linguistically-diverse region. He could not only referee a Pueblo versus Navajo match-up but could also handle the native Spanish teams from the Albuquerque area and Spanish-speaking ones from further south. Joseph elaborates: "They had a lot of teams made up of nationals from Mexico and he was real popular with them. They had their own league—about a six-team league—and they always counted on him to umpire their games because he spoke fluent Spanish." Then his son proudly adds, "He was still umpiring when he was 80 years old." In fact, well into the age where most feel lucky to get out of bed in the morning, Joe the Umpire could still throw some serious smoke. At an old-timers game in 1960, he managed four innings of no-hit ball.[53] And on the table are two small photos of him, pitching at another old-timers game in the 1980s. In one, he is beginning his windup and the other shows him just before the ball's release. His form is that of a very much younger man.

An Isleta team during World War II. Standing, far left, is Joseph Abeita and kneeling, far right, is his father, "Joe the Umpire." Not only did Joseph follow his illustrious father to the pitcher's mound, they were both highly respected umpires. Other players are (standing) Melo Lucero, Eddie "Short" Jojola, and Paul Shattuck, Jr. The gentleman in hat and tie is unidentified (courtesy Joseph and Francis Abeita).

And throughout that lengthy career, he earned a reputation for remarkable patience and equilibrium on the field. As the 1961 *Journal* article pointed out, "He has the remarkable distinction of never having ejected anyone from a ballgame." Jimmy Abeita asks Joseph if he ever pitched games that his father called and Joseph nods. Jimmy says, "I remember Tata umping for our games. The thing that is most memorable to me is the respect. I mean, he was an icon. They respected him enough to allow him to call his son's games."

As Joe the Umpire's career slowed down, his son's was really just beginning. Joseph says that, as a child, when he and his father played catch, Joe the Umpire always encouraged him to throw as hard as he possibly could. From years of this kind of drilling, Joseph became the kind of hurler who attracted attention. He started pitching at the Albuquerque Indian School in the mid-'40s. In one game there, he struck out 19 batters and was later approached by the owner of a local Ford dealership with the offer of a job and a place on its semipro team. "After the war, baseball really picked up around here," he says and describes a schedule that included nightly practice. Joseph played for various Isleta teams, namely the Bees and, in the late '50s, when the All-Indian League was formed, he played in the Southern Division for Cochiti Pueblo (his mother's tribal affiliation). He also competed in the Laguna tournament and remains impressed by the far-flung tribes that attended. Like everyone else, he remembers the dust-ups, which he politely refers to as "arguments." Jimmy interjects, chuckling, "They were a little more than arguments," and Joseph is forced to agree, going on to recall one between Isleta and Barstow in which the game had to be stopped. In 1958, Joseph began double duty by calling games that he wasn't pitching in.

As the one person who undoubtedly watched the father and son—as pitchers and umpires—more than anyone else, Francis is an authority on their skills. She talks about her husband saying, "I think he followed in his father's footsteps in his technical style of pitching. In those days, there were no actual marked fields like they have nowadays. Now they have grass and lines and pitcher's mounds and boxes. In those times, it was all sandlot and they had to have a good eye to throw the ball and make it curve or whatever else they did to it. They practically made that ball *sing*. They knew what it was gonna do the minute it left the glove." And as far as umpiring, she seems almost prouder of their abilities in that realm. "They were really articulate in the game itself. The men that played knew them and they knew the players. I don't think I ever saw Joseph throw anybody out in all those years. They were Indian men—they could call a ballgame a ballgame. It wasn't shoddy, there were no favorites—they called it as they saw it."

Francis and Joseph Abeita. "Our kids are sandlot kids," Francis says. "We'd pack them up and here we'd go umpiring—every single night" (Belinda Winn).

Francis married into her love of the game. "I went into it because I didn't want to become a baseball widow. I wasn't a sports fanatic until I married him," she laughs, nodding at her husband. "In Albuquerque he called for the City-County League. He was an umpire for years and years. We had three daughters and we took them *everywhere*. Our kids are sandlot kids. We'd pack them up and here we'd go umpiring—every single night. That was our life." She describes a social network of baseball families much like her own and obviously misses that part of her life. In fact, she paints a picture of a lost community spirit, one that was centered in the local ballpark. "It was the camaraderie. After the games, we'd have picnics and share food. Everybody would bring their little kids. It was a way of getting together with the other baseball families and enjoying each other's company. It was a way of life here." But while Francis and the other women in the stands may have been enjoying conversation, they kept a fierce eye on the field. "The women were very excitable, very adamant about what their husbands or sons did. They knew how they batted, they knew how they ran — they were true-blue supporters." Even away from the field, the games were the primary topic of conversation. "We never got tired of talking about baseball. When we'd get together, what did we talk about all night? Baseball." When asked about her own behavior when she disagreed with her husband's call, she beams, saying, "I sat behind him and harassed him. I'd say, 'Hey ump — you need another pair of glasses!'"

Jose Manuel or "Joe the Umpire" Abeita. His nearly seven-decade career in baseball finally ended with knee surgery in his eighties. Years after his death, he is still widely revered throughout the area, not only for his playing and calling baseball but as a force in the world of Pueblo tradition (courtesy Joseph and Francis Abeita).

As for her father-in-law, it took knee surgery to finally end Joe the Umpire's calling days. Still, the iron man refused to slow down. Francis studies a photograph of him and shakes her head in amazement. "I don't think his dad ever had one idle moment. When he gave up calling baseball, he took up moccasin-making. He made moccasins for every woman in the village. And some men. Then, in his late eighties, he took up drum-making." He was an important spiritual figure among the people of Isleta. "Tata was involved in so much tradition in our village. He was the one that led the people in our traditions. He danced at Cochiti in one-hundred degree heat up until he was about 85. All day long he danced for their feast."

She and Jimmy have uncovered another remarkable picture in the pile and animatedly discuss it, lapsing — sometimes mid-sentence — into and out of Tiwa, a language that has a silky quality to it. Then she begins talking about her father-in-law's gifts as a storyteller. She laughingly re-tells one of Tata's favorite stories about a 1930s semipro team from Chicago that desperately wanted to bring an Indian team to the Windy City for a game, so they contacted Isleta. The Chicagoans were willing to pay all travel expenses for the Pueblo club and wanted only a photograph of them, presumably for advertising. "They took the picture but, at that time, most of the players had long hair — real barbaric looking. So they sent the picture to Chicago and they never heard from them again!" She continues, laughing, "Tata was a storyteller, in more ways than one. Sometimes he'd make 'em up!" Joseph Abeita smiles sweetly and looks over the table top, obscured by almost a century of photographs, newspaper clippings and awards, the legacy he shares with Joe the Umpire.

* * *

Between the blinding gypsum of White Sands and the Texan flatness of eastern New Mexico, the Sacramento Mountains rise up in alpine splendor. The high altitude insures pleasant summer days with cool evenings and enough winter snowfall for skiing. Nestled on the range's eastern side is the Mescalero Apache reservation, created by executive order in 1873. Having survived the horrors of the Bosque Redondo, the Mescaleros made their home in this Eden and were eventually joined by the Chiricahuas of Fort Sill and the Lipan Apaches. It is a proud nation and richly steeped in tradition.

To the outside world, Mescalero is probably best known for its resort, the Inn of the Mountain Gods, which has been stunningly wrought to showcase the glories of the surrounding landscape. On any given day, a visitor to the Inn may be greeted at the entrance by a handsome man, dressed in a sport jacket adorned with various impressive accents— medals and beaded sashes— that reveal a weighty tribal role. This is Paul Ortega, and he is the tribe's ambassador. Not only is he the face of Mescalero Apache to the first-time guest, but he is a revered medicine man as well, the knowledge and ritual inherited from his mother's side of the family (about that job he laughs and says, "If it doesn't work, it's generally your fault"). To expand on an already impressive career, Paul Ortega is also an artist and internationally known musician, having fused rhythm and blues with traditional Apache lyrics and melodies to create something utterly unique and entirely listenable. In summing up Paul Ortega, one writer said, "He is a living bridge between art and science, spirit and technology, tradition and innovation, Apache medicine and modern medical practices."[54] That, and in his youth, he was a mean center fielder.

If the Navajo had observed American soldiers at the Bosque Redondo playing baseball, it's a short leap to think that the Mescaleros did as well. By 1899, the tribe had developed a pretty competitive team that played in the area around the reservation.[55] With the arrival of the Chiricahuas from Fort Sill, the tribe was able to field a fairly spectacular nine, one that in 1913 vanquished the nearby Cloudcroft town club in one game by a score of 22–2.[56]

The Mescaleros' love of baseball flourished over the years. By the time Paul Ortega began to play in the 1950s, it was a mainstay of tribal recreation. "It had a lot to do with families, okay? Families were the ones that were involved with baseball and softball. If you're in New York, you would talk about basketball. But in the Southwest, it was always baseball," he says. He describes the games as uproarious familial festivities, attended by every member of the tribe. "Oh we had the best field in the world! It was really nice because we had a guy and his buddy from the BIA (Bureau of Indian Affairs) and they used to have *grass* and everything. I can't tell you another field that looked like that. We had a grandstand in a sense but we also had the side of a hill where the seats were all cut into it. Generally people sat in certain areas there; it belonged to their family. That's where whole families would park their carcasses," he grins. A game inevitably meant a picnic in the gouged-out seats, and Paul waxes nostalgic about fry bread, tortillas with meat, beans and chile, all washed down with cokes and lemonade. As so often was the case, the women of the tribe were outspoken fans, given to white-hot anger when they disagreed with a call, usually making their sentiments known with megaphones. "They had all kinds of horns—horns they blew. Some made their own. They looked like bullhorns but they didn't have the electrical stuff or the battery stuff. Oh yeah, the women were the meanest. They'd throw stuff at you—they'd throw that *horn* at you." Families were known to get deeply involved emotionally, a memory which obviously delights Paul who cackles as he says, "Oh yeah, we had big crowds and a lot of fights too. If a guy runs into second and he takes a dive at the second baseman and knocks him down, before you know it, the whole family comes running out. And then boom-boom-boom until it quiets back down. The referee don't get involved when it's happening, he gets involved after it's over with and then yells 'PLAY BALL!'"

With that kind of highly-charged audience, the games naturally called for an umpire who could reign in the emotions. At Mescalero, the choice made was a wise one. "We had different people but mostly we had elders umpire because nobody would bother them. That's one thing with elders, you always keep your distance—no bad talk, no nothing. Look at him cross-eyed, that's all you can do."

The team that Paul describes—sometimes called the Indians, sometimes the Apaches—was a game one, ready for any comers. They played teams from the surrounding area—Ruidoso, Roswell, Tularosa, Las Cruces, Cloudcroft and then, on the Fourth of July, of secondary importance only to the Apache Maiden ceremonies were the ballgames, as teams from much farther away would come. "Two or three teams would come from Oklahoma. They'd come celebrate, have a powwow, Indian dance and in the meantime, you got the baseball going. Baseball was a big thing back in the '50s." Typically, the Mescaleros would pass the hat for visiting teams to help defray the cost of coming to play. But it was never done for the Mescalero team. "Everybody would put money up, like once a month, three or four dollars, towards equipment. And I had a band back then and we used to play on Saturday nights and would charge 25 cents to come in and dance. That money was generally for the baseball team." And there was generally no money for uniforms. "Our thing was to play baseball, not what we were wearing. But, being a team, we had to look kind of alike. What we did was, we had T-shirts and we'd draw a design on 'em. Or have a cap. Other than that, we wore Levis. If you could find somebody who sold cleats, you'd buy them. But some of us couldn't, so you just wore shoes, you know? But as long as you had your own good baseball glove..." he trails off, with a smile.

Paul and his teammates were a mixed bag of ages, sizes and strengths. They kept no scorecards and couldn't be bothered by a man's age or the numbers he put up. "We generally just looked at who could play and who couldn't play. Statistics wasn't our thing. It was a matter of winning *that game, that day*. The last ten years didn't matter. It's not how old you are — if you can play good, get out there! We had a lot of older men that really knew how to play." He recalls one in particular, a lefthander. "We had an old man — Andrew Little. He was Chief Judge for the Mescalero Apache tribe and played baseball. I remember him clearly because I always thought he threw the wrong way, hit the wrong way and caught the wrong way."

The Mescalero were gritty players, their arms well-trained by youths spent ambushing motorists as they drove across the reservation. Paul was expert at hurling a rock through the passenger window and out through the driver's. He proudly remembers hearing one past victim of this skill warning another about the Mescaleros. "'Don't mess with them, they're rock-throwers!'" Paul howls at this and continues. "'They can throw a rock through a wall!'" The Mescalero players obviously put that talent to good use on the diamond. "There were some very gifted guys. A guy like Donald Blake could throw the ball all the way from left field to home plate and that was something a lot of people couldn't do. He had strong arms — strong, long arms, you know?" As for pitchers? "We intimidated. The very first pitch let them know, 'Hey, we're in charge.'" As for his own skill, Paul gives a wicked laugh, saying, "They

Paul Ortega played baseball for Mescalero teams in the 1950s. "Baseball was a big thing back in the '50s," Paul says. "It was a matter of winning that game, that day" (Belinda Winn).

say I was the best. I was a good catcher, I was fast and I could throw the ball. Plus," he adds, "I was a heavy hitter."

Paul Ortega and his teammates enjoyed a good brawl and often spent weekends seeking one out.[57] But the fact that they were Native Americans in southern New Mexico's cowboy country (that area is sometimes referred to as "Little Texas") meant that they could sometimes attract fights they never sought. In those instances, a tough guy image was essential, effectively masking a frightened young man. He tells the story of one fight that terrified the team at the time, but delights him in retrospect. "We used to go down to Juarez and play ball on Saturdays and Sundays. That's when weekends were always taken up with sports. We were coming back at night in our old beat-up bus. We had a manager, Fryen (a little guy, about 5' 3" or 5' 4"), who took care of the equipment and stuff. Anyway, over between Alamogordo and El Paso is a place called Orogrande. Well, Orogrande had two bars. Fryen says, 'Man, stop the bus—I gotta go to the bathroom.' We pulled into one of those bars because it was the only thing open way late at night and he went in. We were waiting in the bus and all of a sudden, Fryen comes flying out of the door. They threw him out, right? Everybody sat up, said, "Look, look, look—what the hell's going on?' Fryen got in the bus and said, 'They tried to beat the shit outta me!' We asked how many were in there and he said about five. Well, you know, being Mescalero, there was always this prejudice back in the '50s. There was a hatred kind of a thing, especially for Mescaleros. We traveled in bunches but they didn't know that." Paul stops here to give a wicked chuckle. "All of a sudden, everybody gets out of the bus and in goes Fryen, looking around the bar, with about fifteen Mescaleros behind him. The people inside got scared and said, 'We're ready to leave,' but one of us said, 'Nobody's leaving. The only ones that's gonna be leaving *alive* from here is us—the Mescaleros!'" At this point, Paul adds an aside, chuckling, "He shouldn't have said that but he did anyway. So Fryen went to town on the one that hit him then said, 'We're gonna park that bus down the road here and wait. If you guys come out before fifteen minutes, you've had it.' Then bam! We got out of there and into the bus and drove—as far as we were concerned—about 200 miles an hour towards Alamogordo. We were all saying, 'What if they call the police? What if they do this, what if they do that?' Man, we thought of everything possible that could happen and scared ourselves. We even went around the backside of Alamogordo, not through downtown, and around the backside of the mountain and came back to Tularosa and bought coffee. We were still shaking when we got there. We were still shaking when we got to Mescalero!"

On this bright morning, as he surveys the mountains he loves from the luxurious surroundings of the inn, Paul Ortega—ambassador, musician, medicine man, artist—looks fondly on the past. "Back then people worked and lived together. It was a different world. Today nobody gives hoot for anybody else—they're in it for themselves. Back then everybody was involved, everybody helped each other." Then, he breaks into an irrepressible grin and it's not entirely clear whether he refers to baseball or to his youth when he says, "Yeah, we were the Mescaleros. We always thought we were the best. In order to beat us, you had to be somebody special."

* * *

When Jacoby Ellsbury set fire to the outfield of Fenway Park in 2007, a buzz began concerning his ancestry. As the first Navajo to make it to the big leagues, he became an instant sensation, not only in sports blogs worldwide but among his mother's people in the Southwest. As he told the *New York Times*, "I definitely have a following and am proud of my heritage and am trying to set a good example for my community.... I'm trying to be a role model on and off the field."[58] One careful observer of Ellsbury's progress is Dineh Benally. During business hours, he is a civil engineer for the Bureau of Indian Affairs. When he leaves his Crownpoint office, however, he is the owner of and instructor at Naa'taanii Baseball Academy, a program which focuses primarily on ballplayers from the Navajo reservation. The word *naa'taanii* translates to "leaders" in English and, indeed, Benally and his staff at the academy are dedicated to molding responsible citizens as well as fine athletes. A visit to the website will show that emphasized as much as athletics is a list of core values that focuses on teamwork and integrity, service to others and leading by example.[59] For the students of Naa'taanii, this training begins at a highly impressionable age, as the academy's youngest players are in the Sandy Koufax division (ages 13–14); also represented is the Mickey Mantle division (15–16 year olds), Connie Mack (17–18) and the academy fields a Junior Olympic tournament team.

Dineh Benally is the first to admit that one of the toughest battles he faces is getting Navajo kids interested in baseball, which has traditionally drawn few takers on the reservation. The turn-of-the-century Indian school rosters were filled with Navajo players but, unlike the Pueblos, which had fairly populated central villages, the seventeen-million-acre Navajo reservation (which extends into Arizona and Utah and includes the non-contiguous New Mexico reservations of To'hajiilee, Alamo and Ramah) is the largest in the United States and, outside of municipalities, homes and families can be spread out very thinly over that vastness. Between Gallup and Shiprock, for instance, along New Mexico 491, the sparse and uniquely beautiful landscape will be punctuated only rarely by small clusters of homes or villages. Yet even these thinly-concentrated areas of humanity cannot convey the isolation of the endless miles of tribal lands that are hidden from view. While the population centers might form baseball teams—and some were good enough to compete in the Laguna All-Indian Tournament—it's not surprising that in the more remote areas, they have historically been very hard to organize.

In addition to logistical problems, Dineh Benally says there have been other obstacles to Navajo baseball, namely a preference for other forms of recreation. "The problem we have is competing against other sports like rodeo—which is very popular out here—and basketball." The emphasis on rodeo has deep cultural roots as the Navajo have always kept livestock. Not only do they raise cattle but sheep as well, the source for wool needed to weave the beautiful rugs for which the Diné are justly famous. In fact, Dineh Benally admits that he, at age 32, is the first in his family to be so interested in the sport, his father and grandfathers preferring the rodeo. His frustration with the lack of attention paid to baseball is evident. "I think rodeo and basketball are a lot easier—I don't want to say to perform—but easier to access than baseball." And then there's what he considers a general lack of understanding and appreciation of the game among Navajos. "Most people think it's boring. That's how I see the perception of it. But you've got to understand the game, you've got to understand how much the mental part goes into that game, the strategy of both teams when they have quality athletes. It comes down to strategizing. That's what interests me about the sport. For most Navajo folks, it's fairly new—very new. I don't think we've been exposed to the game as much as outside society has. The interest is not there yet but I think it *can* happen if the government school and the BIA schools start promoting it at the lower levels, like sixth grade and higher." He sighs and says, "But they're exposed more to basketball. And every weekend there's a rodeo going on." It is with the slightest hint of envy that he mentions the Pueblos' ongoing devotion to the game. At the same time, Dineh Benally is something of a perfectionist and somewhat persnickety about Pueblo brand of play. "It's not played at the level it should be. But they just go out and have fun."

Dineh pitched in high school and also at junior college at the New Mexico Military Institute in Roswell. He tried out for the team at New Mexico State University in Las Cruces. He didn't make it but was inspired by the level of competition there and came away with a passion to help others get at least that far. "Really, the way I started was because of my little brother. He was at that age and I thought, 'I need to start coaching.' It's my pride and joy." His college experiences, both successes and failures, gave him valuable insight into encouraging young talent. "I learned a lot being around the Division I level, seeing the type of athletes that Division I wants. Based on that knowledge, I've built Naa'taanii. The goal is to get more Navajo kids to play at the next level, like college and professional. So I take these kids to these showcases and try to get them exposed to a higher level of baseball. Because, yeah, we play baseball but not at the level that's outside the reservation."

Every year, Dineh Benally has Naa'taanii players in the Farmington Connie Mack League. They play in beautiful Ricketts Park from the end of May until mid–July, when the league tournament takes place. The winner of that is the host team for the renowned Connie Mack World Series. "Our goal there is to be the host team for the World Series. We've come close several times—we've been doing it since 1999—but the closest we've been was in 2003. The past few years we've made it to the championship day but ended up losing that night. What I run into, bringing those kids in from the reservation and expos-

The young players of the Naa'taanii Baseball Academy. Coach Dineh Benally stands at right. Benally believes that his school may be the best opportunity for young Native players to advance to the world of professional baseball (courtesy Naa'taanii Baseball Academy).

ing them to that level of tournament, regardless of the talent they have, for some reason, they seem to choke under pressure. Because of the environment and because they've dreamed about it. They all know about the Connie Mack World Series. They have grown up seeing this series—since, like, they were six years old. That's where we're losing—mentally. So I have to try to get these kids to want it more than they have. Hopefully we'll get there." While admitting that his kids can be overwhelmed at the very thought of the World Series in Farmington, he also thinks that they have an advantage in being local boys. "It's a tradition for Farmington and those kids that live there, and well, if you try to take someone's tradition away, they're gonna fight you for it," he laughs. "So it's pretty competitive, pretty demanding."

While the environment of Farmington and Ricketts Park may be somewhat daunting to the young players, especially those who live on the reservation, Dineh is gladdened by the reception that his boys receive from the people there. "Especially if the majority of my kids are Native American. People say, 'If you ever get a team into the World Series, you'll break all attendance records.' And I believe them. Just because of the name Naa´taanii—'leaders.'"

Asked about aspirations to the majors leagues—his own and those of his kids—Dineh Benally replies with practicality and feeling. "Every kid who plays baseball has that dream. I wish I had been exposed to some of the training techniques they have today. That's what we don't have here on our reservation and that's what we need. That's what baseball requires. But there's not a training facility out here in Navajo country or even in Pueblo country. As soon as that happens, I think you'll see more Navajos playing at the next level. They're building a training facility at Gallup High School. Also trying to start one in Shiprock, but it's a work in progress. Funding is always an issue. We've just gotta keep plugging away and hopefully, people will see what we're doing and think, 'Hey, I want to help that program.'" He looks at the history of Native Americans in baseball and has hope for a future in which their presence will be more widely felt. "I firmly believe that this sport is something that Native Americans can excel in. They could use it to at least go to college like I did. Basketball? I just can't see it—Native American–wise—no way." But with baseball, he feels like Native athletes may have innate skills that give them an advantage. "The mentality of it is one [skill]—being mentally strong. They have pride in themselves and I know how they focus. They stay more composed and the reason I say this is because I've seen it. That's the key in baseball. You can have all the athletic ability in the world but if you don't have that mental toughness, you're going to lose."

When he played in high school and college, he utilized what he considers to be that special Native American focus. "You just concentrate. Before I'd go on the mound, I'd pray to the spirits of my ... the Lord ... to give me the strength to do well. And I'd just get into the zone. When you get into the zone, and you feel that glove right in front of your face, you just touch it where you want that pitch to be and that's where it'll go. It's amazing when that happens. That's why I loved pitching—I loved getting into that zone." He believes that it's easy to detect someone who's "in the zone." "It's in the eyes and the body language. You know that person is going to win. His opponent will know. It's just human instinct." He involves the Naa´taanii players in psychological exercises to help them achieve that zen of the zone which will, as he puts it, "prepare them for the battle."

Of course the issue of performance-enhancing drugs is the noxious cloud that floats through every locker room these days. When asked how he handles the topic with his young players, Dineh approaches it less with righteous indignation and more with simple horse sense. "It takes more than steroids to hit a baseball. It takes hand-eye coordination and that's god given. If you don't have it, I don't care what you put in your body—you're just not going to have it."

In addition to his work at the academy, Dineh Benally serves as the coach for the Navajo team in the Native American All-Star Game, an annual event since 2003, which pits the Navajo players against a team composed of players from the Pueblo leagues. The game takes place near the end of July at Isotopes Park, Albuquerque's Triple-A facility. But long before July rolls around, Dineh is getting his team ready for the famous grudge match. He has been involved since its inception. "It came up as a fundraising mechanism for New Mexico Highlands University [the Native American Athlete Scholarship Fund]. They wanted to raise money somehow and figured, 'Why don't we have an all-star game? Have the tribes bring in their best players possible to play against each other?'" One of the founders was Mike Koldyke, the principal owner of the Isotopes and Dineh is full of praise for the effort put into the event by the organization. "The Isotopes have supported this program since it first started. They provide the facility and even help develop the tickets." The state, he explains, is another sponsor of the game. But he feels that, due to the proximity of the southern Pueblos to Albuquerque and Isotopes Park, advertising is aimed more at them than on the fans on the distant Navajo reservation. As a result, it is much harder to keep the Navajo nation informed on the event. Plus, there is the travel aspect that can hurt. "Navajo attendance can do very well but I want to get on board helping the state of New Mexico promote the All-Star game out here. They expect it to grow by just promoting it in the Albuquerque area and just having the local tribes come. But they need to advertise it out here to get a good crowd." He would also like to see the state coming out to the Navajo reservation to help him get the young ball players and their families cranked up and organized early so that a team could start training months before the game. "Because they kind of say, in the last month, 'Where's your team? We need your team,' instead of organizing it properly." Dineh Benally is obviously a man who needs careful planning and organization and time to get his boys in shape for the All-Star game. Anything less is unacceptable. With unmistakable passion he explains himself, saying, "I think it's an honor to play at Isotopes Park."

Where the All-Star game is concerned, he's also not immune to a certain amount of tribal pride, one that is peppered with opinions with which the Pueblo teams (and Pueblo citizens in general) might take issue. "As Navajos, we're a big nation and supposed to be the role model, from government to culture to way of life. When we go down there to play in the All-Star baseball game, it's like a sibling rivalry, like big brother versus the little brother. The Pueblos are the little brothers and they want to beat up on the big brother. For the Pueblos, it's a very big deal to win the game. For us, we treat it just like another game. That's the difference. The past two years, we've seen them really celebrate when they win. Hopefully we'll step it up a notch this year."

As far as a potential stepping stone for his students, Dineh Benally thinks that the All-Star game might attract a couple of college coaches but that is most likely the extent of any scouting. He wishes that the level of attention paid by influential reconnaissance men to the game was higher but understands that they have to be enticed. "The only way that's gonna happen is with quality athletes. This game is so competitive. Money is involved. It takes money to travel out there to watch kids play. So when contacts come out, they want to be able to see the next Jacoby Ellsbury." (Dineh also manages a junior Olympic team and, while in Oregon recruiting Native American kids for it, he met Ellsbury who was in his teens at the time. They stayed in touch for awhile but lost track of each other after Ellsbury's sensational debut. He thinks the Boston outfielder may be making a dent in the rodeo and basketball monopolies on the reservation. With a laugh, Dineh says, "You see a lot more kids wearing Boston Red Sox uniforms.")

As for the 19-man roster of nervous teenagers, when they arrive at Isotopes Park, a handsome Triple-A field from whence springs many a Los Angeles Dodger, what is their reaction? After all, for most of them, this may be the closest they come to playing in a green cathedral. "They're happy and amazed," their mentor says. "They can't believe it — it's a once in a lifetime experience."

Many decades ago, the Reverend Berard Haile of the St. Michaels, Arizona, mission school described nineteenth century Navajo baseball for an ethnology report. He said that the only position that had a name was the pitcher or *atch'i'náalni,*' which he translated to mean "he throws toward him."[60] To the kids of Naa'taanii, Dineh Benally is throwing a lot of ideas, a lot of dreams, all countered by just as many demands. He asks nothing less of his students than their very best. His ambitions for them include seeing them play for a fine college team or in the minors. Of course, the pinnacle would be to see one of his boys in the big leagues. But — and perhaps this is most important — he obviously hopes that each one of them will feel the same way he says he does about the game. "I have great respect for playing on baseball fields or coaching on baseball fields. When I step onto it I always give thanks. Not many people have the opportunity. Regardless of whether you're a Native American team or a major league team or a minor league team, you've gotta be thankful to be on that field."

* * *

Back at Isleta Pueblo, the lunch dishes have been cleared away and there are just a couple of guests left to enjoy the Abeita's hospitality. Jimmy sits at the kitchen table and shares a memory from his past. It is the tale of any teenager the world over, one of restlessness, hopes and fears, and perhaps a bit of loneliness. It is also a love story, a generations-old passion, nurtured by the feel of raised seams against the palm, the smell of an oiled glove, the satisfying *thwok* of fastball meeting mitt. And it is a peculiarly American love story. But this one is played out in the vastness of an Indian reservation in the desert Southwest.

"At the height of my baseball career, the San Francisco Giants were my favorite team. I was such an avid fan, especially when the Dodgers/Giants series were played in Los Angeles at night." He points to a rise of mountains in the distance and continues. "I would drive to the foothills east of Isleta just so I could catch the voice of Vin Scully on the airwaves." One can almost picture the young man, slouched uncomfortably behind the steering wheel of his Mercury. Above him is the miracle of the New Mexico night sky, with its incomparable canopy of stars almost tangibly close. They provide the only light. Almost a thousand feet below him, the Pueblo spreads out in almost total darkness—no streetlights, few headlights, only the dim glow from a handful of lit windows. He is entirely alone and yet at this moment, in this isolation, he is strangely connected with the larger world that will soon lure him away from home. "I had never attended a major league game in my life, but Vin Scully put me right there in Dodger Stadium. He made every game exciting."

In the hours that he sat there, listening to the startlingly powerful signal that brought each play from California, the car battery would drain and die. But he always knew to park on an incline. So, leaving behind the bright and hectic joy of Dodger Stadium, he'd give the Mercury a push, pop the clutch and coast down the steep mountainside to the sleeping village.

Epilogue

In Charles Van Loan's 1912 short story "The Phantom League," an ambitious scout from the majors thinks he's stumbled upon a rare poaching opportunity when he learns of a heretofore unknown circuit called the Northern New Mexico League. The numbers put up by its powerhouse teams seem almost too good to be true and, in fact, they are. Because the league is a mythical one, invented solely for the amusement of few baseball-loving friends in an isolated village in the Sangre de Cristos. The men — a Jicarilla Apache, an African American and a couple of tubercular Anglos, keep themselves and the mostly Hispano community enthralled for a summer by playing out a season with a mechanical board game. The scout, having made an arduous journey to the remote area, is furious to discover the truth, whereas all the participants consider the whole story — from their tabletop stadium to his big league gullibility — nothing short of hilarious.

Mr. Van Loan couldn't have written the story without having spent considerable time in New Mexico. He has perfectly captured the state personality and its attitude toward life. Beginning with the first New Mexican to bring down a wooly mammoth, the inhabitants of the state have found survival a struggle, a continuing saga of extremes — meteorological, geo-political, socio-economic. What I already knew about the New Mexican people is that they combine flexibility with a streak of fatalism to create an admirable inability to take anything — including themselves — too seriously. And what I learned in the process of this research was that, throughout the decades, they have consistently brought this quality to the baseball diamond. While they have played the game ardently, humor — on the part of players, managers, fans and sportswriters — has been a constant of baseball since the beginning. For contemporary evidence of New Mexicans' tendency to mingle their natural sense of comedy with baseball, one need look no further than the Albuquerque Isotopes, named by the citizens of that city, in a moment of inspired hilarity, after an episode of the television show *The Simpsons*. At the same time, and perhaps it is because of New Mexico's tradition of nineteenth-century unruliness, there has been a renegade sensibility to the game — it's just a little grittier and rougher around the edges, and frequently played just a tad outside the law. How could a culture that included highwaymen, saloons, gambling, guns and hangings inspire anything but a slightly more puckish version of the sport?

Another significant aspect of the game in New Mexico—and perhaps it is unique to this very diverse state—has been the opportunity that it has historically afforded the state's myriad peoples to assert an identity, whether racial, linguistic, geographical, occupational or religious. By what was emblazoned across their chests, players could identify themselves as being a part of a unit, far more specific than just Tiger or Slugger. The New Mexican players have been Miners and Drillers and Apprentices and, with a nod to the past, Pioneers. Only the state's Native Americans wore jerseys with words like Braves, Redskins, Warriors and Tewas. There were Dons and Dukes, and endless family and place names that hearkened back to Iberia. Teams of Monarchs, along with Black Giants and Black Pioneers, signaled a growing African American presence in the urban centers. Clubs playing under a martial banner were some of the very first, with the McArthurs of the nineteenth century naming themselves after their living leader while, during the second World War, another group of soldier-players would salute a fallen hero by taking his name. The uniforms of the post-war Bombers of Los Alamos openly glorified what had put that town on the map. The name of a prison team, the Rocks, was self-explanatory and certainly one of the most proudly borne. At times there have been teams of Saints and even Christians. And now we have the Isotopes, their atomic-age logo cheerfully identifying the Duke City as the only legitimate heir to that name. In the melting pot that has been baseball in the state, the team name identified a player as belonging to a very particular, and very proud, group of New Mexicans.

What I have always found most delightful about New Mexico is the vivid role that its legendary characters continue to play in contemporary life. For history-loving citizens of the state as well as entranced visitors, the ghosts of figures long departed still walk the narrow streets of old Santa Fe or ride their spectral ponies through desert and mountain pass. Some of these luminaries were native born, while others came to New Mexico on a collision course with destiny. Tales of Coronado, Geronimo, Bonney, Pyle, Oppenheimer and O'Keeffe are told and told again, never losing their appeal. And as naturally as New Mexico lends itself to legend, so, of course, does baseball, a pastime steeped in nearly mythical beings and the legacies they have left behind. For the true devotee, the Mathewsons, Gehrigs and Robinsons still loom with a holographic realism that dwarfs living players. In that sense, New Mexico and baseball were made for one another, as each cherishes its own pageant of ghosts. When the southwestern version of the game was still in dewy youth, stars of the local diamonds were already becoming heroes and in smaller communities, legendary players of a half century ago are still discussed in reverent tones.

As this is a tale of the Land of Enchantment, we are given license to imagine the New Mexican ballplayers of the distant past. They join the conquistador and cowboy in the narrative of this place, perhaps not altering its history, but adding texture and richness. We can almost see them, taking their positions on a lonely desert field, a legion of spirits of every color and circumstance, clad in laced-front jerseys and ankle boots or baggy flannel knickers. Shouting, signaling, sliding, spiking, swinging — they are doing what New Mexicans have done for a hundred and fifty years, playing the beloved game on the ancient soil.

Chapter Notes

Chapter 1

1. Odie B. Faulk, *Destiny Road: The Gila Trail and the Opening of the Southwest* (New York: Oxford University Press, 1973), p. 11.

2. Marc Simmons, *New Mexico: An Interpretive History* (New York: Norton, 1977. Reprint, Albuquerque: University of New Mexico Press, 1988), p. 134.

3. Today, many question whether these merchants were actually the first Jews to have settled in northern New Mexico. One school of thought suggests that some northern Hispanos are, in fact, descended from Spanish crypto-Jews who after 1492 adopted Christian names and customs in order to survive, but secretly kept their religious beliefs and practices. As Christians, they were allowed to immigrate to the New World. Some were exposed as "hidden Jews," arrested and burned at the stake in Mexico City. As a result, others found it expedient to head north to New Spain, settling in the isolated northern mountains, where they attempted to maintain their religious traditions. "Those Spanish Jews who converted, but continued to practice their old faith surreptitiously, gradually lost touch with normative Judaism." [Henry J. Tobias, *A History of the Jews in New Mexico* (Albuquerque: University of New Mexico Press, 1990), p. 12.] Today, some northern New Mexicans cherish enigmatic memories and heirloom legends that support their belief in a Jewish ancestry.

4. Simmons, *New Mexico: An Interpretive History*, pp. 140–141.

5. W. Eugene Hollon, *Frontier Violence: Another Look* (New York: Oxford University Press, 1974), p. 178.

6. *Ibid.*, p. 191.

7. *Albuquerque Tribune*, February 15, 1974, p. 52.

8. For over twenty years, a mainstay of *New Mexico Magazine* has been a column called "One of Our Fifty Is Missing," which indignantly celebrates the incidents—and there are many—wherein United States citizens have been confused as to New Mexico's statehood and location.

9. Peggy Pond Church, *The House at Ottowi Bridge: The Story of Edith Warner and Los Alamos* (Albuquerque: University of New Mexico Press, 1960), p. 5.

10. David L. Caffey, *Land of Enchantment, Land of Conflict: New Mexico in English-Language Fiction* (College Station: Texas A&M University, 1999), p. 9.

Chapter 2

1. Emory Upton was a noted general and military strategist during the Civil War.

2. *Albuquerque Journal*, September 14, 1882, p. 2.

3. Harold Peterson, *The Man Who Invented Baseball* (New York: Charles Scribner's Sons, 1969), p. 111.

4. *Mining Life*, September 6, 1873. At that time, one of the residents of Silver City was the boy who would become Billy the Kid. He was fourteen and an active, popular local boy. In a small town, it's not a leap to think he might have been one of the boys involved in or attending that practice match.

5. *Rio Grande Republican*, July 19, 1884, p. 3.

6. *Thirty-Four*, December 18, 1878, p. 3.

7. *Ibid.*, July 16, 1879, p. 2.

8. *Ibid.*, March 17, 1879, p. 3.

9. *Ibid.*, January 15, 1879, p. 3.

10. Faulk, *Destiny Road*, p. 173.

11. *Thirty-Four*, January 1, 1879, p. 3.

12. *Rio Grande Republican*, July 11, 1885, p. 3.

13. Dee Brown, *The Gentle Tamers: Women of the Old Wild West* (Lincoln and London: University of Nebraska Press, 1958), p. 93.

14. *Thirty-Four*, December 18, 1878, p. 2.

15. *Ibid.*, December 25, 1878, p. 2.

16. *Ibid.*, March 10, 1880, p. 6.

17. Hollon, *Frontier Violence*, p. 183.

18. Warren Goldstein, *Playing for Keeps: A*

History of Early Baseball (Ithaca and London: Cornell University Press, 1989), p. 4.

19. George B. Anderson, *History of New Mexico: Its Resources and People* (Los Angeles, Chicago, New York: Pacific States, 1907), p. 472.

20. *Albuquerque Tribune*, March 28, 1969, p. D-10.

21. *Albuquerque Daily Journal*, June 14, 1882, p. 4.

22. *Albuquerque Tribune*, March 28, 1969, p. D-10.

23. *Albuquerque Journal*, May 13, 1883, p. 5.

24. *Ibid.*, October 7, 1883, p. 5.

25. *Ibid.*, June 22, 1884, p. 4.

26. *Ibid.*, April 28, 1884, p. 7.

27. *Thirty-Four*, February 5, 1879, p. 2.

28. *Rio Grande Republican*, August 21, 1886, p. 3.

29. *Albuquerque Journal*, August 30, 1884, p. 4.

30. *Ibid.*

31. *New Mexican*, September 22, 1887, p. 1.

32. *Ibid.*

33. *Rio Grande Republican*, September 12, 1885, p. 3.

34. *Ibid.*, July 7, 1883, p. 2.

35. *Ibid.*, July 11, 1885, p. 3.

36. *Ibid.*

37. *Ibid.*, August 22, 1885, p. 2.

38. Goldstein, *Playing for Keeps*, p. 38.

39. *Rio Grande Republican*, July 5, 1884, p. 2.

40. *Ibid.* This Rynerson is undoubtedly related to, perhaps the son of, William Logan Rynerson, who came to Las Cruces in 1866. In 1868, the almost seven-foot-tall Rynerson killed the chief justice of New Mexico at La Fonda, a hotel still in business in Santa Fe. He gained power under the unscrupulous Santa Fe Ring and was made District Attorney and boss of Doña Ana, Lincoln and Grant counties. In this role, he was instrumental in the Lincoln County Wars and made certain that Billy the Kid never received the pardon promised to him by Governor Lew Wallace.

41. *Ibid.*, December 13, 1884, p. 3.

42. *Ibid.*, July 5, 1884, p. 3.

43. *Ibid.*, September 5, 1885, p. 1.

44. *Ibid.*, May 15, 1886, p 4.

45. *Ibid.*, December 11, 1886, p. 1.

46. *Ibid.*, July 24, 1886, p. 3.

47. *Ibid.*, November 27, 1891, p. 3.

48. *Ibid.*, July 8, 1892, p. 5.

49. *Ibid.*, April 17, 1891, p. 4.

50. *Ibid.*, January 12, 1900, p. 3.

51. *Ibid.*, January 26, 1900, p. 2.

52. *Ibid.*

53. *Albuquerque Journal*, October 12, 1903, p. 12.

54. *Ibid.*, October 14, 1903, p. 1.

55. *Ibid.*, October 17, 1903, p. 10.

56. *The Sporting News*, August 10, 1955, p. 34.

57. *Albuquerque Journal*, October 18, 1903, p. 10.

58. *Ibid.*, October 7, 1903, p. 8.

59. *Ibid.*

60. *Rio Grande Republican*, April 15, 1892, p. 1.

61. *Deming Headlight*, February 22, 1895, p. 4.

62. *Silver City Enterprise*, June 27, 1913, p. 1.

63. *Ibid.*, February 3, 1899.

64. *Ibid.*, March 17, 1899.

65. *Albuquerque Journal*, October 8, 1903, p. 2.

66. *Ibid.*, October 12, 1903, p. 9.

67. *Ibid.*, October 14, 1903, p. 6.

68. *Ibid.*, October 19, 1903, p. 2.

69. *Ibid.*, October 15, 1903, p. 6.

70. *Ibid.*, October, 18, 1903, p. 10.

71. *Ibid.*, October 19, 1903, p. 2.

72. *Ibid.*

73. *Ibid.*

74. *Ibid.*

75. *Ibid.*, October 19, 1903, p. 8.

76. *Ibid.*, October 19, 1903, p. 2.

77. *Ibid.*

78. *Ibid.*, July 18, 1911, p. 6.

79. *Ibid.*, April 3, 1911, p. 3.

80. *Albuquerque Tribune*, March 28, 1969, p. D-10.

81. Until its appropriation by the Nazi Party, the swastika had been an important symbol, with positive connotations, throughout history and in cultures worldwide. In the Southwest, it had long been a part of Hopi and Navajo symbolism. Besides being adopted by the baseball team, it was prominently displayed in the newspaper advertisements of the St. Louis, Rocky Mountain and Pacific Railway Company. In 1919, Swastika Fuel Company, owned by the railway, opened a coal-mining camp of the same name near Raton, New Mexico. It was called Swastika until 1940 when it was deemed a good idea to change the name.

82. *Albuquerque Journal*, June 16, 1911, p. 3.

83. *Ibid.*, June 2, 1911, p. 3.

84. *Ibid.*, April 2, 1911, p. 3.

85. *Ibid.*, April 30, 1911, p. 3.

86. *Ibid.*, May 1, 1911, p. 3.

87. *Ibid.*, May 4, 1911, p. 3.

88. *Ibid.*, May 7, 1911, p. 3.

89. *Ibid.*, June 25, 1911, p. 3.

90. *Ibid.*, May 8, 1911, p. 3.

91. *Las Vegas Daily Optic*, August 7, 1905, p. 2.

92. This was not the team from the Uni-

versity of Waseda which played extensively throughout the United States that year, the first of an every-five-year tour in partnership with the University of Chicago that lasted until 1936. The Illinois team first visited Japan in 1910, likewise returning every five years. In May 2008, the tradition was resurrected when the Maroons of the university played games in three Japanese cities. (athletics.uchicago. edu/baseball/bb-japantour2008.htm)
    93. *Albuquerque Journal*, April 27, 1911, p. 3.
    94. *Ibid.*, May 16, 1911, p. 3.
    95. *Ibid.*, April 17, 1911, p. 3.
    96. *Ibid.*, April 20, 1911, p. 3.
    97. *Ibid.*, May 9, 1911, p. 3.
    98. *Ibid.*, May 11, 1911, p. 3.
    99. *Ibid.*, May 14, 1911, p. 3.
    100. *Ibid.*, May 15, 1911, p. 3.
    101. *Ibid.*, May 29, 1911, p. 3.
    102. *Ibid.*, May 19, 1911, p. 3.
    103. *Ibid.*, June 1, 1911, p. 3.
    104. Bob Rives, "Joe Wilhoit," *The Baseball Biography Project*, Society for American Baseball Research, http://bioproj.sabr.org/bioproj.cfm?a=v&v=1&pid=15190&bid=30.
    105. *Albuquerque Journal*, June 4, 1911, p. 3.
    106. *Ibid.*, June 16, 1911, p. 3.
    107. *Ibid.*, June 5, 1911, p. 1.
    108. *Ibid.*, June 12, 1911, p. 8.
    109. *Ibid.*, June 2, 1911, p. 3.
    110. *Ibid.*, June 24, 1911, p. 3.
    111. *Ibid.*
    112. *Ibid.*, June 26, 1911, p. 3.
    113. *Ibid.*, July 11, 1911, p. 3.
    114. *Ibid.*, June 27, 1911, p. 3.
    115. *Ibid.*, July 2, 1911, p. 3.
    116. *Ibid.*
    117. *Ibid.*, July 20, 1911, p. 3.
    118. *Ibid.*, July 27, 1911, p. 3.
    119. *Ibid.*, July 29, 1911, p. 3.
    120. *Ibid.*, July 30, 1911, p. 3.
    121. *Ibid.*, July 31, 1911, p. 3.
    122. *Ibid.*, August 2, 1911, p. 3.
    123. *Ibid.*
    124. *Ibid.*, August 9, 1911, p. 3.
    125. *Ibid.*, April 10, 1911, p. 3.
    126. *Ibid.*, August 7, 1911, p. 3.
    127. *Ibid.*, August 31, 1911, p. 3.
    128. *Ibid.*, September 2, 1911, p. 3.
    129. *Ibid.*, September 3, 1911, p. 3.
    130. *Ibid.*, August 27, 1911, p. 3.
    131. *Ibid.*, September 4, 1911, p. 3.
    132. *Ibid.*, September 6, 1911, p. 3.
    133. *Ibid.*, September 8, 1911, p. 3.
    134. *Ibid.*, September 9, 1911, p. 3.
    135. *Ibid.*, September 8, 1911, p. 3.
    136. *Ibid.*, September 11, 1911, p. 3.
    137. *Ibid.*, September 18, 1911, p. 3.
    138. *Ibid.*, August 20, 1911, p. 1.
    139. *Ibid.*, October 16, 1911, p. 3.
    140. *Ibid.*, October 11, 1911, p. 3.
    141. *Ibid.*, October 10, 1911, p. 3.
    142. *Ibid.*, September 29, 1911, p. 3.
    143. *Ibid.*, October 12, 1911, p. 3.
    144. *Ibid.*, September 28, 1911, p. 3.
    145. *Ibid.*, September 29, 1911, p. 3.
    146. *Ibid.*, October 1, 1911, p. 3.
    147. *Ibid.*, October 8, 1911, p. 3.
    148. *Ibid.*, October 10, 1911, p. 3.
    149. *Ibid.*, October 8, 1911, p. 3.
    150. *Ibid.*
    151. James A. Riley, *The Biographical Encyclopedia of the Negro Baseball Leagues* (New York: Carroll & Graf, 1994), pp. 622–623.
    152. *Albuquerque Journal*, October 6, 1911, p. 3.
    153. *Ibid.*, October 10, 1911, p. 3.
    154. *Ibid.*, October 11, 1911, p. 3.
    155. *Ibid.*, October 13, 1911, p. 3.
    156. *Ibid.*, October 15, 1911, p. 3.
    157. *Ibid.*, October 16, 1911, p 3.
    158. *Ibid.*
    159. *Ibid.*, October 12, 1911, p. 1.

Chapter 3

    1. Marc Simmons, *The Last Conquistador: Juan de Oñate and the Settling of the Far Southwest* (Norman: University of Oklahoma Press, 1991), pp. 10–11.
    2. Simmons, *New Mexico: An Interpretive History*, p. 23.
    3. James E. Sherman and Barbara H. Sherman, *Ghost Towns and Mining Camps of New Mexico* (Norman: University of Oklahoma Press, 1975), p. 189.
    4. *Deming Headlight*, October 31, 1913, p. 2.
    5. *Silver City Enterprise*, August 26, 1887.
    6. John M. White, "Championship Baseball in the Copper Country," *New Mexico Magazine*, October 1957: p. 15.
    7. *Deming Headlight*, April 13, 1914, p. 3.
    8. *Las Vegas Daily Optic*, February 10, 1914, p. 5.
    9. *Deming Headlight*, July 3, 1914, p. 2.
    10. *Silver City Enterprise*, August 17, 1914.
    11. *Lincoln Daily Star*, June 19, 1916, p. 7.
    12. *The Sporting News*, January 11, 1917, p. 7.
    13. *Ibid.*, March 1, 1917, p. 3.
    14. *Galveston Daily News*, August 5, 1917, p. 8.
    15. *Oakland Tribune*, July 17, 1917, p. 10.
    16. *Ibid.*, July 18, 1917, p. 19.
    17. Chino Copper Company Papers (Terry Humble Collection).
    18. *Silver City Independent*, March 27, 1917.

19. White, "Championship Baseball in the Copper Country," pp. 14–15.
20. *The Capital Times*, July 25, 1918, p. 6.
21. Ibid.
22. *The Sporting News*, August 15, 1918, p. 3.
23. *Silver City Independent*, June 14, 1927, p. 4.
24. *Deming Headlight*, August 30, 1918, p. 1.
25. Lee Allen, *The National League Story: The Official History* (New York: Hill and Wang, 1961), p. 149.
26. *Deming Headlight*, August 30, 1918, p. 1.
27. George Vecsey, *Baseball: A History of America's Favorite Game* (New York: Random House, Modern Library, 2006), p. 59.
28. *Fresno Bee*, April 6, 1925, p. 4.
29. *Santa Fe New Mexican*, July 7, 1923, p. 3.
30. www.bevillsadvocate.org/histweb/CHAPTER2.html.
31. Ibid.
32. *El Paso Times*, March 31, 1926, p. 5.
33. Ibid., May 4, 1926, p. 6.
34. Ibid., May 11, 1926, p. 9.
35. Ibid., May, 26, 1926, p. 6.
36. Ibid., July 17, 1926, p. 6.
37. www.bevillsadvocate.org/histweb/CHAPTER3.html.
38. Allen, *The National League Story*, p. 163.
39. *The Sporting News*, November 25, 1925, p. 5.
40. Ibid., June 17, 1926, p. 4.
41. *El Paso Times*, July 21, 1926, p. 6.
42. *Chester Times*, September 7, 1926, p. 15.
43. www.bevillsadvocate.org/histweb/CHAPTER3.html.
44. *El Paso Times*, August 4, 1926, p. 5.
45. Ibid., January 26, 1927, p. 6.
46. Ibid., January 31, 1927, p. 7.
47. *San Antonio Light*, February 20, 1927, p. 47.
48. *The Sporting News*, April 5, 1928, p. 7.
49. Ibid., March 22, 1928, p. 4.
50. *Albuquerque Journal*, April 13, 1925, p. 4.
51. Richard D. Loosbrock, "The Changing Faces of a Mining Town: The Dual Labor System in Elizabethton, New Mexico," *New Mexico Historical Review* 74 (1999): p. 356.
52. Sherman, *Ghost Towns and Mining Camps of New Mexico*, p. 148.
53. *Albuquerque Journal*, May 18, 1930, p. 6.
54. Ibid., June 8, 1930, p. 6.
55. *Santa Fe New Mexican*, June 3, 1984, p. C-4.
56. *Albuquerque Journal*, August 11, 1930, p. 2.
57. *Silver City Independent*, September 14, 1926.
58. *Albuquerque Journal*, September 15, 1929, p. 6.
59. Ibid., May 5, 1930, p. 9.
60. Ibid., August 11, 1930, p. 2.
61. Ibid., September 15, 1930, p. 2.
62. *Las Vegas Daily Optic*, June 10, 1933, p. 3.
63. *Albuquerque Journal*, August 24, 1931, p. 3.
64. Ibid., September 11, 1933, p. 3.
65. Leon McDuff, *Tererro* (Victoria, British Columbia: Trafford, 2006), p. 9.
66. *Santa Fe New Mexican*, October 17, 1976, p. 63.
67. McDuff, *Tererro*, p. 41.
68. Ibid., p. 129.
69. That store, named "Pick's," worked on the scrip system, one of the reasons the miners went on strike in 1936. Sherman, *Ghost Towns and Mining Camps of New Mexico*, p. 207.
70. *Albuquerque Journal*, July 29, 1934, p. 2
71. McDuff, *Tererro*, p. 145.
72. Sherman, *Ghost Towns and Mining Camps of New Mexico*, p. 207.
73. *Albuquerque Journal*, July 9, 1934, p. 2.
74. Ibid., July 29, 1934, p. 2.
75. Ibid., September 22, 1934, p 6.
76. Ibid., July 28, 1935, p. 6.
77. Ibid., August 12, 1935, p. 2.
78. Ibid., August 26, 1935, p. 2.
79. Ibid., September 2, 1935, p. 2.
80. Ibid., September 6, 1935, p. 7.
81. Ibid., September 9, 1935, p. 2.
82. Ibid., September 16, 1935, p 4.
83. Ibid., September 23, 1935, p. 2.
84. McDuff, *Tererro*, p. 65.
85. *Las Vegas Daily Optic*, April 30, 1936, p. 1.
86. *Santa Fe New Mexican*, July 21, 1936, p. 4.
87. Ibid., July 29, 1936, p. 4.
88. McDuff, *Tererro*, p. 171.
89. David Grant Noble, *Pueblos, Villages, Forts and Trails: A Guide to New Mexico's Past* (Albuquerque: University of New Mexico Press, 1994), p. 35.
90. *Albuquerque Journal*, September 16, 1937, p. 6.
91. *Albuquerque Tribune*, June 15, 1955, p. 17.
92. *Albuquerque Journal*, August 28, 1955, p. 26.
93. *The Gallup New Mexico Independent*, August 11, 1976, p. A-8.
94. *Albuquerque Tribune*, July 1, 1957, p. 17.
95. *Albuquerque Journal*, June 29, 1958, p. 25.
96. Ibid.
97. Ibid., January, 26, 1961, p. B-1.

98. Ward Churchill, *Struggle for the Land: Native North American Resistance to Genocide, Ecocide and Colonization* (Winnipeg: Arbeiter Ring, 1999), pp. 248–9.
99. In 2009, Mount Taylor was listed as one of that year's most endangered historic places by the National Trust for Historic Preservation. To the joy of the Native Americans who had battled to save it, in June of the same year, the New Mexico State Register of Cultural Properties listed it, protecting it from future uranium mining.
100. Churchill, *Struggle for the Land*, p. 416.
101. *El Paso Times*, October 3, 1926, p. 10.
102. Sherman, *Ghost Towns and Mining Camps of New Mexico*, p. 149.
103. *Albuquerque Journal*, February 17, 2004.

Chapter 4

1. *Santa Fe New Mexican*, March 12, 1923, p. 6.
2. *Rio Grande Republican*, March 5, 1887, p. 2.
3. *Ibid.*, February 27, 1891, p. 3.
4. *Deming Headlight*, February 21, 1891, p. 2.
5. *Ibid.*, August 25, 1922, p. 4.
6. *Albuquerque Journal*, April 18, 1911, p. 1.
7. Although Hulmes' and Fall's incarcerations were separated by more than four decades, they are bound together in a byzantine tangle of machinations. Ada Hulmes, who was prosecuted by the same William Rynerson who helped deny Billy the Kid his amnesty, had on her defense team Albert J. Fountain (who had defended the Kid in 1881 on a murder charge). In 1896, Fountain and his young son disappeared under highly mysterious circumstances, their bodies never found. The suspects in that probable murder killed a member of the posse that pursued them, one organized by Sheriff Pat Garrett. The suspects were successfully defended by Fall, who employed them as thugs in his infamously dirty political machine. Twelve years later, Fall's legal expertise was again successfully utilized when he defended the man accused of killing Pat Garrett.
8. Seymour, *Baseball: The People's Game*, p. 397.
9. *Ibid.*, p. 413.
10. *Albuquerque Journal*, October 10, 1903, p. 3.
11. *Santa Fe New Mexican*, January 31, 1918, pp. 6–7.
12. *The Swastika*, December 5, 1924, p. 1.
13. *Albuquerque Journal*, March 18, 1934, p. 5.
14. *Ibid.*, July 12, 1942, p. 4.
15. *Ibid.*, July 4, 1942, p. 4.
16. *Ibid.*, July 20, 1942, p. 5.
17. *Santa Fe New Mexican*, March 25, 1946, p. 6.
18. *Ibid.*, May 1, 1946, p. 8.
19. *Albuquerque Journal*, June 3, 1947, p. 3.
20. *Santa Rosa News*, May 14, 1948, p. 1.
21. *Albuquerque Journal*, January 31, 1931, p. 4.
22. *Santa Fe New Mexican*, May 12, 1953, p. 6.
23. *Ibid.*, April 21, 1961, p. 8.
24. *Hobbs Daily News-Sun*, March 15, 1963, p. 1.
25. *Albuquerque Tribune*, July 15, 1971, p. 44.
26. *Albuquerque Journal*, October 26, 1969, p. F-4.
27. *Ibid.*, August 28, 1977, p. F-11.
28. *Ibid.*, September 14, 1977, p. C-1.
29. *Santa Fe New Mexican*, December 4, 1968, p. 2.
30. *Ibid.*, December 3, 1968, p. 2.
31. *Ibid.*, December 5, 1968, p. 6.
32. *Ibid.*, December 4, 1968, p. 1.
33. *Las Vegas Daily Optic*, January 9, 1976, p. 1.
34. Roger Morris, *The Devil's Butchershop: The New Mexico Prison Uprising* (New York, London, Toronto, Sydney: Franklin Watts, 1983), p. 47.
35. *Ibid.*, pp. 43–44.
36. *Santa Fe New Mexican*, September 19, 1977, p. 12.

Chapter 5

1. *The Sporting News*, December 22, 1948, p. 23.
2. *Big Spring Daily Herald*, March 15, 1937, p. 4.
3. *Ibid.*, June 10, 1936, p. 2.
4. *Ibid.*, March 13, 1937, p. 5.
5. *Clovis News-Journal*, April 5, 1938, p. 6.
6. *Ibid.*
7. *Ibid.*, April 7, 1938, p. 6.
8. *Ibid.*, April 8, 1938, p. 6.
9. *Ibid.*, April 7, 1938, p. 6.
10. *Ibid.*, June 12, 1938, p. 6.
11. *Avalanche-Journal*, September 18, 1938, p. 11.
12. *The Sporting News*, November 3, 1938, p. 2.
13. *Clovis News-Journal*, June 22, 1951, p. 2.
14. *The Sporting News*, May 2, 1946, p. 27.
15. *Ibid.*
16. *Big Spring Daily Herald*, May 15, 1939, p. 3.

17. *Abilene Reporter-News*, June 7, 1939, p. 14.
18. *Big Spring Daily Herald*, December 29, 1939, p. 3.
19. *Ibid.*, September 10, 1939, p. 8.
20. *Ibid.*, October 1, 1939, p. 8.
21. *Ibid.*, April 18, 1940, p. 9.
22. *Avalanche-Journal*, June 1, 1941, p. 7.
23. *Las Cruces Sun–News*, September 6, 1940, p. 8.
24. *Avalanche-Journal*, June 1, 1941, p. 7.
25. *Clovis News-Journal*, July 3, 1941, p. 3.
26. *Ibid.*
27. Dave Henry, "The Show," *Pride of the Plains: 50 Years of the Panhandle Sports Hall of Fame*, edited by Mike Haynes and Dave Wohlfarth (Amarillo: Cenveo Printing, 2008), p. 51.
28. *Big Spring Daily Herald*, August 10, 1941, p. 6.
29. *Ibid.*, August 31, 1941, p. 6.
30. *Albuquerque Journal*, January 29, 1942, p. 4.
31. *Ibid.*, May 9, 1942, p. 4.
32. *Morning Avalanche*, June 25, 1942, p. 6.
33. *San Antonio Light*, July 3, 1942, p. 7.
34. *Clovis News-Journal*, July 6, 1942, p. 3.
35. *Avalanche-Journal*, September 14, 1942, p. 11.
36. hardballtimes.com/main/article/the-west-texas-new-mexico–league/
37. *The Sporting News*, July 9, 1947, p. 40.
38. *Lubbock Evening Journal*, October 1, 1947, p. 8.
39. *Amarillo Globe*, September 7, 1948, p. 12.
40. *Ibid.*
41. *The Sporting News*, December 22, 1948, p. 23.
42. *Avalanche-Journal*, September 17, 1950, p. 16.
43. hardballtimes.com/main/article/the-west-texas-new-mexico–league/
44. *The Sporting News*, May 2, 1946, p. 27.
45. *Amarillo Daily News*, September 10, 1946, p. 4.
46. *Amarillo Globe*, June 30, 1947, p. 6.
47. *Amarillo Daily News*, September 6, 1947, p. 2.
48. *Avalanche Journal*, February 12, 1950, p. 13.
49. *Ibid.*
50. *Morning Avalanche*, May 30, 1950, p. 9.
51. *Lubbock Evening Journal*, August 9, 1950, p. 22.
52. *Morning Avalanche*, August 9, 1950, p. 14.
53. *Lubbock Evening Journal*, June 8, 1950, p. 11.
54. *Abilene Reporter-News*, March 22, 1951, p. 24.
55. *Santa Fe New Mexican*, June 17, 1951, p. 2.
56. *Ibid.*
57. *Amarillo Daily News*, June 16, 1951, p. 9.
58. *Ibid.*
59. *The Sporting News*, October 27, 1948, p. 25.
60. *The Abilene Reporter-News*, December 5, 1948, p. 18.
61. *Clovis News-Journal*, April 24, 1949, p. 8.
62. *Ibid.*, January 30, 1949, p. 7.
63. *Ibid.*, March 29, 1949, p. 8.
64. *The Sporting News*, July 20, 1949, p. 36.
65. *Clovis News-Journal*, March 31, 1950, p. 6.
66. *Ibid.*, April 30, 1950 p. 13.
67. *Ibid.*, June 22, 1951, p. 3.
68. Ibid, June 22, 1951, p. 2.
69. *The Abilene Reporter-News*, June 24, 1951, p. 35.
70. *Clovis News-Journal*, June 27, 1951, p. 4.
71. *Ibid.*, June 29, 1951, p. 9.
72. *Ibid.*
73. *Ibid.*, July 12, 1951, p. 2.
74. *Ibid.*, October 12, 1951, p. 4.
75. *Ibid.*, August 8, 1951, p. 4.
76. *Abilene Reporter-News*, June 17, 1952, p. 11-A.
77. *Clovis News-Journal*, December 2, 1951, p. 37.
78. *Albuquerque Tribune*, February 13, 1952, p. 14.
79. Clovis News-Journal, September 7, 1952, p. 19.
80. *Abilene Reporter-News*, April 29, 1952, p. 4.
81. *Ibid.*
82. *Ibid.*, June 19, 1952, p. 38.
83. *Abilene Reporter-News*, June 17, 1952, p. 11-A.
84. *Albuquerque Journal*, July 20, 1952, p. 12.
85. *The Sporting News*, September 17, 1952, p. 37.
86. *Ibid.*, October 21, 1953, p. 13.
87. *Big Spring Daily Herald*, June 26, 1955, p. 11.
88. *El Paso Herald Post*, January 10, 1955, p. 22.
89. *Clovis News-Journal*, January 19, 1955, p. 1.
90. *Abilene Reporter-News*, April 19, 1955, p. 45.
91. *Clovis News-Journal*, June 13, 1955, p. 5.
92. *Ibid.*
93. *Albuquerque Journal*, June 19, 1955, p. 28.
94. *Ibid.*, June 19, 1955, p. 28.
95. *Clovis News-Journal*, June 21, 1955, p. 7.
96. *Abilene Reporter-News*, August 5, 1955, p. 35.

97. *The Corpus Christi Times*, September 24, 1955, p. 9.
98. *Big Spring Daily Herald*, April 2, 1956, p 9.
99. *El Paso Herald Post*, August 9, 1956, p. 18.
100. *Ibid.*, February 14, 1957, p. 18.
101. *Big Spring Daily Herald*, February 7, 1957, p. 6-A.
102. Henry, "The Show," p. 51.
103. *Big Spring Daily Herald*, February 3, 1957, p. 10.
104. *Ibid.*, February 7, 1957, p. 6-A.
105. Henry, "The Show," p. 51.
106. *The Amarillo Globe-Times*, June 18, 1957, p. 11.
107. *Amarillo Daily News*, June 16, 1951, p. 9.

Chapter 6

1. www.wsmr.army.mil/wsmr.asp.
2. *Las Cruces Sun–News*, August 8, 1943, p. 1
3. *Santa Fe New Mexican*, March 21, 1946, p. 6.
4. www.history.navy.mil/library/online/indians.htm.
5. www.kirtland.af.mil/library/factsheet/factsheet.asp.
6. *Albuquerque Journal*, March 21, 1942, p. 8.
7. *Ibid.*, April 27, 1942, p. 5.
8. *Ibid.*, April 26, 1942, p. 4.
9. *The Sporting News*, May 27, 1943, p. 8.
10. *Albuquerque Journal*, May 19, 1942, p. 2.
11. *Ibid.*, May 29, 1942, p. 4.
12. *The Sporting News*, June 11, 1942, p. 6.
13. *Albuquerque Journal*, June 27, 1942, p. 5.
14. *Ibid.*, June 26, 1942, p. 2.
15. *Ibid.*, June 29, 1942, p. 5.
16. *Ibid.*, July 17, 1942, p. 8.
17. *Ibid.*, July 20, 1942, p. 5.
18. *Ibid.*, July 23, 1942, p. 5.
19. *Ibid.*, August 3, 1942, p. 5.
20. *Ibid.*, August 5, 1942, p. 4.
21. R.J. Lesch, "Doc Crandall," *The Baseball Biography Project*, Society for American Baseball Research, http://www.bioproj.sabr.org/bioproj.cfm?a=v&v=1&pid=2974 &bid=990
22. *Albuquerque Journal*, August 31, 1942, p. 5.
23. *Ibid.*, September 18, 1942, p. 9.
24. *Ibid.*, May 13, 1943, p. 4.
25. *Ibid.*, September 21, 1942, p. 5.
26. Vecsey, *Baseball: A History of America's Favorite Game*, p. 110.

27. *Santa Fe New Mexican*, April 19, 1943, p. 2.
28. *Ibid.*
29. *Albuquerque Journal*, June 20, 1943, p. 4.
30. *Lubbock Morning Avalanche*, May 22, 1943, p. 4.
31. *Las Vegas Daily Optic*, April 19, 1943, p. 6.
32. *Clovis News-Journal*, April 20, 1943, p. 4.
33. *Albuquerque Journal*, May 3, 1943, p. 5.
34. *Ibid.*, May 4, 1943, p. 3.
35. *Ibid.*, May 11, 1943, p. 4.
36. *Santa Fe New Mexican*, May 14, 1943, p. 2.
37. *El Paso Herald-Post*, May 17, 1943, p. 10.
38. *Albuquerque Journal*, May 17, 1943, p. 5.
39. *The Sporting News*, May 27, 1943, p. 8.
40. *Albuquerque Journal*, May 13, 1943, p. 4.
41. *Ibid.*, May 27, 1943, p. 4.
42. *Ibid.*, June 5, 1943, p. 4.
43. *Ibid.*, June 7, 1943, p. 5.
44. *Santa Fe New Mexican*, June 7, 1943, p. 2.
45. *Ibid.*, June 8, 1943, p. 6.
46. *Albuquerque Journal*, June 12, 1943, p. 4.
47. *Ibid.*, June 14, 1943, p. 5.
48. *Ibid.*, June 20, 1943, p. 4.
49. *Ibid.*, July 2, 1943, p. 6.
50. *Ibid.*, July 7, 1943, p. 4.
51. *Ibid.*, July 18, 1943, p. 4.
52. *Ibid.*, July 19, 1943, p. 5.
53. *Ibid.*, July 29, 1943, p. 4.
54. *Ibid.*, August 9, 1943, p. 5.
55. *Ibid.*, August 10, 1943, p. 4.
56. *Ibid.*, August 23, 1943, p. 5.
57. *Ibid.*, April 7, 1944, p. 8.
58. *Ibid.*, June 2, 1944, p. 8.
59. *Ibid.*, May 25, 1944, p. 6.
60. *Ibid.*, June 2, 1944, p. 8.
61. *Ibid.*, June 8, 1944, p. 6.
62. *Ibid.*, August 29, 1944, p. 4.
63. *Ibid.*, May 12, 1945, p. 4.
64. *Ibid.*, May 6, 1945, p. 9.
65. *Ibid.*, May 20, 1945, p. 6.
66. *Ibid.*, June 3, 1945, p. 5.
67. *Ibid.*, June 29, 1045, p. 8.
68. *Ibid.*, August 5, 1945, p. 4.
69. *El Paso Herald-Post*, September 12, 1945, p. 10.
70. *Fresno Bee*, October 1, 1945, p. 8.

Chapter 7

1. Simmons, *New Mexico: An Interpretive History*, p. 16.
2. William Lorenz Katz, *Black People Who*

Made the Old West (New York: Thomas Y. Crowell, 1977), p. 156.
  3. *Thirty-Four*, November 12, 1879. p. 2.
  4. *Ibid.*, November 19, 1879, p. 5.
  5. *Santa Fe New Mexican*, March 18, 1916, p. 4.
  6. William Lorenz Katz, *The Black West: A Documentary and Pictorial History* (Garden City, N.Y.: Doubleday, 1971), p. 183.
  7. Simmons, *New Mexico: An Interpretive History*, pp. 139–40.
  8. Riley, *The Biographical Encyclopedia of the Negro Baseball Leagues*, p. 622.
  9. *Albuquerque Journal*, May 8, 1911, p. 3.
  10. *Albuquerque Tribune*, December 7, 1961, p. E1.
  11. Bazz Owen Smaulding Papers, Collection #1981–027, New Mexico State Records Center and Archives, Santa Fe.
  12. *Albuquerque Tribune*, December 2, 1961, p. 1.
  13. *Ibid.*, December 7, 1961, p. E1.
  14. *Albuquerque Journal*, June 25, 1934, p. 2.
  15. *Santa Fe New Mexican*, June 27, 1936, p. 5.
  16. *The Sporting News*, March 7, 1951, p. 30.
  17. *Amarillo Daily News*, March 2, 1951, p. 18.
  18. *Morning Avalanche*, April 25, 1942, p. 6.
  19. Riley, *The Biographical Encyclopedia of the Negro Baseball Leagues*, p. 450.
  20. *Abilene Reporter-News*, March 20, 1951, p. 12.
  21. *Ibid.*, April 18, 1951, p. 7-B.
  22. *Albuquerque Journal*, July 8, 1953, p. 15.
  23. Bruce Adelson, *Brushing Back Jim Crow: The Integration of Minor League Baseball in the American South* (Charlottesville and London: University of Virginia Press, 1999), p. 36.
  24. *Abilene Reporter-News*, May 26, 1951, p. 7-A.
  25. *The Sporting News*, July 2, 1952, p. 36.
  26. *Albuquerque Journal*, April 22, 1954, p. 17.
  27. *Ibid.*, July 5, 1952, p. 8.
  28. *Ibid.*, July 8, 1953, p. 15.
  29. *The Sporting News*, April, 29, 1953, p. 34.
  30. *Santa Fe New Mexican*, May 23, 1922, p. 4.
  31. *Ibid.*, June 28, 1943, p. 3.
  32. *Big Spring Daily Herald*, June 25, 1952, p. 10.

Chapter 8

  1. Bob Rives, "Joe Bauman," *The Baseball Biography Project*, Society for American Baseball Research, http://bioproj.sabr.org/bioproj.cfm?a=v&vI&pid=16945&bid=739.
  2. *Long Beach Press-Telegram*, November 2, 2008, p. C-1.
  3. *Big Spring Daily Herald*, July 9, 1954, p. 7.
  4. *Clovis News-Journal*, July 19, 1954, p. 5.
  5. *Ibid.*
  6. *Lubbock Evening Journal*, August 31, 1954, p. 8.
  7. *Long Beach Press-Telegram*, July 26, 1981, p. S2.
  8. *Ibid.*
  9. *Roswell Daily Record*, September 3, 1954, p. 10.
  10. Robert Obojski, *Bush League: A History of Minor League Baseball* (New York: Macmillan, 1975), p. 299.
  11. *Long Beach Press-Telegram*, July 26, 1981, p. S2.
  12. "Rocket Man," www.abqjournal.com/sports/163819sports04-18-04.htm.
  13. *Life*, September 20, 1954, p. 145.
  14. www.nytimes.com/2005/09/22/sports/baseball/22Bauman.html?_r=l&sq=joe bauman.

Chapter 9

  1. *Las Cruces Sun–News*, March 19, 1950, pp. 1 and 6.
  2. Arthur R. Gomez, "Urban Imperialism in the Modern West: Farmington, New Mexico, vs. Durango, Colorado, 1945–1965," In *Essays in Twentieth Century New Mexico History*, edited by Judith Boyce DeMark (Albuquerque: University of New Mexico Press, 1994), p. 137.
  3. *Albuquerque Tribune*, August 15, 1963, p. E-2.
  4. Myles Schrag, *Diamond in the Desert: The Story of the Connie Mack World Series in Farmington, New Mexico* (Farmington: Adina, 2000), p. 15.
  5. *Albuquerque Tribune*, August 9, 1963, p. A-8.
  6. *Ibid.*
  7. Schrag, *Diamond in the Desert*, p. 26.
  8. *The Sporting News*, August 20, 1966, p. 38.
  9. *Santa Fe New Mexican*, August 26, 1965, p. A-9.
  10. *Las Cruces Sun–News*, March 15, 1966, p. 9.
  11. Schrag, *Diamond in the Desert*, p. 155.
  12. *Ibid.*, pp. 20–21.
  13. *Ibid.*, p. 20.
  14. *Ibid.*, p. 28.

Chapter 10

1. Josiah Gregg, *Commerce of the Prairies*, edited by Max L. Moorhead. (Norman: University of Oklahoma Press, 1954), p. 155.
2. William E. Tydeman, "New Mexico Tourist Images," In *Essays in Twentieth-Century New Mexico History*, edited by Judith Boyce DeMark (Albuquerque: University of New Mexico Press, 1994), p. 206.
3. *Albuquerque Journal*, October 14, 1929, p. 2.
4. *Albuquerque Tribune*, March 28, 1969, p. D-10.
5. *Albuquerque Tribune*, May 22, 1958, p. 21.
6. For many a New Mexico community, this was the most common way to watch a game and it had been carried over into the professional leagues. From 1937 until 1969, the Albuquerque minor league teams played in Tingley Field which offered the curious and wonderful feature of a "drive in" section in right field where the family could watch the game from the comfort of the station wagon.
7. The term "green chile" refers to a delicious sauce made from the roasted vegetable. There is also red chile sauce which is made of the dried peppers. They range from fairly mild in some restaurants to blindingly hot in others and are generously ladled on the traditional cuisine of New Mexico. Neither has anything to do with the "chili" made of meat and beans, popular in TexMex cuisine.
8. Before he stepped off the plane to begin his new job that year, Snider had been to Albuquerque only once and that was for an exhibition game between the Dodgers and the University of New Mexico Lobos in 1963. It was during that game that batting icon Snider was stunned with the news that he'd been sold to the Mets. In another interesting aside, Johnny Podres had been loaned out to the Lobos for that tilt and managed the only hit for the college team — off of colleague Don Drysdale. (*Albuquerque Tribune*, December 21, 1966, p. 21.)

Chapter 11

1. Stewart Culin, "Games of the North American Indians," Extract from the Twenty-Fourth Report of the Bureau of American Ethnology (Washington: Government Printing Office, 1907), p. 789.
2. *Ibid.*
3. *Rio Grande Republican*, September 20, 1884, p. 1.
4. Seymour, *Baseball: The People's Game*, p. 380.
5. David Wallace Adams, *Education for Extinction: American Indians and the Boarding School Experience, 1875–1928* (Lawrence: University Press of Kansas, 1995), p. 63.
6. Clifford E. Trafzer, Jean A. Keller and Lorene Sisquoc, eds., *Boarding School Blues: Revisiting American Indian Educational Experiences* (Lincoln and London: University of Nebraska Press, 2006), p. 27.
7. Adams, *Education for Extinction*, p. 185.
8. *The New York Times*, March 3, 1907.
9. *Ibid.* The men listed in this article were Frank Jude, Cincinnati right-fielder in 1906, and Louis Leroy, who pitched for the Highlanders from 1905 to 1910. Charlie Roy pitched and played first base for the Phillies in 1906. According to the *Washington Post* (September 17, 1906, p. 6), Jude and Roy, along with Lloyd Nephew, were all football players at Carlisle as well.
10. *Rio Grande Republican*, December 10, 1892, p. 1.
11. *Albuquerque Journal*, April 16, 1911, p. 3.
12. *Rio Grande Republican*, June 1, 1906, p. 2.
13. *Albuquerque Journal*, April 23, 1911, p. 3.
14. *Ibid.*, April 30, 1911, p. 3. Jimmy Abeita points out that Platero is a common surname among the Navajo of To'hajiilee, formerly known as Cañoncito, a small noncontiguous section of the reservation just west of Albuquerque. A horseback ride from there into town would indeed have lasted for several hours.
15. *Ibid.*, May 25, 1911, p. 3.
16. *Ibid.*, May 31, 1911, p. 3.
17. *Ibid.*, June 4, 1911, p. 3.
18. Diego Abeita, "Ancient Games in Ancient Plazas," *New Mexico Magazine*, July 1936: p. 22.
19. *Albuquerque Journal*, July 25, 1911, p. 3.
20. *Ibid.*, February 2, 1961, p. B-2.
21. *Ibid.*, September 16, 1937, p. 6. Although the 1936 tournament was frequently mentioned as being the first, the *Albuquerque Journal*, on September 20, 1936, p. 2, mentions Isleta winning the previous year's championship.
22. *Ibid.*, September 20, 1936, p. 2.
23. *Ibid.*, June 14, 1937, p. 3.
24. *Ibid.*, June 19, 1938, p. 4.
25. *Ibid.*, July 9, 1938, p. 7.
26. *Ibid.*, July 31, 1938, p. 4.
27. *Ibid.*
28. The *Albuquerque Journal*, on September 4, 1939, mentions Isleta having won the championship for two years in a row but this ignores the fact that they also won the very first tournament held in 1935 (see note 21 above).

29. *Albuquerque Journal*, March 26, 1939, p. 4.
30. *Ibid.*, May 8, 1939, p. 2.
31. *Ibid.*, June 21, 1939, p. 5.
32. *Ibid.*, July 30, 1939, p. 6.
33. *Ibid.*, May 15, 1939, p. 2.
34. *Ibid.*, September 9, 1940, p. 2.
35. *Ibid.*, September 11, 1940, p. 4.
36. *Ibid.*, July 14, 1941, p. 2.
37. *Ibid.*, September 22, 1941, p. 4.
38. *Ibid.*, June 25, 1942, p. 12.
39. *Ibid.*, March 25, 1942, p. 2.
40. Kenneth Townsend, *World War II and the American Indian* (Albuquerque: University of New Mexico Press, 2000), p. 126.
41. *Ibid.*, p. 72.
42. *Albuquerque Journal*, September 23, 1947, p. 3.
43. *Ibid.*, January 26, 1961, p. B-1.
44. *Albuquerque Tribune*, March 19, 1957, p. 19.
45. *Santa Fe New Mexican*, July 15, 1953, p. 9.
46. *Ibid.*, May 23, 1954, p. 2-C.
47. Ann later identifies this team as the Casa Grande Cotton Kings, a remarkable semipro team from the town south of Phoenix. It was the launch pad for a couple of major leaguers, including lefthander Don Lee (son of Thornton Lee) and Filomeno Coronado "Phil" Ortega. In the twelve years that the team existed, it won the National Baseball Congress state title in each (*Casa Grande Dispatch*, May 18, 2004, p. 20).
48. *Albuquerque Tribune*, August 25, 1951, p. 6.
49. *Albuquerque Journal*, February 2, 1961, p. B-2.
50. *Albuquerque Tribune*, August 25, 1961, p. 6.
51. *Albuquerque Journal*, February 2, 1961, p. B-2.
52. *Ibid.*, May 16, 1938, p. 2.
53. *Ibid.*, February 2, 1961, p. B-2.
54. Debra Denker, "Apache Renaissance Man Taps Deep-rooted Wisdom," *New Mexico Magazine*, August 1997: p. 38.
55. Morris Edward Opler and Catherine H. Opler, "Mescalero Apache History in the Southwest," *New Mexico Historical Review* 25 (January 1950): p. 35.
56. John A. Turcheneske, "Disaster at White Tail: The Fort Sill Apaches' First Ten Years at Mescalero, 1913–1923," *New Mexico Historical Review*, 53 (April 1978): p. 112.
57. Paul Ortega's ball team had a well-earned reputation for fearlessness and often employed it to very positive ends. Most of the players belonged to the Mescalero Red Hats, the famous all–Indian firefighting crew. Organized in 1948, they were the first firefighters in the western United States besides forest service employees. They, like other New Mexico Native American firefighting units, travel widely to work and have saved countless lives and many thousands of acres across the country from destruction.
58. www.nytimes.com/2007/07/09/sports/baseball/09ellsbury.html?
59. www.naataaniibaseball.com/about.asp
60. Culin, "Games of the North American Indians," p. 789.

Bibliography

Books and Articles

Abeita, Diego. "Ancient Games in Ancient Plazas." *New Mexico Magazine*, July 1936: 22–23, 43.

Adams, David Wallace. *Education for Extinction: American Indians and the Boarding School Experience, 1875–1928*. Lawrence: University Press of Kansas, 1995.

Adelson, Bruce. *Brushing Back Jim Crow: The Integration of Minor League Baseball in the American South*. Charlottesville and London: University of Virginia Press, 1999.

Allen, Lee. *The National League Story: The Official History*. New York: Hill and Wang, 1961.

Anderson, George B. *History of New Mexico: Its Resources and People*. Los Angeles, Chicago, New York: Pacific States Publishing, 1907.

Bevill, Lynn E. "Outlaw Baseball Players in the Copper League: 1925–1927." Thesis, Western New Mexico University, 1988.

Brown, Dee. *The Gentle Tamers: Women of the Old Wild West*. Lincoln and London: University of Nebraska Press, 1958.

Caffey, David L. *Land of Enchantment, Land of Conflict: New Mexico in English-Language Fiction*. College Station: Texas A&M University, 1999.

Church, Peggy Pond. *The House at Ottowi Bridge: The Story of Edith Warner and Los Alamos*. Albuquerque: University of New Mexico Press, 1960.

Churchill, Ward. *Struggle for the Land: Native North American Resistance to Genocide, Ecocide and Colonization*. Winnipeg: Arbeiter Ring Publishing, 1999.

Culin, Stewart. "Games of the North American Indians." Extract from the Twenty-Fourth Report of the Bureau of American Ethnology. Washington: Government Printing Office, 1907.

Denker, Debra. "Apache Renaissance Man Taps Deep-rooted Wisdom." *New Mexico Magazine*, August 1997: 38–43.

Drumm, Stella M., ed. *Down the Santa Fe Trail and Into Mexico: The Diary of Susan Shelby Magoffin, 1846–1847*. Lincoln: University of Nebraska Press, 1926. Reprint. New Haven: Yale University Press, 1962.

Faulk, Odie B. *Destiny Road: The Gila Trail and the Opening of the Southwest*. New York: Oxford University Press, 1973.

Goldstein, Warren. *Playing for Keeps: A History of Early Baseball*. Ithaca and London: Cornell University Press, 1989.

Gomez, Arthur R. "Urban Imperialism in the Modern West: Farmington, New Mexico, vs. Durango, Colorado, 1945–1965." In *Essays in Twentieth Century New Mexico History*, edited by Judith Boyce DeMark, 133–147. Albuquerque: University of New Mexico Press, 1994.

Gregg, Josiah. *Commerce of the Prairies*. Edited by Max L. Moorhead. Norman: University of Oklahoma Press, 1954.

Henry, Dave. "The Show." In *Pride of the Plains: 50 Years of the Panhandle Sports Hall of Fame*, edited by Mike Haynes and Dave Wohlfarth, 50–51. Amarillo: Cenveo Printing, 2008.

Hollon, W. Eugene. *Frontier Violence: Another Look*. New York: Oxford University Press, 1974.

Horgan, Paul. *Lamy of Santa Fe: His Life and Times*. New York: Farrar, Straus and Giroux, 1975.

Katz, William Lorenz. *Black People Who Made the Old West*. New York: Thomas Y. Crowell Company, 1977.

_____. *The Black West: A Documentary and Pictorial History*. Garden City, N.Y.: Doubleday and Company, 1971.

Lesch, R. J. "Doc Crandall." *The Baseball Biography Project*, Society for American Baseball Research. http://www.bioproj.sabr.org/bioproj.cfm?a=v&v=l&pid=2974 &bid=990.

Levine, Peter. *A. G. Spalding and the Rise of Baseball: the Promise of American Sport*. New York and Oxford: Oxford University Press, 1985.

Loosbrock, Richard D. "The Changing Faces of a Mining Town: The Dual Labor System in Elizabethton, New Mexico." *New Mexico Historical Review* 74 (1999): 353–373.

McDuff, Leon. *Tererro*. Victoria, British Columbia: Trafford Publishing, 2006.

Morris, Roger. *The Devil's Butchershop: The New Mexico Prison Uprising*. New York, London, Toronto, Sydney: Franklin Watts, 1983.

Noble, David Grant. *Pueblos, Villages, Forts and Trails: A Guide to New Mexico's Past*. Albuquerque: University of New Mexico Press, 1994.

Obojski, Robert. *Bush League: A History of Minor League Baseball*. New York: Macmillan Publishing, 1975.

Opler, Morris Edward and Catherine H. Opler. "Mescalero Apache History in the Southwest." *New Mexico Historical Review* 25 (January 1950): 1–36.

Peterson, Harold. *The Man Who Invented Baseball*. New York: Charles Scribner's Sons, 1969.

Riley, James A. *The Biographical Encyclopedia of the Negro Baseball Leagues*. New York: Carroll & Graf Publishers, 1994.

Rives, Bob. "Joe Wilhoit." *The Baseball Biography Project*, Society for American Baseball Research. http://bioproj.sabr.org/bioproj.cfm?a=v&v=l&pid=15190&bid=30.

_____. "Joe Bauman." *The Baseball Biography Project*, Society for American Baseball Research. http://bioproj.sabr.org/bioproj.cfm?a=v&vI&pid=16945&bid=739.

Schrag, Myles. *Diamond in the Desert: The Story of the Connie Mack World Series in Farmington, New Mexico*. Farmington: Adina Publishing, 2000.

Seymour, Harold. *Baseball: The People's Game*. New York and Oxford: Oxford University Press, 1990.

Sherman, James E. and Barbara H. *Ghost Towns and Mining Camps of New Mexico*. Norman: University of Oklahoma Press, 1975.

Simmons, Marc. *The Last Conquistador: Juan de Oñate and the Settling of the Far Southwest*. Norman: University of Oklahoma Press, 1991.

_____. *New Mexico: An Interpretive History*. New York: Norton, 1977. Reprint. Albuquerque: University of New Mexico Press, 1988.

Tobias, Henry J. *A History of the Jews in New Mexico*. Albuquerque: University of New Mexico Press, 1990.

Townsend, Kenneth. *World War II and the American Indian*. Albuquerque: University of New Mexico Press, 2000.

Trafzer, Clifford E., Jean A. Keller and Lorene Sisquoc, eds. *Boarding School Blues: Revisiting American Indian Educational Experiences*. Lincoln and London: University of Nebraska Press, 2006.

Turcheneske, John A. "Disaster at White Tail: The Fort Sill Apaches' First Ten Years at Mescalero, 1913–1923." *New Mexico Historical Review*, 53 (April 1978): 109–132.

Tydeman, William E. "New Mexico Tourist Images." In *Essays in Twentieth-Century New Mexico History*, edited by Judith Boyce DeMark. Albuquerque: University of New Mexico Press, 1994.

Vecsey, George. *Baseball: A History of America's Favorite Game*. New York:

Random House, Modern Library, 2006.
White, John M. "Championship Baseball in the Copper Country." *New Mexico Magazine*, October 1957: 14–15, 44–45.

Newspapers and Magazines

The Abilene Reporter-News
Albuquerque Daily Journal
Albuquerque Journal
Albuquerque Tribune
Amarillo Daily News
The Amarillo Globe
The Amarillo Globe-Times
Avalanche-Journal (Lubbock, Texas)
Big Spring (Texas) *Daily Herald*
The Capital Times (Madison, Wisconsin)
Casa Grande (Arizona) *Dispatch*
Chester (Pennsylvania) *Times*
Clovis News-Journal
The Corpus Christi Times
The Deming Headlight
El Paso Herald-Post
El Paso Times
The Fresno Bee
Galveston Daily News
The Gallup New Mexico Independent
Hobbs Daily News-Sun
Las Cruces Sun–News
Las Vegas Daily Optic
Life Magazine
Lincoln (Nebraska) *Daily Star*
Long Beach Press-Telegram
Lubbock Evening Journal
Lubbock Morning Journal
Mining Life (Silver City)
The New York Times
Oakland Tribune
Rio Grande Republican (Las Cruces)
Roswell Daily Record
San Antonio Light
Santa Fe New Mexican
Santa Rosa News
Silver City Enterprise
Silver City Independent
The Sporting News
The Swastika (Des Moines, New Mexico)
Thirty-Four (Las Cruces)

Collections

Center for Southwest Research, University of New Mexico
Chino Copper Company Papers (Terry Humble Collection)
Farmington Museum
Fray Angélico Chávez History Library, Santa Fe
National Archives and Records Administration, Rocky Mountain Region
Bazz Owen Smaulding Papers, New Mexico State Records Center and Archives, Santa Fe
Silver City Museum

Websites

www.abqjournal.com
www.athletics.uchicago.edu
www.baseball-reference.com
www.bevillsadvocate.org
www.daily-times.com
www.hardballtimes.com
www.history.navy.mil/
www.kirtland.af.mil
www.naataaniibaseball.com
www.newmexicohistory.org
www.nmmining.org
www.nytimes.com
www.wsmr.army.mil/wsmr.asp

Interviews

Abeita, Jim, e-mails and interviews, 2008–2009.
Abeita, Francis, April 24, 2009.
Abeita, Joseph, April 24, 2009.
Abeita, Pablo, June 10, 2009.
Baca, Rowena, July 22, 2009.
Bauman, Dorothy, July 2, 2008, and April 17, 2009.
Benally, Dineh, February 19, 2009.
Carpenter, Danny, June 9, 2008, and August 18, 2008.
Carpenter, Maureen, June 9, 2008.
Cooper, Joe, June 27, 2008.
Green, Alfred, January 8, 2009, and April 25, 2009.
Green, Jean Riley, e-mails and interviews, 2008 and 2009.
Jojola, Emil, September 10, 2008, and April 25, 2009.
Kiro, Ann, April 24, 2009.
Kiro, Paul, April 24, 2009.

Kiro, Paully, April 24, 2009.
Kiro, Terence, April 24, 2009.
Lanier, Buck, February 25, 2009.
Martinez, Anthony R., July 7, 2008.
Martinez, Nick, June 4, 2009.
May, Carol, June 9, 2008.
McDuff, Leon, June 28, 2008.
Moya, Tony, June 29, 2009.
Ortega, Paul, February 27, 2009, and April 18, 2009.
Padilla, Matthew, May 27, 2009.
Padilla-Gutiérrez, Rita, May 27, 2009.
Sanchez, Libby, June 3, 2009.
Schrag, Myles, e-mails, August 18, 2008.
Stowers, Harry Jr., December 15, 2008, and December 17, 2008.
Waldrip, Jim, March 11, 2009, and April 17, 2009.
Williams, Zeak, February 21, 2009, and April 8, 2009.

Index

Numbers in ***bold italics*** indicate pages with photographs.

Abeita, Andy 181, 183–184
Abeita, Bartolo 201
Abeita, Buster 181–183, 188, 201–202
Abeita, Debbie 185, 195
Abeita, Francis 201–206, ***204***
Abeita, Jimmy 185–196, ***186***, 201, 215–216
Abeita, Joe M. (Joe the Umpire) 180–183, 201–206, ***202***, ***203***, ***205***
Abeita, Johnnie 201
Abeita, Joseph 201–206, ***203***, ***204***
Abeita, Juan Ray ***180***
Abeita, Lallo 181
Abeita, Lazaro ***180***
Abeita, Marcelino ***180***
Abeita, Pablo (catcher) 161–162, 165–167, 170–171, 192–193
Abeita, Pablo (Isleta manager) 179
Abeita, Richard 192
Abeita, Tony ***180***
Abilene Blue Sox 104, 106
Acoma Pueblo 16, 20, 79
Adams (El Paso pitcher, 1903) 37
Adelino, New Mexico 160
Alamo Navajo reservation 210
Alamogordo, New Mexico 121, 193
Albuquerque, New Mexico 16–17, 22, 24, 26–27
Albuquerque and Cerrillos Coal Company 64–65
Albuquerque Army Air Base 85, 118
Albuquerque Braves 192
Albuquerque Browns 27–30, ***27***, ***30***
Albuquerque Cardinals 181
Albuquerque City-County League (Greater Albuquerque League) 76, 78, 87–88, 166, 185, 191, 201, 204
Albuquerque Dons 72–73
Albuquerque Dukes 68, 77, 100, 102, 104, 118, 129–131, 148, 163–164, 170
Albuquerque Grays 41–50, 69, 159, 178–179
Albuquerque Happy-Go-Luckys 41
Albuquerque Indian All-Stars 74, 181–183, 202
Albuquerque Indian School ***40***, 41–42, 175, ***176***, 177–178, 185–188, 195, 203

Albuquerque Indian School Employees baseball team 180
Albuquerque Isotopes 23, 164, 214, 217
Albuquerque Monarchs 131
Albuquerque Old Town Browns 41
Albuquerque Pirates 181
Albuquerque Territorial Fair, 1903 35–39
Albuquerque Territorial Fair, 1911 48–51
Albuquerque Tigers 72
Alexander, Grover Cleveland 57–58
All-Indian Baseball Tournament, Laguna Pueblo ***76***, 77, 180–184, 229*n*21, 229*n*28, 193–194, 197, 204
All-Indian League 204
All-Indian Men's League, Laguna Pueblo 80
Allen, Walter 45
Allman, Leroy 182
Almquist, Paul 149
Althouse, Harry 60, 63, 65, 67
Amarillo (Texas) Gold Sox 112, 138
Amarillo (Texas) Longhorns 47
Amarillo (Texas) Monograms 47
American Amateur Baseball Congress 147–153
American Metals Company of New Mexico 70, 74
Anaconda Copper Company 75–80, 198
Anasazi (Ancestral Puebloans) 11
Ancestral Puebloans (Anasazi) 11, 52
Ancho, New Mexico 167
Anderson, Lee 182
Anderson brothers (African American players) 42, 49, 129
Animas River 146
Anson, Adrian, "Cap" 37–39
Anzara, Frank ***180***
Apaches 11, 14, 15, 53, 117, 174
Arico, Sam 120
Arizona Copper League 56–59
Arizona State League 63, 65
Arizona-Texas League ***15***, 100, 103, 120, 181
Armijo Yanks 119, 180
Artesia, New Mexico 136, 140
Artesia Drillers 8
Artesia Giants 97

235

Artesia NuMexers 136
Atchison, Topeka and Santa Fe Railroad 7, 27, 41, 96, 197
Athapascan people 11
Atlantic and Pacific Railroad 28
Atomic Energy Commission 76

Babe Ruth World Series 147–148, 152
Baca, Rowena 167–169, *168*
Baerwald, Rudy 37, 58
Bailey, Bill 49–50
Bailey, Bill (newspaperman) 194
Bandelier National Monument 9, 20
Barngrover, Bill 46–48
Bataan Death March 117–118
Battle of Glorieta Pass 17
Battle of Valverde 17
Bauman, Dorothy 136–137, 141, 144–145, *140*, *144*
Bauman, Joe 104, 136–145, *138*, *139*, *140*
Bayless, Dick 56, 58
Beaumont (Texas) Exporters 98
Beers, Clarence 121–123
Belén, New Mexico 159–160
Bell Park, Clovis 98–99, 114
Benally, Dineh 210–215, *212*
Bender, Albert 176–177
Ben-Hur 7
Benites, Frank 110
Bernalillo, New Mexico 159
Bernalillo Piners 68, 69
Big Spring (Texas) Black Giants 133
Big Spring (Texas) Bombers 102
Big Spring (Texas) Broncs 136
Big State League 112
Biggs Field, El Paso, Texas 119, 125
Billy the Kid 7, 18, 221*n*4, 225*n*7
Birmingham Black Barons 129–131
Bisbee, Arizona 60, 62–63, 65, 120
Bisti Badlands 146
Black cowboys 128
Blake, Donald 208
Bluewater, New Mexico 76
Blumenschein, Ernest 19
Blythe, Dee 98
Boggs (African American player, 1922) 131
Bolling, Frank 143
Bolling, Milt 143
Bonds, Barry 144
Bonney, William (Billy the Kid) 7
Borger (Texas) Gassers 100, 102
Bosque Farms, New Mexico 160
Bosque Redondo 174–175, 206
Boston Bloomer Girls 44
Boston Braves 56, 122, 136
Boston Red Sox 56, 59, 215
Bottarini, John 121
Bowles, Emmett Jerome 65, 67–69, *68*, 72, 74, 178, 181
Bradbury Museum, Los Alamos 116
Brandon, Chick 49

Branham, W. G. 103
Brewer, Tom 143
Bridgens, Warren "Pop" 124
Bright, Harry 105
Bronco Bill 84
Brooklyn Dodgers 104, 120
Brooklyn Robins 58
Brooklyn Superbas 37
Brown, Charlie 72
Brown, Jerry 8
Buchoz, Henry 33
Budzinsky, Tererro (player, 1935) 73
Buffalo Bill 57
Buffalo Soldiers 15, 127–128, *127*, 131
Bunning, Jim 143
Burns, Bill 58
Burro Mountains 56
Butler, Oscar *134*
Butler, Sunshine 133

Cactus League 69
Callahan, Nixey 38
Camino Real 22
Camp Cody 57
Camp Lordsburg 117
Camp Luna, Las Vegas, New Mexico 121, 123–124
Camp Pinedale Interceptors, California 125
Canyon Road, Santa Fe 19
Carisch, Fred 56, 58
Carlisle School 176
Carlsbad, New Mexico 53, 113, 143
Carlsbad Air Base, New Mexico 121–122,
Carlsbad Caverns 9
Carlsbad Potashers 54, 97, 136
Carolina League 119
Carpenter, Danny 149–153
Carpenter, Maureen 153, 155
Carrizozo, New Mexico 167, 193
Carson, Kit 174
Cartwright, Alexander Joy 24
Casa Grande (Arizona) Cotton Kings 230*n*47
Catron County 54
Cavet, Pug 49
Central New Mexico League 63–74, 129, 159, 178, 181–183
Cerrillos, New Mexico 52
Cerro Pedernal *17*
Chaco Canyon 11, 146
Chance, Frank 38
Charles, Ray 133
Chase, Hal 59–62
Chavez, Dee 167–168, *168*
Chavez, Frank 167
Chavez, Juan Manuel 117–118
Chicago American Giants 129–130
Chicago Colts 38
Chicago Cubs 49, 57, 60, 104, 109–110, 121
Chicago Giants 50
Chicago Orphans 38

Index

Chicago White Sox 49, 58–59, 65, 125
Chicago White Stockings 37–38, 43
Chick, Bill 104
Chilocco Indian School 176, 182
Chimayo, New Mexico 10
Chino Copper Company 55–57
Chiricahua Apaches 6, *12*, 11, 54, 206
Cíbola 12, 52, 126
Cicuye 53
Cincinnati Reds 49, 56, 114
Civil War 16–17, 24, 32, 128
Clancy, Albert 42, 44, 48
Clemenson, Bill 122
Cleveland Indians 65, 104
Cleveland Naps 56
Cleveland Spiders 49
Cloudcroft, New Mexico 207
Clovis, New Mexico 96–97
Clovis Baseball Association 108
Clovis Baseball, Inc. 109
Clovis Black Pioneers 131
Clovis Buzzers 97
Clovis Cubs 97
Clovis Pioneers 96–99, 101–103
Clovis Redlegs 114
Cobb, Ty 49
Cóchiti Pueblo 117, 195, 204
Colin Kellys *see* Flying Kellys
College of Agriculture and Mechanic Arts, Las Cruces 35
Colorado Volunteers 17
Colored Infantry *see* Buffalo Soldiers
Combs, Earl 120
Compromise of 1850 16
Confederate States of America 16–18
Connie Mack World Series 146–155, *151*, 211–212
Cooper, Joe 147, 149–150, 152, 155
Copper League *15*, 37, 45, 54–63, 65–67, 80
Corhan, Roy "Binger" 43, 159
Cornish, Doc 44
Coronado League 183
Crandall, Otis "Doc" 120
Crawford (Albuquerque Browns player, 1880s) 29
Cross, Allen 113
Crow, Odel *134*
Crownpoint, New Mexico 210
Crues, Bob 100, 104–106, 138
Curran, Louis R. 62
Curry County, New Mexico 96

Dalton Canyon 70
Danning, Harry 122
Davis, Harry 84
Davis-Monthan Air Force Base, Arizona 122
Dawson, New Mexico 41, 44, 48–50, 65
Dawson Coal Diggers 44–45, 48–50, 54
Deal, Charlie 57
Dean, Dizzy 108–109
Dean, Paul 108–109, 147

de Coronado, Francisco Vasquez 52–53, 96
de la Cueva, Don Francisco Fernandez 26
Deming, New Mexico 37, 44, 55–57, 121
Deming Boosters 56
De Montreville, Gene 38
de Niza, Fray Marcos 12, 13, 126
de Onate, Don Juan 13
de Peralta, Don Pedro 13
de Santa Ana, Antonio Lopez 15
Detroit Tigers 49, 56, 98
de Vaca, Cabeza 126
de Vargas, Don Diego 14
Dial, Red 110–113
DiMaggio, Joe 122–123
Dobernic, Jess 125
Domenici, Pete 166, 201
Domino, Fats 133
Dona Ana County, New Mexico 31
Donahue, Tim 38
Donovan, "Noisy" 45, 49, 58
Douglas, Arizona 59–62
Douglas, Jack 102
Downey, Tom 49
Drexel, St. Katharine 177
Drysdale, Don 229*n*8
Dumont, Ray 87
Durhan, Louis "Bull" 49

Earp Brothers 6
Eastern League 98
Eckerman, Nevins 181
El Cerro, New Mexico 162
Ellis (Western League pitcher, 1911) 49
Ellsbury, Jacoby 210, 214–215
El Moro 13
El Paso, Texas 17, 34, 37–39, 59–63
El Paso Natural Gas Company 148–149
El Turco 53
Estevanico 126
Eusebius, (Father) 86–87, 95
Everitt, Bill 38

Faber (Western League pitcher, 1911) 49
Fabrique, Bunny 57
Fall, Albert Bacon 84, 225*n*7
Farmington, New Mexico 146–155, 211–212
Farmington Hummers 150
Fausett, Cy 130
Federal League 60, 120
Feller, Bob 147
Felsch, Hap 62
Fernandez, Nanny 122
Fernandez, Roberto 105
Fitzgerald (secretary Fort Seldon club) 32
Flack, Max 57
Flood-Smith Resolution 48–49
Flying (Colin) Kellys 85, 118–125
Fort Bayard, New Mexico 16, 31, 55, 59–63, 65
Fort Cummings, New Mexico 128
Fort Marcy, New Mexico 31

Index

Fort Seldon, New Mexico 31–35
Fort Seldon MacArthurs 32–33
Fort Seldon Rising Suns 32
Fort Stanton, New Mexico 117
Fort Sumner, New Mexico 121, 174
Fort Union, New Mexico 17, 18, 31
Fort Wingate, New Mexico **127**
Fortin, Joe 105, 107
Foster, Harold 198
Fountain, Albert J. 225*n*7
Freberg, Ken 186
Frontier League 59
Fruitland, New Mexico 146
Fullerton, Hugh 121

Gadsden Purchase 16
Gallup, New Mexico 41, 210
Gandil, Chick 60–63
Gann, Troy "Cotton" 119, 121
Gantner, Bern 108–110, 113, 148
Garcia, John **68, 69**
Garrett, Pat 7, 35, 225*n*7
Gear, Dale 49–51
Gehrig, Lou 120
Geronimo 6, 15, 25, 54, 127
Ghost Ranch **17**
Gila Mountains 54
Gila River 54
Gila Wilderness **12**
Gilkerson Giants 129
Gilstrap, Harry 104, 106, 113–114
Giomi Brothers 120
Gomez, Lefty 147
Gonzalez, Max 163
Gordon, Joe 124
Graham, Andrew 37
Graham, Bert 43, 49, 57–58
Grant County, New Mexico 54–55, 63
Grants, New Mexico 75
Grants Uranium Belt 75
Greater Albuquerque League *see* Albuquerque City-County League
Green, Al 77, 93, 187–189, 191, **193**, 195–196
Green, Howard 100
Green, Jean Riley 77, 187–189, 195–196, **196**
Green, Robert 138, 140
Greenberg, Hank 98
Greer, Stubby 104
Griego, Tererro (player, 1935) 73
Griffey, Ken, Jr. 152
Griffith, Clark 38
Guadalupe Mountains 9
Gustbrach, Lee 182
Gustovich, George 182

Hacker, Warren 106
Haddican, Bill 121
Haile, Reverend Berard 215
Hair, Bill 110
Hale, Lem 119, 121
Hamilton (African American pitcher) 129

Haney, Jay 129–130
Harris, Calvin **134**
Hartnet, Gabby 121
Harvey, Fred 36
Harvey Houses 19, 157
Haskell Institute 176–177, 181–182, 190
Hauser, Joe 104, 138
Heard, Connie 130
Hearst, William Randolph 36, 37, 39
Heinrich, Steve 83
Hendrix, Nelson 181
Hernandez, Ray 88
Hershiser, Orel 23
Hewitt, Bill 102–103
Hidalgo County, New Mexico 117
Hilton, Conrad 167
Hobbs, New Mexico 131–133
Hobbs Boosters 98
Hobbs Drillers 98
Hobbs Tigers 131–135, **134**
Holliday, Doc 6
Hollocher, Charlie 57
Holly, Buddy 97
Holy Ghost Canyon 69
Homerunners Club 153
Homestead Grays 130
Hopi 11, 183, 197
House of David 103
Howell, Dixie 102
Howes, Russell 68
Hulmes, Ada 84, 225*n*7
Hurley, New Mexico 37, 55, 58, 81

Inn of the Mountain Gods 206
International Union of Mine, Mill and Smelter Workers 73
Interstate League 119
Isbell, Frank 47
Isleta Bees 184, 202
Isleta Braves 181–182, 201
Isleta Indians 201
Isleta Pollys 166, 197
Isleta Pueblo 11, 158–159, 161, 179–180, **180**, 181–196, 200–206, 215–216
Isotopes Park 213

Jackpile Mine 76
Jackpile Miners 76
Jackson, Joe 61–62
Jackson, S.J. **134**
Jansen, Ray 58
Japanese Baseball Association of Los Angeles 42–43, 222*n*92
Jemez Mountains 6
Jemez Pueblo 197
Jewish families in New Mexico 16, 221*n*3
Jicarilla Apache 11, 146, 194
Joe Bauman Stadium (Fair Park Stadium) 144
Johnson, Walter 85
Johnson, Walter, Jr. 85–86, 119
Jojola, Domingo **180**

Index

Jojola, Eddie "Short" **203**
Jojola, Emil 187–195, **188, 191**
Jojola, John 179
Jojola, John T. **180**
Jojola, Mariano 180
Jojola, Sam 180–181, 183, 188, 202
Jones (Native American pitcher) 47, 178
Jones, J.W. "Doc" 148–149, 154
Jones, Oscar 37, 39
Jones, Reuben 129
Jones, Tex 49
Jornada del Muerto 28
Juarez (Ciudad), Mexico **15**, 31, 59–63
Jude, Frank 177, 229n9
Justis Park 151
Justis Supply Company, Farmington 148–149, 154

Kailer, J.D. 112
Kane, Harry "Klondike" 58
Kansas City Athletics 190
Kansas City Blues 49
Kansas City Monarchs 129
Katoll, Jack 38
Kearny, Gen. Stephen Watts 14–15
Keefe, Bobby 58
Kelly, Mrs. Colin 85
Kelly, Joe 106
Kennedy, Vernon 147
Kenneth, Father 188
Kewa (Santo Domingo) Pueblo 13, 195
Kilduff, Pete 57
Killefer, Bill 57
Kiner, Ralph 45
King, B.B. 133
Kiro, Ann 77, 196–200, **200**
Kiro, Antonio 199, **200**
Kiro, Paul 77, 196–200, **199, 200**
Kiro, Paully 77–80, 199–200, **200**
Kiro, Terence 78, 80, 199–200, **200**
Kiro, Wilfred 199
Kiro, Zalin 199, **200**
Kirtland Army Air Field 118–125
Kirtland 29ers 124–125
Koldyke, Mike 214
Krikorkian, Doug 137–138
Kunz (Albuquerque Grays outfielder, 1911) 49

La Conquistadora 21
Laguna Anaconda baseball team 76, 77, 194
Laguna Braves 76, 77, 191
Laguna Indians 183
Laguna Jackpile Miners 54, 194
Laguna Merchants 76, 77
Laguna Pueblo 75–80, **76**, 81–82, 180–200
Laguna Redskins 3, 199
Lajoie, Nap 49
Lamesa (Texas) Lobos 129
Lamesa (Texas) Black Lobos 131
La Mesilla, New Mexico 25

Lamy, Jean Baptiste 16
Landis, Kenesaw Mountain 59, 61–63
Lange, Bill 38
Lanier, Buck 137–140, 144–145
La Plata River 146
Las Cruces, New Mexico 9, 16, 22, 25, 28, 31–32
Las Cruces Blue Jays 32
Las Cruces Montezumas 32, 33
Las Lomas Tigers 180
Laster, James **134**
Las Trampas, New Mexico 156
Las Vegas, Nevada, Gunnery School 123
Las Vegas, New Mexico 6, 16, 18, 25–26, 28
Las Vegas Baseball Association 46
Las Vegas Eat-em-alives 41
Las Vegas Giants 41
Las Vegas Grant 18
Las Vegas Maroons 45–50
Las Vegas Optics 28, 31
Las Vegas Sluggers 41
Lazzeri, Tony 120
Leadville, Colorado 6
Lebeck, Greg 150
Lee, Don 230n47
Lemon, Jim 143
Lempke (Denver pitcher, 1903) 37
Leroy, Louis 177, 229n9
Lester, Joe **134**
Lincoln County Wars 7, 18
Lipan Apaches 11
Little Richard 133
Littlehorse, Marcel 74, 178, 181–182
Llano Estacado 96, 131
Lockhart (Native American pitcher) 43–45, 47–48, 51, 178
Lockhart, Tommy 47, 49
Long Beach Ferry Command, California 122
Longhorn League 112, 136, 138, 141, 143
Lopez, Nancy 141
Los Alamos National Laboratory 20
Los Angeles Dodgers 23, 170–171, 215–216
Los Chaves, New Mexico 159–160
Los Lunas, New Mexico 159–160
Los Trujillos, New Mexico 160
Lowrey Field, Denver 120
Lozan, Roy 131
Lubbock (Texas) Black Hubbers 131
Lubbock (Texas) Hubbers 96, 98–100, 105–106
Lucero, Joe 72
Lucero, Melo **203**
Ludlow, Colorado 64
Luis Lopez, New Mexico 159
Luna County, New Mexico 38

MacArthur, Arthur 32
MacArthur, Douglas 32
Madrid, New Mexico 64–65, 81, 129
Madrid Miners 64–69, 72–76, 93, 120, 181
Maisel's Indian Jewelry Store 183

Mangas Coloradas 15
Manhattan Project 19, 116, 167
Mann, Les 57
Manzano Mountains 172
Markley (El Paso catcher, 1903) 37
Marshall, Slam 61–62
Martin, Billy (Santa Fe baseball club manager and penitentiary official) 38, 84
Martin, Hershel 104
Martin, Pepper 147
Martinez, Anthony 90–95, *92*
Martinez, Nick 162–165, 171
Masterson, Bat 6–7
Mathewson, Christy 159
Matthews, Danny 119, 121, 123
May, Carol 148–149, 155
Mayfield, Jack 112
McArdle, Roy 58
McCarty, Henry (Billy the Kid) 7
McCreight, William T. 27–29, *30, 31*
McDuff, Leon 70–74, 81
McGrath, Barney 47
McKibbin, Dorothy 116
McManus, John 83, 85
Melago, John 119–121
Meloan, Paul 58
Memphis Red Sox 130
Menaul School, Albuquerque 41, 178
Meriam Report 175
Merkle, Fred 57
Mertes, Sam 38
Mesa Verde 11, 146
Mescalero Apaches 192, 206–210
Mescalero Red Hats 230*n*57
Mesilla Valley 16, 31, 116
Mesita, village of (Laguna Pueblo) 77, 194, 196
Meusel, Bob 120
Mexican-American War 31
Mexican War of Independence 14
Micewski, Harry 119
Mid Rio Grande League 160–166, 169–172
Midland (Texas) Cardinals 98
Midland (Texas) Indians 136
Midwest Semipro Baseball Association 63
Miera, Jose 167
Miljus, John 120
Miller, Pud 105
Mills, Buster 99
Milwaukee Braves 164
Mimbres River 10, 54
Mitchell, Charles *134*
Mize, Johnny 99
Moffett, Ben 201
Mogollon culture 10–11, *12*, 54
Monahan (Texas) Trojans 98
Montgomery Billikens 43
Montoya, Candido *164*
Montoya, Rufie *164*
Morton, Ray "Professor" 119–120
Mount Taylor 79, 225*n*99

Mountainair, New Mexico 72
Moya, Tony 169–172
Mullens, Eddie 114
Myers, Hap 56

Naa'taannii Baseball Academy 210–215, *212*
Nail, J.H. 101
Nambe Pueblo 194
Nance, Mickey 73
National Association of Professional Baseball Leagues 34, 103
National Baseball Congress 87, 100, 160, 162
National Baseball Congress Tournament 120, 123
Native American All-Star game 213–214
Navajo 9, 11, 14, 15, *20*, 36, 79, 117, 146, 174, 206, 210–215
Navajo Code Talkers 117
Neal (African American player, 1922) 131
Nell, Gordon 100,
Nephew, Lloyd 177, 229*n*9
New Mexico Copper League 56, 58–59, 63, 81
New Mexico Highlands University, Las Vegas 162–163, 214
New Mexico Military Institute 137, 211
New Mexico State University 31, 211
New Mexico Territorial/State Penitentiary 83–95
New York Giants 49–50, 61, 120, 122,
New York Highlanders 37, 177
New York Lincoln Giants 50
New York Mets 229*n*8
New York Yankees 104, 120, 124
Nichols, "Kid" 37
Norman, Red 103
Norris, Willie *134*
Northrop Bombers, California 120
Nuemeyer, Bugs 48
NuMexer Park 136

O'Connell, Jimmie 61–63, 65, 67, 81
Odessa (Texas) Oilers 98, 136
Ohkay Ohwinge (San Juan) Pueblo 13, 183, 194
Old Laguna, village of (Laguna Pueblo) *76*
Oliver (Albuquerque Indian School pitcher, 1911) 177
Oregon Trail 24
Organ, New Mexico 32
Organ Mountains 9, 31
Orogrande, New Mexico 209
Ortega, Paul 206–210, *208*
Ortega, Phil (Filomeno Coronado) 230*n*47
Ortiz, Matt 72
Ortiz Mountains 64
Otero, Avilio, Josefita, and Manuel *165*
Owl Bar and Café, San Antonio, New Mexico 167

Index

Pacific Coast League 56–58, 60, 120–121
Padilla, Dan 41–42, 45–49, 178
Padilla, Felipe **180**
Padilla, Matthew 161–162
Padilla-Gutierrez, Rita 157–162, 172–173
Paguate (village of Laguna Pueblo) 76, 81, 194
Paguate Warriors 77, 191
Paisano, Abel 183–184, 188
Palace of the Governors 13, 17
Palmer House Baseball Club 129
Pampa (Texas) Oilers 99–100, 105–107, 109, 111–114
Parenti, Babe 166
Parker, Capt. William Thornton 128
Parris, Collier 110, 130
Paskert, Dode 57
Pavlovic, Danny 118, 119, 123–124
Pecos, New Mexico 69, 71, 81, 90
Pecos River 69, 174
Pecos Valley-Panhandle League 97
Pecos Wilderness 69
Penitentiary Grays 85–87, 119
Penitentiary Rocks 87–95
Peralta, New Mexico 158–159
Perry, Earl 141
Perry (superintendent Albuquerque Indian School) 178
Pertica, Bill 59
Peterson Field, Colorado Springs 125
Pettus, Bill 49–50, 128, 159
Pezold, Larry 58
Phelan, Art 49
Philadelphia Athletics 120
Philadelphia Phillies 60, 104
Phillips, Bert 19
Phillips 66 (baseball team) 98
Piazza, Mike 23
Pick's Store, Tererro 224n69
Picuris Pueblo 194
Pittsburgh Pirates 42, 56, 97–99, 120, 122, 176, 190
Plainview (Texas) Ponies 113
Platero (Albuquerque Indian School pitcher, 1911) 178, 229n14
Podres, Johnny 229n8
Pojoaque Pueblo 53, 194
Pope, Judge William H. 44
Powell, Putt 106
Pratt, Captain Richard Henry 176
Price, Jackie 143
Price, Milton 103
Pueblo Indians 11–14, 20, 52–53, 158
Pueblo Revolt 13, 14, 158
Pyle, Ernie 117

Queen City Stars (Seattle) 129
Quitaque, Texas 132
Quivira 52

Raíces del Rio Abajo 159

Ramah Navajo reservation 210
Ramirez, Manny 151
Raton, New Mexico 46–47
Ray, Arizona 56
Reed, Tererro (player, 1935) 73
Richardson, Bill **134**
Richardson, Gov. Bill 144
Richardson, Virgil 110
Rickard (San Marcial player, 1880s) 28
Ricketts Park 149, 153–154, 211–212
Riley, Emerson 77
Riley, Roger 77
Rio Abajo 156–173
Rio Grande Association 97
Rio Grande Gorge 9
Rio Grande Park, Albuquerque 73
Rio Grande River 11, 17, 26, 158
Rio Grande Semipro League 183
Rio Mimbres Irrigation Company 37
Ripp, Bart 88–89
Risberg, Swede 62–63
Robinson, Frank 152
Robinson, Jackie 130
Roche, Jack 58
Rochester Redwings 99
Rockland Park 87, 90
Roosevelt, Theodore 18, 127
Rossi, Chick 68
Roswell, New Mexico 44, 140, 207
Roswell Rockets 97, 104, 136–145
Roswell Sunshiners 98
Rough Riders 18
Rouiller, Johnnie 33
Route 66 22, 27
Rowe, Schoolboy 98
Roy, Charlie 177, 229n9
Ruffing, Red 122–123
Ruidoso, New Mexico 117, 207
Runyon, Damon 61, 120
Ruth, Babe 120
Ruth, Mrs. Babe 147
Rynerson, William Logan 222n40, 225n7

Sacramento Mountains 206
Sacramento Solons 121
St. Catherine Indian School 177, 180, 187, 197, 201
St. Francis Cathedral, Santa Fe 21
St. Joseph, Missouri 9
St. Louis Browns 27–28, **30**, 42, 48–49, 56, 58, 97, 123, 182
St. Louis Cardinals 97, 120
St. Louis Maroons 29
St. Louis Terriers 120
St. Michael's (Arizona) Mission School 11
St. Michael's College, Santa Fe 41
Salazar, Carlos 129
Salazar, Ross 42, 45, 48–49, 159
Salt River All-Indian tournament 198–199
San Angelo (Texas) Colts 136
San Antonio, New Mexico 164, 167

Index

San Antonio Angels baseball team 167–169, **168**
Sanchez, Ernesto 160–161, **161**
Sanchez, Libby 160–161, **161**
Sand, Heinie 61
San Felipe Pueblo 195
San Fernandez, New Mexico 163
San Francisco Giants 215–216
San Francisco Seals 58, 66, 119
Sangre de Cristo Mountains 9, 13, 156, 217
San Ildefonso Pueblo 20, 194
San Jose Sluggers 180
San Jose Victory baseball club 183, **202**
San Juan County, New Mexico 148
San Juan (Ohkay Ohwinge) Pueblo 13, 183, 194
San Juan River 11, 146
San Marcial, New Mexico 28, 47, 159
Santa Ana Air Base, California 122–123
Santa Clara Pueblo 83, 194
Santa Fe, New Mexico 7–8, 13, 16, 19, **23**, 28–31
Santa Fe Apprentices 41
Santa Fe Indian Council baseball team 183
Santa Fe Indian School 177, 183, 194–195
Santa Fe Saints 67
Santa Fe Stationers 72–73
Santa Fe Trail 7, 18, 24
Santa Rita, New Mexico 45, 55–58, 81
Santa Rita del Cobre 55
Santo Domingo (Kewa) Pueblo 13, 195
Santuario de Chimayó 21
Sayles, Hal 112
Schmidt, Henry 37
Schrag, Myles 9
Scully, Vin 215
Seaton, Tom 60, 63
Second Air Force League 125
Secory, Frank 105
Seeds, Bob 108
Seitz, Grover 97, 99–103, **101**, 106–115, **111**, 130
Seldon, Col. Henry Raymond 31–32
Selective Service and Training Act 121
Seligman family 16
Serena, Bill 104
Shattuck, Paul **180**
Shattuck, Paul, Jr. **203**
Sheehan, John (Jack) 57–58
Sherman, Gen. William Tecumsah 16
Sherman Silver Purchase Act 55
Shipkey, Ted 119, 121
Shiprock 9
Shiprock, New Mexico **20**, 198–199, 210
Sievers, Roy 143
Silva, Junior 170
Silver City, New Mexico **12**, 24, 31, 37–38, 55, 80
Simpson, Herbert 130–131
The Simpsons 217
Sioux Falls Marauders 125

Sisk, Richard 88–89
Smaulding, Bazz Owen 129
Smith, Allen **134**
Smith, B. (Native American catcher) 45, 47–51, 178
Smith, Chester **134**
Smith, L. (Native American pitcher) 45, 47–49, 178
Smith, Toby 141
Snider, Duke 170–171, 229n8
Sockalexis, Alex 177
Socorro, New Mexico 17, 159, 163, 167
Socorro Red Stockings 29
Sophomore League 97
South Atlantic League 45, 118
Southern Association 43, 119, 124
Southern League 60
Southern Ute 146
Southwest Texas League 48
Southwestern Air Forces Baseball League 122
Southwestern League 97, 113–114
Spalding, Albert Goodwill 37
Spalding, New Mexico 38
Spanish Inquisition 13
Speaker, Tris 65
Spencer, Frank **134**
Spiegelberg, Solomon Jacob 16
Staab family 16
Stevens, Chuck 122
Stowers, Harry 65–67, **66**, 74–75, 93
Stowers, Harry "Pop" 65–69, **66**, **68**, **69**, 74, 129, 181
Swastika Fuel Company 222n81
Swastikas 41
Sweetwater (Texas) Spudders 136

Tanner, Ray 182
Taos, New Mexico 19
Taos County 53
Taos Plateau 9
Taos Society of Artists 19
Taos Pueblo 11, 194
Tebeau, Patsy 177
Tererro, New Mexico 69–71, 74
Tererro Miners 182
Tererro Sluggers 72–73
Tererro Tigers 72
Tesuque Pueblo 194
Texas League 49, 57, 103, 118, 143
Thornton, Foster "Cowboy" 118, 121, 123
Thorpe, Jim 176
Three-I League 44
Tingley, Clyde 123
Tingley Park 6, 10, 229n6
To'hajiilee Navajo reservation 210, 229n14
Tombstone, Arizona 6
Tomé, New Mexico 158, 160
Tomé-Adelino baseball team 160–163, 165–166, 169–170
Toya, Tony 197–198, **198**

Traction Park 41, 45, 47, 51, 179
Traynor, Pie 98
Treaty of Guadalupe-Hidalgo 14, 31, 158,
Triandos, Gus 143
Trinidad, Colorado 6–7, 25, 47
Trinity Site, White Sands Missile Range 116, 167
Truesdale, Frankie 57
Trujillo, Miguel 184
Trujillo, Willie *172*
Tularosa, New Mexico 207
Turquoise Trail 52
Tuttle, Bill 143
Tyrone, New Mexico 55, 81
Tyrone Miners 56, 58

Union Association 29
University of Chicago 222*n*92
University of New Mexico 41, 66, 169
University of Waseda 222*n*92
Ute Mountain Ute 146

Valdez, Tererro (player, 1935) 73
Valencia, New Mexico 158–159, 162
Valenzuela, Fernando 23
Van Houton, New Mexico 123
Van Loan, Charles 217
Vaughan, Arky 98
Very Large Array 20
Victorio 15, 127
Villa, Pancho 127
Virgin Galactic Spaceport 22
Voyles, Rudy "Pop" 119

Wadell, Rube 159
Wagner, Honus 98–99
Waldrip, Jim 141–145, *142*
Wallace, Lew 7
Walsh, Charlie 51
Waner, Lloyd 98
Waner, Paul 98
Warneke, Lon 121

Washington Senators 49
Weaver, Buck 60–63
Weaver, Hank 121, 123
Weeks, Paul 85
Weeks, Rueben 42–43, 45–47, 58, 178
Weeks, "Young" 42
West Texas League 99
West Texas-New Mexico League 96–115, 118, 129–130, 136
Western Association 35
Western International League 130
Western League 37, 44, 46–47, 49–50, 56, 60, 99, 121,
Wetzel, Dutch 97
White Sands Missile Range 116, 169
White Sands National Monument 9
Whitehead, Milton 29
Whitmore, Robert *134*
Wiley, Joe 131
Wilhoit, Joe 44
Williams (secretary Las Cruces club) 32
Williams, Claude "Lefty" 61, 63
Williams, John Henry, Jr. 132
Williams, Ted 150
Williams, Zeak 132–135, *134*
Williams, Zeak, Jr. 132–135
Williams Air Field, Arizona 123–124
Wingate, J.W. 130–131
Wink (Texas) Spudders 98
Winslow, Arizona 180, 197, 201
Winslow Redskins 197–198, 201
Wolverton, Harry 38
Work, Hubert 175
Wright, Ted 119, 122–123
Wyatt, Ken 102–103

Yale Freshies 44
Yellow Horse, Moses 176
Young, "Young Cy" (El Paso player, 1911) 50
Yuma, Arizona 16

Zuni Pueblo 11, 12, 79, 126, 183

www.ingramcontent.com/pod-product-compliance
Ingram Content Group UK Ltd.
Pitfield, Milton Keynes, MK11 3LW, UK
UKHW041939140426
5217IPUK00014B/558